The Art of Immutable Architecture

Theory and Practice of Data Management in Distributed Systems

Second Edition

Michael L. Perry

Apress®

The Art of Immutable Architecture: Theory and Practice of Data Management in Distributed Systems, Second Edition

Michael L. Perry
Allen, TX, USA

ISBN-13 (pbk): 979-8-8688-0287-4   ISBN-13 (electronic): 979-8-8688-0288-1
https://doi.org/10.1007/979-8-8688-0288-1

Managing Director, Apress Media LLC: Welmoed Spahr
Acquisitions Editor: Jessica Vakili
Development Editor: Laura Berendson
Coordinating Editor: Jessica Vakili

Cover designed by eStudioCalamar

Distributed to the book trade worldwide by Apress Media, LLC, 1 New York Plaza, New York, NY 10004, U.S.A. Phone 1-800-SPRINGER, fax (201) 348-4505, e-mail orders-ny@springer-sbm.com, or visit www.springeronline.com. Apress Media, LLC is a California LLC and the sole member (owner) is Springer Science + Business Media Finance Inc (SSBM Finance Inc). SSBM Finance Inc is a **Delaware** corporation.

For information on translations, please e-mail booktranslations@springernature.com; for reprint, paperback, or audio rights, please e-mail bookpermissions@springernature.com.

Apress titles may be purchased in bulk for academic, corporate, or promotional use. eBook versions and licenses are also available for most titles. For more information, reference our Print and eBook Bulk Sales web page at http://www.apress.com/bulk-sales.

Any source code or other supplementary material referenced by the author in this book is available to readers on GitHub (https://github.com/Apress). For more detailed information, please visit https://www.apress.com/gp/services/source-code.

If disposing of this product, please recycle the paper

To Jenny. I still wouldn't change a thing.

Table of Contents

About the Author

Michael L. Perry is Director of Consulting at Improving, where he applies his love of software mathematics to benefit his clients. He has built upon the works of mathematicians such as Marc Shapiro, Pat Helland, and Leslie Lamport to develop a mathematical system for software development. He has captured this system in the Jinaga open source project. Michael often presents on math and software at events and online. You can find out more at http:// michaelperry.net.

Acknowledgments

As Tolkien reminds us, it's dangerous business going out your door. The first step onto the road that has led to this book being in your hands was a shaky one. I was building my first distributed system and making all of the rookie mistakes. Fortunately, I had good friends to make those mistakes with.

Thank you, Russell Elledge and Jerry Feris, for fumbling alongside me. Together, we the Three Amigos learned all the wrong ways to use TCP/IP and SOAP. Who knew that the three-way handshake was not sufficient to guarantee delivery?

Although those first attempts were rough, we started to figure things out. Russell has been my constant co-conspirator, sounding board, and critic throughout this journey. I need to thank you also for introducing me to Chris Gould, who gave us both the freedom to apply what we had learned since that fateful first attempt. His support enabled us to build just the right solution on a mathematically sound foundation. It was the success of that project that gave me the final confirmation that these concepts can be taught.

To my constant collaborator and enthusiast Jan Verhaegen, thank you for encouraging me to package the system in one comprehensive reference. Thanks also for the motivation to put the system into practice with Jinaga. We are going to build great things together.

A huge thank you goes out to Sean Whitesell for years of support, encouragement, and discussion. You always ask the best questions. Just as importantly, you are skilled at bringing people together. Thank you for building the community that helped me practice communicating the ideas that ended up in this book. And thank you especially for making the final connection to get this project started.

It was also Sean who introduced me to Floyd May. Floyd, you are such a deep thinker in technology, interpersonal relationships, and business. You have challenged me to become a better communicator. I cannot wait to see where your feet sweep you off to.

To all of my friends at Improving: Cori Drew, Harold Pulcher, Barry Forrest, Ben Kennedy, David Vibbert, David Belcher, David O'Hara ... all the Daves. We have grown so much together. I remember the first time I met each of you, and all of the things we learned since then. Thanks especially to Tim Rayburn for helping me grow as a speaker, as an Improver, and as a leader. And now that I know that Devlin Liles has read this far into the acknowledgments, I guess it's OK to tell him that I think he's the most brilliant person in the company. He keeps his ego in check nonetheless.

A special thanks to Joan Murray at Apress for believing in this project, Jill Balzano for seeing me through my first publishing experience, and Shonmirin P.A. for staying with me through the second edition. Thanks, also, to Sander Mak for all of the challenging and insightful remarks. And to Jeff Doolittle for joining the fellowship and sharing the concepts with so many. You all made this process the most fun I've had doing the most difficult job.

And finally, my most sincere gratitude to my family. Dad, you inspired me to build software. You provided not only the Apple II and IBM that saw me through high school but also the introduction to the first person I saw making a living doing what I love. You kept the *Nibble* and *Byte* magazines coming in to quench my thirst and eventually to inspire me to write about what I've learned. I am the man I am because of you.

To Jenny. You have always believed in me. You are my partner and my reason.

And Kaela. You make me proud. I am so happy we finished this project together.

The road goes ever on and on.

Foreword

The only way to keep up in this rapidly changing industry is to develop and maintain a learning posture. I regularly read books on software architecture in order to sharpen my skills. However, the majority of books on the topic focus far too much on tactical details. Tools and technologies, while important, are not the appropriate focus of software architecture from a systems engineering perspective. On the other end of the spectrum, a large plurality of books on the topic offer vague, abstract concepts that are challenging to comprehend and apply. They fail to improve the architect's ability to align with the business or communicate their ideas to developers.

Occasionally I come across a rare book that strikes the right balance of useful guidance that is actionable, broadly applicable, strategically oriented, and aligns architecture with the business and the development team.

This is one of those rare books.

At the dawn of the computing era, storage space was scarce and expensive. The data modelling strategies designed to deal with this situation continue to live on as standard practice in many (most?) software development shops. This leads to less than ideal outcomes. Businesses lose vital information by continuing to rely on updates and deletes. Developers remain shackled to outdated concepts designed for a world with constraints that no longer hold.

We now live in a world of abundance as it pertains to data storage. Developers can greatly improve their communication, velocity, and implementation quality by embracing the techniques described in this book.

Immutable architecture is not about creating architectures that do not change. It is about designing systems that work with immutable data. Embracing the mental model of immutable data provides a host of benefits. This book will add tools to your arsenal for tackling the complex world of distributed systems. Applying the techniques of this

---

book will enable clear communication of the constraints and intent of your data models. Even if you are already familiar with event-driven architectures, historical modelling and immutable runtimes can take your systems to the next level of comprehensibility, reliability, and resilience.

I am grateful to Michael for grounding the techniques in this book on solid mathematical foundations and for writing one of those rare books on software architecture that is well worth your time to read, absorb, and apply.

Jeff Doolittle
Senior Software Architect
Trimble Inc.

Introduction

It was 2001. I joined a team using J2EE version 1.3 to build a distributed gift card processor. The point-of-sale system was written in Microsoft Visual C++ 6.0. We were just learning about this new thing called SOAP, the Simple Object Access Protocol. The running joke was that it was too ill defined to be called a protocol, that it was not about accessing objects, and it was anything but simple. But it did hold some promise for making a C++ client talk to a Java server.

We all added three new books to our libraries. The first was on implementing a SOAP client in C++. The second was on JAXP, the Java API for XML Processing. And the third detailed the operation and limitations of TCP/IP. Armed with these tools, we began to build.

At first, the challenge was just to get the two platforms to talk to each other. When we finally settled on a subset of SOAP that both sides could handle, we thought we were over the hump. Little did we know that on the other side lay mountains.

There were reliability problems with the network. We set up a lab that continually ran transactions every night. We would check the card balances in the morning to find that some machines would have the wrong total. That led to a day of digging through logs, setting up the next test run, and then leaving it going until morning.

Over time, we evolved a message exchange protocol (over SOAP) based on confirmations and acknowledgments. One side sent a message. The next morning, we found messages missing. So next, the recipient confirmed that the message arrived. The next morning, we found duplicates. And so the sender acknowledged the confirmation. Fewer missing messages, but still not perfect.

It took many failed releases and many years of busy holiday seasons to work through all of the problems. We learned about the Two Generals' Problem (TGP) and realized why our message exchange protocol was flawed. Then we learned about eventual consistency and designed a working solution. This solution required that there be some uncertainty about how much money was left on a gift card. We tried to have that conversation with the product owner. Bankers get eventual consistency of money. Our product owner was not a banker.

The lessons we learned from gift cards were learned the hard way. "Guaranteed delivery" does not mean what you think it means. You need to first move data, then process it. Remote procedure calls (RPCs) aren't procedure calls. There is no line of code in a client-server system before which the transaction rolls back and after which it commits. I didn't want to learn those lessons over and over again.

And so I started putting those lessons together and defining a system that I called historical modeling. It was based on the idea that historical facts cannot be modified or destroyed. It relied upon the predecessor/successor relationships among facts. And it identified facts based only on their content, not on their location. I filled a notebook with examples of historical models. Eventually, I gained an intuitive feel for which kinds of solutions could be modeled historically and which could not. That's when I knew that I had to share it. Hopefully I could save someone else the pain of learning these lessons the hard way.

Since then, I have had countless conversations about immutable architectures. I broke the topic down into digestible chunks for conference and user group talks. I produced online courses that taught idempotent and commutative messaging. Yet none of that has truly empowered others to begin practicing immutability themselves. It can't just be adopted in pieces. Taking on only a subset of the ideas leaves gaps that can only be filled with the rest of the system.

Finally, I packaged the entire system in two forms. One, the open source project Jinaga. And two, the book that you are now holding. This is a complete treatment of the system, the patterns, and the techniques. It anticipates the problems that historical modeling creates and provides the solutions that enable a cohesive implementation. Most importantly, it presents the mathematical foundation that makes the technique work.

If you have read this far into the introduction, you have probably faced some of these same problems. You might even have come up with similar solutions. This leaves only a few more questions you probably have about this book. Who should read it? What will I get out of it? How is it organized? And how do I go about reading it?

Glad you asked.

Who Should Read It

This book is intended primarily for three audiences: decision makers, system builders, and tool crafters. You are a decision maker if you identify the problems for which you want to create solutions. Your title might be CTO, product owner, or business systems analyst. There are some problems that you can outsource, some that you can buy solutions for, and some that define your core business value. You need to find just the right team to build solutions to problems of this third kind. To find them, you need to be able to talk to them. And once you've brought them on board, you need to understand what they are doing. If your core business problem looks like the kind of thing that can be solved with an immutable architecture, this book will help you build that team and have those conversations.

Or perhaps you are a system builder. You are a member of the team brought in to deliver value against a core business domain. Your title might be developer, test engineer, or user experience designer. You know how to solve problems. But it would be great to have some ready-made solutions to the most common problems of distributed computing. You want to know that all of the edge cases are accounted for. You desire a common language to talk about solutions with the people who are helping you build them. If your software development challenges require constructing eventually consistent distributed systems, then this book will give you those tools.

Finally, you – like me – might be a tool crafter. You are a force multiplier. The things that you build empower others to build solutions more quickly, more predictably, and more effectively. You might be a solutions architect or an open source maintainer. If you have a team, you want them focused on delivering business value while you take care of the plumbing. If you serve the community, you want consumers to be able to quickly learn and apply your framework to build robust systems. In either case, this book lays out the mathematics, algorithms, and patterns that assure the correctness of your solutions.

What You Will Get Out of It

I have a secret. This is a math book. Don't tell anybody who hasn't read this far into the introduction.

Mathematics is the greatest invention of humankind. It is surprising in its ability to describe the natural world. It is astonishingly applicable to a broad range of problems. And it is the only way that we can be sure of anything.

The way that we normally learn that we have gotten something right is to test it. We'll put our solution in one situation and see if we get the expected result. Then we'll try another scenario and see what it does. If we are really good, then we can imagine a few unexpected conditions and test for those. But the unexpected is really hard to anticipate.

Testing is all about gathering empirical evidence. It only gives you confidence that the system behaves as expected in certain cases. It does not give you any assurance that you haven't missed something.

Knowing requires mathematical deduction. If something is proven mathematically, then you can be sure that it will be true no matter what test case you try. Pythagoras is true for any right triangle. Euclid holds up for all figures on the plane. If your reasoning is sound, you can be sure that you haven't missed any edge cases.

It's not that mathematical truths are universal. It's that they come with known limitations. Division only works for nonzero divisors. Pythagoras only holds on the plane. The rules of deduction tell us how to carry those boundaries through to the solution so that we know precisely where that solution applies and where it doesn't.

This book applies mathematical rigor to the problem of distributed computing. It is not the first to do so, but it does provide a complete and practical solution. If you follow the deductive reasoning over the problem and carry the limitations of distributed systems through your calculations, you will end up with an understanding of the boundaries of the solution. This book is your guide through that process.

How It Is Organized

The book is roughly divided into three parts, analogous to the three primary audiences. Decision makers need only read the first part, which includes the first three chapters. In this part, you first learn why immutability is so important. Then you explore the space of alternatives, eventually landing on historical modeling. Finally, you learn how to read a historical model so that you can communicate more effectively with your team. You can stop reading when we get into some deep math.

System builders will want to continue on to the second part. This includes Chapters 4 through 9. First, we see how to apply immutability to analyzing systems. Then, we get neck deep in the mathematical foundations of immutability, causality, and conflict-free replicated data types (CRDTs). Next, we learn how system operators will compose solutions from these components. And finally, we study patterns for modeling entities, building state machines, and enforcing security rules. These are the tools that you will need to build robust distributed systems.

My people, the tool crafters, will want to read right through to the end. We'll start with techniques for using traditional technologies like relational databases, REST APIs, and message queues. This will help prepare you for a gradual transition from stateful to immutable architectures. After that, we'll see how to construct libraries and infrastructure components purpose built for immutability. We pull it all together and describe an ecosystem made up of collaborative applications generating emergent behavior from shared specifications. That's where we get into the mathematical results that I find truly beautiful and inspiring. I hope you follow me to the end.

How to Read It

Now that you know this is a math book, you might have some reservations about how you are going to read it. Perhaps you struggled through algebra or dropped out of calculus. You might think that math is not for you.

It is my belief that math is for everyone. And it is my goal with this book to prove it. Mathematics is nothing more than applying logical reasoning over symbolic representations of abstract concepts. Programming, on the other hand, is applying logical operations to a symbolic language describing generic rules. In other words, they are the same thing. If you are a programmer, then you are an applied mathematician.

One problem with mathematics is the jargon. In order to efficiently communicate with each other, mathematicians have to come up with words to represent ideas. Unfortunately, natural language is limited, and all of the good words are taken. And so mathematicians either make up new words or use terms that almost mean the right thing. One example is the term "join semilattice." How does the structure of a rose trellis relate to eventual consistency? In this book, I don't use that term even though I talk about that concept. And where I can't avoid jargon, I will clearly define the terms.

Another problem with mathematics is how it is written. Math papers have a predictable form. They start with an abstract. Then they fully define the problem. What follows is section after section of lemmas and propositions building an argument. Every statement is justified by the statements before, until finally, like an M. Night Shyamalan plot twist, one final assertion puts the whole argument into perspective and the result emerges.

While I really enjoy a good math paper, I don't read them the way that they are written. I skim the first few paragraphs for the motivation behind the problem. I scan the headings for the outline of the argument. I want to know why each statement is proven and how it will contribute to the whole. I want to know how the story is going to play out before I invest the time in understanding it.

I wrote this book the way that I read a math paper. In each section, you will understand the motivation behind a certain result. Then you will see a sketch of the basic reasoning. There will be no mystery why each of the steps is there. Then the section will justify each of those steps with the rigor they require.

I fully anticipate that this will impact the way you read the book. If you are after results, you can read just a paragraph or two past the section header. If you want to know why or how, then continue a bit further to understand the argument. And if you need to be convinced, then finish out the whole section. The important thing is that you can stop reading whenever it gets too deep and skip to the next section. You won't miss anything important to you.

If you have read this section without skipping anything, then I am truly pleased to have you. You are one of my people. With your help, we can build the software that the world needs. We will make it reliable, efficient, and correct. And it will give our users the autonomy they need to do their jobs with creativity and confidence, knowing that we have provided the mathematical rigor.

PART I

Definition

CHAPTER 1

Why Immutable Architecture

Distributed systems are hard.

Most of us have used a website to buy a product. You might have seen a purchase page that contains a warning **do not click submit twice!** Maybe you've used a site that simply disables the buy button after you click it. The authors of that site have run up against one of the hard problems of distributed systems and did not know how to solve it. They abdicated the responsibility of preventing duplicate charges to the consumer.

Maybe you've used a mobile application on a train. The train enters a tunnel just as you save some data. The mobile app spins for a few seconds before you realize that you are in a race. Will the train leave the tunnel before the app gives up? Will the app correct itself once the connection is reestablished? Or will you lose your data and have to enter it again?

If you are involved in the creation of distributed systems, you are expected to find, fix, and prevent these kinds of bugs. If you are in QA, it is your job to imagine all of the possible scenarios and then replicate them in the lab. If you are in development, you need to code for all of the various exceptions and race conditions. And if you are in architecture, you are responsible for cutting the Gordian Knot of possible failures and mitigations. This is the fragile process by which we build the systems that run our society.

The Immutability Solution

Distributed systems are hard to write, test, and maintain. They are unreliable, unpredictable, and insecure. The process by which we build them is certain to miss defects that will adversely affect our users. But it is not your fault. As long as we depend upon individuals to find, fix, and mitigate these problems, defects will be missed.

3

© Michael L. Perry 2024
M. L. Perry, *The Art of Immutable Architecture*, https://doi.org/10.1007/979-8-8688-0288-1_1

This book explores a different process for building distributed systems. Rather than connecting programs together and testing away the defects, this approach starts with a fundamental representation of the business problem that *spans* machines. And this fundamental representation is *immutable*.

On its face, immutability is a simple concept. Write down some data, and ensure that it never changes. It can never be modified, updated, or deleted. It is indelible. Immutability solves the problem of distributed systems for one simple reason: every copy of an immutable object is just as good as any other copy. As long as things never change, keeping distant copies in sync is a trivial problem.

The Problems with Immutability

Unfortunately, immutability is counter to how computers actually work. A machine has a limited amount of memory. Machines work by modifying the contents of memory locations over time to update their internal state. So the first problem of modeling immutable data on a computer is how to represent it in fixed mutable memory.

The second problem is that when we look out at the world of problems that we want to solve, we see change. People change their names, addresses, and phone numbers. Bank account balances go up and down. Property changes hands and ownership is transferred. How then are we to model a changing problem space with unchanging data?

Our initial instinct is to model the mutable world within the mutable space of the computer. This is the solution that has led us to build programs and databases based on mutation. Programs have assignment statements; databases have UPDATE statements. When we connect those programs and databases together to create distributed systems, crazy unpredictable behaviors emerge. And we are left with the unending task of testing until all of those anomalies are gone.

Redefine the Process

This book defines a new process by which to build distributed systems. It relies upon a rigorous system of specification, a mathematical proof of correctness, and a mechanical translation into machine behavior.

The first step is to model the business domain as one large immutable data structure. We call this data structure a *historical model*. The goal is not for a single machine or database to house the entire structure. It is instead to share that structure across nodes. The historical model is a description that both humans and machines can understand and reason about, not a concrete implementation.

The second step is to subdivide that model into autonomous components. This subdivision will not be clean; there will be overlap. We will use that overlap to derive the rules, messages, and protocols by which machines communicate with one another.

The third step is to convert these subdivisions into deployable software. This step is mechanical: a machine can do it. We call the system that supports this process an *immutable runtime*. One such runtime – Jinaga – is currently in operation and will serve as the reference implementation. For organizations not yet ready to adopt an immutable runtime, this book describes how to perform this step manually. You can build autonomous components from traditional databases, protocols, and messaging infrastructure. Be careful, however. Without the mechanisms of the immutable runtime, you will still be prone to the errors of human implementation.

This system is based on prior art, most notably conflict-free replicated data types (CRDTs). Throughout this book, we will reference that research in the form of math and computer science papers. Every claim is justified. I humbly add two new claims to this body of work. Both are based on projections — the ways in which you extract information from a replica. The first claim is that replicas will reach consistency after exchanging a subset of updates determined by a set of projections. And the second is that we can determine which projections produce new results after receiving an update. These two claims allow us to automate message passing and cache invalidation in ways that are impossible without the assumption of immutability. The proofs of these claims constitute the last two chapters of the book.

It is my ambition that you build a historical model of your own business domain. From this, you will construct more reliable, resilient, and secure distributed systems, whether using an immutable runtime or by hand. Let's begin by understanding the problem of distributed computing.

The Fallacies of Distributed Computing

Between 1991 and 1997, engineers at Sun Microsystems collected a list of mistakes that programmers commonly make when writing software for networked computers. Bill Joy, Dave Lyon, L Peter Deutsch, and James Gosling cataloged eight assumptions that developers commonly hold about distributed computing. These assumptions, while obviously incorrect when stated explicitly, nevertheless inform many of the decisions that the Sun engineers found in systems of the day.

The fallacies are these:

- The network is reliable.

- Latency is zero.

- Bandwidth is infinite.

- The network is secure.

- Topology doesn't change.

- There is one administrator.

- Transport cost is zero.

- The network is homogeneous.

Although it has been years since that list was written, many of these assumptions continue to be common. I can recall on several occasions being surprised that a program that worked flawlessly on *localhost* failed quickly when deployed to a test environment. The program contained hidden assumptions that the network was reliable, that latency was zero, and that the topology doesn't change. Here are examples of just these three.

The Network Is Not Reliable

One way in which these fallacies appear in modern systems is when a remote API is presented as if it were a function call. Several platform services have promoted this abstraction, including remote procedure calls, .NET Remoting, Java Remote Method Invocation, Distributed COM, SOAP, and SignalR. When a remote invocation is made to look like a local function call, it is easy for a developer to forget that the network is not reliable.

Any time you call a function, you can rest assured that execution will continue with its first line. And if the function makes it to the return statement, you can feel pretty confident that the next line to run will be the one following the function call. Remote procedure calls, however, make no such claims. They can fail on invocation or on return. The calling code will be unable to tell which.

An abstraction that hides the fact of a network hop does a disservice to its consumers. In an effort to make things easier and more familiar, it pretends that an inconvenient truth can be ignored. Such abstractions make it easier for developers to believe the fallacy that the network is somehow reliable.

Latency Is Not Zero

Modern web applications have moved away from the client proxy in favor of more explicit REST APIs. These APIs avoid the mistake of presenting the remote machine as if it were a library of functions that could be invoked reliably. They instead present the world as a web of interconnected resources, each responding to a small set of HTTP verbs. Unfortunately, this style of programming makes it easy to forget that latency is not zero.

Some of the HTTP verbs are guaranteed to be *idempotent*. If the client duplicates the request, the server promises not to duplicate the effect. There is no way for the protocol to enforce that guarantee, but server-side applications typically uphold the contract. Examples of HTTP verbs that are idempotent are PUT and PATCH. An HTTP verb that is *not* guaranteed to be idempotent is POST.

On the Web, HTTP POST is often used to submit a form. When a web application responds quickly, the lack of idempotency guarantee makes little difference. But as latency increases, the user starts to wonder if they actually clicked the submit button. And if that button triggered a purchase, they have to wonder if they will be charged twice if they try again. An end user has no good recourse during an extended latency after clicking a *Buy* button, nor does a client-side application developer have a good response to a timeout on POST.

There is no correct use of an API that features non-idempotent network requests. Because latency is not zero, there will always be a time during which the client is unsure if the server has received the request. As latency exceeds the time that the client is willing to wait, they must make a choice: either abort the attempt or retry. If the client aborts, then they don't know whether the request has been processed. And if they retry, then the effect might be duplicated.

The POST verb is indeed part of the HTTP specification. And that specification makes no guarantee as to its idempotency. But any API that includes a non-idempotent POST is making the incorrect assumption that latency is zero. It forces the client to make an impossible choice when that assumption proves false.

Topology Changes

Most database management systems include a concept that leads developers to assume that topology doesn't change. These databases make it easy to set the identity of a record to an auto-incremented ID. Every time a record is inserted, the database generates the next number in the sequence. This number is used from then on to identify the record.

An auto-incremented ID requires that topology remain constant throughout a multistep process. Imagine a web application that inserts a user's form data into a database and then redirects them to a page representing that new data. To accomplish this with an auto-incremented ID, the browser must wait for the request to go all the way to the database and the response to come all the way back before it can learn the URL of the next page. The application assumes that the topology will not change in the meantime.

This may seem on the surface to be a valid assumption. It will usually be true. Changes to server topology are rare, and network requests are usually fast (invoking the fallacy that latency is zero). However, for a heavily trafficked web application, there will never be a moment during which no requests are in flight. The assumption that topology does not change will be violated for some requests.

Topology may change during a system upgrade. It will certainly change during a disaster failover. And it will change again when reverting back after the disaster is resolved. When topology changes, the database that a request ends up on will not be the same as the one that generated the source page. That database will instead be a replica of the original. If the replica is just a little behind the original, then the change in topology will be noticeable. And it will be behind because, again, latency is not zero.

The use of auto-incremented IDs is ubiquitous. They are the default choice for most application database models. And yet their use belies an assumption that the topology will not change.

Changing Assumptions

The fallacies of distributed computing are easy assumptions to make. We make them because our tools, specifications, and training have led us to do so. The non-idempotent POST verb is a valid part of the HTTP specification. Auto-incrementing IDs are a valuable feature of most database management systems. Almost every tutorial on application development will teach a beginner to use these capabilities. The fact that by doing so they are making an incorrect assumption does not even occur to them.

The tools that we use and the patterns that we follow today all evolved from a time during which assumptions of high reliability, zero latency, and topological consistency were not fallacies. In-process procedure calls are perfectly reliable. Sequential program statements have very low, very predictable latency characteristics. And sequential counters in a for loop will never return to the top of the function to find the code's topology had changed. It's when we evolve these abstractions into RPCs, network requests, and auto-incremented IDs that problems arise. When we apply the languages and patterns of the past to the problems of modern distributed systems, it is no wonder that programmers will make incorrect assumptions.

All of the fallacies of distributed computing stem from one simple truth: distributed systems are built using tools designed to run in a single thread on a single computer. Developers imagine a fast, isolated, unchanging, sequential execution environment and then treat the idiosyncrasies of distributed systems as edge cases. But these are not edge cases; they are the normal operation of a distributed system. A repeated request due to a network timeout is not a bug. An ID collision caused by a database failover is not a defect. These are realities of distributed systems that we cannot code around or test away. They demand a new set of tools, patterns, and assumptions.

Immutability Changes Everything

In 2015, Pat Helland wrote "Immutability Changes Everything,"[1] an analysis of several computing solutions based on immutability. It demonstrates that immutability solves many problems in several layers of computational abstraction. At one end of the spectrum, low-level storage systems use copy-on-write semantics to mitigate against

---

[1] Helland, Pat. (2015). "Immutability Changes Everything." http://cidrdb.org/cidr2015/Papers/CIDR15_Paper16.pdf

media wear. At the other end, applications accrete read-only facts and derive current state. This paper claims no new ideas but only serves to point out the common thread of immutability in all of these solutions.

In the past, computers were slow, expensive, and limited machines that could only operate on small sets of data. Today, they are fast, cheap, and capable workhorses that store an embarrassment of data richness. Where application developers of the past had to optimize data storage by overwriting information when it was no longer needed, today we can afford to save everything. There is little economic need to update or destroy bits.

At the same time, computers of today are much more connected than they were in the past. Rather than co-locating a workload with the data on which it operates, we have moved to a world of microservices and mobile devices that share data far and wide. Many machines share the computational and storage burden of work that used to be performed by one. As a result, coordination has become more expensive, even as computing has become cheap.

And so while in the past it was expensive to keep immutable copies of data, current architectural constraints *require* that we do. Not only is data cheaper than it used to be, but making immutable copies actually *enables* the kinds of solutions that scale to multiple machines. When two machines share mutable data, they need to coordinate as that data changes. They may need to block one another to ensure that only one can change the data at any given time. But when that data cannot change, then no coordination or blocking is required. Cost reduction enables immutability, and immutability enables modern architecture.

Shared Mutable State

Many of the hard problems in computing are problems that we have created for ourselves. Take, for example, the problem of shared mutable state in a multi-threaded system. One thread writes source data into a shared memory location, and another thread performs calculations on it. These two threads must be carefully coordinated to ensure that one does not write to shared memory before the other is finished reading from it. If the first overwrites the data while the second is still calculating, the results would be complete nonsense. We typically solve this sort of problem with a lock, limiting the ability for the program to scale.

But there is a solution that does not impair scalability. Instead of a lock, we could use immutable data structures. Rather than overwriting memory with the next data set, the first thread would simply allocate new memory. When it is finished building the data structure, the first thread passes a pointer to the second. From that point on, no thread can modify the contents of that memory. It remains completely immutable.

On the surface, it appears that we have improved scalability at the cost of memory efficiency. Rather than modifying just one small part of a data structure, it would seem that we have to make an entire copy with every operation. If that were true, it would be hard to justify the trade-off, even with the decreased cost of storage. Fortunately, however, that is not a trade-off we have to make.

Persistent Data Structures

The fact that we intend for data structures to be immutable opens a new possibility. As we build new data structures, we can reuse existing pieces of old data structures. There is no need to copy those pieces, because we have already established that they will not change. We simply create new data elements to represent the ones that have "changed" and let them point to the ones that haven't.

This is a technique called persistent data structures. It's a common optimization for immutable data structures that is *enabled* by immutable data structures. Take, for example, the binary tree shown in Figure 1-1. Each node in the tree contains a piece of data, in this case a number. It also contains two pointers: one to a number that is less than this node and one to a number that is greater. Finding a specific number in this data structure is fast, because you walk down a path asking "less than or greater than" at each stop.

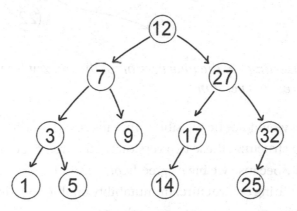

Figure 1-1. A binary tree of numbers

To insert a new number into the binary tree, you first need to locate the place that it belongs. Walking down to where it should be, you will discover either that it is less than a number that has no left path or greater than a number with no right path. Once there, your desire will be to "change" that node to add a new path. However, changing a node is not allowed: they are all part of an immutable data structure. So instead, you create a new node.

This new node should be to the left or right path of a parent, and so you will want to "change" that node as well. But again, changing the parent is not allowed. And so you create a new parent that points to the new child.

Continuing up the tree, you will eventually reach the root, as shown in Figure 1-2. No matter where you insert a new number, you will always end up creating a new root node. This new root node is effectively the new version of the tree. It represents the shape of the tree after the insertion. The previous root node still exists, and the nodes to which it points have not been modified. Any threads running in parallel searching that version of the tree can happily continue to do so. They will be unaffected by the new tree that shares most of its structure with the old one.

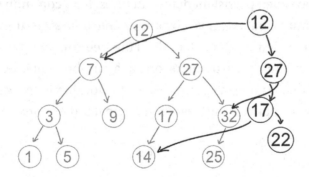

Figure 1-2. *After inserting 22, the new version of the binary tree shares most of its structure with the previous version*

This optimization would not be possible if threads could modify these data structures. By sharing structure, these two versions of the tree become sensitive to modifications. It's only because we have agreed *not* to modify the nodes that we can get away with this deep sharing of structure. Immutability enables persistent data structures, and persistent data structures optimize immutability.

The Two Generals' Problem

Nowhere in computing is immutability more valuable than in sharing data among machines. But before we can truly understand why, we must first understand the scope of the problem. And there is no better way to do that than with the parable of the two generals, as first introduced by Akkoyunlu.[2]

Imagine a besieged city. Within its walls, the defenses are insurmountable. A direct attack is almost certain to fail. Outside of the city are two armies, which have succeeded in cutting off its supply lines. The generals of these armies lie in wait, watching the city slowly weaken under the blockade.

At some point, the city's defenses will be weak enough to attack. The generals of these two armies – one in the East and one in the West – are constantly observing the situation through their network of scouts, spies, and messengers. They determine each day whether the city is sufficiently weak. When the time comes, they will prepare an attack for the following day. This situation appears in Figure 1-3.

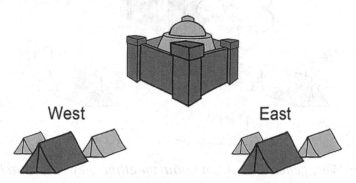

West   East

Figure 1-3. *Two armies encamped outside of a besieged city*

An attack from one army would not be sufficient. The attack would be repelled and the attacking army destroyed. The remaining army would not be able to maintain the blockade, and so it would be routed soon thereafter. Only a coordinated attack from both East and West will win the city.

Now imagine that you are the general of the West army. Your partner to the East is separated from you by enemy territory. You cannot communicate directly. You can only send messengers through hostile terrain with no guarantee of success. Any message

---

[2] Akkoyunlu, E. A.; Ekanadham, K.; Huber, R. V. "Some constraints and tradeoffs in the design of network communications." ACM SIGOPS Operating Systems Review. November 1975.

could be lost, their carrier killed or captured. The two of you must devise a method of reliable communication built from unreliable components.

If you in the West determine that the city is weak enough, and that the time for attack has come, you will begin preparing your army. You will also send a messenger to the East to inform the other general that you will attack in the morning. If the messenger arrives safely, then the East general can begin preparations and join you in the attack. With your combined efforts, the attack is likely to succeed.

But if the messenger is killed or captured, the message will not arrive. If that happens, your army will set out in the morning to mount a lone attack against the city. Your army will be destroyed, and the siege will be lost. As Figure 1-4 shows, you are unsure of how to proceed. And so you must have assurance before the morning comes that the message has been received.

Figure 1-4. *The West general does not know whether they can attack*

A Prearranged Protocol

Let's try to devise a protocol that will give us some assurance that the message was received. Suppose you ask the East general to send a messenger in response confirming that your message was received. Now if you receive the confirmation before morning, you can confidently launch your attack. You know that the East general has received the message and will join you on the battlefield. If, on the other hand, you do not receive confirmation, then you will call off the attack, not knowing whether the original messenger made it through. As the general of the West army, you can be sure that you will not attack unless you know that the East general has received your message.

But while this protocol gives the West general those assurances, it fails to do so for the East general. Imagine now that you are on the East and you have received a message informing you that the West will attack in the morning. You have plenty of time to begin preparations for your army. And, as per the protocol, you respond with confirmation. If the confirmation message reaches the West general, then the attack will proceed as planned.

But if that message is lost, then the West general will not attack. Remember, they are waiting for confirmation to know that you received their message. If you attack in the morning without knowing that the West general has received your confirmation, then your army could be defeated. And so you are left in uncertainty, as in Figure 1-5.

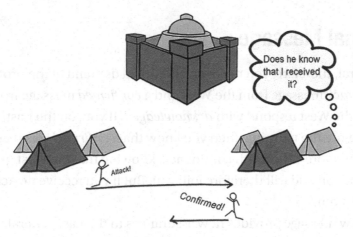

Figure 1-5. *The East general is uncertain*

Reducing the Uncertainty

This protocol is not sufficient. You try different strategies to improve upon it. The first strategy is to simply send more messengers. Instead of relying upon one messenger, you send two. The probability of two messages both being lost is certainly less than the probability of one being lost. But that probability is not zero. And so you try again.

You can send three messengers, four messengers. Choose any number you wish. As you increase the number, the probability of total message loss gets closer and closer to zero. But it never quite reaches it. You can never choose a number of messengers high enough to assure you that the message will be received.

And so you change your approach. You send messengers out at a constant rate until the response is received. From the West, when you decide to attack, you send

15

messengers with the *attack* message once every ten minutes. When you receive the first *confirmed* message from the East, you stop sending messages. As for the general on the East, they will reply with a *confirmed* message every time that an *attack* message is received. As long as they receive a steady stream of *attack* messages, they will respond at the same rate with confirmations. And once that stream stops, they can assume that the confirmation has been received.

Or can they? Can the lack of messages be taken as a signal? Is it possible that six messengers an hour continue to flow from the West, but all are captured? The general on the East has no way of ruling that out. And so they still run the risk of attacking in the morning with no support from the West.

An Additional Message

As the East general, therefore, you make an additional demand of the protocol. In addition to an *attack* message from the West and a *confirmed* message from the East, you require that the West respond with *acknowledged*. If you, on the East, receive *acknowledged* before the morning, then you know that *confirmed* was received in the West. You may therefore attack with confidence, knowing that the West general has received confirmation and will therefore join you. But if you receive no acknowledgment, then you must abstain.

While this new message provides new assurances to the East general, it again confounds the situation on the West. When the West general sends out an *acknowledged* message, they have no way of knowing whether it was received. If it was, then the East general will attack. If it wasn't, then the East general will abstain. And so, as Figure 1-6 illustrates, they have no assurance that their attack in the morning will be supported.

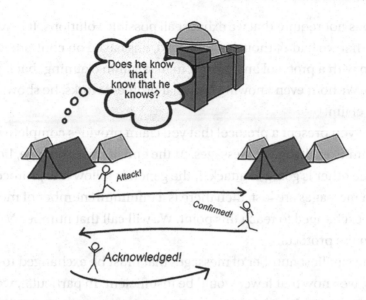

Figure 1-6. *The West general is again not sure if the East will attack*

The addition of one message has only moved the uncertainty to the other side of the conversation. It didn't actually solve the problem. We still have not yet discovered a protocol that will ensure that both armies either attack or abstain, when those two generals can only communicate via unreliable messages.

And indeed, we never will.

Proof of Impossibility

The Two Generals' Problem, as Jim Gray named it in 1978,[3] has no solution. There is no finite protocol that can give both generals mutual assurance of an agreement. I'm not simply saying that no one has found a solution. I'm saying that no solution can exist.

E. A. Akkoyunlu, who published the original problem and the impossibility proof in 1975,[2] named this mutual assurance *complete status*. He described interprocess communication protocols that negotiate transactions between participants. A protocol would ideally provide status to those participants regarding the outcome of every transaction. Akkoyunlu proved that a distributed system cannot achieve complete status in a finite number of messages.

---

[3] Gray, Jim (1978). "Notes on Data Base Operating Systems." Chapter 3. Operating Systems, an Advanced Course. Springer-Verlag, London, UK.

His proof does not require that we exhaust all possible solutions. It leaves no room for clever tricks that we hadn't thought of. Instead, it is based on contradiction. Let anyone come up with a protocol and bring it to Akkoyunlu claiming that it provides complete status. Without even knowing how that protocol works, he shows that it does not uphold that claim.

Suppose that you present a protocol that you claim provides complete status to two generals after a finite exchange of messages. At the end of this exchange, both generals will know that the other is going to attack. If the generals follow this protocol and it happens that no messages are lost, then there is a minimum number of messages that must have been exchanged to reach this point. We will call that number N. The number N is particular to the protocol.

Since N is the smallest number of messages that must be exchanged to reach complete status, we know that fewer would be insufficient. In particular, we have not reached complete status after $N-1$ messages. One of the generals must still be at the point where they are not sure whether the other is going to attack.

Since $N-1$ messages would be insufficient, the Nth message is important. Without it, the protocol would not work. And yet, the message is not guaranteed to arrive. The sender of the Nth message does not know whether it will be received. Therefore, the sender of the Nth message does not have complete status and will not receive complete status as there are no further messages in the protocol. This situation appears in Figure 1-7.

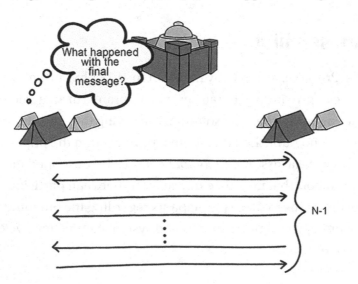

Figure 1-7. *The sender of the final message does not have complete status*

This contradicts your claim that the protocol provides complete status within a finite number of messages. Therefore, we can conclude that no such protocol exists.

Relaxing Constraints

The Two Generals' Problem (TGP) is an analog for many of the problems we try to solve in distributed systems. Using only unreliable networks to pass messages between nodes, we must construct systems that nevertheless reach agreement with a high degree of certainty. The impossibility of the TGP would seem to tell us that this is a fool's errand. Fortunately, however, the problems that we solve in distributed systems are a little bit easier than this fictional analog.

Consider an ATM. A bank customer uses a terminal to withdraw cash from their account. This common everyday transaction appears to be a TGP made real. On the West, you have an ATM terminal with the ability to dispense cash. On the East, you have a bank's central computer, which records the flow of money into and out of customer accounts. In between, the hostile territory of digital communications threatens to interrupt the delivery of messages.

Our desire is to ensure that the transaction either succeeds or fails. If it succeeds, the cash is dispensed and the customer's account is debited. If it fails, no cash is dispensed and no debit appears in the account. We wish to avoid an outcome that has success on one side and failure on the other. Customers would be very upset if their accounts were debited but no cash was forthcoming, and banks would lose money if their ATMs dispensed cash without a corresponding debit.

Redefining the Problem

The impossibility result of TGP tells us that this cannot be accomplished. And yet, millions of ATM transactions are processed every day.[4] Clearly something is out of alignment. What we have failed to recognize in the ATM example is that the constraints on the system are more relaxed than they appear at first. Let's take a closer look at the reason that the full TGP is impossible. From there, we can see how to relax the constraints and create a viable protocol.

---

[4] The 2023 Federal Reserve Payments Study reported 3.7 billion ATM withdrawals in 2021.

The problem as originally stated has two strict constraints:

1. A general will not attack unless they have assurance that the other general will also attack.

2. The attack will come in the morning.

By the first constraint, the behavior of each general is based on what they know about the behavior of the other general. As long as one general is in a state of uncertainty, both remain uncertain. There is no message that can simultaneously change both of their minds.

By the second constraint, there is a deadline. When that deadline arrives, they must achieve consensus. Any messages already en route at that time must have no effect on the final outcome. There will be no further messages to resolve any lingering uncertainty.

If we relax this pair of constraints, we can formulate a problem that has a valid solution. We can indeed find a protocol that exchanges complete status, as long as we allow one party to act in uncertainty and remove the deadline. Doing so destroys the narrative of the Two Generals' Problem, but it fits the ATM example. Indeed, we will find that this relaxed version fits *many* business problems that we solve with distributed systems.

Decide and Act

We will first relax the constraint that a general will only attack if they are certain that their peer will as well. The West general decides that the time is right and prepares to attack regardless of what happens in the East. What is foolish behavior for a general could be a valid compromise for an ATM. When a customer withdraws money from their account through an ATM, one side or the other must act without full knowledge that the other will follow suit. Either the ATM must dispense the cash or the central bank computer must record the debit. Consider the consequences and corrective steps of each decision, should it turn out to be one-sided.

Suppose that the bank records the debit, but the ATM terminal fails to dispense the cash. In that scenario, the customer leaves the terminal with no cash, but the central bank believes that they have their money. The consequence is that the customer is unsatisfied when they discover the problem, and their trust in the bank is eroded. The corrective action is to reverse the debit once the problem is discovered.

Now suppose that the ATM dispenses the cash, but the central bank fails to record the debit. In this scenario, the customer has left happy, and the ATM retries the communication until it is successful. In the meantime, it might be possible for the customer to withdraw money from another ATM, since the bank is unaware that their balance has been depleted. If so, the corrective action is to charge the customer an overdraft fee.

Clearly, one of these scenarios is better for both the bank and the customer. It protects trust, puts the power in the customer's hands, and gives the bank an additional revenue stream. And so in this situation, the designer of the distributed system determines that the ATM will dispense cash even while it is uncertain whether the central bank will record the debit.

Accept the Truth

The designer can only confidently make this decision if they relax the second constraint: that there is a deadline. Assume that the ATM has dispensed cash but then experiences technical difficulties while communicating this fact to the central bank. It may take some time for a technician to repair the ATM terminal, thus reestablishing the communication channel. When the terminal shares with the bank that the cash was dispensed, the bank must honor this truth. It cannot reject the transaction based on the passage of time or the customer's current account balance.

The damage to the ATM may be so severe that the digital record of the transaction cannot be recovered. It may have experienced a full unrecoverable hard drive crash. In this case, additional forensics could be employed: count the cash remaining in the machine and determine whether the last transaction completed. If the ATM, including all of its cash, is totally destroyed, then even this method might not be available. But of course, in that case, the bank has lost more than a single transaction. Accepting the truth means accepting some risk.

A Valid Protocol

Given these relaxed constraints, we can now devise a protocol that eventually achieves complete status. One side (the ATM in this case) reaches a point where it can confidently make a decision. It acts (dispenses cash) and then continues the protocol until it knows that the other side is aware of the decision. It continues to do so no matter how much time has passed, or what conflicting circumstances have intervened.

To reach the point of decision, the ATM communicates with the central bank. It verifies that the account holder has sufficient funds to dispense the requested cash. It also checks its local storage of bills to ensure that it will be able to complete its side of the transaction. In this process, the bank may place a temporary hold on the customer's funds. But this hold only reduces the likelihood of an overdraft; it cannot prevent it. The ATM for its part will put a temporary hold on its repository of bills: only one customer at a time may use the machine. If both of these checks pass, then the ATM dispenses the cash. It makes the final decision.

After it makes the decision, the ATM enters a second phase. In this phase, the decision has happened; the cash has been dispensed. The goal of this phase is simply to communicate this fact with the central bank. There is no time limit on the second phase, and the truth cannot be retracted.

This kind of protocol is what Jim Gray referred to in 1978 as a *Two-Phase Commit* (2PC). In the first phase – commonly known as the *voting* phase – the coordinator receives from each participant confirmation that it can commit to the requested transaction. In the second phase – the *commit* phase – the coordinator informs each participant of its decision. In the preceding example, the ATM plays the role of coordinator and one participant. It is the sole decision maker, once it has gathered enough information to responsibly make that decision.

Examples of Immutable Architectures

The benefits of immutability have not gone unnoticed by distributed systems designers. Some of the most successful distributed systems in use today are built upon this concept. They derive capabilities from immutability that would be difficult to achieve otherwise. Three examples are Git, blockchains, and Docker.

Git is a distributed version control system popular among open source and corporate development teams alike. It offers the benefit of autonomy to each individual developer. A developer can make changes, switch among parallel lines of history, and resolve conflicts all within an isolated replica of the repository. When developers connect their replicas – whether directly to one another or to a shared central repository – they only trade information. No locking or consensus occurs during that exchange, keeping the interaction short.

"Blockchain" is an umbrella term for a collection of related architectures. The first blockchain was Bitcoin, a distributed currency based entirely on cryptographic algorithms. Most blockchains retain the economic aspects of a currency, but some layer additional features onto the core data structure. The prominent feature of a blockchain is a shared immutable ledger, providing assurance of the veracity of a singular, transparent history.

Docker is a technology for executing software within containers, as if the entire operating system and all dependencies were encased within a single isolated execution environment. It is an evolution beyond physical machines that truly ran isolated workloads and virtual machines that simulated that environment for the purposes of portability and scale. Docker achieves efficiencies that virtual machines lacked by a clever use of persistent data structures and immutable disk images. This led the way to further advancement in orchestration such as Kubernetes clusters and mesh computing.

All of these examples use the benefits of immutability to enable their core defining capabilities. Interestingly enough, they all also happen to be open systems. Most likely that is simply a consequence of open software being readily available to analyze and uphold as architectural examples. There is no reason to believe that immutability would not be just as valuable to a closed system as it is to an open one. Let's analyze each one in a little more detail to see how immutability serves its goals.

Git

Git is a distributed version control system that developers use to collaborate on software. In this system, each developer has a complete replica of the repository. The repository is composed of immutable snapshots of source code known as *commits*. Each commit captures the state of the entire code base at a specific point in time.

Each commit contains tree objects that describe file structure and blob objects that describe file contents. It also contains references to its parent commit or multiple parent commits. Changes – or deltas – are derived by computing the differences between commits. The whole of the repository is an ever-growing history of commits accumulated over the life of the project.

Git uses a technique known as *content-addressed storage* to identify blob objects. It hashes the contents – and only the contents – of each file. It then uses that hash code as the name of the blob. This practice enforces the immutability of the blob; if the contents change, the hash changes, and you have a new blob.

Git uses a related technique known as *Merkle Trees* to identify tree objects. The leaves of the tree refer to individual files. These nodes reference the blob objects by hash. Higher nodes of the tree refer to collections of files in directories. The identity of each node in the tree is the hash of the combined hashes of the child nodes. These hashes of hashes continue all the way up to the root of the tree. This helps to ensure that the tree is immutable.

A commit contains the hash of the root of the tree. From this, Git can reconstruct the exact state of the source code. All the while, it employs persistent data structures across commits to minimize the storage required. Git doesn't need to copy a blob if its contents haven't changed. And it doesn't need to copy a tree node if its child nodes haven't changed.

To capture the branching and merging of history, Git includes the hash of the parent within each commit. If a commit represents a merge, then it has two parents. Both hashes are included. This results in an immutable graph of commits like the one in Figure 1-8. Every developer who clones the repository will compute the same hash for each commit, thus making those identities deterministic and consistent.

```
*   249916e - (origin/master, origin/HEAD) Merge pull request #11 from micha
|\
| * 44644f4 - chore(package): update lockfile package-lock.json (5 weeks ago
| * 8aede8a - chore(package): update webpack to version 4.36.1 (5 weeks ago)
|/
| * 26223d5 - (origin/greenkeeper/jinaga-pin-2.3.8) fix: pin jinaga to 2.3.8
|/
| * a8613b0 - (origin/greenkeeper/jinaga-2.4.0) chore(package): update lockf
| * 1e480d3 - chore(package): update jinaga to version 2.4.0 (5 weeks ago) <
|/
*   4037b30 - Merge pull request #8 from michaellperry/dependabot/npm_and_ya
|\
| * a5dc439 - Bump lodash from 4.17.11 to 4.17.14 (5 weeks ago) <dependabot[
|/
*   d91d87d - Merge pull request #7 from michaellperry/dependabot/npm_and_ya
```

Figure 1-8. *A history of commits in a Git repository*

The current state of the source code can be constructed from a commit without reconnecting to the remote host, thus granting each replica autonomy. The developer works disconnected from the server to construct a new set of commits on their own. While they work, they are not connecting to the remote host to lock files or check for the most recent changes. They are working in complete isolation; no round trip to the server is required.

When a conflict occurs, as it often does in source code, the developer finds within their local repository all of the information necessary to resolve it. They have the identity of the collaborators (possibly even themselves) involved in the conflict. They know exactly the context of the change – what the code looked like before it was modified. And they even have from the commit messages some clue as to the intent of each programmer.

Once they have pulled all of this information to their machine, the developer can resolve the conflict themselves. They don't need to further involve the server. In fact, because of the nature of Git branches, they can choose to let the conflict stand as long as they please. There is no immediate need to for the conflict to be resolved before work can continue. But when a resolution *is* made, it is recorded as a merge commit. Once pushed, that commit becomes part of the repository and is replicated to all parties involved. They can all see the conflict resolution.

This mode of working is only possible because every commit is immutable. Every developer who has the same commit knows that their copy is just as good as any other. No other developer can modify the contents or the identity of a commit; all they can do is create new ones. Even rebasing creates new commits with new identities.

Blockchains

Blockchains store information as singular units (transactions, contracts, digital assets) aggregated into *blocks*. A block is simply a collection of these units surrounded by an envelope of metadata. Each blockchain defines its own block data structure, but they all share some common fields.

- A random number called a *nonce*

- A reference to the previous block

- A hash of the block's contents (including the nonce and the reference)

As a result, the current block is just the most recent collection of transactional units. It points back to the previous block, which points back again forming a chain. This chain, as depicted in Figure 1-9, represents the entire history of transactions since inception.

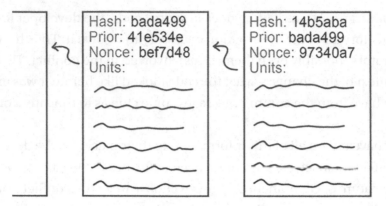

Figure 1-9. Each block in the chain contains a hash and a reference to the previous block

The immutability of a block is a consequence of the hash that is its identity. If the contents of a block were to change, the new hash would be different. Cryptographically strong hash functions are used so that it would be difficult to modify a block in such a way as to leave the hash undisturbed. And when I say "difficult" here, I use the term in the way that cryptographers use it. We are not allowed to say "impossible."

Because a block's hash (and hence its identity) includes the hash of its predecessor, any change to a block will ripple through all subsequent blocks and produce a new alternate history. Such tampering would be easily detected. Every node sees the same copy of every block. This is both the enabling characteristic and the most valuable feature of a blockchain. On the one hand, this enables immediate detection of tampering, and on the other hand, it provides the benefit of a shared public auditable ledger.

Docker

Docker goes beyond the capabilities of virtual machines because it organizes images in *layers*. A layer is an immutable portion of a file system with a reference to the layer below. An *image* is really nothing more than a reference to the topmost layer. For this reason, the other layers are also referred to as *intermediate images*.

For Docker to execute a workload, it creates a *container*. A container is a running instance of an execution environment, complete with its own simulated file system. When a container starts up, Docker allocates to it a special writable layer, which in turn points to the topmost layer of the image. This layer is initially empty.

At runtime, when a container reads from the disk, Docker will forward that read operation to the writable layer. As this layer is initially empty, the read request will fall through to the topmost layer of the image. If the requested data is in that layer, then it will be returned. Otherwise, it will move down to the layer below.

When a Docker container writes to the disk, it only modifies the writable layer. This layer is special, in that it is not shared among any of the other Docker containers and it is not persisted beyond the lifetime of its container. Any information written to that layer is lost when the container is deleted. Even if the container "overwrote" parts of the operating system, the lower layer containing that source data is unaffected.

The identity of a layer is a hash, similar to the identity of a Git commit or a blockchain block. The difference, however, is that it is a hash not of the contents but of the command that created it (including any source files in the case of an ADD or COPY command). The resulting structure is shown in Figure 1-10. To build an image, Docker starts with the base image: a name used in a registry to identify the hash of an existing layer. Starting from this base layer, Docker then scans the commands one by one and computes the hash of the resulting intermediate image. If that image is already in the repository, then it is retrieved rather than being reconstructed.

```
IMAGE                   CREATED BY
3d53cdc8aa80            /bin/sh -c #(nop)  CMD ["pm2-runtime" "npm" ...
8e48995a6b00            /bin/sh -c #(nop)   USER node
e022d570f832            /bin/sh -c npm install pm2 -g
277f48e981fd            /bin/sh -c npm install --production
77178a97af83            /bin/sh -c #(nop) COPY multi:56a9de3a81cb55e...
```

Figure 1-10. *Each Docker image is created by applying a command to the previous image*

Immutable layers allow a single Docker host to run several containers from the same or related images without duplicating the entire operating system for each one. Virtual machines cannot share Virtual Hard Drives when those VHDs are mutable. If one machine modifies a VHD, that change would become visible to the other VMs. But Docker can get away with sharing layers because those layers will not be modified. It's the sharing of layers that allows Docker to support orchestrators and meshes, coordinating several interconnected running containers all formed from a shared repository of images.

Each of these systems has harnessed the power of immutability to provide their own distinct advantages. Just as Pat Helland pointed out in "Immutability Changes Everything," this one idea is a recurring theme appearing at several layers of the technology stack and across many problem domains. As you learn to model business problems based on immutability, you will start to enjoy the advantages of a reliable audit history, just like blockchains. And as you learn to implement immutable data structures within your mobile apps and microservices, you will benefit from the same autonomy found in Git. Let the journey begin.

CHAPTER 2

Forms of Immutable Architecture

There are consequences to designing a system using only immutable records. Some of them are the advantages that we've already explored: overcoming unreliable communication channels, reduced blocking, increased autonomy, and improved auditability. Other consequences are less desirable. Many of them simply require a shift in thinking, while others demand entirely new solutions. As you adopt immutability into your application design, you will need to recognize how the architecture must change in response.

The trade-offs required by the shift to immutability have led to the emergence of different architectural styles. In this chapter, we will examine three of those styles: event sourcing (ES), Asynchronous Model View Update, and historical modeling. All three share the idea that state evolves from historical records. Where they diverge is in the ordering of those records. The first two styles assume that records can be viewed in *sequence*. They expect to be able to enumerate records in order. The third arises from the idea that historical records may be *partially* ordered. It does not allow enumeration. Instead, it trades that capability away to achieve some valuable results.

After this chapter, the remainder of the book will focus on the third style: historical modeling. But it will be important to put that choice into context. Each architectural decision is a trade-off among competing values. Let's explore all three architectures to get a better understanding of what those trade-offs will be. We'll begin with the concepts that they all have in common.

© Michael L. Perry 2024
M. L. Perry, *The Art of Immutable Architecture*, https://doi.org/10.1007/979-8-8688-0288-1_2

Deriving State from History

The art of immutable architecture is finding a balance. On the one hand, there is the recognition that immutable data structures offer significant advantages in parallel and distributed computing. On the other hand, there is the recognition that the world that our systems model is full of mutation. Each of the architectures we will study finds this balance in their own way.

Here, it helps to give things distinct and meaningful names. We will call the things that change *objects* and the things that do not change *records*. These choices are not arbitrary. They are based on concepts that humans have invented to organize information both with and without computers.

Historical Records

Let's go back in time to a world before computers. How was business transacted in this world? Rather than updating the current state of the world in a large database, information was recorded and shared in the form of documents.

Suppose a customer places an order for ten widgets. This decision is captured as a purchase order. The purchase order references the two parties: the buyer and the seller. It also references the product – widgets – by the catalog number assigned by the seller. The result would be a document similar to the one shown in Figure 2-1.

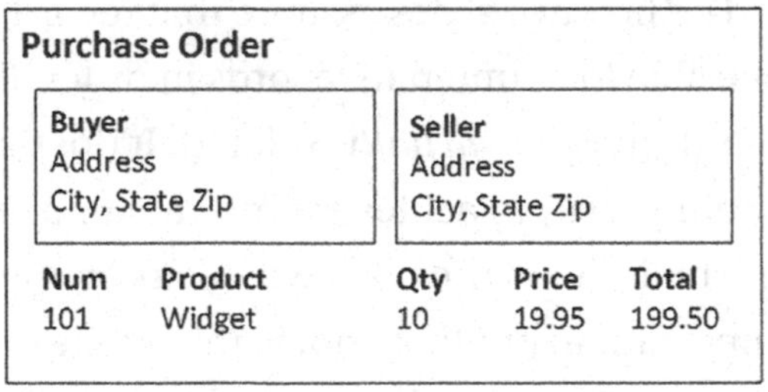

Purchase Order					
Buyer Address City, State Zip			**Seller** Address City, State Zip		
Num	**Product**		**Qty**	**Price**	**Total**
101	Widget		10	19.95	199.50

Figure 2-1. *A purchase order records the intent of a customer to purchase products from a vendor*

Building Upon the Past

The purchase order is a historical record. It is an immutable document that records a decision as it was at a certain point in time. It makes reference to two parties: the buyer and the seller. Neither party can change the purchase order itself. They can only amend this document with another one.

The buyer and the seller are distinct legal entities. These entities were created with their own set of immutable records: documents that were filed with their respective regulating bodies as articles of incorporation. These documents were created well in advance of the purchase order.

The purchase order refers to a few other decisions that came before. For example, it refers to a catalog number. This is the result of a decision to publish the widget in a catalog of available products with a listed price. The catalog, once published, is not changed. It is only amended by publishing subsequent catalogs with ever-evolving lists of products and prices.

Evolution of Understanding

Future documents will in turn refer back to this purchase order. Once the seller receives a copy of this document, they will create an invoice – a new document that requests payment. The buyer will write a document in response, a check that requests that the bank transfer funds to the seller. The seller will create a packing slip, which documents the items to be included within a shipment. The carrier will issue a bill of lading to the buyer, documenting delivery of the goods.

Historical records evolve our collective understanding over time. Each one is in itself immutable. But our view of the world changes as more documents are published.

Mutable Objects

The invention of the computer has greatly scaled up our capacity for handling transactions. But it has also subtly changed the way in which we think about what is true. Before computers, we each had to carry a bank book to calculate our account balance. Now, we can see it immediately on our cell phones. It used to be understood that the idea of "balance" was a derived one and differed based on one's knowledge of which checks had been cashed. Now, at least intuitively, "balance" has become an intrinsic property of an "account" object.

Like functional, modular, and structured programming before it, *object orientation* was one of the great advancements in software modeling. It originated from the observation that software systems exist to model the real world. It sought to first understand the behavior of the objects being modeled and then provide patterns and templates for implementation.

At its core, object-oriented programming assumes that at least *some* objects are mutable. It leaves room for immutable objects but mainly describes the behavior and evolution of mutable objects. This assumption appears most notably in the concept of identity.

Identity

Of the fundamental elements of object orientation that James Rumbaugh defined in 1991, the three we frequently talk about are encapsulation, inheritance, and polymorphism. The one that we fail to mention is *identity*. Rumbaugh defines identity as a distinguishing property independent of identifying attribute. In object-oriented modeling, even if two objects have the same properties, they are different objects. Acting on one will not affect the other.

[T]wo objects are distinct even if all their attribute values (such as name and size) are identical.[1]

When we translate that idea to object-oriented languages such as Java or C++, the concept of identity is mapped to a location in memory. An object becomes a block of memory allocated to store its current state. The identity of the object is the address of that memory. That is why sharing the identity of an object in C++ is achieved by "passing a pointer."

Memory addresses obey the rules of object-oriented identity. They represent uniqueness absent any identifying attribute. At any point in time, the state of two objects might be exactly the same. The chunks of memory at those two addresses might be byte-for-byte equal. But changing the memory at one location will have no effect on the memory at the other. A consumer of one object will perceive no change in behavior based on a modification of the other.

---

[1] Rumbaugh et al. Object-Oriented Modeling and Design. 1991 Prentice-Hall, Inc. ISBN 0-13-629841-9.

As we move further away from a single thread in a lone process on an isolated machine, this implementation decision starts to show its faults. Moving from one thread to many, we must introduce locking to protect the integrity of the data structure against simultaneous mutation. Moving from one process to many, we must map the shared object into independent memory spaces. And going beyond the boundaries of a single machine, the concept of a pointer loses all meaning. Other forms of identity need to be introduced to compensate.

Evolution of State

Rumbaugh's definition of identity solves a problem for objects that can change state over time. But if we introduce the concept of immutability, it becomes less valuable. The reason for an object to have intrinsic identity is so that it can provide consistent, meaningful behavior as it changes over time. If I take a bite out of one apple, another remains whole. It would be a very strange world indeed if a bite appeared in *your* apple, or if I returned later to find mine completely restored.

Rumbaugh's identity is a recognition that objects in the real world change state in response to stimulus. They remember that state. Their observable behavior is based on their current state. For those changes in behavior to make sense in any model of the real world, objects in the model have to have intrinsic identity.

Projections

Our goal now is to use immutable records to model mutable objects. The records clearly are not the objects themselves. That would be insufficient, as records would not allow for the mutability that objects expect to have. Instead, the records must in some way represent *changes* to the objects. The immutable records *are* the mutations of the objects.

To achieve this goal, we will treat immutable records as *observed* state. They represent things that we actually saw and recorded. Objects, on the other hand, are *derived* state. They represent our interpretation of those observations and can change as new observations are made.

Two Kinds of State

Imagine a spreadsheet. In each cell, you can enter one of two things. Either you can enter a value or you can enter a formula. A value represents some basic measurement, an observation of the system you are modeling. A formula, on the other hand, derives a new value from those observations. Formulas represent derived state.

As a mathematician, my favorite analog of this idea is a function. We will often write y as a function of x, thereby producing a plot. You can draw a vertical line anywhere on that plot and you will hit only one point. The same cannot necessarily be said for any horizontal line. We say that x represents the *independent* variable and y the *dependent* variable. You get to choose x, but y is calculated by the function. Independent variables are observed, and dependent variables are derived.

In software, we have other names for this phenomenon. Derived state is sometimes referred to as a *projection* of the observed state. A pure function takes a value as an input and produces an output with no side effects. The output is deterministic, depending only upon the input. Where the input is observed state, the output is derived from that input. It is a projection of that observed state.

In the MVVM pattern, observed state is called the model and derived state is called the view model. The model represents objects in the problem domain. The view model projects those objects onto a view. As the user interacts with the view, the view model translates their actions into model updates. It then re-projects those updates back to the view to display to the user.

Projecting Objects

No matter what you call it – formulas, dependent variables, projections, or view models – derived state is a deterministic transformation of observed state. It adds no information to the system; it only presents the information that's already there in a different way. In mathematics, we say that it adds no new degrees of freedom to the system. In software, you might say that the view model is backed by the model. The important point is that the user gets to directly affect observed state. They can only see the results indirectly projected onto the derived state.

In an immutable architecture, the historical records are observed state. The user gets to create new records directly through their actions. Those records capture decisions that the user has made.

The objects, on the other hand, are merely projections. They are ephemeral. The user does not get to set the state of an object. They can only see those objects change as a result of new historical records. Every one of these architectures has their own way of calculating that projection.

Event Sourcing

Historical records are the observed state of an immutable architecture. They represent past decisions. You could call these past decisions "events" and demand that they are the sole source of truth. That is the origin of the term *event sourcing* (ES).

While the term "event sourcing" could arguably be applied to any architecture that reconstructs state from a history of immutable records, the practice is a bit more specific. As Martin Fowler described it in 2009

> *The fundamental idea of Event Sourcing is that of ensuring every change to the state of an application is captured in an event object, and that these event objects are themselves stored in the **sequence they were applied** for the same lifetime as the application state itself.[2]*

The emphasis on "sequence they were applied" is mine. The idea of a sequence does not necessarily follow from the requirements of immutable historical records. But it is a reasonable assumption, and one shared by all implementations of ES that I have seen. I therefore consider *sequence* a defining characteristic of event sourcing. Be aware that the sequence is applied not at the application level, but at the aggregate level, as we will see shortly.

Generating Events

In an event-sourced application, the user interacts (through a UI and possibly an API) with a domain model. The domain model does not respond immediately to the request. Instead, it validates the request and generates an event. The event is an immutable record of the user's intent. It is named and interpreted as a past-tense statement, as in "this thing happened": `OrderSubmitted`, `PlayerRegistered`, and `ResidentMoved`, for example. The naming convention reflects the truth that an event, once generated, cannot be ignored. Its effect might just be different from what the user intended.

---

[2] `https://martinfowler.com/eaaDev/EventSourcing.html`

By interacting with the domain model, the user experiences the application as if it followed a traditional object-oriented paradigm. They get the impression that objects have properties that change over time and that their actions directly cause that change. The application hides the fact that the object model is both a generator and a projection of a sequence of events.

The advantages that ES provides over a traditional object model begin with the same ones that we've already identified for all immutable architectures: increased scalability and auditability. In addition, they boast the ability to rebuild objects entirely from the stream of events. When a defect is fixed or a feature is added, the application can discard any cached versions of the domain model and reconstruct them using the new code. It also allows an event-sourced application to go back in time and replay only part of a sequence, seeing an object as it appeared in the past. This provides the user of the application with a powerful ability to perform temporal analysis.

Practitioners will often pair event sourcing with both Command Query Responsibility Segregation (CQRS) and Domain-Driven Design (DDD). This pairing is not a requirement for ES, nor are the implementations all in agreement how it is achieved. Some choose to pair just CQRS with ES, or just DDD with ES. This architectural decision affects how an application projects immutable records into mutable objects.

CQRS

Command Query Responsibility Segregation extends the object-oriented principle of Command Query Separation (CQS). Bertrand Meyer defines commands and queries as kinds of methods. He distinguishes them as follows:

A command serves to modify objects, a query to return information about objects.[3]

Where CQS draws a line between methods, CQRS extends that line to segregate objects. In obedience of the single responsibility principle,[4] some objects are responsible for issuing commands and others for issuing queries.

---

[3] Bertrand Meyer. Object Oriented Software Construction, Second Edition. Prentice Hall. 1997. ISBN: 0-13-429155-4.

[4] Robert C. Martin. Agile Software Development, Principles, Patterns, and Practices. Prentice Hall. 2003. ISBN 978-0135974445.

In CQRS, *commands* are responsible for changing the state of the system. These are distinct from *queries*, which request information about current state. Commands and queries follow separate paths and often interact with different architectural components. Commands are often asynchronous, while queries are usually synchronous. In many implementations, they operate against different data stores.

When paired with ES, commands are further distinguished from *events*. Whereas a command is expressed as an imperative statement, an event is a past-tense statement. The command `SubmitOrder` results in the event `OrderSubmitted`. The command instructs the system of record to perform the user's intent. The event, on the other hand, is *produced* by the system of record and must be honored. The system of record is responsible for first validating and authorizing the command. It may choose to fail or ignore the command.

When the command is sent asynchronously, this further removes the user from the effect of their actions. Applications using the CQRS/ES architectural style with asynchronous commands will often expose an *eventually consistent* interaction to the user, making it clear to the user that their request will be processed at a later time.

DDD

When object-oriented programming was first introduced, it held the promise that objects in software could model objects in the world. As it was adopted into enterprise software development, objects started to model the world less and the computer more. Eric Evans refocused object-oriented analysis and design onto the problem domain with his 2004 book *Domain-Driven Design*.[5]

While the book offers advice on many phases of the software development process, we will focus only on the technical aspects. In particular, we will focus on the ontology and relationship of different kinds of objects.

DDD recognizes two kinds of objects: entities and value objects. An *entity* is an object that has identity. As we have already seen, object-oriented identity affords the object the ability to change over time. In contrast, a *value object* has no identity and is therefore immutable.

---

[5] Eric Evans. Domain-Driven Design: Tackling Complexity in the Heart of Software. Addison-Wesley Professional. 2004. ISBN: 0-321-12521-5.

A `Customer`, for example, would be an entity, since it has identity and can change over time. A customer might have a mutable property `ShippingAddress`, the data type of which would be `Address`. An address in turn would have several different properties, like `Street`, `City`, `Country`, and others. But the shipping address is managed as a single unit, not as separate properties on `Customer`. The `Address` data type is a value object and has no identity of its own.

Entities in DDD are organized within hierarchies called *aggregates*. An aggregate is a parent-child relationship. At the top of this hierarchy is the *aggregate root*. For example, an `Assembly` in one domain might be an aggregate containing many `Parts`. Several `Assemblys` are collected under one aggregate root called `Product`. The aggregate appears in Figure 2-2.

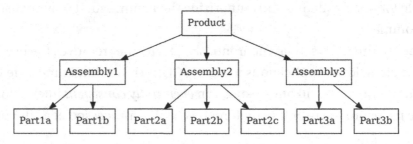

Figure 2-2. *An aggregate root owns its child entities*

As a rule, entities are not addressed outside of their aggregate root. Within the domain that we described previously, it would make little sense to talk about a `Part` without first identifying its `Product`. The `Product` is the aggregate root and therefore the entry point for all external references.

Event sourcing replays past events in order to rebuild objects in the model. But that doesn't mean that the system reconstructs the entire object model on every query. That would not be an efficient way to handle a query of a single object. Most of the events in a model's history will have no effect on that object. So instead, event-sourced applications break that history into independent streams. Each stream affects only a subset of the domain model. When ES is combined with DDD, that subset is the aggregate root.

A query in a DDD/ES application will identify an aggregate root. The application loads the stream of events for that given identity. The stream contains all events that affected the root or any other entity within the aggregate. Individual entities are not reconstructed from their own history; they arise from the history of their root entity.

Taking a Functional View

So far we have been concentrating on object-oriented analysis to describe the effect of events. But there is an equally valid interpretation using the ideas of functional programming. Consider a function that computes the state of a system after applying an event:

$$f(state_n, event) \rightarrow state_{n+1}$$

By "state of the system," we could be talking about a single object, an aggregate root, or even the entire object model. Practically speaking, you will want to choose a smaller boundary. But analytically, the outcome is the same.

The advantage of modeling system state using this function is that state – like events – becomes immutable. The function is a *pure* function: it does not cause side effects. More specifically, it does not change the state of its inputs. The function does not *modify* the incoming state; it returns a new state *derived* from the incoming state.

In functional programming, it is not uncommon to define *higher-order functions*. These are functions that take functions as parameters. One such function is *left-fold* (sometimes abbreviated as *foldl*). *Foldl* takes a binary operation – a function taking two parameters – and applies that operation over every element of a list.

For example, given the binary operation *+*, the starting point *0*, and a list of numbers, *foldl* will compute the sum.

$$foldl(+, 0, [3, 17, 2]) = 22$$

You can think about event sourcing in these functional terms. The binary operation is the function described previously, which takes the current state and returns the state after an event is applied. The starting point is the initial state of the system. And the list is the sequence of events. Greg Young uses functional constructs to describe event sourcing:

> *When we talk about Event Sourcing, current state is a left-fold of previous behaviors.*[6]

---

[6]www.eventstore.com/blog/projections-1-theory

Commutative and Idempotent Events

We will find that the commutative and idempotent properties are useful in distributed systems. The commutative property allows us to apply an operation out of order and get the same result. The idempotent property allows us to repeat the operation without further effect. Since event sourcing is based on a sequence of operations, it is sensitive to both order and duplication. It is up to the application developer to ensure that order is preserved and duplicates are prevented.

The + operator is commutative: $a+b = b+a$. But in general, binary operations don't have to commute. Subtraction is not commutative: in general, $a-b \neq b-a$. Nor are many business operations. Unless you are very careful in your selection of f, *foldl* will be sensitive to the order of items in the list. Event sourcing, therefore, is noncommutative by default. If a system is to respond consistently with respect to out-of-order events, then it is incumbent upon the developer to prove that the event-application function commutes when necessary. To be more precise, if the event-application function satisfies the following equation, then the events commute:

$$f(f(x, e_1), e_2) = f(f(x, e_2), e_1)$$

Just as not all binary operators commute, not all are *idempotent*. The + operator is one such example: $a+a \neq a$ (except in the special case that $a = 0$). And so a left-fold over a sequence containing duplicate numbers will inflate the result. If your distributed system allows duplicate events into the stream, then it is up to you to prove the following equation:

$$f(f(x, e), e) = f(x, e)$$

You can handle order and duplication in front of the event stream or behind it. Either prevent out-of-order and duplicate events from entering the stream or carefully choose your event-application function.

Model View Update

The Elm programming language takes the functional view of a history of events quite literally. This language compiles to JavaScript and runs in the browser. It generates HTML from a source model. A pure function produces successive versions of the model as it handles events. The pattern on which Elm is based is called *Model View Update*.

Inspired by Elm, Facebook created a suite of tools that implement Model View Update in their products. The first of those tools was React, a front-end library for JavaScript that projects a model into HTML. The next was Flux, a unidirectional data flow application design pattern. This defined the way that Facebook designed web and mobile apps. Redux was an implementation of Flux developed outside of Facebook by Dan Abramov. Dan was subsequently brought into Facebook to continue work on Redux, React, and the architecture in general. Finally, there is the back-end architecture, only parts of which are currently open sourced, upon which Facebook develops their APIs.

The Update Loop

When React and Redux are used together, they form a loop. This loop is the core engine of the Model View Update pattern. React transforms the model into the view, and Redux dispatches actions to update the model.

The *model* is simply a data structure. As an application developer, you define the data structure that you need. Since React targets single-page web applications, the model is typically the collection of state that a single user is viewing and manipulating within a page.

The *view* is what the user sees; in React, it is HTML. A function called *render* transforms the model into the view. This function runs first after the model is loaded and then every time a new version of the model is produced. The results of subsequent executions are compared to determine what has actually changed and to update the Document Object Model (DOM). The developer does not have to be concerned with change tracking.

---

render(model) → *view*

Finally, *update* is a function that computes the next version of the model. This is a pure function, so it does not modify the model. Instead, it produces a model as it would look after an *action* is applied.

41

$$update(model_n, action) \rightarrow model_{n+1}$$

A Model View Update application begins with loading a model. It then enters a tight loop in which user interaction generates an action. The update function handles the action producing a new version of the model. The render function turns that new model into a new view. The framework compares the two versions of the view to determine what to change in the browser. The user is presented with the updated user interface, and the loop continues as shown in Figure 2-3.

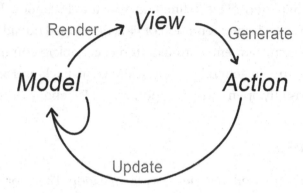

Figure 2-3. *The model-view-update loop found in React and Redux*

Being a pure function, *update* does not modify the model. It produces a new version of the model, which is then rendered to produce a new version of the view. So it is more accurate to depict this loop not as a cycle, but as a spiral as in Figure 2-4.

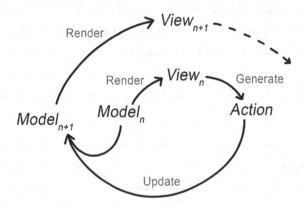

Figure 2-4. *Each iteration produces a new version of the model*

This image makes it more clear that there are no circular dependencies. Each iteration produces a new set of objects. The old objects are still available to support optimizations, such as minimizing DOM manipulation.

Unidirectional Data Flow

Flux and Redux were developed as a reaction to problems found in the *Model View Controller* (MVC) pattern. In MVC, a controller responds to changes in the model by updating the views. It also responds to user input in the view by updating the model. The controller coordinates data flow in two directions: both in from the user and outward from the application.

Bidirectional data flow is very simple to start with. With just a handful of controllers, following the thread of execution from view to model and back again is not difficult. But as more controllers are added, the number of paths increases super-linearly, as illustrated in Figure 2-5. It is difficult to know whether a new feature is going to produce a new edge case that causes cascading updates or circular dependencies.

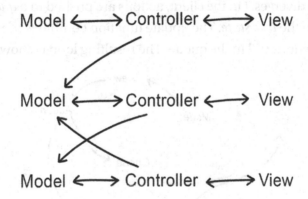

Figure 2-5. *Several controllers coordinating with one another to update their models*

With unidirectional data flow, on the other hand, there is no chance of cascading updates. An action produces an update to state, which produces an update to the view. The view cannot respond to one action by producing another action. There is no possibility of cycles or runaway updates.

Unidirectional data flow also supports better unit testing. Start with a given state. When an action is handled, then the handler produces a new expected state. Initializing the state, applying the action, and verifying the resulting state are all easy to automate.

The operations that are hard to automate – verifying that the view is correctly rendered and that user interaction is properly interpreted – are marginalized. Rendering a view is simply a function on the model, and user input only produces an action. Unidirectional data flow minimizes the manual testing surface area.

Immutable App Architecture

Model View Update as practiced by React and Redux is only half of the picture. The other half happens on the server. While Redux has the luxury of operating on an in-memory store, when a mobile application communicates with its host server, the current state of the model is not always available. Lee Byron presented Facebook's solution at Render 2016.[7] He called it "Immutable App Architecture." But since that name is similar to the general term "immutable architecture" as I've been using it, I will call the pattern he presented *Asynchronous Model View Update*.

The pattern begins just as before with a render function projecting a model into a view. Also as before, the user's interactions with the view produce actions. At this point, however, the pattern diverges. On the client, actions are pushed to a *queue*. On the server, actions are applied to the *true state*. The update function combines the last known true state with all of the actions still in the queue. The resulting loop is shown in Figure 2-6.

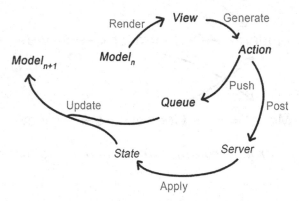

Figure 2-6. *Asynchronous Model View Update*

On the client, the next iteration of the model is not based on the previous iteration. Instead, the client goes back to the last state fetched from the server. If a new state is received from the server asynchronously, then it becomes the new true state. Any actions that are represented within that state are removed from the queue. The state is known to be true; the queue contains actions that optimistically might become true.

The advantage of this architecture for Facebook was that they could more easily reason about new features. To add a feature, a developer needed only to add new actions and propagate them out toward the view. If those actions had an impact on other views, they would simply add the desired effect to the update function. The mobile application could work quickly, even while on a slow network. The effect of a user's interaction would be immediately visible, without waiting on a round trip to the server.

The Asynchronous Model View Update architecture optimistically interprets a series of actions. User actions are validated on-device with the expectation that most of them will succeed on the server. It is assumed that no other actions will intervene and that the result of executing the actions on the server will be the same as on the client. When this optimistic assumption is found to be false, the architecture simply discards the locally computed state and takes the server's version.

Historical Modeling

The immutable architectures that we just examined both make a distinction between immutable historical records and a mutable object model. They also assume that historical events occurred within a fully ordered sequence. But neither of these assumptions necessarily follow from the idea of using immutable records as the source of truth. If we model a system as a collection of related historical facts, we find that we can dispense with the mutable object model altogether and that facts don't have to occur in a fully ordered sequence.

Let's begin with a slight change in terminology. Instead of referring to historical records as *events* or *actions*, let us call them *facts*. The reason for the name change is that facts obey a set of rules that do not necessarily apply to events in event sourcing, or actions in Asynchronous Model View Update. In particular, facts are partially ordered.

Partial Order

The term "partial order" comes from mathematics and is distinguished from the term "total order." Start with a set of objects, be they numbers, words, research papers, data structures, what have you. Define a comparison operation that tells you whether one

---

[7] Lee Byron. Immutable User Interfaces. Render 2016. https://vimeo.com/166790294

object comes before another. We will typically use the less than symbol (<) to represent this operation. If for any pair of objects in the set, we can use < to put one before the other, then the set is totally ordered. If we can only do that for *some* of the pairs, then the set is partially ordered.

Consider the set of research papers. A paper will cite earlier research on which it builds. One way in which a paper "comes before" (<) another is if it is directly cited. For example, in "Immutability Changes Everything," Pat Helland directly cited a Leslie Lamport paper, "The Part-Time Parliament." We can write

---

Lamport 1998. < Helland 2015.

Another way in which a paper "comes before" another is through the transitive property. If a paper is cited by another that comes before a third, then it does to. In our example, Lamport cited "Impossibility of Distributed Consensus with One Faulty Process" by Fischer, Lynch, and Paterson.

Fischer, Lynch, Patterson 1985. < Lamport 1998.

Therefore by the transitive property:

Fischer, Lynch, Patterson 1985. < Helland 2015.

A partial order is more forgiving than a total order. Take any two research papers at random. Chances are neither one "comes before" the other. They are most likely completely unrelated to one another. If we were to define a total order on the papers – say, by their date of publication – then one would come before the other. Instead, by defining a partial order, we get to choose when order matters and when it doesn't.

Whether we are talking about a total order or a partial order, the comparison operator that we choose must have a couple of useful properties. First, it must be transitive.

---

a<b and b<c ⇒ a<c

It must also be nonreflexive. That is to say that an object does not "come before" itself.

$$a \not< a$$

Finally, the comparison operation must be unidirectional. That means that an object cannot come both before and after another one. More formally, this is written as follows:

$$a < b \Rightarrow b \not< a$$

All of these properties hold for a comparison operator that imposes either a partial order or a total order. The thing that distinguishes them is whether for any given pair one must come before the other. In a total order, if two distinct objects are not ordered one way, they must be ordered the other way:

$$a \not< b \Rightarrow b < a \text{ (for a and b distinct)}$$

This is not the case for a partial order. A partial order will allow both $a \not< b$ and $b \not< a$. Total and partial orders can be found for many sets. This includes the set of historical records, or *facts*.

Predecessors

The way in which historical modeling puts facts into a partial order is to identify *predecessors*. For each fact, a historical model makes explicit which other facts must have come before. These aren't simply the list of all other facts that have occurred earlier in time: that would put facts into a sequence – a total order. Instead, predecessors are facts that must have happened before in order to make the current fact make sense.

If we return to our purchase order example, we can see a few predecessors in evidence. A purchase order is a document of the decision by a buyer to purchase items from a seller. The example purchase order from earlier in the chapter appears again in Figure 2-7.

Purchase Order

Buyer Address City, State Zip	**Seller** Address City, State Zip

Num	**Product**	**Qty**	**Price**	**Total**
101	Widget	10	19.95	199.50

Figure 2-7. *A purchase order from a buyer to a seller*

The purchase order is a *fact*. It is a historical record that documents a decision. It is immutable: neither party can change the purchase order itself. They can only amend this document with another one.

The purchase order fact refers to a few other facts that came before. It refers to the buyer and the seller as distinct legal entities. These entities were created with their own set of historical facts – documents that were filed with their respective regulating bodies as articles of incorporation. These facts were created well in advance of the purchase order.

The purchase order fact also refers to product. The order specifies precisely which product the buyer wants. The diagram in Figure 2-8 illustrates the relationship of the purchase order with all of its predecessors. The arrows point up to emphasize that the purchase order refers to its predecessors, not the other way around.

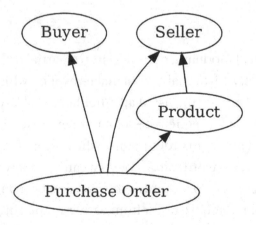

Figure 2-8. *Buyer, seller, and product are all predecessors of purchase order*

In this model, there is no predecessor relationship between purchase orders. It does not record that one purchase order was submitted earlier in time than another one. Predecessors are not simply facts that occurred earlier in time; they are prerequisites: things that must have been true for this fact to make sense.

Successors

It is useful to talk about the opposite direction of the predecessor relationship. A fact that refers to another one is its *successor*. Successors help us to evolve our understanding of a system over time. We cannot change a historical fact, but we can create successors.

Let's continue the story of the buyer and the seller. The seller receives a copy of the purchase order and then sends the buyer an invoice. The invoice is another historical fact. The predecessor of this fact is the purchase order. The successor of the purchase order is the invoice, as shown in Figure 2-9.

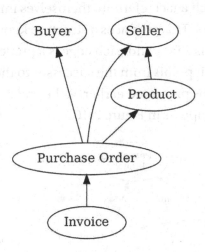

Figure 2-9. *Invoice is the successor of a purchase order*

The presence of a successor does not change the predecessor. Issuing an invoice does not alter the historical record that is the purchase order. However, the successor changes our *interpretation* of the predecessor. When we see the invoice, we now know that the state of the purchase order has changed. We know that it has been invoiced, and it would be incorrect to issue a second one.

It is important to recognize that there is no mechanism within a historical model to *prevent* the creation of additional successors. The model itself must allow for multiple invoices to the same purchase order. If we carefully control *who* can create those invoices, and on what machine, then we can avoid this situation in any practical scenario. But the model itself has no ability to lock the purchase order, or to prefer one invoice over another.

A fact does not know about its successors. New successors are added over time. To fully understand the state of a fact, we must query the historical model to discover if new successors have been created. Compare this with the DDD/ES approach of replaying a portion of history to update an aggregate. The current state of historical model is simply the collection of known successors.

Immutable Graphs

Like an event in event sourcing, a historical fact is immutable. But unlike an event, a fact refers to its predecessors. Taken together, these properties have interesting consequences.

The predecessors to which a fact refers are themselves immutable facts. Those facts can in turn have predecessors. This produces a structure known as a *directed graph*. Each vertex in this structure is a fact, and each edge is a predecessor relationship. This relationship has a direction: it points from the successor to the predecessor. We've seen examples of these graphs presented earlier as they relate to purchase orders and invoices. Another example appears in Figure 2-10.

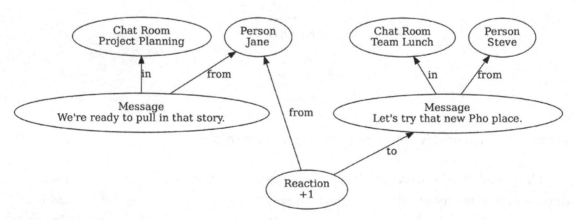

Figure 2-10. *A fact refers to its predecessors, which in turn refers to still more predecessors*

Since a fact refers to its predecessors, and the fact is immutable, it follows that a predecessor cannot be added to an existing fact. That predecessor relationship is *part* of the fact, and the fact cannot be modified. And so while it is possible to add successors to a fact, it is not possible to add predecessors. This is in keeping with our use of the predecessor relationship to define what comes before in the partial order. All predecessors must be known facts, recorded before the new one.

From any given fact, we can trace the graph along the predecessor paths. We will select a subgraph that includes the starting fact, all of its predecessors, and all of *their* predecessors recursively. This process produces the *transitive closure* of the starting fact. If we compute the transitive closure of the reaction, we end up with the subgraph in Figure 2-11.

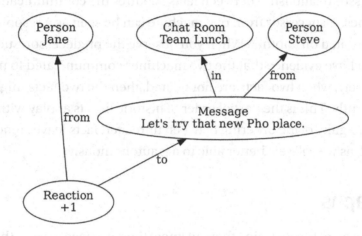

Figure 2-11. *The transitive closure of a fact contains every fact's predecessors*

To build the transitive closure, we started from one immutable fact and followed arrows only in a direction that cannot change. The subgraph is therefore immutable. For any given fact, the transitive closure will always be the same. Adding new successors to any of the facts in the graph will not change it. Those successors would never get added to the transitive closure.

Conversely, the transitive closure *identifies* the starting fact. There is no other fact for which the transitive closure would produce this same set. While comparing sets, include all values contained in the facts, as well as the edges leading to their predecessors. In a historical model, this is the *only* way to identify a fact. They do not have globally unique identifiers (GUIDs) or sequence numbers outside of this structure. The contents of the facts in the transitive closure are all you've got to tell one fact apart from another.

Collaboration

Machines within a distributed system can communicate by exchanging graphs of historical facts. As they do, they must be sure to send the transitive closure of each fact. They have to know that the recipient is aware of all of the predecessors at every step.

When a machine records a new piece of information – a decision that a user has made or the outcome of some business process – it does so by creating a new fact. It cannot create that fact based on predecessors of which it is not yet aware. It must either create those predecessors first or have learned about them from its peers.

The predecessor relationship between facts captures the communication structure between machines. A successor from one machine can be seen as a response to its predecessor generated on another. When you observe the predecessor/successor relationship, you have evidence that the two machines communicated to make that happen. Conversely, when two facts are not related, then the two facts might have been created concurrently. This is the partial order of historical facts at play within distributed systems. The ambiguity of the ordering between unrelated facts leaves machines less constrained and, as we will see, better able to act autonomously.

Acyclic Graphs

The immutability of facts constrains them to know their predecessors at the time of creation. But there are two more constraints that we have to put on the system. First, we have to be able to construct the graph one fact at a time. And second, we cannot allow a fact to refer to itself as a predecessor. We must disallow both simultaneous creation and self-reference, lest we introduce cycles.

Every graph starts empty. It contains no facts. The first fact added to the graph therefore can have no predecessors. There is no existing knowledge upon which to build. The first fact is a root. A graph containing only one root has no cycles, because there are no edges.

Let time pass, and let more facts be added to the graph. Assume that the graph still contains no cycles. As I add a new fact to the graph, that fact may refer to any of the existing facts as predecessors. However, those existing facts may *not* refer to this new fact as a predecessor. I cannot change their predecessor relationships, and this new fact did not yet exist. I therefore cannot introduce a cycle by adding a single fact.

If we were to allow self-reference, then we could introduce a trivial cycle. And if we were to allow simultaneous insertion, then we might introduce two facts that have each other as predecessors. Since neither of these operations is allowed, the resulting graph of facts will not contain cycles. In mathematics, this kind of structure is known as a *directed acyclic graph* and has many interesting properties. As we get deeper into the analytical and implementation details of historical modeling, we will take full advantage of the acyclic nature of the graph.

Timeliness

In a system based on the exchange of historical facts, not all parties will know about all facts at the same time. This is one of the greatest strengths of historical modeling, but also one of its important limitations. It is impossible to reject a fact based on the time at which you learn of it. The reason is that other parties will have learned about it earlier and would therefore have come to a different conclusion about the fact. For every party in the system to eventually reach the same conclusion, that conclusion cannot be based on timeliness.

This causes significant problems in systems that do not recognize this limitation. Several legal documents, such as tax forms, checks, and invoices, have explicit due dates or expiration dates. If the form is received after the required date, then it will not be honored. The sender must go to great lengths to prove that the document was written and transmitted on time, or suffer the consequences of a failed transaction. In such situations, the sender believes one thing – that they met the deadline – while the recipient believes something else. Only by arbitration of a central authority can these situations be resolved.

To design a system that does not rely upon a central authority, we must respect that documents will be received late. In a truly historical model, a fact is not rejected based on the time at which it was received. At best, we can record the fact that a fine was levied or an opportunity was lost due to the failure of information to arrive at a certain place by a certain time. But we cannot prove that the information did not exist somewhere else at that time. And when the fact arrives later, we must decide how we are to react to it. All parties must honor the existence of the facts, no matter when they learned about them, and draw the same conclusion. Perhaps that conclusion is that the sender still owes a fine. But timeliness alone did not determine that outcome.

These, therefore, are the rules of a historical model. They follow logically from the desire to capture the full history of a system with several parties, separated by time and space, exchanging historical facts.

- Facts are immutable.

- Facts reference their predecessors.

- Two facts having the same values and predecessors(and therefore transitive closure) are the same fact.

- We cannot guarantee that there is only one successor for any given fact.

- We cannot change our interpretation of history based on the timeliness of our knowledge of it.

These rules impose constraints on the way we build systems. With those constraints come significant advantages, but also certain limitations.

Limitations of Historical Modeling

For the remainder of the book, we will focus our attention on historical modeling. The other forms of immutable architecture are documented elsewhere, but historical modeling requires a bit more study. Historical modeling, as we will see, offers many advantages over the other forms: autonomy, scalability, and conflict resolution to name a few. But it is not without its limitations. We have already mentioned a few, but let us now explore them in better detail.

With the power of historical modeling comes some constraints. These constraints make it inappropriate to apply historical modeling to certain types of systems. In these situations, it is best to model all or part of the system statefully and integrate where appropriate. Fortunately, good integration strategies are available.

We will often find that we can pair a historical model with a stateful model. The stateful model is mutable, centralized, and can enforce serialized access. Relational databases are good stateful models, as they have a long track record of supporting efficient locking.

No Central Authority

A historical model allows for decisions to be made with autonomy. Each decision is recorded in the local history and eventually shared with the rest of the system. As a result, the system cannot reject facts based on age or current state.

Decisions that were made in the past are approved locally, with only the information available at the time. No remote part of the system needs to be consulted. That decision cannot be rejected post facto.

This makes historical modeling inappropriate for parts of a system that model scarcity. For example, a conference room reservation system will need to know with certainty whether a room was available at a certain time. When a reservation is approved, the approver needs to know that no other reservation for the same room at the same time has been approved. That decision must be made by a central authority.

A historical model may be applied around the edges of a central authority, so long as that central authority itself implements scarcity. The historical model can capture the fact that a request has been made. This occurs at the point of request, such as at a user's workstation or a device mounted by the door of the conference room, and these facts find their way to a central authority. The historical model can also capture the fact that a request was approved. This occurs at the central authority and moves out to the devices at the edge. But a historical model alone cannot say for certain whether a room is available at any given time. That would require that the model know that a reservation has not been approved, which is impossible given a subset of history.

The central authority need not be a single machine; most likely it is a cluster. It can implement scarcity in a number of ways. All machines in the cluster could all have access to a shared common database. Or they could be running a consensus algorithm such as Paxos. They might even employ proof of work on a blockchain. As long as the members of this cluster have a means by which to agree, they can act with singular authority.

Of the available options, the least expensive is the shared stateful model. It needs a locking mechanism to help this cluster coordinate their actions and transaction support to ensure consistency and atomicity. Relational databases work well as shared stateful models.

Once the central authority has reached agreement that one thing happened and not another, it will record approval or rejection of the request as a successive fact. This fact will find its way back to the client from which the request came. The historical model provides communication, auditable history, and eventual consistency. The one component that is better modeled statefully is the one that requires scarcity.

No Real-Time Clock

A time-sensitive request must be fulfilled within a specified period of time. If it is not, the request is invalid. Such requests are common in real-time systems such as factory automation. A request for a door to open or a robotic arm to move must be fulfilled within a narrow span of time. If the message does not arrive in time, then the request must be rejected.

Facts in a historical model, however, are honored no matter what the time frame. The decision is made at the time that the fact is recorded and cannot be rejected thereafter. It may take an indeterminate period of time to transmit the fact. The recipient is simply informed of something that has already happened in history.

While it might be appropriate to model the input or output of a real-time factory automation system historically, the software that runs the factory itself should use a real-time model. These models are specifically designed to provide time-sensitive fail-safe behavior. If a message fails to arrive at the right time, the system defaults to safe operation. And once the message does arrive, late as it is, the system ignores it so as not to cause any damage.

No Uniqueness Constraints

Uniqueness is a special case of scarcity and therefore cannot be modeled historically. In a historical model, any query for successors of a fact might return multiple results. It is not possible to constrain a query to return only one result. The consequence of this is that a domain that requires at most one result cannot effectively be modeled historically.

For example, a login that requires a unique username should be supported by a stateful model. A historical model would be unable to enforce the uniqueness of a username.

At best, a historical model might include a fact containing only the username. Because a fact is uniquely identified by its value, there is logically only one fact with this exact username. However, the fact could contain nothing that could differ from one user to the next. If it contained information in addition to the username, then two or more facts could again exist with the same name. They would no longer be unique.

To correlate a distinct username with a user, therefore, would require a successor fact. Identifying the user for a given username would require a query for the successors of the username fact. Such a query cannot be guaranteed to return at most one fact. The possibility always exists for it to return more.

To model a system that requires uniqueness constraints, you must use a stateful model. The model can be consulted to determine if the desired value is already in use. The indexing and transactional features of a relational database once more come into play.

That stateful model must also be centrally located. A replica of a stateful model cannot enforce uniqueness. An insertion into one copy would need to block in order to consult the others. Only if that unique value is not reserved in a quorum (usually a simple majority) of replicas can it be accepted. A consensus algorithm such as Paxos can be employed to reach a quorum.

If uniqueness is required, such as registering for a username, a historical model could be used for registration requests, as well as for acceptance or rejection responses. The requests can be recorded as facts by clients at the edge of the system. These facts will make their way to a central authority that has access to a stateful model. The stateful model enforces uniqueness constraints. That central authority will decide whether to approve or reject the request based on the stateful model and then record that decision as a successor fact.

The response will find its way back to the client from which the request came; only then will the client know whether the requested username is unique. They will query for successors to the request fact – the acceptance or rejection. Once they have one successor, they will know the answer to the uniqueness question. However, there is no guarantee in the historical model itself that the request will have no further successors. That assurance comes only from the trust that a central authority is making the decision, with the help of a stateful model that can enforce uniqueness.

No Aggregation

After a certain amount of activity, a system might be expected to provide an aggregate or summary of that period's activity. For example, a financial ledger could be closed at the end of a day, a month, or a quarter. The system would then produce a summary that records the total of that period's transactions. From that point forward, no additional transactions would be allowed into that period.

A historical model cannot guarantee that all facts within a given period have been seen. The system responsible for generating the aggregate might not have all of the period's records at the required time. If it receives a fact after computing and recording the summary, then it is not permitted – by the rules of historical modeling – to reject it. The decision was made elsewhere, and the fact of that decision was merely shared.

Three strategies exist for dealing with aggregation of historical facts: central ledgers, map-reduce, and blockchains. A central ledger is by far the simplest of the three. A central ledger uses a stateful model to tally which facts have been included in which period. For example, it determines which financial transactions are part of which date of business or quarterly summary. It makes that decision within the tally as the facts arrive, regardless of when they occurred in history. The tally is a stateful model. The central authority uses this stateful model to guarantee that a transaction is not double counted, in other words, included in more than one period.

Map-reduce decentralizes the stateful model. No longer does a single stateful model have to contain all of the financial transactions that occur within a date of business. Instead, the transactions are distributed among several stateful models, called shards. To compute an aggregate for a date or a quarter, a coordinator sends a request to each of these shards. Each shard computes their own aggregate and then shares that result with the coordinator. The coordinator combines all of the aggregates into one final answer. This works because no transaction is ever duplicated between shards. If it were, that duplication would lead to over-counting in the final result.

A blockchain is more complex but avoids the need for a central authority. At many points within the system, individual facts are gathered into candidate blocks. The hash of each block is computed and tested for some arbitrary condition (e.g., a certain number of leading zeros). This arbitrary condition is a proof of work that ensures that satisfactory blocks are found at a desired frequency. Each candidate block contains the hash of its predecessor, and no fact may appear in more than one block in a chain. Nodes within the system will honor the longest chain of satisfactory blocks.

When designing a system that requires aggregates over history, add a stateful model – whether singular or sharded – to the historical one. Model individual transactions historically. At a central authority, collect a list of ongoing historical facts into the stateful model. At regular intervals, close the tally of facts and compute a summary – either as an aggregate function or via map-reduce. This preserves the logical and technical benefits of historical modeling while also allowing for aggregation.

CHAPTER 3

How to Read a Historical Model

Throughout the rest of this book, we will be exploring many examples of historical models. To do so, we will need a language for describing them. This language will be part visual and part textual. The visual aspect of this language will aid in overall understanding, while the textual part will provide specificity.

The goal of the modeling languages, whether visual or textual, is to achieve a shared understanding about the decisions we are collectively making and the consequences of those decisions. Business analysts, product owners, and information architects will uncover the language and rules of the domain. Developers and system architects will describe the consequences of various decisions. And user experience designers will map the model to task-driven interfaces.

Throughout the process, the team is communicating using a common language. That language needs to be as free as it can be from jargon and implementation details. It should not talk about databases, APIs, services, or repositories. Instead it should focus on the entities and actions of the problem domain.

And yet, the language must also be precise. This is the foundation for both mathematical proof and immutable runtimes. There is no room for ambiguity. Later in this book, we will prove two important theorems using the modeling language. And runtimes that implement provably correct behavior will use internal representations of this language.

Starting from the baseline of immutable architecture, we can define just such a specification language. It carries with it enough constraints to ensure that a correct implementation will have desirable characteristics, like performance, scalability, security, and autonomy. And since one of those constraints is immutability, reasoning about the model will be possible.

© Michael L. Perry 2024
M. L. Perry, *The Art of Immutable Architecture*, https://doi.org/10.1007/979-8-8688-0288-1_3

The modeling language that we will describe has two graphical components and one textual component. We will begin with the first of the graphical components: the *fact type graph*.

Fact Type Graphs

Within the visual language, we will create two kinds of graphs. One will represent the types of facts, and the other instances. Fact *type* graphs will be the more common of the two, so let's describe them first.

In a fact type graph, the type of a fact is represented as a labeled ellipse, as in Figure 3-1.

Figure 3-1. *A single fact type*

An arrow between two fact types indicates a predecessor/successor relationship. The type at the head of the arrow is a predecessor of the one at the tail. Figure 3-2 shows an example.

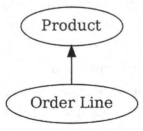

Figure 3-2. *Arrows point up toward predecessors*

In any predecessor/successor relationship, a predecessor can have zero or more successors. There is no way in a historical model to limit the number of successors to any given fact. Even though the graph shows only one order line type, it implies that a product can have many order line instances.

The predecessor side of the relationship, however, can be constrained. In the preceding graph, an order line is associated to exactly one product. With additional notation, we can indicate other cardinalities. In Figure 3-3, we indicate zero or one predecessor with a question mark.

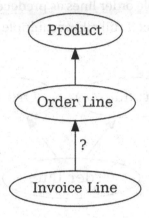

Figure 3-3. *A question mark indicates an optional predecessor*

In this graph, an invoice line may or may not refer to an order line. The reference is optional. Some invoice lines are charges for specific products ordered and would therefore have an order line. Others are fees or discounts unrelated to a specific order line. These would have no predecessor.

The third cardinality that can be depicted on a fact type graph is zero or more (a.k.a. many) predecessors. To indicate this relationship, we use an asterisk as in Figure 3-4.

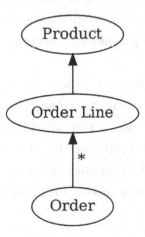

Figure 3-4. *An asterisk indicates multiple predecessors*

This graph says that an order refers to zero or more order lines. Because the tail of the arrow always allows for multiples, this is a many-to-many relationship.

There is more than cardinality at play in this graph. It also represents the order in which facts can be created and the degree to which changes can be applied. The arrow in Figure 3-4 allows multiple order lines as predecessors. The arrow in Figure 3-5 is reversed and has no asterisk. Yet it still allows multiple order lines, only now as successors.

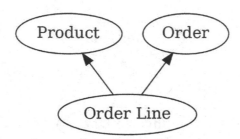

Figure 3-5. *Successor relationships always allow multiples, so this model still allows multiple order lines*

In Figure 3-5, the direction of the predecessor/successor relationship between order and order line is reversed. The successor end of an arrow always allows zero or more facts, and so both graphs indicate many order lines to an order. The distinction, however, is related to immutability. In Figure 3-4, the many order lines are predecessors of the order. They were known at the creation of the order. New order lines cannot be added to the order after the fact. Existing order lines cannot be removed after the order is created. The collection of order lines is immutable. When we wish to call out this immutability, we will often say that the successor *captures* its predecessors, as in "An order captures many order lines."

In this domain, we want to lock down the order lines in an order, and so we will choose to make order line the predecessor (as in Figure 3-4). We will reject the model in Figure 3-5. However, we do want a mechanism by which a user can build an order line by line. To accomplish this, we will introduce the concept of a cart. The cart is the predecessor of the order line; new order lines can be added. The order lines are predecessors of the order; the order captures the order lines. The resulting model appears in Figure 3-6.

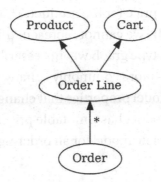

Figure 3-6. *A cart allows the addition of order lines*

It is important to choose the model based on the direction of the predecessor/ successor relationships, not just based on cardinality.

For some patterns that we will study shortly, it makes sense for a fact to refer to other facts of its own type. We indicate this as a loop, as in Figure 3-7.

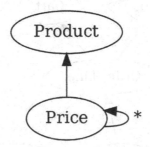

Figure 3-7. *A loop indicates that the previous prices are predecessors*

A price refers to not only a product as a predecessor but also zero or more prices that came before. This indicates that a price replaces previous values. Even though this relationship introduces a cycle into the fact type graph, it does not allow cycles of fact instances. A given instance of a price cannot refer to itself as a predecessor. It can only refer to a previous price, the one that it is replacing.

Keep in mind that a price in this context refers to a fact, not a value. A fact is uniquely identified by its values and predecessors. Two prices having the same value will nevertheless be different price facts if they have different predecessors. This applies to the product as well as the prior prices. As a consequence, two products will have different price facts even if they cost the same amount. And a product can be marked up and then subsequently discounted to its original amount. Since the final price fact will include the intermediate price fact as a predecessor, it will be distinct from the original price fact.

There must have been a first price for the product. That fact instance would have no price predecessors. That is why we cannot represent this as a one-and-only-one relationship. Loops within a fact type graph will necessarily include an arrow that is either optional (zero or one) or – more commonly – many (zero or more). Because these references are the only way to model properties that change over time, we will often refer to them as "mutable," as in "A product has a mutable price."

Putting it all together, a complete model for an ordering domain appears in Figure 3-8.

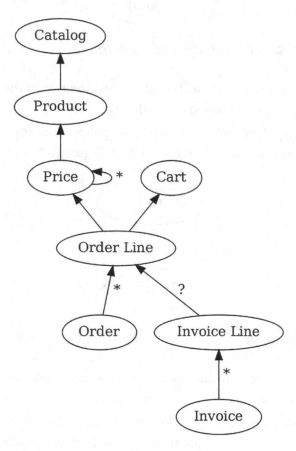

Figure 3-8. *A fact type graph showing various decisions for cardinality*

A product in a catalog has a mutable price. An order line in a cart captures a specific price for a product. An order captures a set of order lines. Order lines can be added to a cart, but the order is closed. An invoice line may or may not refer to an order line, and an invoice captures a set of invoice lines.

You may be wondering why an invoice does not refer to an order as a predecessor. After all, a customer must submit an order before we can invoice them. The answer lies in the subtle consequences and inferences that we might draw from such a relationship. If an invoice refers to an order as a predecessor, must it include invoice lines for all order lines? What if we don't bill for an item until we can ship it? Might we end up with partial invoices? And would it be possible to invoice a customer for multiple orders placed in close succession? An invoice to order relationship would imply a certain causality that might not actually be present in the domain.

The fact type diagram expresses both the cardinality and the causality of the domain. Reading through it reveals a narrative of how a system came to be in a particular state and exposes the constraints on how that system can and cannot evolve.

A Chess Game

When I first started thinking about historical modeling, I drew a few models to convince myself that it would be a useful way to analyze software. The first model that I drew was of a single chess game. Chess is a game between two players. The players are chosen before the game begins. Players are therefore predecessors of the game, as shown in Figure 3-9.

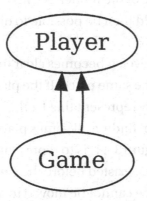

Figure 3-9. *A chess game has two players*

This immediately revealed that I needed a way to talk about different predecessors of the same type. At first, I thought about perhaps allowing an array of players and using the index to indicate the order of play. As I got into further models, I realized that predecessors had to be *sets*, not *arrays*, which invalidated that idea. Furthermore, the game supports precisely two players. An array would allow invalid games of 0, 1, or 3+

65

players to be represented. The natural conclusion was that predecessor relationships should support labels, as in Figure 3-10.

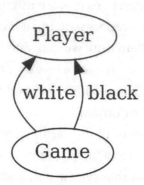

Figure 3-10. *The players in a chess game have labels*

When no disambiguation is required, the labels can be omitted. The label always describes the predecessor, not the successor.

Important Attributes

In chess literature, the place at which a game is played is often used in the title. It represents an important attribute of the model. My first instinct was to record this attribute in the game fact. It would then be possible to display that information as part of the title of the game.

Upon further reflection, however, it becomes clear that that would not be quite right. Several games will be played at the same place. If the place is simply a field of the game, then the model does not faithfully represent that truth. The name of a place is not the place itself. And there is no way of finding all games played in a particular location.

The solution, as shown in Figure 3-11, is to represent place as a fact. The place is a predecessor of the game; the place existed before the game was played, and the game knows about that location. A game cannot be moved to a different place. The place is immutable and part of the game's identity.

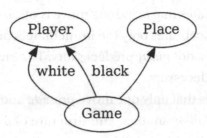

Figure 3-11. *Place is important enough to be extracted from game and become its own fact*

With this change, the model accurately represents the importance of place. It is a fact in its own right. It stands apart from any game, but it also provides a way to find a set of games. If an important attribute is hidden away as a field in another fact, then we have no way of talking about such a query. But if the important attribute is represented as a separate fact, then we can reason about it appropriately.

A Chain of Facts

The next part of the game that I needed to model was the moves. Considering that a predecessor is a thing that happened before, I decided to represent move order using predecessor relationships. The result was the diagram in Figure 3-12.

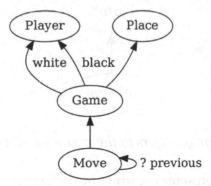

Figure 3-12. *A move refers to the previous move as its predecessor*

The question mark indicates that previous move is optional; the first move would have none. The predecessor captures only the immediately previous move, as previous allows *optional* predecessors, not *many* predecessors. The entire history of the game can be found in the chain of predecessors.

While the model requires that only one move *precede* another one, it does not require that only one move *follow* another. The structure of the model does not prevent a player from cheating by playing two possible moves.

The structure also does not prevent a move from following a move from a different game. There is no constraint that the prior move belongs to the same game. This will have to be expressed in a validation rule.

After analyzing this model, I was not particularly happy with the previous relationship. I realized that later moves in the game would be identified by a long list of previous moves. It seemed wasteful. Instead, I decided to add an index to the move fact. Starting at zero, white would play the even moves and black the odd moves. This flattened the model into the one in Figure 3-13.

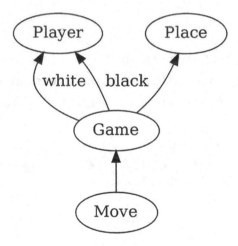

Figure 3-13. *A move no longer refers to the previous move as its predecessor*

The model no longer represents the structure of the game. It does not record the idea of one move following another. But then again, given the inability to disallow forks, the structure wasn't providing much value. Furthermore, removing the previous reference eliminated the possibility of moves crossing games. Modeling is a trade-off between the rigor of the type system and the brute force of validation. Validation of sequential move order makes for a simpler model.

Sequential move order is part of the chess domain. As we analyze other domains, we will find that sequences are often not an intrinsic component. We have no constraint, for example, that the next fact must come from one particular user the way that we do in a turn-based game. If we can't rely on such a constraint, then this trade-off is not available to us. When modeling mutable properties, in particular, we will come to rely upon prior references.

Endgame

The last part of the chess game to model was the outcome. Was it a win for white (1-0), a win for black (0-1), or a draw (½-½)? The simplest solution is to create an outcome fact and record that value as a field, as shown in Figure 3-14.

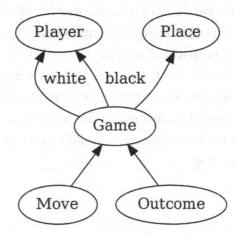

Figure 3-14. *A new fact records the outcome of the game*

I found two problems with this simple solution. First, the outcome is not related to the player fact. This makes it more difficult to find games that a certain player has won without searching all of their games. This might be an important query, so the model should support it. And second, it allowed for moves to continue past the outcome. The outcome should lock the moves into place.

To solve the first problem, I decided to separate the Outcome fact into two different types: Win and Draw. A Win refers to one of the two players. The Draw – to help with the query – refers to both. This changes the model to the one in Figure 3-15.

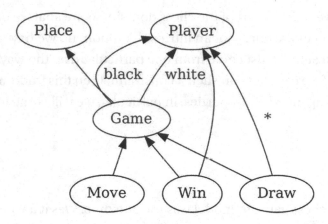

Figure 3-15. *A game concludes with a win for one player, or a draw for both*

The model again requires validation to enforce that the winner must be one of the players from the game. But on the plus side, it is much easier to query for all wins and draws by a player. This could help with things like computing score.

To solve the problem of moves continuing past the outcome, I took advantage of the fact that predecessor relationships were immutable. If an outcome records all moves of the game as predecessors, then those moves are locked down when the game concludes, as Figure 3-16 illustrates. Sure, future Move facts could be recorded, but they would not have contributed to the outcome.

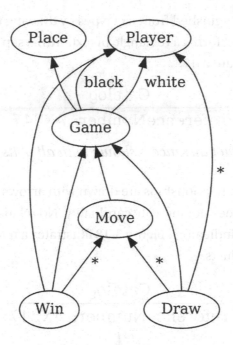

Figure 3-16. *A win or a draw locks in a set of moves*

As this example shows, the act of modeling a problem historically exposes several decisions that might otherwise be deferred as implementation details. The correct option is not always clear. But the choice has important downstream effects. One path might lead to a simpler model, but a difficult query. Another might constrain the system to render invalid inputs unrepresentable, only to put too much of the burden on the type system. Take the time to draw out several alternatives, and analyze each on its own merits.

Fact Instance Graphs

So far, the graphs we've drawn refer to fact *types*. The visual language of historical modeling also includes a kind of graph that represents fact *instances*. We will use this kind of graph less frequently. The goal of a fact instance graph is to illustrate a specific example of the state of a system at a certain point in time and at a certain node. It includes more details about the fact instances observed but typically contains only a small number of facts.

Fact instances are distinguished from fact types by drawing them without a border. Instead, the body of the fact forms a rectangle of text, with a separator between the type and the contents, as in Figure 3-17.

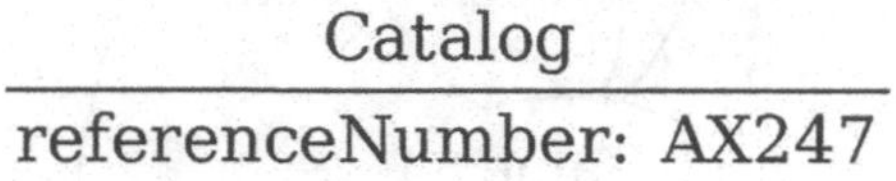

$$\frac{\text{Catalog}}{\text{referenceNumber: AX247}}$$

Figure 3-17. *A catalog fact instance is shown with all of its values*

Predecessor/successor relationships are drawn with arrows as in the type diagram, but an instance diagram does not indicate cardinality. No relationships include the asterisk or question mark indicators. Figure 3-18 illustrates a relationship between a catalog and one of its products.

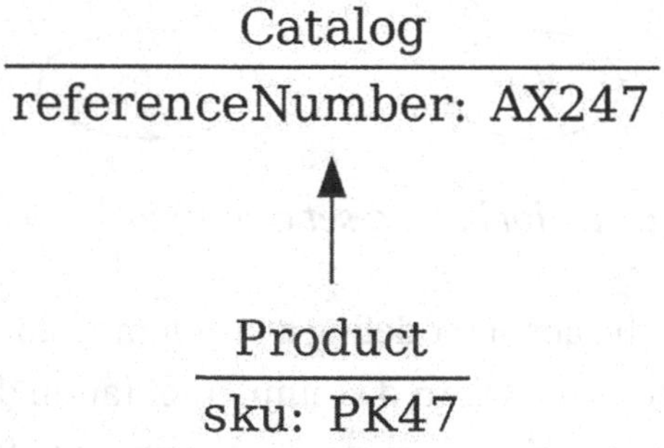

$$\frac{\text{Catalog}}{\text{referenceNumber: AX247}}$$

$$\uparrow$$

$$\frac{\text{Product}}{\text{sku: PK47}}$$

Figure 3-18. *A product points to its predecessor catalog*

When a predecessor reference is "optional" or "many," it allows zero predecessors. If an instance has no predecessors in this role, then the diagram will typically simply have no edge with that label. However, you may choose to emphasize that the role is empty. You can show this with a terminating line. If the role is optional (?), then the terminator represents a null reference. If the role is many (*) as in this example, then the terminator represents an empty set.

Terminators are helpful to illustrate the changes in a mutable property. The root instance, or initial value, of a mutable property will have no predecessor. Subsequent instances will form a chain from the root, as in Figure 3-19.

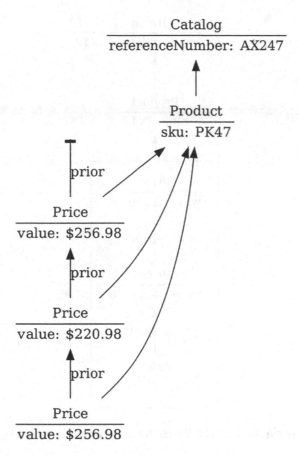

Figure 3-19. *The first price has no prior price*

Recall that the fact *type* diagram depicted only one price node. A small loop indicated that a price had zero or more prior prices. Now in the fact *instance* diagram, we see what that loop really means. It doesn't indicate that the model allows cycles. It means only that instances of a given type can refer to other instances of the same type. The loop has turned into a chain.

A fact instance diagram does not admit cycles. A fact never refers to itself as a predecessor, nor can facts refer to predecessors that in turn refer to the original, directly or indirectly.

Since all instances of the price refer to a common predecessor product, a shorthand can be used to group the common relationships. A box is drawn around all members of the group, as in Figure 3-20. In this example, we drop the terminator as the root of the chain becomes more obvious. The predecessor reference common to all members of the group is shown as a line from this box.

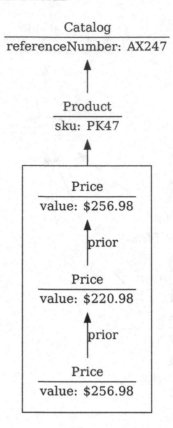

Figure 3-20. *A box indicates that all instances share a common predecessor*

If a successor referred to all members of the group, it would be represented as an inward arrow. Figure 3-21 illustrates an order capturing a group of order lines.

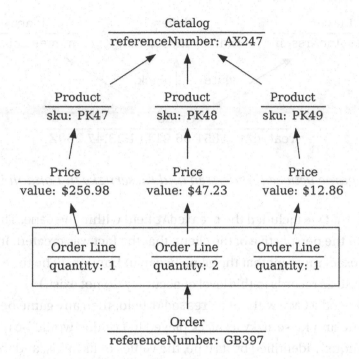

Figure 3-21. *An order refers to all of its order lines as predecessors*

Whereas fact *type* diagrams are general descriptions of a model, fact *instance* diagrams show specific examples. Instance diagrams help to illustrate the consequences of different modeling decisions. They offer a form of debugging prior to a model having been implemented. Let's walk through a specific example and show how it helps us reason through design decisions.

The Immortal Game

Previously, we imagined what any chess game might look like. Now, we will draw a specific instance of a chess game using that model. Before the game begins, we have two players: Anderssen and Kieseritzky. They meet in London. As Figure 3-22 shows, the game is a fact that joins those two players at that place at a certain point in time.

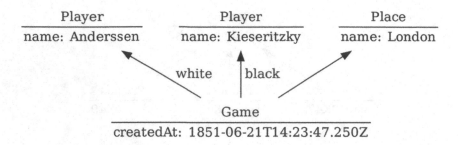

Figure 3-22. *A game between Anderssen and Kieseritzky in London in 1851*

It's important that we included the `createdAt` field within the `Game`. This represents the moment, from the perspective of the client, that the fact was created. In this example, we are using the exact moment that the game began in London. (The time of day in this example is fictional, as records to this level of accuracy do not exist.)

If we had modeled a `Game` without a `createdAt` field, then any game between Anderssen as white and Kieseritzky as black played in London would be the same game. A fact is uniquely identified by its type, the values of its fields, and the set of its predecessors. This model makes the reasonable assumption that two players will not simultaneously start two different games.

It is also important that `createdAt` represents the moment at which the fact became a fact, not the moment at which it became known to any particular computer. Of course, at the time there were no computers in London to capture the fact. Nevertheless, it existed. In modern systems, this creation time is often captured as a timestamp on the client machine. After that, however, other machines that learn of this fact must honor that timestamp, no matter how much time has passed.

Collecting Moves

Now that the fact of the game is recorded, the players begin making moves. We can capture these moves as facts referring to the `Game`. Figure 3-23 shows the game after the first three moves.

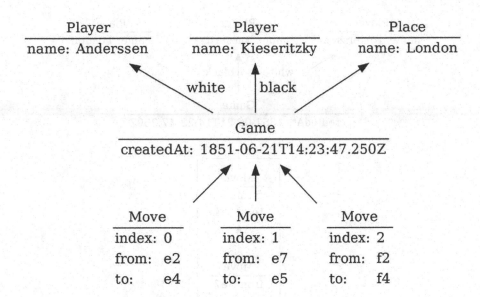

Figure 3-23. *Moves are recorded as successors of the game fact*

In a previous iteration of the model, we considered representing the relationship between a move and its previous move as a predecessor. This had the advantage of being accurate: a move *is* the predecessor of the one that follows. But it had the more significant disadvantage of creating long chains. Had we chosen this model, the game after three moves would look like Figure 3-24.

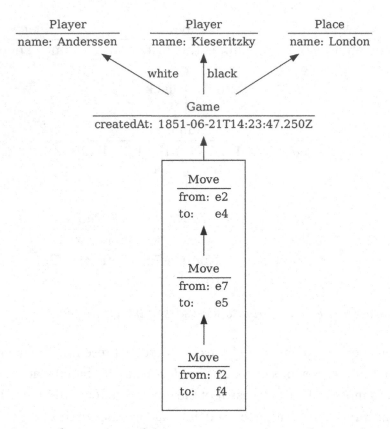

Figure 3-24. *In an alternate model, moves are represented as predecessors of one another*

As the game progresses, the chain would get longer. Understanding that the 20th move *is* the 20th move requires traversing this entire chain. Even *identifying* the 20th move means talking about the entire history, as predecessors are *part* of identity.

Because of the practical drawbacks of recording moves as a chain, we decided to model the system as having individual moves, each with an index. And so, we abandon Figure 3-24 and go back to Figure 3-23. That leaves us with the chore of validating those indexes to ensure that we have no gaps and no duplicates. We can simply add this to the validation that would already have to occur to defend against illegal moves such as moving into check. The model can only go so far to make invalid state unrepresentable.

As we collect more and more moves within the game, representing them as individual facts on the diagram becomes tedious. So instead, we group them together. The group has a common predecessor: the Game. Within the box, we can simply draw the set of moves as a table, as shown in Figure 3-25.

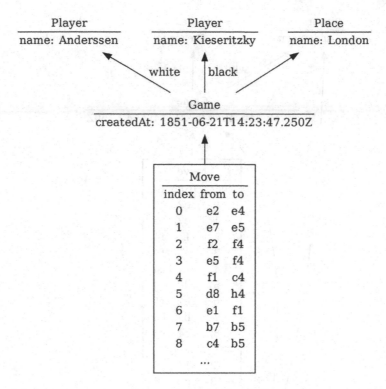

Figure 3-25. *Moves are grouped together under their common predecessor*

The grouping does not change the fact that each move is a separate record. The order of moves within the grouping does not imply any relationship between the facts. This is simply a convenience to constrain the size of the illustration.

A Brilliant Win

In the game that we are modeling, Anderssen sacrificed material brilliantly to secure a win for white. We will represent that win in Figure 3-26 with a fact that captures the game, the winner, and the set of moves as predecessors.

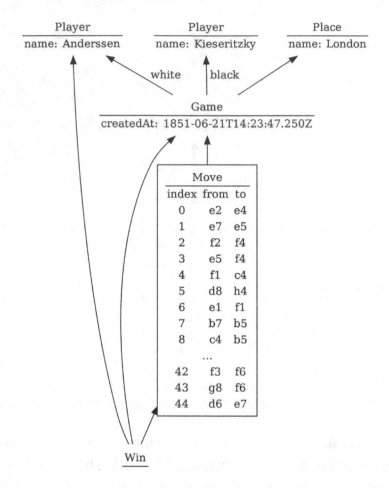

Figure 3-26. *A win captures several predecessors, including all moves of the game*

The Win fact has no fields. It needs no additional information. It says all that it needs to say with the predecessors it gathers together. We draw the predecessor set of moves as an arrow pointing toward the entire group. Every Move in the group is a predecessor of the Win.

As this example shows, fact instance graphs are quite different from fact type graphs. They represent individual instances of facts, complete with their type and fields. They show predecessor/successor relationships between facts rather than the roles between types. Whereas a fact type graph allows cycles between types, an instance graph does not permit cycles among instances. A cycle in the fact type graph unrolls into a chain in the fact instance graph.

Fact type graphs and fact instance graphs are used for different purposes. A fact type graph makes general statements about all possible models of given fact types. We use them to reason through the causality of a domain. A fact instance graph, on the other hand, illustrates a specific example data set. We use them to try various scenarios and debug a model before implementation.

Because fact type graphs better describe the general causality of a domain, we will rely more heavily upon them than on fact instance graphs. Fact instance graphs are often too specific to make general statements. In the remainder of this book, they will be used sparingly and only to illustrate specific patterns.

The Factual Modeling Language

While the visual language of historical modeling is useful for understanding the relationships within a model, it is not sufficient for rigorous reasoning. It cannot specify a model to such a degree that assertions can be proved, or code generated. To satisfy this need, we use the Factual Modeling Language, or Factual.

Using the Factual Modeling Language, we can write precise specifications. It describes all the data that is part of the model, the ways in which those data elements relate, and the rules by which we can query it. It even describes the rules by which data is secured and validated. This precise specification language allows us to reason about the requirements of a system and determine far in advance what we will be able to implement.

When using an immutable runtime, Factual becomes much more than a form of communication. It is the representation by which the runtime derives provably correct behavior. An immutable runtime converts types and specifications from the source language into the Factual Modeling Language. It then applies rigorous transforms in order to update user interfaces, invalidate caches, optimize data transport, and secure data access.

Declaring Fact Types

Types of facts are declared in Factual using the fact keyword. The body of the type, enclosed in brackets, includes a list of fields and predecessors. Fields are declared in a style reminiscent of Pascal and related programming languages: a field name is followed by a colon and a type. Fields have native data types, such as string, int, and bool.

```
fact Catalog {
  referenceNumber: string
}
```

Predecessors are similarly declared. The primary difference is that a predecessor refers to another fact type. Predecessors can appear before, after, or interspersed with fields.

```
fact Product {
  catalog: Catalog
  sku: string
}
```

Cardinality indicators modify predecessor declarations. Singular predecessors have no modifier (as shown earlier). Optional predecessors are declared with the question mark modifier, and multiple predecessors are declared with an asterisk.

```
fact InvoiceLine {
  orderLine: OrderLine?
  total: decimal
  description: string
}
```

```
fact Invoice {
  lines: InvoiceLine*
  subtotal: decimal
  tax: decimal
}
```

A predecessor can refer to a type that has not yet been declared. It can even refer to the type in which it is declared. Such self-referential predecessors, as we discussed previously, are frequently used to refer to previous versions of mutable properties. Remember, while this introduces a cycle in the type graph, it does not permit cycles within the instance graph:

```
fact Price {
  product: Product
  value: decimal
  prior: Price*
}
```

The fact declaration syntax is designed to be familiar to developers. It is also simple enough to be a communication mechanism between developers and nondevelopers. It contains no behavior, no access modifiers, nothing that could be confused for code. And yet, it is precise and expressive enough to describe the fundamentals of a model.

Consider each fact as a decision that a person or another actor is making. The fact captures the details of that decision. It also shows which decisions came before in the form of predecessors. By stepping through the creation of facts, analysts tell the story of how a system evolves to solve business problems.

Querying the Model

As powerful as it is to declare the types of facts in a system, a useful application must also answer questions based on those facts. The Factual Modeling Language includes syntax for querying a model to find its current state. This is accomplished with a specification. Let's take a look at a simple example.

```
productsInCatalog = (c: Catalog) {
  p: Product [
    p→catalog = c
  ]
}
```

In natural language, you can read this specification as "given a catalog c, find all products p such that p has a predecessor catalog c." Indeed, previous versions of the Factual Modeling Language used the more natural syntax. The version I use today relies instead on punctuation.

You can see in this specification that there are three forms of grouping punctuation. Parentheses (()) indicate *givens*. Braces ({}) indicate *unknowns*. And brackets ([ ]) indicate *conditions*. Let's take these one at a time.

The set of givens represents the inputs to a specification. Each is a *label*, consisting of a name and a type. The labels are placeholders for facts. As givens, these facts are known at the time the specification is used. In this case, we know the catalog in which we want to find products.

The set of unknowns describes the facts that we seek. Each unknown is a label and a set of conditions. In this specification, we seek to discover the products.

Finally, the set of conditions describes how those unknown facts relate to other labeled facts. In this example, we describe a path by which to get from a product to a catalog. The path uses an arrow (→) to indicate a predecessor. This specification relates a predecessor of an unknown to a given. It therefore requires that we find *successors* in order to satisfy that condition.

Conditions constrain the relationships between labeled facts. The specification matches tuples of labeled facts that simultaneously meet all conditions. The preceding specification finds all products within a given catalog c. It produces every tuple (c, p) such that p has a predecessor in the role "catalog" equal to c.

There will be multiple such tuples, since a product is a successor of a catalog. A historical model allows for any number of successors.

Changing Direction

Specifications that match predecessors are just as useful as those that match successors. We can reverse the direction of the path by moving the arrow to the other side of the equals sign. Here is the reversed specification:

```
catalogsOfProduct = (p: Product) {
  c: Catalog [
    c = p→catalog
  ]
}
```

Given a product, this specification finds all catalogs that are the product's catalog. You might reasonably expect that there is exactly one such catalog. The product type as defined previously restricts the cardinality of the catalog predecessor to one and only one.

However, when reasoning about specifications, we are motivated not to make this assumption. For one thing, we don't know about the cardinality restriction unless we further inspect the types. It is useful to limit our knowledge to just the specification at hand. And for another, other versions of the types might allow for other cardinalities. Specifications are to be deployed in an immutable runtime. Types can change over time and across nodes in a network. While types change, facts do not. We must honor facts from prior versions and from other nodes. And so we stipulate that even this specification produces any number of tuples (p, c).

As with any equation, the left- and right-hand sides of a condition can be swapped. By convention, however, we choose to write a path condition with the unknown on the left. Following this convention makes it more obvious in which direction we are walking the graph. An arrow on the left implies that the condition matches successors, while an arrow on the right implies predecessors.

Jumping Levels

Conditions are not limited to following a single predecessor reference. By chaining additional predecessor references, a path can reach further down the successor graph. For example, a line on an order captures a specific price of a product. In the model that we defined earlier, the product is a predecessor of the price. The order line therefore can only reach the product indirectly through the price fact. To find all order lines for a particular product, we traverse those two relationships in the opposite direction.

```
orderLinesForProduct = (p: Product) {
  ol: OrderLine [
    ol→price→product = p
  ]
}
```

Since the relationship between OrderLine and Product is indirect, the specification follows the intermediate predecessor. Starting at a Product, we match all OrderLines where the price's product is the given. Let's overlay the specification onto the fact type diagram, as shown in Figure 3-27, to see how this jumps levels.

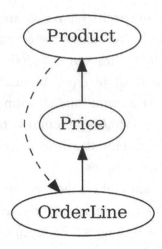

Figure 3-27. *A specification matches successors two levels down*

Common Ancestors

As you might expect, a path condition can contain arrows on both sides of the equals sign. This has the effect of matching facts by a common ancestor. For example, to find all invoices related to a specific order, we look for common order lines.

```
invoicesForOrder = (o: Order) {
  i: Invoice [
    i→invoiceLine→orderLine = o→orderLine
  ]
}
```

To evaluate this specification starting from the order, we would first follow the predecessor step to the order lines. From there, we would follow the successor steps to invoice lines and then to invoices, as shown in Figure 3-28.

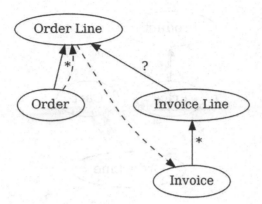

Figure 3-28. *A specification finds related facts via their common ancestor*

When joining this way, it is not necessary to label the common ancestor. But going in the other direction requires a new unknown.

Multiple Unknowns

The braces in a specification may contain multiple unknowns. Each one defines a new label and a new set of conditions. This is necessary to bounce back up from a shared successor. We can use this, for example, to find all of the carts containing a given product.

```
cartsContainingProduct = (p: Product) {
  ol: OrderLine [
    ol→price→product = p
  ]
  c: Cart [
    c = ol→cart
  ]
}
```

Notice that the arrows in the first condition all appear on the left of the equals sign. That implies that it matches successors. Starting from the given, this path traverses arcs down to the unknown order line. Then, in the second condition, all of the arrows appear on the right. This one traverses arcs back up to the unknown cart. The full specification, jumping down to order lines and then back up to carts, appears in Figure 3-29.

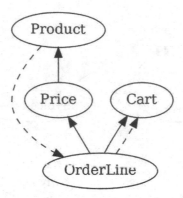

Figure 3-29. *A specification matches predecessors of intermediate successors*

Since this specification contains one given and two unknowns, the results are three-tuples. The specification yields every combination (p, ol, c) that matches all conditions.

Joining via a common ancestor does not require a new label. But joining via a common successor does. It may seem like an arbitrary consequence of the syntax that we've selected that one direction is treated differently than the other. As it turns out, however, this difference foretells an important observation that we will use when computing inverses. This will help immutable runtimes to optimize user interface updates and cache invalidation. We will cover those optimizations in greater detail later in the book.

The syntax we have just described is sufficient for traversing down any number of successors, up any number of predecessors, and bouncing off of facts to explore different directions. This covers the entire graph of connected facts. If one fact is in some way related to another, then a specification could be written to describe that relationship.

Existential Conditions

Often, we find it necessary to exclude results from a specification. Rather than listing all related facts, we want to instead focus on a subset that is in a certain state. The state of a fact is not intrinsic to the thing itself; facts are immutable after all. Rather, the state of a fact is determined by the presence or absence of successors. We therefore constrain specifications using existential conditions.

Existential conditions appear alongside path conditions within square brackets ([ ]). They take the form of either an exists (∃) or not exists (∄) operator followed by a set of unknowns in braces ({ }). For example, let's use a negative existential condition to look for lines remaining in a cart.

```
linesRemainingInCart = (c: Cart) {
  ol: OrderLine [
    ol→cart = c
    ∄ {
      o: Order [
        o→orderLines = ol
      ]
    }
  ]
}
```

The preceding specification finds all of the lines in a cart that are not yet part of an order. It shows only the unordered lines, which might be useful for updating the user interface or generating a new order. When an Order is created referring to the order line, it is removed from the specification results. The specification, complete with the not exists clause, appears in Figure 3-30.

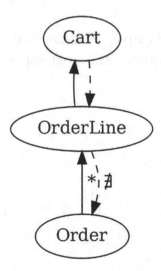

Figure 3-30. *A specification matches successors for which a second-level successor does not exist*

The results of a specification do not include labels inside of existential conditions. The preceding specification only produces tuples (c, ol). It does not produce orders. Indeed, it could not, since the results only include order lines for which no matching order yet exists.

Projections

The specifications we have examined so far have produced tuples of facts. The following specification, for example, produces the product and price for each order line in a cart:

```
linesInCart = (c: Cart) {
  ol: OrderLine [
    ol→cart = c
  ]
  pc: Price [
    pc = ol→price
  ]
  p: Product [
    p = pc→product
  ]
}
```

To update the user interface in this application, we don't want a list of tuples. We want data from the facts in those tuples. And so we append a projection using the double arrow symbol (⇒).

```
linesInCart = (c: Cart) {
  ol: OrderLine [
    ol→cart = c
  ]
  pc: Price [
    pc = ol→price
  ]
  p: Product [
    p = pc→product
  ]
```

```
} ⇒ {
  sku = p.sku
  price = pc.value
  quantity = ol.quantity
}
```

The braces following the double arrow have a different meaning than those before it. The first set of braces describes a set of unknowns. The second set of braces describes the shape of a projection. This is analogous to objects or structures in many programming languages.

The projection describes how to populate the fields of an object from fields of the resulting facts. They use the dot operator (.) to select one field from a labeled fact. Projections cannot navigate to predecessor facts. An arrow (→) cannot appear within a projection.

Nested Specifications

A projection may contain other specifications. In the preceding example, we select the product SKU and price. These are immutable fields of the labeled facts. We would also like to show the description of the product on the user interface, but the description is not immutable. It is recorded in successor facts.

A projection can describe fields that are themselves the results of other specifications. These child specifications can have projections of their own, to any depth required. We can add the product description as shown here:

```
linesInCart = (c: Cart) {
  ol: OrderLine [
    ol→cart = c
  ]
  pc: Price [
    pc = ol→price
  ]
  p: Product [
    p = pc→product
  ]
} ⇒ {
```

```
sku = p.sku
price = pc.value
quantity = ol.quantity
descriptions = {
  d: Product.Description [
    d→product = p
    ∄ {
      next: Product.Description [
        next→prior = d
      ]
    }
  ]
} ⇒ d.value
}
```

Don't worry if you are confused about the negative existential condition in the descriptions specification. It is using the Mutable Property pattern. We will cover that pattern in more detail later in the book. For now, just notice that it is using a nested specification having its own projection.

Nested specifications don't introduce their own givens. Instead, they rely upon labeled facts in the parent specification. The preceding projection produces the descriptions of each product in its results.

Also notice that we used the plural name descriptions for the projected field. Remember, a specification can always produce *any* number of results. We cannot prove that the specification will produce one and only one value. As we will see later, this is a reflection of the realities of working with distributed systems. This projection will therefore produce a list of possible descriptions for each product.

Factual in Immutable Runtimes

The Factual Modeling Language is powerful enough to be the foundation for implementation. It is understood by and manipulated within an immutable runtime. Programmers and analysts alike will use Factual to communicate with these runtimes.

There are two ways in which people will interact with runtimes. First, they will type specifications directly using the Factual language outside of any application programming language. This mode of interaction is often called an *external domain-*

specific language or external DSL. Second, programmers will code in an application programming language. The runtime will convert this language into Factual. This technique is often called an *internal* or *embedded* DSL.

When using Factual as an external DSL, developers and analysts will need to type specifications and projections. Some of the symbols that we used to build specifications and projections are not readily available on a keyboard. The arrow ($\rightarrow$), double arrow ($\Rightarrow$), exists ($\exists$), and not exists ($\nexists$) symbols are important shorthand. Yet they are not easy to type.

An immutable runtime will accept simple replacements for these symbols. An arrow or double arrow can be represented with a pair of characters: (->) and (=>). Indeed, these are common multi-character operators in many programming languages. An existential operator can be represented by a capital E. Its negative can be expressed using an exclamation point – a common character for the Boolean *not* operator – followed by an E (!E).

When using Factual as an internal DSL, developers will use the capabilities of their application programming language. The runtime will translate these expressions into Factual. C# has a built-in query language called LINQ (for language-integrated query). A .NET immutable runtime can translate LINQ directly into Factual specifications. For other languages, a combination of fluent interfaces and lambda expressions is sufficient.

When analysts and programmers express their intent in the form of Factual specifications, the runtime can convert that intent into useful behavior. Most directly, the runtime can execute the specification and projection to produce results. This capability is similar to that of GraphQL. It allows a client app to shape the results to fit their needs. But an immutable runtime can do better.

Based only on the Factual specifications, an immutable runtime can determine how a fact influences results. Projections determine how a user interface is rendered. Their results are also stored in databases to provide search and aggregation capabilities. And they are translated into API calls to integrate with third-party systems. When a new fact is recorded, an immutable runtime can determine mechanically which views to update, indexes to refresh, and APIs to call. We will see these capabilities in action in Chapter 6.

And finally, Factual specifications determine which facts a particular node is interested in. An immutable runtime can turn specifications into feeds. It sets up channels to automatically deliver tuples of facts over these feeds to interested parties. Those nodes then execute the projections themselves to process the results. This is how immutable runtimes replicate data so that each node can operate autonomously. And they do it all from Factual specifications with no further human intervention.

Historical Modeling in Analysis

We will be using both the visual and the textual language of historical modeling throughout the remainder of this book. The visual language will be the primary tool for understanding a model. We will lean most heavily upon the fact type graph. The textual language will be employed to reason through a system's behavior. This form will help us to prove assertions and implement immutable runtimes.

As you apply historical modeling in your work, you will find yourself starting with the visual language. You will start at a whiteboard making rapid changes to a model using fact type graphs. This captures the important objects and user actions and shows how they are related. Then you will write out some examples using fact instance graphs. This helps validate the model as you explore specific scenarios. Then finally, you take the time to express in the Factual Modeling Language the specific structure and rules of the system. This will let you implement and interact with the running system. You will even convert Factual models back into graphs to complete the round trip. The Factual Modeling Language will be your tool for building working models and sharing them with others.

Now let's explore historical modeling as a tool for analysis. Our goal is communication. We want to unambiguously describe the desired behavior of a system. Using the rules of historical modeling, we can be certain that the behavior that we describe can be efficiently implemented within a distributed system.

PART II

Application

CHAPTER 4

Analysis

What is the most important decision made in your business?

It might be the decision to offer a product for sale. It might be the pricing of the product. It might be an internal decision like hiring a key employee.

The most important decision might not even be made within your organization. Maybe it's the decision to *buy* a product. Or maybe the decision to file a claim.

This is how I like to start a conversation I call a historical modeling workshop. Assemble a group of key stakeholders and get them to think about the web of decisions made within their business processes. The idea is similar to event storming, a practice developed by Alberto Brandolini. Whereas event storming centers the discussion around domain events, a historical modeling workshop uses historical facts. It explicitly documents the causal relationships among those facts.

The question about the most important decision seeds the conversation by focusing on decisions, not technology or procedures. Ask stakeholders to write down their answer before sharing with the group. The answers you get will be diverse. The more diverse, the better.

Historical Modeling Workshop

When you reveal and compare the most important decisions in the organization, you will discover some disagreement. Different stakeholders might naturally assume that the decisions most closely aligned with their function will be most important. Or they might show humility by placing other people's decisions above their own. If you do see consensus, then it probably indicates that one particularly influential stakeholder has imposed their values on the group. Take this opportunity to identify that behavior and move past it. Collect a few more "most important" decisions.

© Michael L. Perry 2024
M. L. Perry, *The Art of Immutable Architecture*, https://doi.org/10.1007/979-8-8688-0288-1_4

You now have a collection of decisions. Maybe you don't have agreement on which is *most* important, but you know that they are all important. Critically, you know that they are all *decisions*. These are not steps in a process. These are not outputs from an automated procedure. Somebody had to think about them. And they could have chosen differently.

Which Came First

Now that you have a collection of decisions, you can start to relate them. This works best if you write each one on a note that you can move around. Ask which decisions must come before which others. Focus on *causality*. We are less concerned that a decision is usually made earlier than another. Relate decisions only if they could happen in no other order.

Perhaps you are meeting with stakeholders of a restaurant. They list important decisions in their business. A customer orders a meal. A customer decides to eat at our restaurant rather than another. The chef adds a meal to the menu. And marketing purchases an ad in the local paper. They write these decisions on sticky notes and post them on a whiteboard, as shown in Figure 4-1.

Figure 4-1. *Important decisions as identified by restaurant stakeholders*

Some of these decisions are clearly related. A customer must decide to eat at our restaurant before they can order a meal. And they can only order a meal if the chef had previously added it to the menu. Organize these decisions with the causes above the effects. Draw arrows up toward the prerequisite decisions, as shown in Figure 4-2.

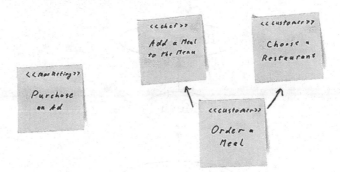

Figure 4-2. *Decisions are arranged with prerequisites above successors*

Other decisions are not so clear. A customer might decide to eat at our restaurant because they saw an ad. Or they might make that decision based on word of mouth, convenience, or any unknown reason. We cannot draw a definitive causal relationship between the ad and the customer's arrival. Leave that one off to the side.

Complete the Process

Important decisions usually occur in the middle of a process. There are preparations that must have come before. And there are future steps taken to wrap things up. Focus on a specific decision and identify the process in which it is embedded.

Let's focus on the decision that a customer makes to order a meal. What must have happened before? We have already identified that the chef must add the meal to the menu. What happened before that? There must have been a menu to add it to. And before that, there must have been a decision to open a restaurant. Carry this all the way up the chain, as illustrated in Figure 4-3.

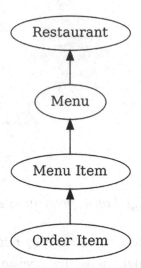

Figure 4-3. *Other historical facts preceded the customer's order*

Consider the steps that must follow. Add those to the diagram. The meal is prepared and then delivered to the table. The customer pays the check and leaves. Then the table is bussed for the next customer.

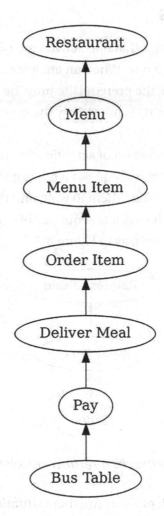

Figure 4-4. *A sequence of steps outlines the usual business process*

At this stage, you will often find sequential chains of events. The chain represents the happy path. The business process usually progresses in this order. Allow the group to build these chains. Then lead them past the sequential phase by identifying and then challenging assumptions.

Validate Assumptions

Each arrow in the diagram indicates that one activity is a prerequisite of another. The prerequisite relationship is a strict one. When an analyst draws a line from one decision to its prerequisite, they claim that the prerequisite must be completed before the subsequent activity can begin. If that is not strictly the case, then the relationship should not exist.

Consider, for example, the typical set of activities that happens when a customer enters a restaurant. First, the customer requests a table, giving the size of their party. The host finds them a table, possibly asking them to wait, and then seats them. Once seated, a server takes their order. Given that typical sequence of events, you might draw each activity as the prerequisite of the next, as in Figure 4-5.

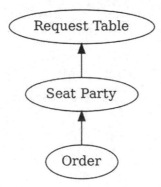

Figure 4-5. *A sequence of activities in a restaurant system*

But is this really the correct depiction? Are there situations in which a server can take a party's order without them being seated? What about a to-go order, a catering order, or a customer at the bar? Seating a party is not truly a prerequisite to taking their order. It is only an activity that *usually* comes earlier and only in some scenarios. A more accurate analysis of this problem would be the one shown in Figure 4-6.

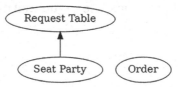

Figure 4-6. *Taking a party's order is not predicated upon seating them*

In addition to being strict, the prerequisite relationship carries information forward. A prerequisite provides information to subsequent activities. There is no need to duplicate the information from a prior activity into a later one. If a subsequent decision does not rely upon the information in the prerequisite decision, then perhaps that relationship should not exist.

In the earlier example, the request for a table includes the size of the party. That provides information that constrains the task of seating the party. The very relationship between Seat Party and Request Table indicates that we know the number of people to seat. An example instance diagram appears in Figure 4-7.

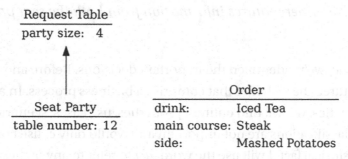

Figure 4-7. *Seat party has available to it the party size from request table. Take order does not need that information*

The Order activity did not require knowing where the customer was seated. As long as a server can communicate with a customer – even if it's over the phone or at the bar – they can complete the Order activity. This is another indicator that tells us that seating the party is not a prerequisite.

Delivering an order to a table, however, *does* require that we know where they are seated. Extending this example, Figure 4-8 shows that this new activity requires information from both of its predecessors.

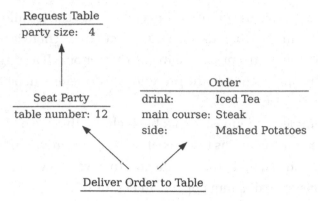

Figure 4-8. *Deliver order requires information from both the seat party and order activities*

In the workshop, we've identified the important decisions. Before and after these decisions, we captured the activities that comprise a business process. In addition to decisions and activities, we will find entities, properties, use cases, scenarios, commands, and events. The classifications are not important and would only cause confusion. Each one is simply a historical fact. I will use the word *fact* to refer to any of these objects.

There is only one relationship between facts. A fact is a *predecessor* of another if it necessarily comes before. The arrows in the preceding diagrams point toward the predecessors. The fact at the tail of an arrow is called the *successor*. A successor knows about its predecessors. And from this simple relationship, we can derive some very compelling behavior.

Data

After we leave the workshop setting, we iteratively refine our model. The first pass of an iteration will focus on the data carried within each fact. Gather a few practical examples of business processes completed manually or with prior versions of the software. Then lay this data out among the facts and see if everything fits.

We've seen how the data from predecessor facts is available to its successors. This allows us to analyze how information accumulates as we chain more facts together. We can further analyze that information content to discover identifiers, cardinalities, and mutation.

Identifiers

Hidden within many data structures are values that identify people, objects, or other entities. When you find an identifier hidden within some data, consider extracting it to a separate fact. Replace the field with a predecessor relationship pointing toward that fact.

Continuing our analysis of the restaurant system, we can see an identifier in the form of the table number. We decide to elevate this concept to its own fact, moving the table number into it to serve as its identity. When we replace the identifier in the Seat Party activity with a predecessor relationship, we end up with the diagram in Figure 4-9.

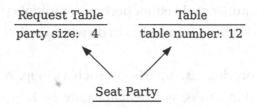

Figure 4-9. *Table number is elevated to its own fact*

Elevating an identifier to a fact creates a new point of interest in the application. This accomplishes two things. It first allows us to observe all of the successors of this new fact. We can identify, for example, which parties were seated at a table over time. But perhaps more importantly, it gives us an anchor to say more things about the identified entity. In this case, we now have a place to say which server is assigned to a table. This helps us to understand who is responsible for attending to the party, as well as to balance future seating so that all servers have a roughly equal workload. The result appears in Figure 4-10.

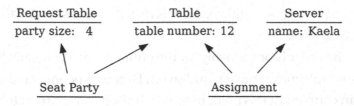

Figure 4-10. *A server is assigned to a table*

As you elevate identifiers to facts, you will find that the model contains a mixture of activities and entities. The activities came from use cases, broken down into their atomic decisions. The entities are identified people, objects, places, or concepts that those decisions are about. The distinction between activities and entities is not important.

They are all facts. Furthermore, the diagram contains only one kind of relationship: predecessor. A predecessor fact is either a prerequisite decision – one that must have come before – or an entity involved in that decision.

Cardinality

Continuing our analysis of a set of decisions, we can identify groups that have zero, one, or many parts. These indicate points of cardinality that need to be addressed in the model. A group that allows only zero or one part becomes an optional (?) predecessor. A group that allows any number could either become a multiple (*) predecessor or a successor. The difference between the two has to do with whether new parts can be added after the fact.

The `Order` fact in the previous example is just such a group. We originally modeled it as a single unit having multiple rows, as shown in Figure 4-11.

Order	
drink:	Iced Tea
main course:	Steak
side:	Mashed Potatoes

Figure 4-11. *An example order fact having multiple rows*

In this example, it made sense to label each of those fields as `drink`, `main course`, and `side`. This particular order was made up of those three parts. But in general, we don't need to enforce that every order has exactly those three things. Some orders will have appetizers. Some will have desserts. Some might have two sides. While a typical order might follow a pattern or template, there is no value to restricting the items in the order to specific categories.

Furthermore, the order is presumably for the entire party. We are likely to have multiple drinks, multiple main courses, and so on. Different people might even order appetizers as main courses. At this point in the analysis, it is important to ask whether these distinctions are relevant for the solution you are modeling. Is it important to know which person ordered the steak, or will the server simply ask when they reach the table? Is it important to model when to deliver the salad, or will the server keep track of each course on their own?

The decisions you make while analyzing the cardinality of the model determine the relationships you will emphasize. These will reflect the values of your product owner. One valid restaurant model would allow the flexibility of adding items to an order at any time. A different but equally valid model would lock an order down so that it can be controlled at each part of the preparation, delivery, and payment. If the product owner values flexibility over control, then you would come up with a model such as the one in Figure 4-12 that allows successors to be added at any time.

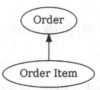

Figure 4-12. *An order allows multiple items to be added as successors*

A fact can always have multiple successors. We do not indicate that cardinality on the diagram, as it is implied. An example of facts in that structure appears in Figure 4-13.

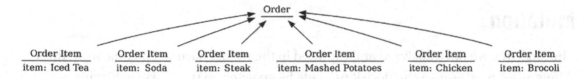

Figure 4-13. *Multiple items represented as successors to the order*

The decision to model items as successors emphasizes the fact that new items can be added to an order at any time. If the product owner makes a different set of decisions, then you might choose a different model. For example, in a fast food restaurant, the order is taken in its entirety, prepared, and then delivered. Modifications cannot be made along the way. That may cause you to instead make the Order Items predecessors of Order as in Figure 4-14.

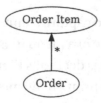

Figure 4-14. *Multiple order items are predecessors of an order*

Since Order Item is a predecessor, we *do* indicate the cardinality. Order items cannot be added after the fact. The asterisk (*) indicates that multiple order items are present when the order is captured. An example set of facts matching this model appears in Figure 4-15.

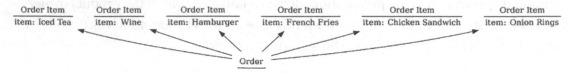

Figure 4-15. *A strict organization of items as predecessors, which cannot be changed*

Simply saying that an order has many items is not quite enough to capture the nuances of the process. Knowing whether items can be added afterward is an important part of the model. These reflect the values of the product owner and translate into capabilities of the product. Capturing them in the model is an important first step toward analyzing the consequences of those decisions.

Mutation

The facts that we have analyzed and captured in the model have so far come from three different sources. Some were decisions made by an actor on the way to achieving a goal. Others were identifiable entities about which those decisions were made. And still others were smaller parts of those decisions and entities that appeared from analysis of cardinality. In every case, these facts are immutable. The past decision, identity, or part will not change.

This does not always match our intuition. When we look at the state of a system, we imagine that it is changing over time. We see state as mutable. But what we have modeled so far is a succession of decisions that have *caused* the apparent evolution of state change. The model represents those past decisions; it does *not* represent the state itself.

At some point, we will just need to capture a mutable property. We might, for example, just want to record the name of a menu item. The name can change over time. But we are not interested in the various decisions that led to the chef selecting those names. We just want to know what to print on the menu.

Modeling mutable state should be considered a last resort. If you can imagine a property being the consequence of a set of business decisions, then model those decisions. The total of a restaurant check, for example, is a consequence of the items ordered, the taxes and gratuities applied, and any discounts that the restaurant might be offering. Properties such as check total should not be represented as mutable state. Only use this pattern for values that are not an outcome of the business process being modeled.

Let's model the name of a menu item. We do so by writing the property as a fact separate from the entity that it describes. This property has a reference back to itself called `prior` that allows many predecessors (*). The pattern is illustrated in Figure 4-16.

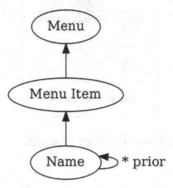

Figure 4-16. *The name of a menu item is a mutable property*

We saw this pattern in the previous chapter: a small loop that points back to the same type. In the last chapter, the loop was on the price of a product. You might be concerned that the loop allows cycles in the model. But as we saw in the price example, the loop disappears when we examine the data. Figure 4-17 shows that the name of a menu item has changed over time.

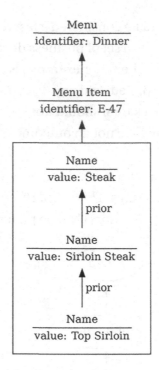

Figure 4-17. *A menu item has had multiple names*

Current State

As you document the facts in a model, you will want to explain how to find the current state of the system. This is where the Factual Modeling Language comes in. Start by describing the state of data structures built using collections and mutable properties.

Let's say that we are displaying a menu so that the server can take the customer's order. We can write a specification that shows the menu items for a given menu.

```
itemsOnMenu = (m: Menu) {
  mi: MenuItem [
    mi→menu = m
  ]
}
```

This specification lists all menu items related to the given menu. For each menu item, we want to display the current name. Let's make that a projection of the menu items.

```
itemsOnMenu = (m: Menu) {
  mi: MenuItem [
    mi→menu = m
  ]
} ⇒ {
  names = {
    n: MenuItem.Name [
      n→menuItem = mi
    ]
  } ⇒ n.value
}
```

The projection would include all names of the menu item, even the ones that have been superseded. We want to exclude those from the results. To do that, we can introduce an existential condition.

Take another look at Figure 4-17. You can clearly see that the current name should be "Top Sirloin". It is at the end of the chain. How can you express that condition using only existential qualifiers? The secret is in the arrows. We want to eliminate all of the names at the head of an arrow.

For each name that was superseded, there exists a next name. That next name has a prior reference to the superseded one. We want to eliminate those names. In other words, we only want the names for which a next one does *not* exist.

```
itemsOnMenu = (m: Menu) {
  mi: MenuItem [
    mi→menu = m
  ]
} ⇒ {
  names = {
    n: MenuItem.Name [
      n→menuItem = mi
      ∄ {
        next: MenuItem.Name [
```

```
            next→prior = n
        ]
      }
    ]
  } ⇒ n.value
}
```

This is a common pattern that arises when modeling data historically. I call this the *mutable property* pattern. This allows a model to represent the changes to a property over time. It returns only the most recent versions of that property.

Like all specifications, this one can return multiple results. This will happen because historical models exist in distributed systems. In a distributed system, we cannot eliminate the possibility that multiple users edited a property simultaneously. When the specification returns only one value, then there have been no concurrent edits. But when more than one value is returned, they are the candidate values. We will examine mutable properties in greater detail in later chapters.

Views

After modeling the decisions, entities, and properties of a domain, we have a good understanding of its basic structure. The model so far captures how a process evolves over time. Each decision builds upon those of the past in a latticework of increasing knowledge.

In order to make a decision, a user of the system needs to have access to that knowledge. The job of the system is twofold: provide that information and capture the resulting decision. That new decision becomes a new fact and contributes to the information that users will receive in the future. The views that a system presents to its users can therefore be expressed as a function of their past decisions. One of our jobs as an analyst is to describe that function.

Finding a Place to Start

To pull data out of a historical model, we need to identify a starting point. We cannot simply query the entire model as a whole. Fortunately, we usually have a few good candidates.

Most applications require a user to log in. As soon as they do, we have a starting point: the user themselves. Once in the application, they will navigate from page to page. As they do, they will change their starting place. The application will provide them information based on that point in the model. From there, they can continue to navigate or make a decision that will be captured in the model.

Let's continue building our restaurant model to see how the user can be the initial starting place. A server will log into the system at the start of their shift. From there, they will see all of the tables to which they are assigned. By logging in, the server has identified the starting point of the model, which is outlined in Figure 4-18.

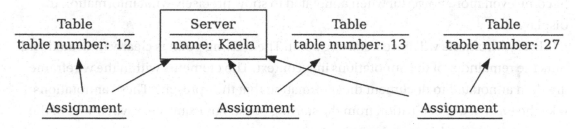

Figure 4-18. *A server logs into the system to see their table assignments*

Even when an application does not require the user to log in, it usually has a clearly defined starting place. This is typically a top-level entity that defines the scope of the application. For example, if the restaurant guest has a device at their table for ordering drinks or appetizers, they will typically not need to log in first. The starting point of the information that they can search is the menu. From here, they can navigate through menu items, as shown in Figure 4-19.

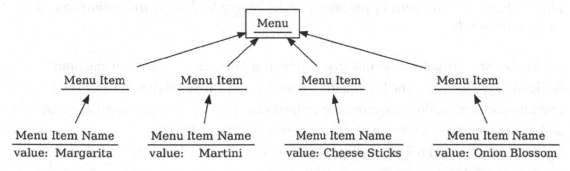

Figure 4-19. *A guest starts with the menu to search through menu items*

Once we have identified a starting place, we can describe the information that will be presented to the user. We will use wireframes and specifications to do so. These will in turn lead to refinements of the model in an iterative inward spiral of analysis.

Annotated Wireframes

Wireframes are a powerful tool for communicating the information that will be presented to the user. They are applicable to any system that displays information on a screen. They are effective for web, mobile, and desktop applications alike. And they become even more powerful when annotated to show precisely what information to display.

Every wireframe will have a starting point. The starting point is clearly indicated and puts the remainder of the annotations into context. The elements within the wireframe are then annotated to document the information that they present. These annotations take the form of a specification from the starting point. For example, a wireframe of the server's home page is shown in Figure 4-20.

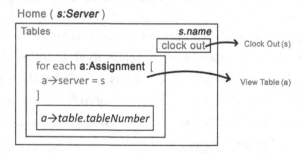

Figure 4-20. *A wireframe of the server's home page includes annotations on various elements*

As the user navigates from one page to the next, they select a new starting point. Navigation appears as a line leaving the wireframe and carries with it the new starting point for that destination. Sometimes it is the same (as in the navigation to `Clock Out`), and sometimes it drills into a narrower context (as in `View Table`).

Annotations need not be represented directly on the wireframe the way that they are depicted in Figure 4-20. They could be shown as footnotes to keep the wireframe simpler, or to allow space for sample text. The important idea, though, is that the annotations be precise. The Factual Modeling Language conveys just the right precision to ensure that behavior is unambiguous and assumptions are made explicit.

Removal from Lists

Historical facts cannot be deleted. Views are projections of historical facts. Yet any view that simply grows unbounded will soon become useless. The specification for a view needs a way for items to be removed from lists. This operation is accomplished with a negative existential condition.

Consider the host making the decision to seat a party. What information do they need to make that decision? They need to know the tables available, the parties waiting, and the capacities and sizes of each. With this information at hand, they can perform a few tasks. They can enter a request for a table, seat a party, or indicate that a waiting party has walked out. That information might be displayed in a view such as the one wireframed in Figure 4-21.

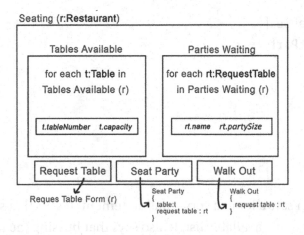

Figure 4-21. *A host sees the tables available and parties waiting and can take appropriate actions*

The "Request Table" button takes the host to a form where they can capture the details of an arriving party. It initiates a navigation. The "Seat Party" and "Walk Out" buttons, on the other hand, immediately create new facts. They record the decisions related to the selected table and table request. These decisions will influence the information displayed on the view.

But exactly *how* will these facts influence the view? What are the events that lead to a table becoming available? What makes it no longer available? These answers become clear when we define the specifications referenced in the wireframe: `tablesAvailable` and `partiesWaiting`. Let's start with the first.

Consider the list of tables that are available for seating. We aren't simply adding to and removing from a list; there's a business process taking place. When the restaurant opens, all tables are available. One is removed from the list when a party is seated. It is added again when the table is bussed. We can model this process with a single specification:

```
tablesAvailable = (r: Restaurant) {
  t: Table [
    t→restaurant = r
    ∄ {
      s: SeatParty [
        s→table = t
        ∄ {
          b: BusTable [
            b.seatParty = s
          ]
        }
      ]
    }
  ]
}
```

This specification says a lot in a very small statement. It says that seating a party removes the table from the available list. It also says that bussing the table puts it back. It makes clear that we need to have a relationship between a table and a restaurant so that we have a starting point for the specification. And it tells us that we need a relationship between Bus Table and Seat Party. The revised model is shown in Figure 4-22.

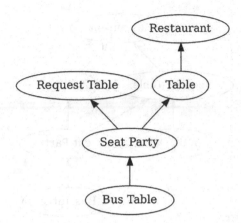

Figure 4-22. *New relationships suggested by the need to show tables available*

Following similar logic, we can analyze what adds and removes parties waiting for a table. A party is added to the list when they request a table. They are removed when they are seated. The party is also removed when they walk out. This leads us to define the view of parties waiting with the following specification:

```
partiesWaiting = (r: Restaurant) {
  rt: RequestTable [
    rt→restaurant = r
    ∄ {
      s: SeatParty [
        s→requestTable = rt
      ]
    }
    ∄ {
      w: WalkOut [
        w→requestTable = rt
      ]
    }
  ]
}
```

These additional facts and relationships further refine our model. We can now see that Request Table must be within the scope of a Restaurant. We can also see how Walk Out is related to Request Table. The more complete picture appears in Figure 4-23.

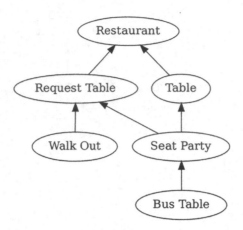

Figure 4-23. *A request for a table happens within the scope of a restaurant and can be aborted with a walkout*

Taking these two specifications together, we can find implied requirements. We can see, for example, that two parties should not be seated at the same table at the same time. This can be inferred from the fact that a table will be selected from the list `tablesAvailable`, which does not contain any tables with a current `Seat Party`. More subtlely, the specifications reveal that seating a party removes both the party and the table. This is apparent because `Seat Party` appears in the ∄ clause of each specification.

Other systems of analysis would require us to consider these activities in terms of cause and effect. Requesting a table *causes* the party to be added to the list. Seating a party *removes* the party and the table. We end up defining a state machine describing how events change the state of aggregates. It is easy to forget to update the view state in response to an event, thus leading to incomplete specifications and bugs.

The precise nature of the Factual Modeling Language reveals assumptions about how state evolves with the introduction of new facts. Had the requirements for these views been expressed in prose, it would be easy to overlook these assumptions. A product owner familiar with the process of running a restaurant might not even see the assumptions that they are making. Of *course* two parties can't be seated at the same table. Why *wouldn't* you remove both the party and the table upon assignment?

A less precise form of specification would require the analyst to discover these unstated assumptions and raise the questions. If the analyst misses them, then the developers might run into edge cases. And if developers miss them, then testers might file a defect. If we demand precision, then our analysis will uncover assumptions, make behaviors explicit, and avoid waste.

Collaboration

As the model continues to evolve, we will want to take note of which actors are responsible for which decisions. Labeling the model with the actors gives us a clear picture of how the system will ultimately be used as a collaborative tool. People will work together *through* the system. It will be their means of communication.

In a use case diagram, actors are drawn external to the system as stick figures. Arrows indicate which use cases particular actors are responsible for undertaking. While this is an accurate depiction – actors *are* outside of the system – it obfuscates points of collaboration within the model. It is much clearer to draw lines of responsibility within the model itself.

Regions

In my own work as an analyst, I have used several tools to indicate which actor is responsible for which decision. On a whiteboard or using sticky notes, I might assign each actor a color. In a notebook, I might jot a small annotation at the top of each fact. But the most versatile method, and the one that we will use here, is to divide the model into regions.

A region is an area of real estate within the model having clearly demarcated boundaries. All of the facts in a region are decisions for which a single actor is responsible. Compare this to bounded contexts from Domain-Driven Design. The concepts are similar in that they subdivide the model. But whereas bounded contexts are demarcated according to many factors – including domain language, organizational structure, and human judgment – regions are strictly concerned with identifying the responsible party.

It is common practice in process modeling systems to use swimlanes to organize regions of responsibility. While regions in a historical model do not have to be swimlanes, the practice carries over quite naturally for those that are accustomed to it. When used, swimlanes are typically oriented vertically, because time progresses down the page.

Let's switch to a different model to illustrate this concept more clearly. Imagine a system that helps conference organizers to select speakers and then schedule their sessions for attendees. In this system, there are several actors, each making different decisions. The organizer is primarily responsible for putting on the conference and selecting the presentations. The speaker proposes presentations for the conference.

And the attendee chooses which sessions to attend, rating them afterward. Figure 4-24 illustrates each of these three actors as a separate region.

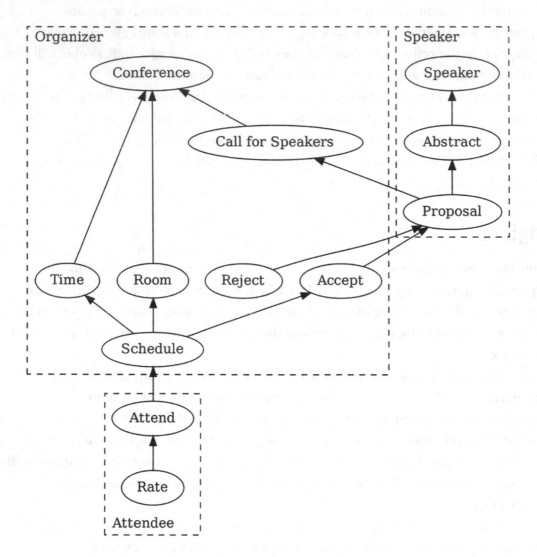

Figure 4-24. *Conference organizers, speakers, and attendees all have different responsibilities within a single model*

The organizer and speaker regions are roughly vertical swimlanes containing the decisions for which they are responsible. The process begins with the organizer creating the `Conference` and the speaker creating the `Abstract`. The organizer puts out a `Call for Speakers`, and speakers submit `Proposals`. If the proposal is accepted, then the organizer schedules the talk. The attendee only comes in at the tail end of the process to `Attend` and `Rate` sessions. Rather than showing the attendee's actions in a vertically distinct swimlane, Figure 4-24 depicts them in a small region. This choice still conveys the important information: who is responsible for each decision. It also makes it clear when a line crosses a responsibility boundary.

Crossing Boundaries

Once the regions of responsibility are clearly arranged, an important feature of the model emerges. It takes the form of an edge crossing the boundary from one region to another. A decision that depends upon one outside of the decision maker's control is an important point of collaboration. It indicates that one actor made a decision and then published it so that another actor can respond. These points in the model are referred to as *pivots*.

When a pivot appears in the model, we know that the information provided by one actor needs to be made visible to others. We have two examples in Figure 4-24: sending out a call for speakers and publishing a schedule. The conference organizer is responsible for both of these decisions. In the first, the organizer advertises the speaker call on mailing lists, social media, websites, and through their professional network. In the second, the organizer deploys the schedule to their website and mobile app and hands out printed pages. The audience for each publication is indicated by the tail of the arrow: the call for speakers is targeted toward speakers, while the schedule is intended for the attendees.

In a computer system, pivots often appear as interfaces between interdependent subsystems. This is especially true if the actors on each side of the pivot are members of different organizations. In this scenario, it is not uncommon for a pivot to be expressed as an API. The receiving actor – the one at the tail of the arrow – makes an API available to business partners so that they can publish facts such as the one at the head of the arrow. This would be the case if a conference organizer used an API for a CFP (call-for-papers) website or social media platform to publish the call for speakers.

Even when actors are members of the same organization, pivots will often manifest as connections between subsystems. If actors are in different departments, for example, it is not uncommon for their systems to collaborate through message passing. In these scenarios, the fact at the head of the arrow will take the form of a message published to a topic or queue. This might also be accomplished with an internal API, a shared database connection, or a batch file. As an analyst, it is important to understand the connections that already exist and the opportunities available to interface with legacy systems.

Consumer-facing pivot points are also important features of a model. However, they often take very different forms within a deployed application. A public pivot point like the attendee's arrow into schedule can simply appear as information on a web page. The information may be searchable, or it might be listed in its entirety. Usually, a page refresh is required to update the view, but for some pivot points, the website or mobile app may choose to provide notifications. Annotate the model with these requirements so that the development team can choose the correct implementation of the pivot.

Conversations

In some models, several pivots appear between two actors. Usually, the pivots will swap directions and form a chain of facts traveling back and forth between the two. These represent conversations happening between two actors *through* the system. One actor publishes some information, another actor responds to it, and the original actor builds upon that response. These conversations usually provide the greatest value of the system and are therefore the most important features to analyze.

The model in Figure 4-24 contains one example of a conversation. After the conference organizer publishes a `Call for Speakers`, the speaker responds with a `Proposal`. The organizer then responds with `Accept` or `Reject`. This represents a back-and-forth collaboration between the organizer and each speaker. The organizer is presumably having these conversations with many speakers simultaneously. Each conversation carries with it the entire context: which call for speakers, which proposal, and whether it was accepted or rejected.

Publishing Facts

Conversations indicate that a multistep process must occur between two actors. Each actor is made aware of the decisions made on the opposite side of that conversation. This is even true of the last decision – the one for which there is no further response. In the preceding example, either `Accept` or `Reject` is the final decision in this conversation. Yet even though the speaker has no response in this model, they are made aware of the decision. Such will usually be the case with any conversation. Nevertheless, the model does not make that explicit. Use an annotated view or some other form of Factual specification to make this assumption explicit.

Whereas the first pivot in the conversation is published to a wide audience, subsequent messages are directed to specific actors. The `Call for Speakers` is published on social media, but the subsequent acceptance or rejection takes place via direct message or email. This narrowing of scope can be inferred from the structure of the diagram. The Speaker is an indirect predecessor (an ancestor) of the Proposal. This relationship indicates that the speaker is particularly interested in responses to that proposal. That interest implies that the system needs some form of direct notification targeting a speaker. We will formalize this concept and explore the mechanisms to implement it in later chapters.

Integrating Subsystems

When the actors on opposite sides of a conversation are using different subsystems, each subsystem will usually need to carry a copy of the entire conversation. Whether they are in different organizations, or simply in different departments, their respective applications or microservices will store their own version of all of the data exchanged. The model shows what information this might include: follow the arrows up from the facts involved in the conversation. All of the facts in this upward cone – called the *transitive closure* – are likely to be duplicated to some degree between the systems. Figure 4-25 illustrates how this set can be found. If you discover that any information *outside* of the transitive closure is shared between the systems, then you have cause for concern. This information may change and will require other conversations if it is to be kept in sync.

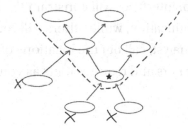

Figure 4-25. *The transitive closure includes all predecessors and their predecessors. It does not include successors*

On each side of the conversation, consideration must be given to data ownership and security. There may be requirements governing the movement of data outside of a country's jurisdiction. Regulations and standards such as Europe's General Data Protection Regulation (GDPR), the United States' Health Insurance Portability and Accountability Act (HIPAA), the Payment Card Industry Data Security Standard

(PCI-DSS), or the California Consumer Privacy Act (CCPA) will determine how data is controlled, stored, secured, and accessed. These guidelines may even include policies under which data must be destroyed. While destroying data is typically *not* allowed within a historical model, exceptions must be made to accommodate these requirements. Fortunately, the model helps identify the set of all records that must be expunged: it is the cone extending *down* from the entity to be erased or forgotten, as depicted in Figure 4-26. When this cone crosses from one region into another, then the system requires policies to ensure that partners are in compliance.

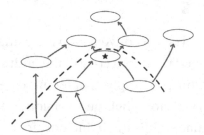

Figure 4-26. *The records to be deleted from a historical model include all successors and their successors*

Pivot points are important features of a model to analyze. They are opportunities for the application to interact with external systems. While the job of the analyst is not to design that integration point, it is important to understand where they are and how they will manifest. Different forms of interfaces will constrain the system in different ways. Some will provide real-time notification, while others will require scheduled polling or the occasional refresh. As an analyst, call out the locations of pivots, and gather as much information about their constraints and requirements as you can assemble.

Valid Orderings

In building the model, we have assembled a graph of related decisions. Each arrow indicates that two decisions must be made in a certain order: the predecessor always occurs before the successor. But equally telling are the pairs of decisions between which there are no arrows. These are the places where order is fluid. Two facts may have a common ancestor, but as long as there is no path from one to the other, those two facts can occur in either order.

Look back at the model for seating and table assignment at a restaurant (Figure 4-27). The two facts `Seat Party` and `Assignment` have a common ancestor: `Table`. And yet, there is no way to walk in the direction of the arrows from one to the other. This indicates that a party can be seated at a table before or after that table is assigned to a server. The order of these two decisions is not constrained.

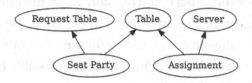

Figure 4-27. *No arrow or chain of arrows leads from seat party to assignment, or vice versa*

Each of these two valid orderings – the party is seated before the table is assigned, or the table is assigned before the party is seated – implies a different requirement. First, because parties might already be seated when a server receives their table assignments, they should be told which tables are already occupied. And second, because parties might be seated afterward, a server should be notified when a party is seated at one of their tables. Either order is valid, but they evoke different behaviors from the system.

Eliminating Race Conditions

In this simple example, we have only two valid orderings. But in a more complex system, the number of orderings can grow significantly. Finding and accounting for all possible permutations of events can be a daunting task. An analyst might find that the job gets cumulatively more difficult as each new requirement is added. What starts as a simple list of a few possibilities eventually explodes into a labyrinth of edge cases, each one being revisited and expanded with every new feature.

It is important for an analyst to understand how a system behaves under different valid orderings of events. Describing each of the permutations will help testers identify scenarios that must be examined. Explaining the possible behaviors will help developers code for edge cases. And most importantly, comparing the outcomes of different valid orderings will help uncover race conditions. A *race condition* arises when the final state of a system depends upon the order in which events occurred. To avoid race conditions, the analyst must demonstrate that all valid orderings converge to the same state.

Fortunately, the Factual specifications with which we annotate our views provide the proof that we need. When we express the behavior of the system using a Factual specification, rather than a series of cause and effect, we are guaranteed that the state converges to the same set of results no matter which valid ordering occurred.

Furthermore, those specifications also provide a mechanism for enumerating all valid orderings. They reveal the events that could possibly affect the information presented to a user. Moreover, they show us how to respond to each of those events. They indicate how to use facts that have come before to update the view or notify the user. From a single specification, we can derive the correct behavior for any possible ordering of events.

Responding to Different Valid Orderings

Let's revisit the view that shows the server their table assignments. Earlier, we only identified each assigned table. But now, let's augment the view to also display the size of any party seated at that table. The modified annotation appears in Figure 4-28.

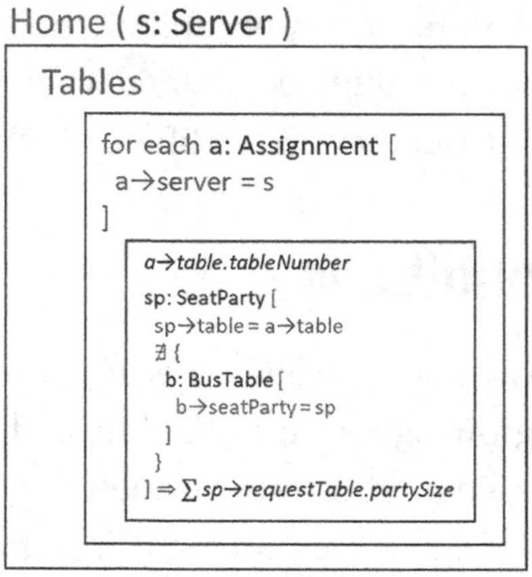

Figure 4-28. *The annotated server home view now shows the total party size at each table*

Concatenating the two annotations gives us a specification for all of the parties assigned to a server. Let's write that as a Factual specification so we can better understand how this view behaves.

```
partiesAssignedToServer = (s: Server) {
  a: Assignment [
    a→server = s
  ]
```

```
sp: SeatParty [
  sp→table = a→table
  ∄ {
    b: BusTable [
      b→seatParty = sp
    ]
  }
]
}
```

When read directly, the specification gives instructions on how to populate the view. First, find all assignments for the server. Then for each assignment, find all parties still seated at the table. This interpretation of the specification gives us the initial behavior of the system. It executes the specification when the view is loaded to find all seated parties.

Now let's examine the specification to see how we should respond to changes. Because the results of the specification are displayed to the server, we want to notify the server when the results change. Let's look at the structure of the specification to determine which events can cause that change.

The specification contains three labels, one each for `Assignment`, `SeatParty`, and `BusTable`. This is a clue that any of these three events can lead to a notification. We can split the specification along these seams to determine which servers to notify of these events.

The first clause tells us that the view will change when there is a new `Assignment`. When the manager assigns a table to a server, the specification will be affected *for that server*. The server will need to be notified. The assignment tells us exactly *which* server to notify. Any parties already seated at the assigned table will appear in this view as a result. More formally, we can write the following Factual specifications to give us the server to notify and the parties that were added:

```
serversToNotify = (a: Assignment) {
  s: Server [
    s = a→server
  ]
}

partiesAdded = (a: Assignment) {
  sp: SeatParty [
```

```
    sp→table = a→table
    ∄ {
      b: BusTable [
        b→seatParty = sp
      ]
    }
  ]
}
```

This pair of specifications describes the behavior of the system when an Assignment occurs *after* a SeatParty. Using the second specification, we find all existing parties still seated at the newly assigned table. If the result is not empty – meaning that the table is occupied – then the first specification tells us which server to notify.

But there is another valid ordering that the partiesAssignedToServer specification tells us about. The second clause of the specification implies that the view will change when there is a new SeatParty. Upon seating a party, we have to notify the server assigned to that table. We can find the server by *inverting* the specification. For completeness sake, the query giving the party added is listed as well.

```
serversToNotify = (sp: SeatParty) {
  a: Assignment [
    a→table = sp→table
  ]
  s: Server [
    s = a→server
  ]
}

partiesAdded = (sp: SeatParty) {
}
```

Notice that the second specification simply returns the new SeatParty fact. It has no additional clauses. In particular, it does not mention the BusTable fact, which would ordinarily remove it from the results. The reason for this is that this specification describes how the system responds when a new SeatParty fact is created. At the moment of creation, there can be no BusTable fact: there has not been time for any successors to be created. The formal justification for this decision is given in Chapter 13.

Using the inverted specification, we can determine the behavior of the system when `Assignment` happens *before* `SeatParty`. Given the fact that a party is being seated, we find all assignments for that table. Each assignment gives us a server. We notify each server that they have a new party: the one that was just seated.

The third label – the `BusTable` fact – does not lead to the addition of parties. It leads to removal of parties from the server's attention. If our goal was updating the view, we would need to include that scenario in our analysis. But as we are currently concerned with notification, we can make the decision only to notify servers of parties *added*, not *removed*. We will therefore skip the third scenario.

At first, you may need to convince yourself that this pair of behaviors gives all of the servers that need to be notified for each event, as well as all parties that the server needs to learn about. They cover all valid orderings of the events and let nothing fall through the cracks. You might want to reason through several different scenarios to determine why this is true.

Later, however, we show that inverting a specification is a mechanical process. It can be done for *any* specification, and it always produces a complete and correct result. Immutable runtimes compute the inverse automatically. You will learn how this works in Chapter 13. The important takeaway for now is that analyzing a system from the perspective of Factual specifications will reveal *all* of the valid orders of events. It describes exactly how the system should behave in each of those permutations. And it always converges to the same outcome.

Consequences

You have iterated over your model several times, and each pass has refined the facts a little bit more than the last. You have a clear picture of how the use cases break down into individual decisions. You know how those decisions relate to one another. You have identified the actors responsible for each decision. From that, you have identified pivots and conversations within the model that support points of collaboration. You've expressed the information that those actors see in terms of specifications and from those identified which events lead to notifications and updates.

Now you can answer some very real questions about the capabilities of your model. From the design decisions that have led to this point, you can derive the constraints under which the resulting application will perform. You can determine the consequences of your modeling decisions. This will help you decide if these consequences are satisfactory and, if not, show you what compromise you need to make before you build the system.

The consequences of historical modeling are not arbitrary constraints. They limit our capabilities to only those things that can be easily done in a distributed system. If there is something that the model does not allow, then that is because implementing that feature in a distributed system would be prohibitive. It would cause blocking, loss of autonomy, or reduced scalability. Consider carefully whether you need that feature. If you do, you will need to implement it with a stateful model. You should be aware of the compromise that you are making when you do so. Let's examine three of these constraints in detail: indexes, number of results, and order of results.

Indexes

The first constraint that you will need to consider will be how the historical model can be indexed. This will affect uniqueness, navigation, and searching. For uniqueness constraints, consider that you cannot enforce that only one fact in a distributed system has a given value for one of its fields, unless that is the only field that it has. For navigation, consider that you cannot query for facts based on only one of its fields. The best you can do is to reconstruct a fact given all of its fields and then query for successors. Searching, on the other hand, is an activity best done outside of a historical model; determine what should be searchable and annotate how the information will be sourced.

Uniqueness Constraints

Uniqueness constraints are often quite desirable and yet difficult to implement in a distributed system. In an accounts receivable system, for example, you may wish to impose a uniqueness constraint on invoice number. If you have identified the invoice fact to have extra fields in addition to the invoice number, then you will not be able to enforce this constraint in a distributed system. You will need to collect all invoices into the same place and only then verify that no two have the same number.

In a historical model, the entire collection of fields – including predecessors – uniquely identifies a fact. Let's use this premise to model an invoice with a uniqueness constraint. Invoice numbers are not universally unique; they are only unique within the scope of a single vendor. And so our Invoice fact would also have a Vendor predecessor. The combination of Vendor and invoice number is sufficient to identify an invoice. It must also therefore be sufficient to *construct* an Invoice fact, as illustrated in Figure 4-29.

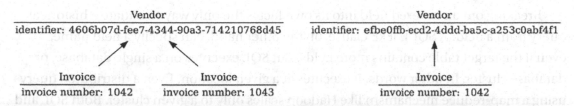

Figure 4-29. *An invoice that has a unique invoice number per vendor cannot have any other fields*

And so to model an invoice that has a unique invoice number, you would need to ensure that the invoice number was the only field in the fact, aside from the Vendor predecessor. The fact could have no additional fields, such as shippingAddress or a Customer predecessor. Adding these fields would weaken the constraint on the invoice number and allow invoices with different addresses or for different customers to have the same number.

Invoice numbers are an example of a *generated* unique identifier. Not only must the uniqueness of the identifier be enforced, but a new invoice must also be given a new invoice number. Even if the unique identifier is isolated, as in Figure 4-29, generation must still occur in a single place. Make a note in your model that a certain field is generated, and define the rules by which it will be unique.

Navigation

Next, let's examine the effect of indexes on navigation. As we saw previously, facts are the starting point for specifications in a view. As the user navigates from one view to the next, they select a new fact as the starting point of the next view. We cannot query from a field; only from a fact. If we *want* to start from a field, then we must be able to construct the corresponding fact. In other words, such starting points must be the *only* fields in their corresponding fact.

We observed this first when we extracted table number from the Seat Party fact to create the Table fact. Because of this choice, the table number can now be used as an indexed field. It isn't the field that the system indexes, but rather the entire Table fact. Servers can navigate the data model as they select one table or another to drill into more detailed views.

Breaking out an indexed field into its own fact is the only way to initiate a historical query from a field. A SQL WHERE clause, on the other hand, can specify a field name, even if the target table contains more fields. But SQL executes on a single database, or database cluster. In other words, it executes at a given location. Even a distributed query using a map-reduce mechanism like Hadoop scales only to a given cluster. Both SQL and NoSQL queries alike are outside of the more constrained historical specification. Make a note in the model if this kind of query is required so that the development team can integrate accordingly.

Searching

And finally, let us examine how indexing affects searching. Searching differs from other indexed query activities in that it allows much more flexibility. A search can match against part of a field, as in a prefix, substring, or SOUNDEX search. Searches can also include composition, such as Boolean operators or conditionals. Search engines typically have complex and expressive query languages.

Searching is an inherently location-dependent activity. All of the records that you search need to be in the same location. That single "location" may indeed be a cluster of distributed nodes, but we consider it a single location for a number of reasons. First, the nodes tend to be homogeneous: each one was created specifically to be a member of the cluster and therefore tends to run the same operating system, search engine, and data store. Second, the nodes tend to be co-located. They are rarely geographically dispersed and almost never operated by different organizations. And third, the number of nodes tends to be well-known or constrained. The distributed search algorithm needs to have a good idea when all of the nodes have reported in so that it can aggregate and present the results.

Stateful data stores are best suited for search. Good examples include Elasticsearch or other Lucene variants. These data stores are optimized for indexing complex records or documents using a multitude of different kinds of indexes. Some indexes are designed for numerical data, allowing range filtering and sorting. Other indexes are optimized for filtering chunks of text for substring operations. To use these systems effectively, a team must understand how documents are to be fed into the search engine and the various ways in which they will be indexed. This is where analysis can provide a great deal of value.

Write a specification that produces a projection of searchable records. No user will execute that specification and view all of the results; there will simply be too many. Instead, a service will use that specification to add the projected records to the search index. This service can then run continuously, looking for additions, modifications, and deletions of documents that must be applied. Document the source specification and the projection into searchable documents.

Expected Number of Results

The second constraint that a historical model imposes upon our system is the number of results that we can expect from any given specification. In a SQL query, it is feasible to write a WHERE clause that you know will match at most one record. This occurs when the filter is based on a unique index or primary key. The database management system enforces these constraints and implicitly applies the assumption of a single result to the query. Developers will often carry this assumption into their code and ignore any subsequent rows that the query might return. Occasionally, they will take the extra precaution of logging or raising an exception when more than one result is returned. But they will almost never adjust their code to allow for more results.

A historical specification, however, cannot restrict the number of expected results. The reason is the same as the analysis we just performed previously: the lack of uniqueness constraints. Since uniqueness cannot be scalably verified in a distributed system, historical models offer no such guarantee. This forces you to consider what should happen if a specification returns multiple results when you only expect one. Should the data be aggregated? Should the multiple results be listed? Should the view highlight more than one result as an issue to be resolved?

Sometimes a combination of factors makes it extremely unlikely that a specification will return more than one result. We have seen a good example of this in the restaurant system. Recall that the host view removed a table from the list when a party was seated. This was accomplished by sourcing that list from the following specification:

```
tablesAvailable = (r: Restaurant) {
  t: Table [
    t→restaurant = r
    ∄ {
      s: SeatParty [
        s→table = t
```

```
        ∄ {
          b: BusTable [
              b→seatParty = s
          ]
        }
      ]
    }
  ]
}
```

Because this specification is one of the sources for the command that creates
SeatParty, this view will not construct two SeatParty facts with the same Table – at
least not until the first seating has been bussed. This would therefore lead us to conclude
that the specification for parties seated at a given table would return at most one result.

```
partiesAtTable = (t: Table) {
  s: SeatParty [
    s→table = t
    ∄ {
      b: BusTable [
        b→seatParty = sp
      ]
    }
  ]
}
```

The model, however, makes no such guarantee. Our confidence in this constraint is
based only upon the behavior of a single view. Consider other possibilities that would
circumvent that view. Is it possible that another subsystem could assign parties? Could
two different hosts have the view open at the same time? If we allow such flexibility,
then it is possible that two seatings for the same table might occur. In the server view
in Figure 4-28, we opted to allow for multiple results by summing the party sizes (note
the Σ). Other valid choices might have been to list the parties, or alert the server of
a potential problem. No matter what your choice, you must acknowledge that every
specification can return multiple results.

No Implicit Order

The final constraint on distributed systems – as exposed by the historical model – is that specification results are not ordered. Even when two nodes have reached consensus and return the same set of facts from a specification, they could return those facts in very different orders. We would like to believe that the order in which facts appear is the order in which they were created. But in a distributed system, there is always the possibility that two decisions were made concurrently, each without knowledge of the other. When this happens, the nodes on which those decisions were first captured will certainly disagree to the order in which they were made.

Implicitly, the results of specifications are sets, not lists. Sets have no order, only membership. There is nothing that can be inferred from the order of the results, only from the presence or absence of facts. Software, however, is full of lists. Iterating over a collection in order is a common feature of most languages. We cannot even present an unordered set to the user; it will always appear as a list. If we iterate over the results of a specification, then we will find that they are in *some* order. We just have to be careful not to depend upon *which* order.

One goal of a distributed system is to have different nodes reach a consistent state. When we build a system based on the principles of historical modeling, we can use CRDTs (conflict-free replicated data types) to prove that we will reach consistency, as we will see in Chapter 5. The data type that we will choose is the *set*, not the *list*. If we choose to use lists, the math will not work out. With sets, we will prove that our replicas will converge. The final step is to prove that the *projections* of those sets – the information that we display to the user – will converge as well.

Aggregates

The projections that we present will be one of two kinds: aggregates or iterations. Let's examine aggregates first. An aggregate is simply a value computed from an ordered collection. The sum of a list of numbers is an aggregate. Maximum, product, and standard deviation are also aggregate functions that can be computed over a list of numbers. One important feature of all of these aggregate functions is that they are *commutative*. The sum is the same no matter the order of the numbers you add. The same can be said for maximum, product, and standard deviation. Commutative aggregates are useful because they ignore the order of the list.

Other kinds of aggregates are not commutative. One example that appears frequently is string concatenation. Given a list of strings, it is common to append them to one another, separated by commas. While this aggregate is useful, it is not commutative; the result of string concatenation depends upon the order of those strings. As a result, two nodes may compute different results. Before using this kind of aggregate, you should first sort the facts in a deterministic order.

Iterations

This brings us to the second kind of projection that we need to consider: the iteration. Iterations appear on the user interface as lists. They also appear as noncommutative aggregates such as string concatenation. An iteration makes it apparent to the user when there is more than one result and implies a certain order to those results. Since the results don't have an implicit order, an iteration needs to impose one.

Find some feature of each fact that can determine an order. For example, you might order Table entities by their table number. Before presenting the results to the user, order by that field. As long as every node orders results in the same way, the iteration (or noncommutative aggregate) will appear to be consistent.

You might find that you want to put facts in order according to a mutable property. Being mutable, these fields are not members of the facts themselves. They are members of successor facts, which might not be present at every node at the same time. When this is the case, be sure to document a projection that returns these property facts. Express the order of the main results in terms of the projected value. As you do so, remember that the projection *also* returns multiple results, and so it too needs a commutative aggregate or deterministic ordering.

Creation Order

Finally, there is one way to deterministically order events in a historical model by creation time: record the creation time as a field. This is certainly the simplest and most direct way to impose a deterministic order on results. However, this has two consequences. First, it requires that the clocks on the source nodes be synchronized. To the extent that the clocks are out of sync, new facts might be inserted before older ones. Second, and more importantly, this forces the creation time into the identity of the fact. Two facts that are created at different times, but would otherwise have the same field values, will now be considered as discrete facts. Sometimes this is desired behavior; other times it is not. Only include the creation time in a fact if you need an extra identifier, as discussed in the "Identity" section in Chapter 5.

The choices you make while analyzing a problem will have consequences upon the final implementation. Some things that are easy to say are not easy to implement. Even thinking about the problem in terms of a small set of nodes or collaborators is not sufficient to expose all of these assumptions. Distributed systems impose their own unique set of constraints.

The rules of historical modeling are deliberately restrictive so that the consequences of these choices become clear. Rather than allowing uniqueness or search on any field, historical models can only be indexed on the fact itself. Rather than being able to restrict the number of possible results, historical specifications always allow multiples. And rather than implying an order, historical results require that projections either be commutative or explicitly sorted. Augment your analysis with the extra information necessary to clarify your assumptions so that the team understands any compromises they might have to make before they write a single line of code.

CHAPTER 5

Location Independence

In the not too distant past, most programs ran on a single computer. After the proliferation of JavaScript in the web browser, apps on mobile phones, and microservices in the cloud, most programs that we write today run across many computers. Whereas distributed systems used to be a specialty, today they are the default. We need to update other defaults to meet that demand.

One of the defaults that we need to update is the assumption that data has a location. Some systems try to treat remote objects as if they are local. DCOM uses object identifiers to make a proxy look like a local instance of a remote object. Remote procedure calls (RPCs) try to hide the reality of network communication behind an interface that looks like a normal function. The problems with these systems have been well covered elsewhere, so I will not rehash them here.

The assumptions of locality that I want to examine are a bit more subtle. Even when we replace RPCs with messages, and object identifiers with URLs, it is easy to assume that data has a location. We make that assumption whenever we identify a "source of truth" or a "system of record." We rely upon location whenever a single node generates unique identifiers. Our default mode of programming what happens *at a machine* leaks into the behaviors that we program into the system as a whole.

So many of the behaviors that we've come to expect from our systems depend upon location. We expect items to be sequentially ordered. We expect the system to reject duplicate names. We expect that when the user updates a property of an object, it will have the value that they just assigned. Indeed, the expectation that properties even *have* single values is a location-dependent assumption.

A system that depends upon location will misbehave when that location becomes unavailable. If we strive instead for location independence, we will construct systems that are more responsive, resilient, and reliable. They can act autonomously without communicating with remote nodes. They can tolerate network failures without introducing defects. And the decisions that a user makes in isolation will be honored when other nodes and users learn of that decision.

© Michael L. Perry 2024
M. L. Perry, *The Art of Immutable Architecture*, https://doi.org/10.1007/979-8-8688-0288-1_5

Modeling with Immutability

At its core, the assumption of location is all about mutability. A variable is a place that stores a value. Programs use the variable to address that location and read its value. After the variable is updated, we expect the program to read the new value the next time it looks. Scale this up to the level of the distributed system, and you have location dependence. A system depends upon data being in a location specifically because that data is allowed to change.

If we search instead for a model of computing that is based on immutability, then dependence upon location fades away. If an object cannot change, then every copy of it is just as good as any other. There is no need to know where the object is stored, where it was created, or which subsystem is the source of truth.

Of course, we need to model domains that change over time. So the concepts of time and change need to be re-examined in the light of immutability.

Synchronization

It's not uncommon to talk about managing data in distributed systems as a synchronization problem. But even this term comes from a place of putting data in a location. Synchronization is the task of changing data in two or more places at more or less the same time. When the data in two locations differs, those locations are out of sync. A location-dependent system will seek to synchronize them.

When data no longer has location, concurrent changes are allowed to happen. A temporary disagreement between two nodes is not a synchronization problem to be solved, but an opportunity for them to converge over time. A location-independent system uses a different definition of time so that it can describe concurrency. It relaxes its assumptions so that changes are no longer linear. This helps the system to ensure that concurrent changes don't cause conflicts.

A location-independent system is not concerned with synchronization, but with causality. It seeks to understand which events caused which other events. Where synchronization describes the agreement of data structures stored in different locations, causality describes the history of the data itself, no matter where it is stored. Causality is a weaker constraint than synchronization, but one that is much easier to achieve.

140

Guarantees

In this chapter, we will take a tour of some important guarantees that a distributed system can ensure. These will include some simple and obvious ones like "I expect to read what I just wrote." We will also see some very elusive and powerful ones like "All nodes eventually converge to the same state." We will see what it takes in general to ensure one of these guarantees. Along the way, we will make trade-offs to give up some guarantees in order to gain others.

What we will find is that the guarantee that we think we want – the one equivalent to the assumption that data has a location – is not achievable in many situations. Instead the guarantee that we trade this off for will be one that permits access to data independent of location. If we recognize when we've made the assumption that data is stored in a location, we can choose instead to expect a different guarantee.

Identity

The first task in the quest for location independence is to separate the identity of an object from where it is stored. When location is part of identity, objects have a certain affinity for machines at that location. To achieve the best results, users should be able to identify objects just as easily from any location, without the need to communicate.

Let's examine common mechanisms of identity. We will start with location-specific options, like auto-incremented IDs and URLs. Then we will compare location-independent options, such as GUIDs and hashes.

Auto-incremented IDs

Whenever a relational database is involved, you are likely to find auto-incremented IDs. Most database management systems include a mechanism for generating them on INSERT. The most common way to identify an object is to use the number that was generated when it was inserted into a table.

The auto-incremented ID is a great way to produce unique primary keys. They are monotonically increasing, which makes them ideal for clustered indexes. You will never split a page when inserting a new record with an increasing primary key. They are perfect foreign keys, much more compact than any other column that the referenced table might have. And they do not change. Most database management systems take precautions to discourage or prevent updates of auto-incremented columns. That helps preserve their uniqueness and utility as references.

So it would seem that an auto-incremented ID would be the ideal identifier for an object in a system backed by a relational database. But while these IDs are perfect for representing identity *within* a database, they are poor choices for extending identity *beyond* the database. The convenience of doing so has made them the default choice for identity but has caused many problems upstream.

The core of the issue is that an auto-incremented ID is generated at a certain location. It only has meaning within a single database. While it's true that that single database may be clustered and spread across several machines, it is still logically a single location. It is accessible by a single connection string and may easily become unavailable to remote clients.

Environment Dependence

If you have ever promoted software from a development environment, to testing, to staging, and then to production, you are well aware that the IDs generated in each environment do not translate to the others. The object that gets ID 1337 in test will not be the same as object 1337 in production. This can be mildly annoying when you back up the testing database to restore to development in order to replicate a bug. After the restore, all IDs refer to the same objects in each environment. But as you start working with one system or the other, the IDs start to diverge. That means you cannot easily import incrementally more data from testing without dropping the development database.

It becomes more than mildly annoying when moving data between staging and production. A common practice is to back up production data and restore it in a staging environment. Then you can update the staging environment to the latest version of software, applying any necessary database updates simultaneously. After a quick smoke test, you are assured that the deployment was successful. It would be desirable at that point to just swap the staging environment into production, but that won't work unless production was taken down during this process. If it was still up, then most likely new data have been inserted into the production database, receiving new auto-incremented IDs. These IDs are meaningless in the staging database.

Auto-incrementing IDs cross the threshold from annoyance to impediment when we try to implement a warm standby disaster recovery solution. The goal is to have a replica of production data in a geographically isolated datacenter to mitigate against a localized outage. Before the outage occurs, records stored in the production database are shipped to the remote database with as low a latency as reasonable. Latency needs to be low in order to ensure a minimum of data loss in the event of a failure. When a failure occurs, the application should "fail over" to the remote replica. Before the failover, the production database is responsible for generating IDs. After the failover, the remote database becomes responsible.

Just as the latency of the data transfer should be low, the time required for the failover should also be low. Unfortunately, latency cannot be zero, and the cut over can never be instantaneous. It is difficult to get the timing just right of importing all of the production data before turning on ID generation. Reducing latency, especially between geographically dispersed locations, becomes more expensive the closer we get to zero. Losing data during a failover can be even more costly. And the longer we wait for the data to arrive, the longer we have to postpone generating new IDs.

I have been on many long, costly projects to set up disaster recovery. Some of them have even been successful. After a few false starts, we managed to get the system to fail over reliably. But "failing back" is a much bigger challenge. After resolving the original production issue, we had to run the entire process in the opposite direction. I've never seen this done without taking the system offline for an extended period of time. It would be much easier to do if we didn't put the extra burden of generating location-specific IDs onto the database.

Parent-Child Insertion

The awkwardness of using an auto-incremented ID as identity becomes apparent when dealing with parent-child relationships. The parent record has a primary key. The child records each have a foreign key. The database enforces referential integrity of foreign keys, so the parent record must be inserted before the children. Child insertion cannot begin until the parent insertion has completed and produced the auto-incremented ID.

We don't often think about the database and the application as being two separate locations, but that is in fact what they are. The application produces INSERT instructions and transmits them to the database for execution. Under normal circumstances, the application could produce multiple INSERT statements and ask the database to execute them in a batch. But with a parent-child relationship, the application must wait until the parent insertion completes before it can learn its primary key. Only then can it generate the batch of child insertions.

Object-relational mappers (ORMs) perform, among other things, the task of inserting parent-child relationships. From the outside, it looks as if we can build a graph of objects and then execute a single command to save the changes. But within the ORM, that single operation is spread over several batches of INSERT commands, sent to the database in just the right order.

ORMs hide this behavior from applications as well as they can, but it does leak through the abstraction. When an object exposes the primary key as a property – so that it can use that as an external identity – that primary key is initially zero or a negative number. After the command to save the objects to the database, that primary key becomes positive. The primary key of an object is not supposed to change, but the necessity of going to a different location to generate an auto-incremented ID forces the ORM to violate that invariant.

When an application is close to its database, we can attempt to hide the truth of auto-incremented IDs within ORMs. But as a node gets further away from its central database, the dependence upon location becomes harder to conceal.

Remote Creation

Consider a mobile application. It has its own local database to store a copy of the user's data for quick access, even when the device is on a slow network. Let's further assume for simplicity that this local data has a similar schema as the central database.

When the device fetches data from the central application, it stores the objects with the provided IDs. From then on, it can present that data quickly by performing local queries against its own copy. The user can even make changes. Those updates are applied first to the local copy and then stored in a queue to be sent to the central application.

Everything is working well for queries and updates. But the problem arises when we try to insert new objects. The local database cannot use an auto-incremented ID to create new records. If it did, it would often generate an ID that the central database has already used for a different object. So if the auto-incremented ID was used as the identity of the object, the application would have to make a round trip to the central database in order to get a correct ID.

For this reason, the simple solution is often not the one used in mobile applications. They will instead choose a local database that does not rely so heavily upon foreign keys. This at least allows the mobile client to create entire structures of objects before knowing their identity. That postpones the problem of location-specific identity far enough for most applications, but it is not a complete solution. A complete solution would remove the location-specific component – such as the auto-incremented ID – from the identity entirely.

URLs

Web applications that follow the REST architectural style tend to use Hypermedia as the Engine of Application State (HATEOAS). Every operation that the application performs is a request against a resource. With each request, the application transitions to a different state. When hypermedia is used as the engine of that state, the identities of available resources are returned as references within each response.

Identity in the REST architectural style is defined by a Uniform Resource Identifier (URI). This is a hierarchical identity so that the generator can ensure that new URIs are unique. A common practice is to use the domain name of the generator as the first level of that hierarchy. A domain name identifies a small collection of nodes that are often closely located.

For an application to select and issue the next command, and so transform into the next state, it needs some way to send the command to the correct host. For this reason, the URIs used in HATEOAS are often not just identifiers, they are Uniform Resource Locators (URLs). A URL has the same hierarchical structure as a URI, but now it has an additional constraint. A URL must be addressable. It must carry enough information for an application to send a command to the host that will execute it.

URLs carry the domain name, not just as an identity namespace but also so that a client can resolve the domain name to an IP address. That IP address must be capable of routing the subsequent command to a host that will execute it. So the domain name is closely tied to the location of the resource.

When URLs are used as the identity of resources, it can be very difficult to move a resource from one location to another. Either that new location must be addressable using the same domain name or the identity of the resource must change. Ideally, identity would never change. It should be immutable. But on the Web, the identity of a resource changes every time the server responds with a 301 or 308 permanent redirect. The client is expected to update its reference to that resource and use the newly provided identity from then on. Unfortunately, the old identity must remain addressable to serve those 301 or 308 responses, as there is no way to know when all clients have updated their references. Clients must contact the remote server to learn the canonical form of the URL.

Location-Independent Identity

We've examined just a couple of ways that the identity of objects in an application is often coupled to their location. When identity is based on an auto-incremented ID, that ID only has meaning in a specific location and can only be generated there. When identity is based on URLs, the location of the node that responds to subsequent commands is given right in the identifier. When identity is dependent upon location, objects show a certain affinity for their location of origin. Applications start to have trouble using those objects when their locations become unavailable.

The ultimate solution to each of these problems is to identify objects without respect to location. A location-independent identity has three useful properties:

- It can be generated from any node.

- It is immutable.

- It can be compared.

Generating a unique identity from any node solves the problem of latency during remote inserts. Whether it is a geographically remote disaster recovery datacenter, or a mobile device on a slow network, a node that is capable of generating its own identities can work much faster. Immutable identities solve the problem of keeping old domains addressable indefinitely. And comparison between identities allows clients to know when they are talking about the same object. If they had to contact the origin location to learn the canonical form of the identity before comparison, they could not complete their transaction in isolation.

With a little extra thought, we can come up with identities that meet these three conditions. Such identities are not location specific and support continued operation of isolated nodes. The following are just a few examples.

Natural Keys

Probably the simplest example of a location-independent identity is the natural key. Examine the domain that you are modeling in your application. Does it already have an attribute that uniquely identifies concepts in that domain? Is that attribute immutable? If so, consider using that as a natural key within the model.

Room numbers may change over time, but a scheduling app already takes time into account. A new room number means a new room, but past events already took place in the old room. The application doesn't care that the old room was in the same physical space.

Applications that manage articles, stories, or questions will often assign them tags. A good natural key is the canonical name of the tag in a primary language (e.g., English). The name can be canonicalized by converting all letters to lower case, dropping punctuation marks, and replacing spaces with hyphens to make them more URL friendly. A mapping will be necessary to convert the tag `fermats-last-theorem` to the full phrase "Fermat's Last Theorem," or to provide translations into other languages. But the natural key is easier to generate on any machine than a synthetic ID would be.

Some natural keys are primary keys generated by an external system. If you are integrating with the US tax system, you will probably identify people and companies by their tax ID. If you receive an invoice from a vendor, a good natural key for that object would be the vendor-provided invoice number. There is usually no good reason to generate a new identity when the system on the other end of an integration has already provided one.

GUIDs

When a natural key is not available, we have mechanisms for generating IDs that do not collide across machines. These are universally unique identifiers (UUIDs). Or if, like me, you came to them via Microsoft COM, globally unique identifiers (GUIDs). Whether you call it a UUID or a GUID, it is a 128-bit number represented in hexadecimal in a hyphenated format that is recognizable to most developers.

Originally, GUIDs were generated using the MAC address of the originating machine and a timestamp. Then, as GUID generation became more frequent, the timestamp was replaced with a counter. Finally, it was recognized that random GUIDs were probably just as good.

While some systems use a GUID to represent every row in a database, my practice has been a bit more reserved. I generate a GUID only for the most rarely created objects at the highest level and then only if natural keys are not practical.

Timestamps

One of the easiest ways to identify an object that a user has created is to use the time at which the user created it. For example, some cameras or video recording devices use a timestamp as a file name. This works well at human scales, especially when there is only one human involved. The granularity of timestamps should be less than a second to ensure that even the fastest of human-generated actions gets a unique value. Millisecond granularity is reasonable and often achievable.

While it is tempting to compare timestamps to determine which event happened before another, this should be avoided. Timestamps are only increasing within a single machine. And even then, the clock of the machine may be adjusted forward or backward. Adjustments such as daylight saving and crossing time zones are not the concern; timestamps should always be captured in UTC. But small corrections to fix clock drift should be allowed.

Timestamp alone is not sufficient to identify objects in a system with a large number of users. They should only be used in combination with other forms of identity.

Tuples

Using just one identity, like a timestamp, is often not enough to avoid collisions. But bring different forms of identity together, and the combination is stronger than any of its parts. A tuple is an ordered list of values, where each member has its own type and meaning.

Tuples are often written as a parenthesized list: (`that-conference`, `day-2`, `10:00`, `136`). But it is just as valid to write a tuple as a path: `/that-conference/day-2/1000/136`. This gives them a hierarchical feel that makes them suitable for use in URLs. (Yes, URLs can be used in an application, just not as identities of objects.) The hierarchy implies that the object has just one owner, which is identified by the tuple having one fewer element. In the preceding example, the session held in room 136 is owned by the 10:00 time slot on day 2.

The transparent nature of tuples makes them susceptible to human interpretation. This is both a benefit and a drawback. While it is often useful to be able to see the implied relationships between objects just by their identities, this can sometimes cause confusion. In some cases, a strict hierarchy does not exist, yet the tuple implies one by its choice of values and order. And in other cases, the values in the tuple represent mutable concepts. For example, a session could be moved to a different room, or even a different time slot. We can choose either to change these values, and thus change the identity of an object, or to keep the old values and risk confusion.

Hashes

To avoid the confusion caused by a transparent data structure like a tuple, we can instead choose an opaque structure like a hash. A hash function takes a tuple as an input and produces a value. The function is deterministic: the same tuple will always produce the same hash. But ideally, the function should also be unpredictable: it should be hard to find a tuple that produces a given hash.

Hashes have additional benefits over their source tuples. Where a tuple contains elements of variable length, like strings, hashes are always the same size. Furthermore, while tuples tend to chunk data together, hashes tend to spread it apart. And while tuples can be easily reverse engineered, hashes are one way. This makes them better suited to problems that require a degree of security.

Many systems that use hashes for identity choose to do so for one of these reasons. Blockchains use hashes to identify transactions so that the contents cannot be easily altered. Changing one element of a transaction – such as the sender, recipient, or amount – will alter the hash. And finding a different transaction that produces the same hash is an intractable problem.

Git uses hashes to identify commits. It doesn't do so for reasons of security. Instead, since Git is based on the file system, having an identifier of constant size helps them fit into file names and data structures. The tuple that it starts with includes the name and email of the author (natural keys), the contents of the files, and a timestamp (to the second). That source tuple is of variable length and can be quite large for significant code bases. The resulting hash, however, is 256 bits, or 64 hexadecimal digits.

Public Keys

In keeping with the security theme, public keys are excellent ways to identify principals such as individuals or corporations. Public keys are often used to digitally sign messages, proving their authenticity. Only someone with access to the private key could produce the signature.

A certificate is a fully vetted identifier for a principal, often including their name, physical location or legal jurisdiction, and identity of the vetting party. Certificates form their own kind of hierarchy, as the identity of the party who signed the certificate is provided as a public key.

Blockchain systems use a public key as the only means of identifying a party. Each transaction records the sender and recipient by their public keys. To pay someone in Bitcoin, you need only know their public key. That is sufficient to identify them uniquely to any node within the distributed network.

Random Numbers

When other forms of identity are not available, an application can always fall back on random numbers. Public keys are really nothing more than two random numbers that have been verified to be prime and then multiplied. And modern GUIDs are often generated completely at random, rather than using MAC address or timestamp. So it is a valid choice to simply use random numbers directly, as long as they are big enough and random enough.

Like timestamps, random numbers should never be used as the only form of identity. They should be combined with other identifiers to create a tuple. Since the random number is not fit for human interpretation, producing a hash of that tuple is often the next step. In cryptography, a random number added to a tuple prior to hashing is called a "nonce," a number used once. In this case, we are using the nonce to distinguish an object from others that share the same tuple values.

When choosing a random number generator, it is best to stick with a cryptographically strong algorithm. Algorithms used to generate public keys, shared secrets, and nonces are specifically selected to produce unpredictable results. While you will most likely not be relying upon these random number generators for securing data, you will be using their output as part of an object's identity. Having two nodes use the same predictable random number generator means that the chance of a collision is high.

Choose the most appropriate mechanism for generating unique identities for objects. Whatever method you choose, avoid anything that would tie the identity of an object to the location that generated it. Instead, choose a generator that meets the following criteria:

- Any node should be equally capable of generating identities without consulting a central database.

- Identity must be immutable.

- Peers should be able to compare identities to know when they are talking about the same object.

Identity is the first step to location independence. The next step is to ensure consistent behavior without respect to location.

Causality

As we begin to reason about the behavior of a distributed system, we are going to try to construct a chain of events. Our goal is to predict the effects of local actions upon distant nodes in the future. We want to understand cause and effect.

Causality itself is a hard concept to measure. You can say that tipping one domino caused the next one to fall. But would the second one have fallen on its own? We would like to say for certain that it would not. However, as anyone who has built a large domino chain knows, that is a hard claim to assert.

The causes of many events in a distributed system can be just as complex and inscrutable as a chain of dominoes. And yet we still desire some predictability from the system. And so, we have to find a reasonable stand-in for causality that is easier to measure and useful for making predictions.

While we cannot always say with certainty that one event caused another, we can say for certain that the cause happened before the effect. As this book is being written, time travel is still impossible. Perhaps "happened before" is enough. Maybe it is sufficient to use the order of events as a stand-in for causality. Let's apply this notion of causality to steps in a program and compare this with our intuition.

Putting Steps in Order

We often think about a program as a sequence of steps. The steps happen in order as the program executes. It is easy to look at two steps executing in the same program, such as the one in Figure 5-1, and say that one happened before another.

```
for i = 1 to 100
    if i mod 15 == 0
        print "Fizbuzz"
    else if i mod 3 == 0
        print "Fizz"
    else if i mod 5 == 0
        print "Buzz"
    else
        print i
```

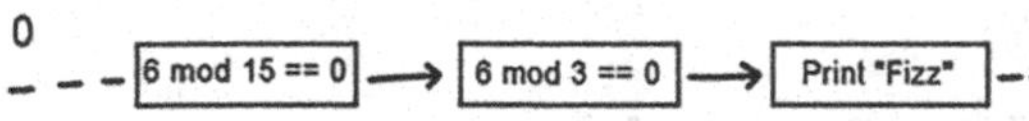

6 mod 15 == 0 → 6 mod 3 == 0 → Print "Fizz"

Figure 5-1. *Steps in a process*

Using the order of steps as a stand-in for causality leads us to say that one step in a program causes the next. In some sense, this is true. A program executes sequentially, so it's reasonable to say that executing one step will cause the computer to then execute the next one. Even if the two steps operate on different objects and do not depend upon one another, they are at least temporally coupled. The program would not get to the second step without having executed the first.

You may be thinking that a goto statement that jumps over one step to get to another violates this notion of causality. The program executes the target step without having executed the one preceding it. However, in this situation, we would observe that the goto happened before the target step. It is not the order in which the steps appear in code that is interesting to us. It is the order in which they occur at runtime. And so it was the goto that caused the step to occur. This agrees with our intuition about a statement that causes execution to jump to another. "Happened before" is looking like a good measure of causality.

When we try to generalize steps in a single program to multi-threaded or multi-process systems, things get a little trickier. We cannot say quite so clearly which of two steps executing in different processes happened before the other. The processes can be running on parallel threads or even on different machines. There is no single clock that can help us to put those steps in order.

We can, however, observe that two processes running independently do not cause any behavioral changes in one another. They are not causally connected. As long as they don't communicate, nothing that happens in one can influence the other.

When they *do* communicate, causality is clearly asserted. If one process sends a message, and another process receives it, then we know that the *send* step happened before the *receive* step. And in a very real sense, the sending of a message caused its receipt. With this fact in hand, we can start to causally order steps that have occurred in different processes. This is precisely how Leslie Lamport defined the order of events in his 1978 paper on distributed systems.[1]

The Transitive Property

The relationship that one step happened before another has another useful property: it is *transitive*. That is, if one step happened before a second, and the second happened before a third, then we know that the first happened before the third. This is easy to

---

[1] Leslie Lamport. Time, Clocks, and the Ordering of Events in a Distributed System. Communications of the ACM, 21(7):558–565, July 1978.

see when all of the steps are in the same process. Those steps are in sequence. But the transitive property holds just as well when we cross process boundaries.

Take, for example, a web browser. The user commands the browser to navigate to a given URL. The browser has just executed two steps: input a URL from the user and send a request to the web server. Since these steps happened in the same process, we know that one happened before the other: "input URL" happened before "send request."

Now let's look at what happens in the web server. When it receives the request, it will load the requested file from the hard drive. The receipt of the request and the loading of the file are two steps within the same process. We can therefore say that the receipt happened before the load.

Since these two processes are talking to each other by passing messages, we can also put some of the steps across processes in order. We can say for certain that the send of the request happened before its receipt, even though they happened in different processes. As Figure 5-2 illustrates, the transitive property allows us to then chain these events together. We can say for certain that the user input happened before the file load.

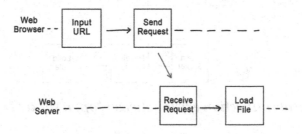

Figure 5-2. *Order of steps in two processes*

Because we are using "happened before" as a stand-in for causality, what we are really asserting here is that the user input *caused* the file to be loaded. This fits well with our intuition. We can imagine that the user intended for the web server to load the file, and so this causal chain of events served to realize the user's intent. We might also assume that the web server probably would not have loaded that particular file, had the user not entered the URL. But intent and might-have-been are difficult to reason about. "Happened before," however, is very clear.

We can clearly state when we know one step happened before another. We can also clearly state when we have no idea.

Concurrency

While it was possible in our previous example to say for certain that user input happened before loading a file, it will not always be the case. Some steps happening in different processes will not be so easily put in order, even using the transitive property.

Take, for example, the step where the web server opens a socket. As Figure 5-3 demonstrates, "open socket" happens before "receive request" and is executed in the same process. And as we saw in the previous analysis, "input URL" also happened before "receive request." But the transitive property does not allow us to say which of "open socket" and "input URL" happened before the other. They both happened before "receive request," but that doesn't imply anything about their relative order. Lamport called two steps that cannot be put in order *concurrent*:

Two distinct events a and b are said to be concurrent if a ↛ b and b ↛ a.

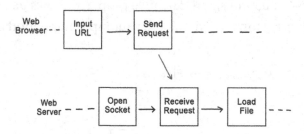

Figure 5-3. *No causal connection exists between "open socket" and "input URL"*

This definition of concurrent is a bit different than in common language. Concurrent operations in a multi-threaded system might be running in parallel. In common use, if two events are concurrent, then they happen at the same time.

By Lamport's definition of concurrent, we don't know whether two steps indeed happened at the same time. They could have been separated by a large span of actual time on a physical clock. It could be, for example, that the web server opened the socket hours before the user input the URL. In fact, that is quite likely. But what could be and what is likely do not hold sway in this conversation. It is precisely the fact that *we cannot know* that makes these two events concurrent according to Lamport.

In a very real sense, concurrency is what makes distributed systems so difficult to think about. If there were no concurrent steps, we could put all of the steps in order. If every step can be ordered relative to every other step, then we would end up with a totally ordered sequence. It would be much easier to think about that kind of system, because it always behaves as if the whole network is running on a single machine.

While a totally ordered system would be easier to think about, it would not have the properties that we desire in a distributed system. It would not scale as we added more hardware, since totally ordered steps cannot be run in parallel. It cannot autonomously serve clients in different locations, because the steps the program takes to serve one client would need to be put in order with others in real time. And it would not allow for disconnected operation, since the steps running on the disconnected computer would be out of sequence with the rest of the network. And so, concurrency is both the hero and the villain of this story.

Partial Order

If you were to compare any two steps running in the same process, you could tell which of the two came first. Those steps are *totally ordered*. They happen in sequence.

If, however, you compare two steps running in different processes, you *might* be able to tell which came first. If one preceded the sending of a message, the receipt of which preceded the second, then the transitive property tells us that the first happened before the second. But if that is not the case – if the two steps are concurrent – then you cannot tell which came first. Because sometimes you can tell and sometimes you can't, the execution of steps in a multi-process system is said to be *partially ordered*.

Since we are using "happened before" as a stand-in for causality, we can say that causality itself is partially ordered. Some things are causally related: we can clearly say which is the cause and which is the effect. The user input of a URL into a browser caused the web server to load a file. But some things are not causally related. The web server opening a socket did not cause the user to input a URL, nor did the input of the URL cause the web server to open a socket.

Partial order imposes fewer constraints on a system than does total order. It frees up some steps to happen in parallel. It permits devices to act autonomously while disconnected. It gives nodes the ability to act independently without constant synchronization. Recognizing that causality is partially ordered gives us a powerful tool for analyzing distributed systems. We can better understand their capabilities as well as their limitations. And we can make better choices about trade-offs between the two.

Now that we have a better understanding of identity and causality, we can define the guarantee we most seek from our distributed systems: consistency. We'll find that there are many useful definitions. The one that we'll start with comes from Eric Brewer's CAP Theorem.

The CAP Theorem

Probably the most famous mathematical idea in all of distributed systems is the CAP Theorem. It was postulated by Eric Brewer at the 2000 Symposium on the Principles of Distributed Computing.[2] Formally proven by Seth Gilbert and Nancy Lynch in 2002,[3] the CAP Theorem relates the ideas of consistency, availability, and partition tolerance. It is often quoted as saying you can only have two of the three.

Consistency means different things in different contexts. Unfortunately, as it usually appears, it doesn't have a very useful definition. For example, if you're familiar with relational databases, then you probably first heard of consistency as it relates to the ACID properties of a transaction: atomic, consistent, isolated, and durable. Atomic is easily defined as all or nothing. Isolated simply means that concurrent transactions don't affect one another. And durable means that the change persisted.

But consistent in this context is not so easy to define. The working definition is that a consistent transaction is one that does not violate any invariants. It "commits only legal results."[4] The trouble is that the invariants that define a legal result come from two sources: the database management system and the application. Database management system invariants include guarantees like "primary keys are unique" and "foreign keys reference rows that exist." Application-defined invariants, when they exist at all, are defined in terms of the problem domain, such as "all balances are zero or positive." If we were talking only about the well-defined guarantees generally adopted by database management systems, we might have some chance of proving some generally applicable theorems. But with all of the choices that an application can make in determining its own domain-specific invariants, we find it very difficult to write a meaningful proof. Therefore, we will use a more precise definition of consistency.

---

[2] E. Brewer, "Towards Robust Distributed Systems," Proc. 19th Ann. ACM Symposium on the Principles of Distributed Computing (PODC 00), ACM, 2000, pp. 7–10.

[3] Seth Gilbert and Nancy Lynch, "Brewer's conjecture and the feasibility of consistent, available, partition-tolerant web services," ACM SIGACT News, Volume 33 Issue 2 (2002), pp. 51–59.

[4] Haerder, T; Reuter, A. December 1983. "Principles of Transaction-Oriented Database Recovery." Computing Surveys. 15 (4): 287–317.

Defining CAP

The definition of **consistency** that the CAP Theorem uses is specifically related to nodes in a distributed system. It says that if I ask two different nodes for a value, they will give me the same answer, as illustrated in Figure 5-4. If the nodes are consistent, then their answers will agree. If the answers disagree, then the nodes are not consistent.

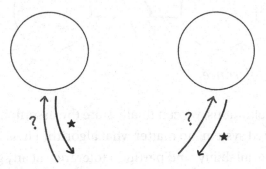

Figure 5-4. *Consistency*

That's very different from the definition used in ACID. In fact, you could argue that it's closer to atomic than to consistent. Either both of the nodes have the latest version of a value or neither does. But where atomic – and indeed each of the ACID guarantees – is about changes to a single database, consistent in CAP is about nodes in a distributed system.

Continuing on, the A in CAP is for **availability**. A node is available if it responds in a reasonable amount of time to any request, as shown in Figure 5-5. This leaves one to ask: "What is a reasonable amount of time?" The answer depends upon the domain and the user's tolerance for latency.

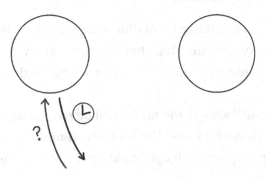

Figure 5-5. *Availability*

Finally, the P in CAP is **partition tolerance**. A network partition is a condition that prevents messages from flowing in a network, indicated in Figure 5-6. Partitions are only temporary, however. After some period of time, the connection will be restored. But in the meantime, partition tolerance promises that the system will continue to function.

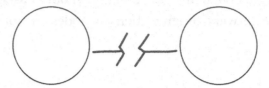

Figure 5-6. *Partition tolerance*

Armed with these definitions, we can finally state the assertion of Brewer's conjecture. No distributed system, no matter what algorithm it uses, can simultaneously guarantee consistency, availability, and partition tolerance at any given interval. If the network is partitioned for the duration of that interval, then the system will either be inconsistent or unavailable.

This is one of those delightful theorems that challenge you to find an algorithm that works, like Gödel asking you to write a formula that determines whether another expression is true, or Turing imploring you to write a program that determines whether another program terminates, or two generals commanding you to find a reliable way for them to communicate. The proof doesn't have to guess what you might come up with. It can simply demonstrate, by pain of logic, that whatever you've dreamed up will not be equal to the task.

Proving the CAP Theorem

Imagine that you have a system made up of different computers, which we'll call nodes. Each node has its own internal state. That state, however, is invisible to us. The only thing we can do as an outside observer is to send messages to the nodes and see how they respond.

The message that we will send to the nodes will be *read* and *update*. If we send a node a *read*, it will send us back a value. If we send it an *update*, it will presumably write down the value and then respond with confirmation. I say *presumably* because we can't really see its internal state.

The only way we can observe a node is by sending it messages. And the messages have the following contract: if I *update* a node in isolation, and then after it confirms, send it a *read*, it will return the value that I just updated, as in Figure 5-7. The node is acting as if it is saving the state for us to later retrieve.

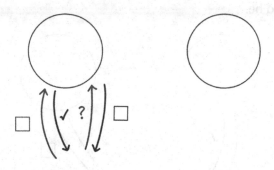

Figure 5-7. *Update and read*

Be careful here. We can't really tell what these nodes are doing. Their internal operation is left unconstrained. That is important for the proof to be general. If we dictated that they truly *were* storing internal state, that would limit the kinds of algorithms we could make assertions about.

Similarly, the messages *read* and *update* do not constrain our choice in the algorithm either. The algorithm does not need to be composed of reads and updates. In fact, the algorithm might not even use these two messages at all. They only exist as a way of setting up a test.

Test an Algorithm

And so, this is the challenge. I ask you to provide an algorithm. You can devise any algorithm you like. You choose the steps. You choose the data structures. I will load this algorithm into two nodes. They communicate with one another by passing messages between them. You choose what messages they will use.

Then, I'll run a test. I will begin by observing that the nodes are initially consistent. I can tell that they are consistent by sending *read* messages to each and observing that they return the same answer.

Next, I'll send one of them an *update* and wait for it to respond with confirmation. Since it confirmed, I can test the contract by sending that same node a *read*. If it is behaving properly, it will return that value I just sent it. In about half of the tests, I'll perform this check. I'll reject your algorithm if it ever fails to uphold the contract.

In the other half of the tests, I'm going to turn to its neighbor to perform the *read*, as in Figure 5-8. If I get the same value that I just *update*d, then the system is demonstrating *consistency*. If both the *update* and the *read* return within a certain interval of time, then the system is demonstrating *availability*. To be completely fair, I will even let you tell me what the interval should be.

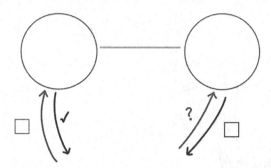

Figure 5-8. *Test the algorithm*

But that's where I play my trick. During the test, I will create a network partition. The two nodes will not be able to communicate with one another during this interval. The partition will last just a little bit longer than the duration you defined. While communication will eventually be restored, it will not be fast enough for the algorithm to exhibit availability and still be consistent.

And so, the algorithm is going to have to choose one of three behaviors, illustrated in Figure 5-9.

1. The first node might block during *update* until it can communicate the value and then confirm the result. If so, then *update* takes longer than the specified interval, and so the system is not available.

2. The second node might block during *read* until it can retrieve the value from the first. If so, then *read* takes longer than the specified interval, and so again the system is not available.

3. The system might decide to return before the interval has expired. If so, there was no way that the value I *update*d will be able to propagate to the second node to be *read*. The second node cannot return the same value as the first, and so the system is not consistent.

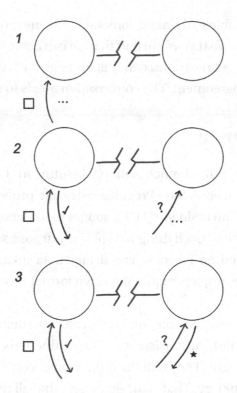

Figure 5-9. *Three possible behaviors when the network is partitioned*

During this interval of network partition, the system cannot be both consistent and available. And so, it seems that we are doomed to choose.

Eventual Consistency

If we cannot expect different nodes within a distributed system to have the same state, then what can we hope to achieve? How can we get any work done if we get a different answer from every node that we ask?

Consistency at any given instant may be out of our reach, but all hope is not lost. We can achieve consistency if we wait long enough. Eventually, nodes will come into agreement with one another. This is a concept referred to as eventual consistency.[5]

---

[5] Terry, D. B.; Theimer, M. M.; Petersen, K.; Demers, A. J.; Spreitzer, M. J.; Hauser, C. H. (1995). "Managing update conflicts in Bayou, a weakly connected replicated storage system." Proceedings of the fifteenth ACM symposium on Operating systems principles – SOSP '95. p. 172.

While it might be desirable to demand consistency at any given instant, it might not be practical. If we loosen our constraints, we find that we can achieve a much more palatable trade-off. Instead of insisting upon consistency at every given instant, perhaps we can tolerate a lesser degree of agreement. The conversation needs to get a bit more nuanced.

Kinds of Consistency

Marc Shapiro, a researcher at the French National Institute for Computer Science and Control Science (Inria), and Nuno Preguiça, associate professor at Faculdade de Ciências e Tecnologia da Universidade (FCT), sought to understand consistency trade-offs at a formal level. They had each designed special-purpose solutions to achieve eventual consistency, including Treedoc, a replicated data structure for collaborative text editing.[6] Each one of these projects required its own formal proof. They wanted a more general result.

Based on their prior results, Shapiro and Preguiça, together with their colleagues, identified three different kinds of consistency.[7] The distinctions among them led to the general result that they sought. They redefined the kind of consistency used in the CAP Theorem as **strong consistency**. That is the guarantee that all nodes will report being in the same state at any given time. They used the term **eventual consistency**, on the other hand, to mean that nodes will eventually reach the same state, as long as they can continue to talk to one another. This may require some additional consensus algorithm, such as conflict resolution.

The reliance upon consensus algorithms introduces more than a small degree of overhead. The nodes might need to elect a master to make the final decision, introducing a bottleneck. Or they might run a complicated and chatty algorithm like Paxos to determine by majority decision what the final state shall be. For these reasons, Shapiro and Preguiça decided to distinguish a third kind of consistency. **Strong eventual consistency** promises that all nodes reach the same state the moment they all receive the same updates. The nodes do not need to talk among themselves after receiving those updates to reach a consensus and resolve conflicts.

---

[6] Nuno Preguiça, Joan Manuel Marquès, Marc Shapiro, Mihai Leţia. A commutative replicated data type for cooperative editing. 29th IEEE International Conference on Distributed Computing Systems (ICDCS 2009), Jun 2009, Montreal, Québec, Canada. pp. 395–403, ff10.1109/ ICDCS.2009.20ff. ffinria00445975.

[7] Shapiro, Marc; Preguiça, Nuno; Baquero, Carlos; Zawirski, Marek. Conflict-free Replicated Data Types. Institut National de Recherche en Informatique et en Automatique, No 7687, 2011.

The CAP Theorem showed us that strong consistency is incompatible with availability. Allowing for consensus algorithm means that the eventual consistency may incur some undesirable overhead. And so, we, like Shapiro and Preguiça, will focus our attention on strong eventual consistency (SEC).

Strong Eventual Consistency in a Relay-Based System

With SEC as our stated goal, let's construct a useful example. Let's build a distributed system based on relaying messages and see what properties it must have to satisfy SEC.

This distributed system is made up of nodes connected in some kind of network. The network is connected, which is to say that, unless the network is partitioned (which will occur from time to time), there is a path from any node to any other node. These paths don't have to be direct; they may go through any number of intermediate nodes.

Some nodes receive new information from outside of the network. When they do, they formulate a message that they themselves process and then send along the network to neighboring nodes. When a neighbor receives the message, it processes it and relays to *its* neighbors. Each node is running some kind of algorithm to determine when to forward a message and to whom. That algorithm guarantees that eventually, every node will receive every message.

It's important to observe that we are explicitly *not* requiring that every node receive each message exactly once, nor are we requiring that every node receive the messages in the same order. Whatever forwarding algorithm we come up with only has to ensure eventual delivery.

Now let's consider the internal state of a node within the distributed system. As the node processes a message, it transitions from one state to another. The message can be viewed as a function, taking the starting state as an input and producing the resulting state as the output. The system is strongly eventually consistent (SEC) if, after seeing all of the messages, all nodes arrive at the same state. We can determine what properties those functions must have in order to achieve SEC.

First, every node's response to each message must be **idempotent**. If a node sees the same message twice in a row, then it must end up in the same state as if it had seen it only once. And second, every node's response to each *pair* of messages must be **commutative**. If the node sees two messages in one order, it must end up in the same state as if it had seen them in the opposite order.

Taken together, idempotence and commutativity are sufficient to prove SEC. So long, that is, as every node eventually sees every message at least once. This result is only valid for the kind of relay-based distributed system that we defined. It assumes that messages are forwarded exactly as they are, not filtered, altered, or summarized. We will find a more general result in the next section, but for now, let's examine this relay-based system.

Idempotence and Commutativity

Mathias Verraes joked on Twitter (Figure 5-10).

Mathias Verraes
@mathiasverraes   •••

There are only two hard problems in distributed systems: 2. Exactly-once delivery 1. Guaranteed order of messages 2. Exactly-once delivery

1:40 PM · Aug 14, 2015

💬 82   ↻ 7,209   ❤ 6,813   🔖 99   ⬆

Figure 5-10. https://twitter.com/mathiasverraes/status/632260618599403520

Like all good jokes, this one is absolutely true. It is hard to guarantee that a message is delivered exactly once – not lost and not duplicated. It is even harder to guarantee that messages will arrive in the order in which they were sent.

Network protocols have been invented to specifically try to address these two hard problems. AMQP, for example, is a messaging protocol that can be configured to deliver a range of guarantees. It can be used as a best-effort transport, in which the message is guaranteed to be received no more than once. It can also be tuned up to reliable delivery, which guarantees that a message will be received at least once, but possibly more than once and possibly out of order. With a bit more overhead, it can perform deduplication, which attempts to guarantee exactly once delivery. And with a herculean amount of effort, it can serialize messages in a channel, guaranteeing that they will be delivered in the same order they are sent, though you wouldn't be happy with the performance.

Authors of infrastructure components that rely upon AMQP, such as RabbitMQ, often advise that a consumer be written to tolerate duplicate messages.[8] The cost of running a message queue with deduplication or serialized channels can be prohibitive. Instead, they recommend that you make your downstream nodes tolerate messages that arrive multiple times, or out of order. That's precisely what idempotence and commutativity mean.

A downstream node that tolerates duplicate messages is *idempotent*. It will remain in its current state upon seeing the duplicate message. A classic example of an idempotent node is an HTTP server receiving a PUT message. The message carries the desired state of the resource given by the URI. If it receives the PUT message a second time, the HTTP server simply sets the desired state again, as demonstrated in Figure 5-11. The end result is the same as if the HTTP server had received only one PUT message.

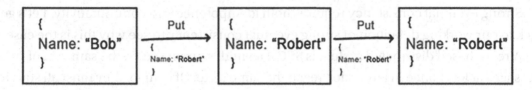

Figure 5-11. *Idempotent PUT*

A downstream node that tolerates out-of-order messages is said to be *commutative*. This comes from the mathematical commutative property, which says that an operator has the same result no matter which way its operands are given. The commutative property of addition says that $a+b = b+a$. Multiplication is also commutative, but subtraction and division are not. In a similar sense, a node is commutative with respect to two messages if it ends up in the same state no matter which message it sees first.

Deriving Strong Eventual Consistency

It is possible for a node to be idempotent with respect to a set of messages but not commutative. For example, an HTTP server receiving two different PUT requests for the same resource will behave differently based on the order. The resource will end up in the state described by the last message it sees. Change the order of the messages, and you change the final state of the resource, as in Figure 5-12.

---

[8] "[C]onsumer applications will need to perform deduplication or handle incoming messages in an idempotent manner." RabbitMQ Reliability Guide. www.rabbitmq.com/reliability.html

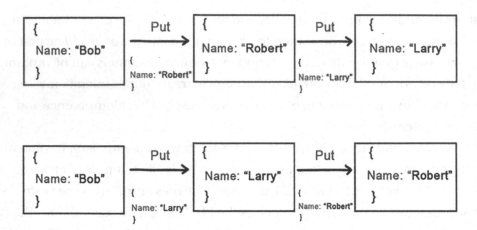

Figure 5-12. *Noncommutative PUT*

Strong eventual consistency requires both idempotence and commutativity. Let's go back to our working definition of strong eventual consistency to see why this is the case.

A relay-based distributed system is SEC if all nodes, upon seeing the same set of messages at least once in any order, reach the same state. Of course, they must all start in the same state. If the set of messages was empty, the problem would not be interesting: all nodes would still be in the start state. And if the set contained only one message, eventual consistency would only rely upon idempotence. Nodes that receive duplicate copies of that one message will remain in the same state.

And so, we only need to carefully consider the case in which the set contains more than one message. Let's consider how this might play out. If every node received each message exactly once, then we could argue based on commutativity alone that they would all reach the same state. Or, if every node received each message in order, but some were doubled or tripled, then we could argue based only on idempotence. It's the fact that things can get jumbled up that causes us to have to stop and consider the possibilities.

Take, for example, a pair of PUT requests to an HTTP server. As we noted previously, PUT is idempotent, but it is not commutative. So, if an HTTP server sees the same PUT message duplicated immediately, it will not change state. However, if there were some intervening messages in between the duplicates, then we have a problem. If a second PUT was received *between* the first one and its duplicate, as in Figure 5-13, then the HTTP server would overwrite its change when the duplicate arrives. In order to behave in an eventually consistent manner, the node would have to ignore the duplicate altogether.

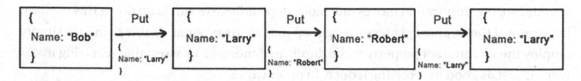

Figure 5-13. *Intervening PUT*

And so for a given set of messages *{ m1, m2, m3, ... }*, the scenario that we have to carefully consider is if *m1* is duplicated after having received some number of intervening messages. We would like to say that

m1+m2+m3+m1 =

m1+m2+m3

As it turns out, we can indeed prove this for an idempotent and commutative set of operations. First, we observe that the duplicated message (*m1*) is commutative with the message that was received just before it (*m3* in this example). We can therefore swap their places without changing the state of the node. And so

m1+m2+m3+m1 =

m1+m2+m1+m3

We just swapped the *m1* and *m3* at the end. This moves the duplication of the message one step earlier in the sequence.

But now, we observe that we can use the commutative property again, this time with *m2*. That is to say

m1+m2+m1 =

m1+m1+m2

And so, the duplication moves one more step earlier. We can keep doing this until we have moved the duplicated message right up next to the original. At this point, we simply employ the idempotent property of the duplicated message to assert that receiving it twice is just as good as receiving it once. In other words

$$m1+m1 =$$

$$m1$$

And so, we have shown that, because the node is both idempotent and commutative with respect to the set of messages, it will reach the same state after seeing one of the messages duplicated, no matter how many other messages have intervened:

$$m1+m2+m3+m1 =$$

$$m1+m2+m3$$

And this generalizes to any number of messages. This reduces the problem back down to receiving some set of messages in any order, but with no duplicates. We only need to rely upon commutativity to ensure that any such sequence will yield the same result.

And that is why our PUT example does not exhibit strong eventual consistency. While it is idempotent, it is not commutative. Both properties are required to achieve SEC in a relay-based distributed system.

The Contact Management System

A friend and I created a contact management system, back in the days when personal digital assistants (PDAs) connected to your workstation via RS-232 serial port. At the time, the state of the art was Microsoft's ActiveSync. We thought we could build a better product.

The solution we came up with was a message store-and-forward system where the nodes (workstations and PDAs) processed messages in an idempotent and commutative fashion. The messages included things like "add contact," "update contact," and "delete contact." Contacts were uniquely identified by GUID, which made add operations trivially idempotent and mutually commutative.

Delete operations took a little more work in order to commute with adds. If the delete is processed first and the add second, the result should be the same as if they were handled in the usual order. That is to say, delete followed by add should result in the contact being absent. We accomplished this by keeping a list of all contact GUIDs that had been deleted, even if the contact itself was not present at the time. And then, when the add was processed, if its GUID was in the list (what is commonly referred to as a tombstone, shown in Figure 5-14), then the contact was not added.

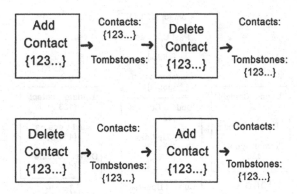

Figure 5-14. *Tombstones*

Update operations were the hardest to get right. As with HTTP PUT, the trivial implementation of update is idempotent but not commutative. To solve this problem, we assigned each update message a GUID as well. Each node kept track of the GUID of the most recent update that set a contact's properties. It would also keep a list of update GUIDs that it saw in the past. When the user changed a contact, it would add the current GUID to the list of past GUIDs and then generate a new current GUID. It then sent an update message including the updated state, the current GUID, and the list of past GUIDs.

When a node received an update, it would first check whether that update's current GUID was already in its own list of past updates. If so, it would ignore the update. If not, it would perform the opposite check: was its current GUID in the message's list of past GUIDs? If not, it would accept the update and merge the past update GUIDs into its own list.

As long as one of these two checks passes, then updates commute with one another. When received out of order, the future update will deliver the GUID of the past update. The past update would subsequently be ignored.

If both checks fail, however, there is more work to do. In this scenario, a concurrent update is detected. The user had modified the same contact on two different nodes while they were disconnected. Our response to this was to merge the two sets of properties. Where a field, such as phone number, was the same, we kept that value. Where they were different, we just concatenated them. That meant each of the fields allowed for multiple values. Fortunately, it's already understood that a contact can have multiple phone numbers. Figure 5-15 shows examples of these three scenarios.

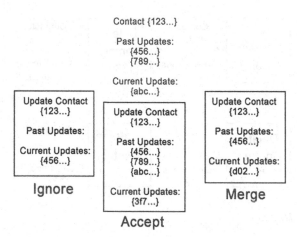

Figure 5-15. *Compare past and current GUIDs*

In addition to merging the properties, the node would also merge the GUIDs. The list of past GUIDs was the union of the current and incoming lists. And the current GUID? That's where our data structure was a little more complicated than what I first described. The current GUID was also a list. Usually it contained only one element. But after a merge, it contained two (or even more if additional concurrent updates were detected).

This merge is commutative (ignoring concatenation order, which we were happy to do). Each side of the concurrent update would perform the merge upon seeing the other's message. They would both get the same list of past GUIDs, and they would both get the same list of current GUIDs. When the user subsequently edited this merged contact, both of the current GUIDs would be added to the past list. And so both sides would happily replace its automated merge with the user's manual one.

Replaying History

This solution worked pretty well. It was strongly eventually consistent (though we didn't know that term at the time). We proudly showed prospective buyers that we could disconnect a PDA, make changes, and then sync it back up. After all of the messages flowed back and forth, all clients had the same list of contacts in the same state.During the synchronization process, however, things looked a little sketchy. If a large number of changes had happened on one side, all of those edits would replay before our eyes on the other. Given the speed of networks at the time, you could easily read the list of names as they were added, modified, and subsequently deleted while history replayed on the device.Adding a new device to this system revealed the full extent of the issue. Since it was based entirely on processing messages exactly as they had been originally sent, the entire history of messages was persisted in a central repository. We referred to this as the transaction pipeline. When a new device was introduced to the transaction pipeline for the first time, as in Figure 5-16, it would pull down and process every one of those messages. That means that it would see all of the past edits. It would even see contacts that had long since been deleted. As history grew, the time required to add a new device grew proportionally.

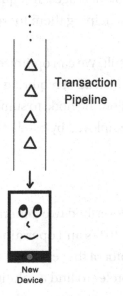

Transaction
Pipeline

New
Device

Figure 5-16. A new device is introduced to the transaction pipeline

My friend and I never sold an installation of this contact management system. In the end, it proved to be just as clunky as the Microsoft product that we were competing against. Perhaps we could have found a way to prune history, or to download snapshots. But if we had known about conflict-free replicated data types, they would have offered a better solution.

Conflict-Free Replicated Data Types (CRDTs)

We achieved a useful result for a distributed system based on processing and forwarding messages. If every node sees every message, and nodes forward the messages unaltered, then two properties are sufficient to achieve strong eventual consistency (SEC):

- Idempotence (ignore duplicates)

- Commutativity (don't depend upon order)

Prove these properties about the way nodes process messages, and you already have a very reliable system. I have built many systems using exactly this technique. It pairs well with infrastructure components such as Amazon SQS, RabbitMQ, and MSMQ that ensure broadcast and delivery of messages. It requires only a minimum set of guarantees from those components, helping them to work at scale without becoming over-constrained.

But this isn't the most general result. We can optimize our distributed system further if we allow nodes to modify messages. Instead of requiring that a node forwards exactly the same messages it received, we can allow the node to summarize its knowledge and send fewer messages. This is the strategy employed by conflict-free replicated data types (CRDTs).

State-Based CRDTs

Shapiro, Preguiça, and colleagues described two general solutions to the strong eventual consistency problem: state-based CRDTs and operation-based CRDTs. Operation-based CRDTs require a delivery protocol that ensures once-and-only-once delivery and preserves causal order. We would prefer to find a solution that does not place so high a constraint on infrastructure components. Fortunately, state-based CRDTs have no such restriction. State-based and operation-based CRDTs can each emulate one another and are therefore equivalent. For these reasons, we can put aside operation-based CRDTs for this discussion and focus entirely on the state-based variety.

A conflict-free replicated data type is a data structure that exists not at one location, like a typical abstract data type; it exists in multiple locations. Each node in a distributed system has its own replica of the CRDT. Operating on a replica of a CRDT closely meets the requirements for location independence with which we opened the chapter. Each replica can serve queries in isolation, without communicating with other replicas. And each replica can process commands that immediately alter its state. The effects of these commands will be shared with other replicas in an eventually consistent manner. All replicas will converge to the same state when all updates have been delivered.

The key is to understand what it means for an update to be delivered.

Partially Ordered State

Each replica of a state-based CRDT has internal state. As an application designer, you get to choose the form of that internal state. It is based on the problem you are trying to solve. But that state has to satisfy a few conditions.

- It must support a "happened before" (causality) relationship that defines a *partial order*.

- All updates must *increase* the state in that partial order (the previous version "happened before").

- It must support a *merge* operation that takes two states and produces a new one that is the lowest possible value that is greater than or equal to both of them (both previous versions "happened before" the merged version).

To be useful, the "happened before" relationship should help us detect concurrent updates. We want to avoid creating a total order and instead capture the partial order inherent in causality.

Unlike our relay-based distributed system, updates do not have to be idempotent or commutative. That's because updates will be executed only on a single replica. Within a single process, we can easily control how many times and in what order updates are applied. A state-based CRDT does not rely upon message relay like the system we just analyzed.

Shapiro, Preguiça, and colleagues proved that these three conditions are sufficient to guarantee SEC. All replicas will converge to the same state after all updates are delivered. So what does it mean for an update to be delivered to a replica?

Causal History

When we examine the state of a replica within a single process, we will find only two operations that cause it to change: updates and merges. An update occurs when that node executes some command from outside the network. Perhaps the node is running a client application and responding to user input. A merge occurs when another node shares the state of its replica. This happens on the *receive* operation of a network communication.

Recalling Leslie Lamport's definition of causality, we can say that the state of a replica after an update is *caused by* the update; the update is in its *causal history*. Lamport also showed us that the *send* operation of a network communication causes the *receive*. And so, the updates that occurred on the origin node before the send, illustrated in Figure 5-17, are in the causal history of the merged state.

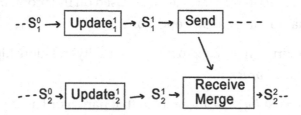

Figure 5-17. *Both updates are in the causal history of s_2^2*

Following this logic, the causal history of a replica includes

1. All updates that have occurred previously in that node

2. All updates in the causal histories of the states that were merged from other nodes

Remember, the updates themselves are not shared between nodes. Only the resulting states. Those states contain all of the information about the updates that caused them.

And so now we can finally answer the question. What does it mean for an update to be delivered to a replica? It means that that update is in the causal history of its current state.

Vector Clocks

That's a lot to process. Let's make it a bit more concrete. How could we have implemented the contact management system as a CRDT? For simplicity, we will look only at the update contact case, which changed the properties of a contact. We'll represent each contact as a CRDT, where each workstation, PDA, and server node has its own replica. Recall from the "Partially Ordered State" section that the conditions of a CRDT's internal state are that

- It supports a partial order

- Updates increase the order

- Merges produce the *least upper bound*

Let's start by defining the state. Each contact is going to have a set of properties, like name, phone number, and email address. We will store those in the state.

By the partial order condition, the state needs to support a "happened before" operator to give us causality. Clearly just looking at the properties of a contact, we cannot tell which of two versions came first. For that, we will need to keep some sort of version number. A simple monotonically increasing version number would satisfy the increasing order condition. We will be able to see which version came first, and we will increase the version number with each update.

Unfortunately, a simple version number does not help us to identify concurrent updates. It does not capture the true partial order of causality. So instead, we will keep a separate version number for each node. This is a data structure known as a *vector clock*.[9] Figure 5-18 shows an example.

---

[9] Friedemann Mattern. Virtual time and global states of distributed systems. In Int. W. on Parallel and Distributed Algorithms, pages 215–226. Elsevier Science Publishers B.V. (North-Holland), 1989.

```
{
    Node 1:3
    Node 2:1
    Node 3:7
}
Name:"Robert"
Phone:"555-1212"
Email:"rob@email.com"
```

Figure 5-18. *A vector clock as part of the contact CRDT*

To compare two vector clocks, we compare each node's version number. If all of the version numbers in the first vector clock are less than or equal to the second, then the first one "happened before" the second. This is a partial order, because it's possible for one node's version to be lower in one, while another node's version is lower in the other. When this happens, the two clocks are not causally related.

When a node updates a contact, it increments its own version number in the vector clock, as demonstrated in Figure 5-19. This ensures that the new version has a greater version, as required by the increasing order condition. State moves forward in causal time with every update.

```
{                              {
    Node 1:3                       Node 1:3
    Node 2:1                       Node 2:2
    Node 3:7                       Node 3:7
}                              }
Name:"Robert"                  Name:"Robert"
Phone:"555-1212"               Phone:"555-1212"
Email:"rob@email.com"          Email:"robert@email.com"
```

Figure 5-19. *Node 2 updates the email of a contact and bumps its own version number*

When a node merges state from a remote node, as in Figure 5-20, it takes the maximum of each of the version numbers. This ensures that the new vector clock is greater than each of the two original vector clocks. Strictly speaking, if one vector already "happened before" the other, then the merge will just give us the greater of the two. In this case, it is not greater than, but equal to the later version. What this operation is really doing is computing the least upper bound of the two vectors, thus satisfying the last of the SEC conditions.

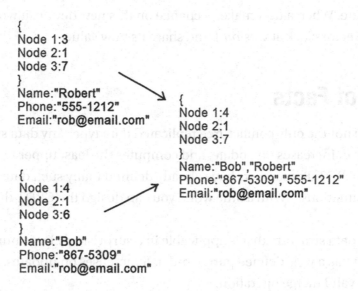

Figure 5-20. *Merging two contacts takes the maxima of all version numbers*

We can see that vector clocks satisfy the necessary conditions for SEC. Since we put a vector clock into the state of our CRDT, we have a way to compare two versions to see which one happened before. Incrementing one version number when we update produces a vector clock that is greater than the previous one, so updates increase the state. Merging two vector clocks produces a set of numbers that are all greater than or equal to the previous two vector clocks, and so merge produces the least possible state that is greater than or equal to the source states.

Most importantly, vector clocks capture the causal history of the replica. During a merge, we can detect concurrent updates. If all version numbers in the vector clock of one of the two states are greater than or equal to the other one, then that state represents the more recent version. The values of the contact's properties will simply be copied from the greater of the two. But if neither vector clock "happened before" the other, then a concurrent update has occurred. That tells us that we need to merge the contact's properties.

A vector clock is a tool for building state-based CRDTs. It gives us a way to define a partial order between states that supports update and merge operations. When used properly, replicas that include a vector clock will converge to the same value, once all updates appear in their causal history.

If my friend and I had built the contact management systems using vector clocks, then introducing a new device to the system would be a simple download. It would get only the current state of each contact and the vector clock representing the causal history of that state. When a user makes a change on this new device, it would simply add itself to the vector clock at version 1 and share its new value.

A History of Facts

Vector clocks are not the only conflict-free replicated data type. Any data structure that is partially ordered, increases on update, and computes the least upper bound on merge can be used as a CRDT. Researchers have already defined many such data structures for use in different situations.[10] With a little work, you can design the CRDT that is exactly right for you.

There is one data structure that is applicable in a surprisingly large number of circumstances. It has a well-defined partial order. It increases on updates. And it comes equipped with a valid merge operation.

I'm talking, of course, about the humble set.

Sets

A set is a collection of items that has a couple of interesting properties:

1. It contains no duplicates.

2. It is unordered.

The first property means that an element is either in the set or it is not. The set does not remember how many times we tried to add an element. The second property tells us that no element comes before or after any other element. The set doesn't remember the order in which we added the elements.

---

[10] Marc Shapiro, Nuno Preguiça, Carlos Baquero, Marek Zawirski. A comprehensive study of Convergent and Commutative Replicated Data Types. [Research Report] RR-7506, Inria – Centre Paris-Rocquencourt; INRIA. 2011, p. 50. ffinria-00555588f.

It's interesting to observe that set insertion satisfies the two conditions necessary for SEC in a relay-based system. Because of the first property, set insertion is idempotent. If we try to insert an element that is already in the set, it remains unchanged. And because of the second property, set insertion is commutative. Inserting elements in the opposite order yields the same set. These two properties mean that set insertion behaves well in the face of duplicated or out-of-order messages.

Idempotence and commutativity are not required for using a set as an state-based CRDT. The properties that are required for CRDTs are partial order, increasing updates, and a merge that computes the least upper bound. As long as we do not allow elements to be removed from a set, we can easily achieve all three.

Partial Order

Sets are partially ordered under the subset relationship. One set is a subset of another if it only contains elements that can be found in the other one. If we use subset as "happened before," then we have defined a partial order.

Take, for example, the set {🚗, 🛵, 🚃}. It is a subset of {🚗, 🛵, 🚙, 🚃}. Every element in the first is also in the second.

Now consider a third set {🛵, 🚙, 🚃}. It is also a subset of the second. But neither the first nor the third is a subset of the other. The first set contains an element not found in the third (🚗), and the third contains an element not found in the first (🚙). Therefore, they are not related under the subset relationship.

The fact that some sets can be put in relative order while others cannot is what makes this a partial order. We can use that partial order to represent causality. A subset "happened before" a superset.

Update

The only update operation that we will allow on a set is an insert. If you try to insert an element that the set already contains, then the set is unchanged. But if the element was *not* already in the set, then the new set has everything that was in the old set plus one additional item. So set insertion, when it modifies the set, increases its value within the partial order.

If you think about the set as containing all of the knowledge of a replica, you can see how set insertion increases that knowledge. The replica still knows everything that it knew before. But after the update, it now knows a little bit more.

179

This also illustrates how a set can represent the causal history of a replica. Recall that the causal history of a replica includes all of the updates that have occurred in its past. By enumerating the elements of a set, you can clearly see all of the insertions that have occurred in the past.

Merge

A valid merge operation in a CRDT will compute the least upper bound of the two values. The least upper bound of two sets under the subset partial order will be the set that contains every element from both sides. It will be a superset of each one. To compute the least upper bound, we simply have to take the set union.

Consider again the two sets {🚗, 🏍️, 🚞} and {🏍️, 🚙, 🚞}. Neither is a subset of the other. But we can compute the smallest set that is a superset of both of them. That will be the set union: {🚗, 🏍️, 🚙, 🚞}.

This follows our intuition about a merge, as well as the conditions required for SEC. If one node merges all of a remote node's knowledge into its own, then it ends up with the union of the two. Knowledge grows as a result of that merge.

Thinking of this as the combination of two causal histories also makes intuitive sense. The causal history after a merge includes all of the updates that occurred both locally and remotely.

Historical Records

Let's formalize this intuition about a set representing the causal history of a replica. Instead of looking at sets of transportation emoji, let the elements in the set be actual historical records.

When a user performs an action at a node, we capture that action as a historical record. We make note of what they were trying to do, what they were trying to do it to, and what options or parameters they chose while doing it. The record is simply a structure that collects all of this information. It captures all of the pertinent data that was part of the user's decision.

When we put these historical records into a set to form a causal history, we will notice four things:

1. We need to distinguish between similar records.

2. We cannot remove a record once it is inserted into the set.

3.   We cannot change a record that is already part of the set.

4.   Some of the records are related to one another.

These four observations give rise to the rules of historical models that we examined in previous chapters. Let me list those rules again. First, we have three laws:

- Facts are immutable.

- Facts reference their predecessors.

- Two facts having the same values and predecessors (and therefore transitive closure) are the same fact.

Then we have two restrictions:

- We cannot guarantee that there is only one successor for any given fact.

- We cannot change our interpretation of history based on the timeliness of our knowledge of it.

Let's see how the rules of historical modeling arise from building a causal history.

Distinguishing Between Records

Revisiting the contact management system, we can identify the first action that a user might perform at a node. They will want to create a new contact. When a new contact is created, it doesn't have any properties. Those can be changed later.

The causal history that a user creates will look something like this:

{ ContactCreation }

When they try to create a second contact, however, they run into a problem. The record *ContactCreation* already exists in the set. It cannot be inserted again.

To insert more records of contact creation into the causal history, we need to distinguish among them. This is where a location-dependent system would use an auto-incrementing identifier. It would produce a causal history that looks like this:

{ ContactCreation(1), ContactCreation(2) }

The problem with this strategy becomes apparent when we merge one node's causal history with that of another. Merge is accomplished with a set union. If they were both generating identifiers using an auto-incrementing counter, then they would produce the same identifier for different contacts. The set union would merge different contacts into one.

So instead, the node will choose a location-independent identifier. A natural key would be best, but in this case, we don't have an immutable natural identifier in the problem domain. We aren't asking contacts for their date of birth, government ID number, and DNA sample. We will just have to be satisfied with a GUID.

{ ContactCreation(74aac247-a86a-4af8-9db4-cf1387f8a1fb),

ContactCreation(5853e3fe-059a-4180-af0a-f969260be882) }

And so, we have derived one of the three laws of historical modeling. Two facts having the same values, predecessors, and transitive closure are the same fact. A fact has no other identifier. This is to ensure that causal histories merge in a location-independent manner.

Removing a Record

The next action that a user of the contact management system wants to perform is deleting a contact. The most natural way to represent a deletion is to remove the creation of the contact from causal history. Removing the second contact (5853...) from the set would bring us down to this:

{ ContactCreation(74aac247-a86a-4af8-9db4-cf1387f8a1fb) }

But this strategy won't work. It violates the second condition of a state-based CRDT. Update operations may only increase the state of a replica within the partial order. Removing an element from a set creates a subset, not a superset. This takes the state backward in causal time.

It becomes apparent that we've made a mistake when we share state with other nodes. Suppose the user creates a contact and then their device shares its state with another node. That contact creation is now part of the other node's replica.

Now suppose that the user removes that contact, and the node incorrectly represents that by removing it from the set. When the remote node at some point in the future shares its state with the user's node, the replica sets will be merged. The contact that they had deleted will suddenly reappear. Just search for "deleted contact reappears" in your favorite search engine to see just how common this bug is.

Instead of removing a historical record from the causal history, we have to instead create a new historical record. That new record represents the deletion of a contact.

{ *ContactCreation(74aac247-a86a-4af8-9db4-cf1387f8a1fb)*,

ContactCreation(5853e3fe-059a-4180-af0a-f969260be882),

ContactDeletion(5853e3fe-059a-4180-af0a-f969260be882) }

We have restored the condition that updates increase state within the partial order. This new set is a superset of the prior one. And merging state with other nodes will never cause the contact to reappear.

This gives another law of historical modeling. Facts are immutable. By immutable, we mean that it cannot be modified or deleted. A record can *represent* the deletion of an entity. But its creation cannot be removed from causal history.

Changing a Record

The next action that a user might want to perform at a node will be setting the properties of a contact. When they do, we'll record a historical record of their actions. It includes which contact they are modifying and the values they set for those properties. The resulting causal history looks something like this:

{ *ContactCreation(74aa...)*,

ContactModification(74aa..., "Bob", "555-1212") }

On the second edit, the naive solution will be to modify the record within the set:

{ ContactCreation(74aa…),

ContactModification(74aa…, "Robert", "555-1212") }

We can already see why that doesn't work. The new set is not a superset of the original one. This violates the second condition: updates must increase state in the partial order. We have, in fact, created a new set that is not causally related to the old one.

To fix this problem, we can partially order the modification records. One way to do this is to add a vector clock:

{ ContactCreation(74aa…),

ContactModification(74aa…, [node1: 1], "Bob", "555-1212"),

ContactModification(74aa…, [node1: 2], "Robert", "555-1212") }

We have discovered that once a record is part of history, it cannot be modified. We can add a new record that *represents* a modification to an entity, but the old records must remain.

Since we already have a complete set of the historical records, the vector clock is a bit redundant. Remember, vector clocks help us to turn a simple data structure into a CRDT. It captures the partial order of causality. But now that we are working with a *set* of simple data structures, we can rely upon the set to capture causality. We have the opportunity to optimize a bit.

Records Are Causally Related

Looking carefully at the set of historical records reveals several relationships. The most obvious one is that the *ContactModification* records contain the GUID of the *ContactCreation* record. As Figure 5-21 shows, we can represent this relationship directly by drawing an arrow from the modification to the creation.

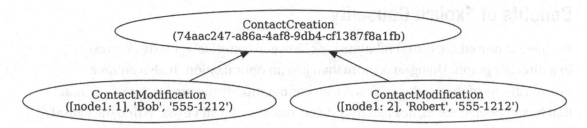

Figure 5-21. *Contact creation precedes contact modification*

This graph is still a set. Every vertex of the graph is a historical record in the set. All we have done is replaced the implied relationships of common GUIDs with explicit arrows.

The second observation we can make is that the vector clocks are actually references to one another. The clock [node1: 2] represents an update that occurred on node 1 bringing its version from 1 to 2. It refers to the previous clock [node1: 1] by inference. As Figure 5-22 shows, we can replace the vector clocks with arrows.

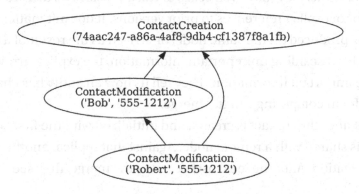

Figure 5-22. *Vector clocks are replaced with explicit arrows*

Changing the vector clocks to arrows preserves the partial order between modifications. It is still easy for us to compare two *ContactModification* records to see which one came before the other. If we can trace a path from one to the other along the arrows *in the correct direction*, then the record at the head of the last arrow "happened before" the record at the tail of the first one.

This gives rise to the third and final law of historical modeling. Facts reference their predecessors. The graph thus produced captures the partial order of causality.

Benefits of Explicit Causality

We have captured the causal relationships between historical records as arrows in a directed graph. Doing so is more than just an optimization. It also enforces preconditions of the user's actions. A user cannot modify the properties of a contact that hasn't been created, nor can they delete one that doesn't exist. When the causal relationships between records were only implied by a shared GUID, the data structure did nothing to help us ensure that these preconditions were met. But now that it explicitly captures the arrows, these preconditions are enforced by the existence of the record at the head.

Another benefit is that we have just traded away less important information for more important information. The vector clock included the names of the nodes at which modifications were made. It needed this information only so that a node knew which version number to increment on update. After that, the names of the nodes are unimportant. Over time, they may even cease to exist. The arrows discard the names of the nodes in favor of explicit references to prior versions. It doesn't matter whether that prior version was produced on the same node, or arrived as the result of a merge.

In exchange for discarding unimportant information, the explicit arrows provide us with much more important information. They tell us how an entity has changed over time. This is useful in computing a better merge.

Suppose that after the contact is created and initialized with the first contract modification, it is shared with a remote node. Against that replica, another user makes a different modification. After the local user receives the merge, they see the graph in Figure 5-23.

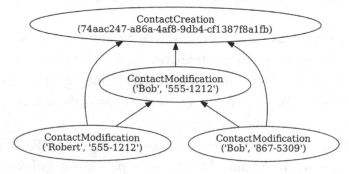

Figure 5-23. *A graph after merging concurrent modifications*

The partial order among modifications shows us that the two leaves of the graph are not causally related. Neither one happened before the other. We therefore need to merge the two sets of properties to display to the user.

The concatenation-based merge that we did before would produce a contact with two names and two phone numbers. If all we had were two data structures and two vector clocks, this is the best we could hope to achieve. But having the graph gives us a third data point. We can see the *nearest common ancestor* of the two leaves.

Comparing the left branch with the nearest common ancestor, we can see that the local user changed only the name. And comparing the right branch reveals that the remote user changed only the phone number. This allows us to perform the much more reasonable merge of displaying the most recent name and the most recent phone number.

---

name: "Robert"

phone: "867-5309"

This three-way merge happens only on display. The set (or graph) of historical records is not modified in any way. Furthermore, all nodes perform this three-way merge in exactly the same way. They all have the same graph, so they will all compute the same result. So even when the history captures causally unrelated records, it does not result in a conflict. Every node converges to the same value.

Accepting Constraints

The requirements of CRDTs are sufficient to prove strong eventual consistency. The data structure that we just constructed ensures that every node will converge to the same state once all of the updates have been exchanged. Nodes do not require any extra communication to reach consensus.

Strong eventual consistency is a valuable property that stakeholders should be reluctant to give up. To faithfully defend this property, we must accept two constraints.

The first constraint is that we cannot guarantee that there is only one successor for any given fact. The merge operation forbids it. To disqualify other successors would require a vote. The system would need a central authority, an elected master, a consensus algorithm, or proof of work to uphold that guarantee. It does not arise from the rules of conflict-free replicated data types.

The second constraint is that we cannot change our interpretation of history based on the timeliness of our knowledge of it. Some nodes will learn of updates before others. For example, nodes might attempt to resolve conflicts by applying the "last writer wins" rule. Different nodes would receive writes in a different order and would therefore have different opinions on which was the last writer. If nodes based their interpretation on timeliness, then those interpretations would not be eventually consistent.

With this, we have re-derived historical modeling from the mathematics of CRDTs. This system follows logically from the desire to capture the full causal history of a system with several parties, separated by time and space, exchanging historical facts. These, again, are the rules of historical modeling:

- Facts are immutable.

- Facts reference their predecessors.

- Two facts having the same values, predecessors, and transitive closure are the same fact.

- We cannot guarantee that there is only one successor for any given fact.

- We cannot change our interpretation of history based on the timeliness of our knowledge of it.

Historical Facts

Because these records are no longer simple flat data structures, I hesitate to call them records anymore, nor do I like referring to them as historical *events*, as that evokes event sourcing. Event sourcing captures a totally ordered sequence of historical events but does not capture explicitly the relationships *between* historical events. And so I refer to these elements of the causal set as *historical facts*.

The arrows point toward the *predecessor* of a historical fact. The earlier fact preceded the latter one. The latter, I call the *successor*. Arrows are only inserted into the graph with the successor, never afterward. This enforces preconditions, preserves the partial order of the causal relationship, and has the extra benefit of preventing cycles. The contents of a fact combined with its set of predecessor arrows are all that distinguish it from other facts. Because facts have no extrinsic identity, nodes can refer to facts in a location-independent manner. The entire causal set is what I call the *historical model*.

A historical model is a state-based CRDT that captures the causality among historical facts as a directed acyclic graph. The arrows of the graph impose a partial order that shows which facts happened before which other facts. Facts in the graph can be referenced, queried, and used with no dependence upon the location of the node.

The graph supports two operations: insert and merge. Inserting a new historical fact moves the graph forward along the causal timeline, because the resulting graph is a superset of the original. Merging two historical models computes their least upper bound and therefore helps remote replicas achieve strong eventual consistency.

Conclusion

We have identified the properties that a distributed system must have in order to be location independent. They must exhibit location independence both in identity and in behavior.

A location-independent identity does not imply any affinity of an object upon its location of origin. Any node should be able to generate and compare a unique immutable identity for a new object without communicating with other nodes. This reduces latency and increases autonomy of isolated nodes within a distributed system.

Location-independent behavior permits a node to query and transact with replicas of objects in isolation. These replicas achieve strong eventual consistency when all replicas converge to the same state once all updates are delivered. This can either be achieved by means of an idempotent and commutative relay system or by a more sophisticated conflict-free replicated data type.

From these constraints, we derived a set of rules that help us to define systems that operate in a location-independent fashion. These are the rules of historical modeling. The reasoning laid out in this chapter demonstrates that a historical model satisfies the requirements for strong eventual consistency.

CHAPTER 6

Immutable Runtimes

Now that we have the tools to model a problem historically and the math to reason about it, let's build some working software. This is where we make a choice. On the one hand, we can use familiar tools such as databases, API gateways, and message brokers. On the other hand, we could invent a new set of tools that take full advantage of the rigor of historical models.

Using familiar tools is a safe route. You get to gradually add immutability to an existing application. You get to grow a team into the practice of thinking immutably. This is a low risk way to introduce these concepts. I cover this path in Chapters 10 and 11.

But inventing a new set of tools holds incredible promise. This is the only way that we can achieve the goals introduced in Chapter 1. Let's replace the practice of testing away defects with a rigorous system of first representing and then generating solutions. Let's construct an immutable runtime.

We'll start by imagining that we have an infrastructure component based on conflict-free replicated data types (CRDTs). If we had such a component, what could we do with it? What benefits would it give us over familiar traditional tools? And what attributes must it have?

Then we will take a closer look at what it would take to make such a component a reality. How would we construct such a thing? What new math is required to imbue it with the desired attributes? And can we perhaps build it out of the very components we wish to replace?

Let's begin by taking a critical look at those familiar components. Perhaps there is something about the way we use them that leads to brittle architecture.

© Michael L. Perry 2024
M. L. Perry, *The Art of Immutable Architecture*, https://doi.org/10.1007/979-8-8688-0288-1_6

When Architecture Depends Upon the Domain

The traditional approach to software design is to mirror the application domain directly into code. We take words from the domain model and use them to describe software components. This results in a system architecture that depends upon the domain. When the domain changes, the architecture is invalidated.

Consider the API for interacting with an education system. You will expect to see endpoints associated with semesters, courses, and students. You will find JSON objects representing these concepts in the requests and responses. The API uses the language of the domain and therefore depends upon the domain.

Then take a look at the database. You will find tables for teachers, tests, and report cards. The columns of those tables describe the properties of those entities. The storage mechanism of the system mirrors the domain model.

And finally consider the message broker. It will notify components when a student enrolls in the school or registers for a course. Inspect the infrastructure and you will find queues tied to enrollment and registration. To expand the capabilities of the application, system operators will deploy new infrastructure components.

Eventually, the infrastructure will reflect the needs of the domain. Our goal is not to completely avoid that. Instead, our goal is to delay infrastructure decisions until the latest responsible moment. Rather than building domain-specific APIs, database schemas, or message consumers into the application, let's allow the system operator to deploy application components in different configurations as the domain evolves.

The application domain changes rapidly. Product owners run experiments to determine if a different process will improve or harm business. If infrastructure depends upon the domain model, then these changes will be slow and error prone. We can do better.

An immutable runtime requires infrastructure components that are ignorant of the application. Some infrastructure components like APIs are custom built for each application. They have domain knowledge built in. Any immutable runtime must replace custom APIs with an application agnostic communication mechanism.

But other infrastructure components such as databases and message brokers are shipped with no domain knowledge. If only they could remain application agnostic, then they could respond easily to change. Alas, the very first thing we do after installing them is to imprint domain knowledge upon them. Before we can begin using a database, we describe to it the tables, columns, and constraints of our application. And as we deploy new versions of the application, we have to update that metadata.

Instead, let's define an infrastructure component that adapts on the fly to changes in the domain model. Let's take inspiration from schemaless databases and operate on a generalized form of data. But rather than mutable documents, these components will store graphs of immutable facts. They will obey the mathematics of CRDTs to guarantee consistency as they securely move subsets of graphs where they need to go.

This is a replicator.

Replicators

The unit of infrastructure in an immutable runtime is the *replicator*. A replicator provides storage, security, and communications for your model. Traditionally, these functions are implemented by separate infrastructure components. The database provides storage. The identity provider and API gateway collaborate to provide security. And the message broker and application interface work together to provide communications. When these are separate components, a human needs to configure their interactions. But when they are combined, the replicator can automate their collaboration.

Replicators do not represent a wholly new infrastructure component. Instead, they are composed from existing components. Encapsulated within a replicator is a database, a network interface, and a message broker. The vision of the immutable runtime is not to replace these components, but instead to orchestrate them. It provides a provably correct way of storing, securing, and transporting information. The replicator provides a discrete deployable unit of orchestration.

Let's see what system architecture would look like if we had replicators. How would they work together with an immutable runtime to solve common infrastructure problems? We'll begin with traditional components and then transition to a replicator-based solution. Then we'll gradually add system requirements and see how the infrastructure evolves.

Scaling Up Traditional Infrastructure

We'll start with a simple problem. The system provides a website with which students can enroll and register for classes. This site produces server-rendered pages containing data from the course catalog.

The traditional starting point for such an application is to deploy a single web application with a single database, as shown in Figure 6-1.

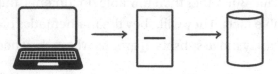

Figure 6-1. *A single instance of a web app serving data from a database*

This topology is great for developing an application. But it is insufficient for a production system. It will not scale as our student user base grows.

To support additional load, the operator will deploy multiple instances of the web application. They will configure all of them to connect to the same database. Since the developers created the web app to be stateless, the operator can make this change without affecting the behavior of the app. We're off to a great start.

Scaling up the number of web servers controls the load on the web application. But all of those requests still flow through to the database. The operator wants to install another infrastructure component to absorb this load. So they introduce a distributed cache for the apps to store results that are unlikely to change. The modified infrastructure appears in Figure 6-2.

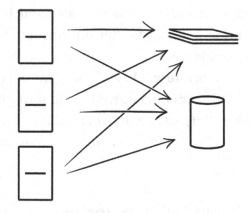

Figure 6-2. *Multiple instances of a web app share a distributed cache to support a large number of users*

The operator makes this cache available, but the developer must change the web app to take advantage of it. They decide what information belongs in the cache. They have to guess what will be used often enough to see the benefits from skipping the database hit and will also change infrequently enough that the cache remains valid. Based on their domain knowledge, they decide that the course catalog can be cached for 30 minutes at a time. They make the change, and the database load drops considerably.

Notice how the application developers used domain knowledge to make an infrastructure decision. They modified their application code in order to get better system behavior. How could this be improved with an immutable runtime and replicator?

Scaling Up an Immutable Runtime

Let's look at the same system, but instead built with immutable components. First, let's consider the client library with which the application is built. Immutable runtimes obey the rules of conflict-free replicated data types (CRDTs). They are quite different from the data access library or object-relational mapper (ORM) that the traditional application is built upon.

A traditional data access library connects to a remote database. It makes a network request for every query. It has no local cache and has no mechanism for keeping a local copy fresh if it did.

A CRDT, however, operates locally. Recall the operations that a CRDT implements: they are update, merge, and query.[1] All three of these operations are performed on a local replica. Queries are served from the local store. Updates are applied locally. Even merges are performed on the local replica, albeit with state fetched from a remote.

An application developer working with an immutable runtime is using a CRDT. The client library has a built-in cache, which is kept consistent with a remote replicator. Rather than making a network request for every query, the runtime serves application state directly from its own store. The client carries its own miniature replica to hold the subset of application state needed for the client's operation.

Let's update the diagram. With apologies to Alistair Cockburn, I will use a hexagon to represent a replicator. I'll also add a small hexagon to the web servers to show that the apps each have an in-memory replica of their own. The updated diagram is in Figure 6-3.

---

[1] Shapiro, Marc; Preguiça, Nuno; Baquero, Carlos; Zawirski, Marek. Conflict-free Replicated Data Types. Institut National de Recherche en Informatique et en Automatique, No 7687, 2011.

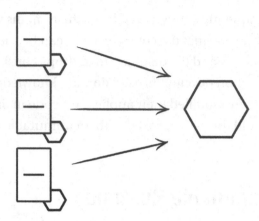

Figure 6-3. *Multiple instances of a web app connect to a common replicator*

You'll notice that the diagram no longer includes a distributed cache. It's not that the cache has disappeared. It's that the cache is no longer a separate piece of infrastructure. Caching is a natural feature of a CRDT and is therefore encapsulated within the immutable runtime.

But something else truly remarkable has changed, and this difference is not obvious from the diagram. The decision about what to cache and for what duration has been removed from the developer. They no longer write application code to control infrastructure components. The runtime works with the replicator behind the scenes to exchange state. When new state is available, it merges it into its own local replica. There it is ready for the application the next time it needs to serve a page. We'll talk about the mechanism it uses to do that shortly.

It may be tempting to remove the central replicator altogether, replacing it with a gossip protocol. After all, the web servers each have a replica. However, the purpose of those replicas, like the cache that they replace, is lower latency, not persistence. The web server replicas are in-memory. The central replicator is persistent. Moreover, we will improve its persistence by making it redundant.

Redundant Storage

Let's return our attention to the system operator. They have deployed redundant web application instances to handle load at scale. But web apps are not the only place where redundancy is useful. As is common practice with databases, replicators can be clustered. The goal of this kind of redundancy is protection against data loss as a result of hardware failure. Each replica takes a copy of the whole database.

Traditional databases do not have the consistency guarantees of CRDTs. They must therefore employ some form of consensus algorithm to ensure that all replicas agree. Often this includes electing a primary database that handles all write requests. The other replicas can only handle reads, as shown in Figure 6-4.

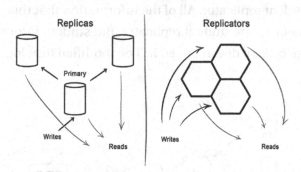

Figure 6-4. *A cluster of databases elect a primary to handle writes, while a cluster of replicators can all respond to writes*

Replicators, however, do not need to elect a primary. They can guarantee that the replicas will reach consistency, even when writes occur at multiple nodes. New replicators can be added to the cluster without risking inconsistency or invoking an election.

Keep in mind the limitations of replicators. A replicator cannot enforce uniqueness constraints. It cannot guarantee that only one consumer receives a scarce resource. It does not provide searching or aggregation. For any of these capabilities, keep the traditional database. For the rest of your data, the cluster of replicators will be simpler and more reliable.

Legacy Integration

Immutable architectures do not exist in a bubble. They integrate with legacy systems. Let's see how an operator connects replicators to control the flow of information.

Suppose the course catalog is managed in a legacy system. Faculty and staff use this system to define courses and assign professors to offer courses in each semester. The programmatic interface to this legacy system is based on uploads and downloads of data interchange files via FTP.

Application developers write an adapter in the form of a lambda function that integrates with the legacy system. The lambda uses an immutable runtime. Its job is to turn all of the data in the interchange files into facts.

To support this integration, the system operator deploys a course catalog replicator downstream of the student replicator. All of the information that this replicator receives from the lambda flows up to the student replicator. But student information does not flow down. The course catalog doesn't need it. The modified topology is shown in Figure 6-5.

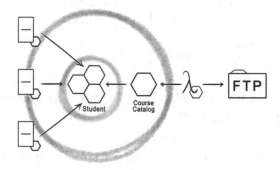

Figure 6-5. *A replicator feeds course catalog data upstream to the student cluster*

All facts flow upstream toward a centralized replicator. But only certain facts flow downstream. Let's evolve the system a little more to illustrate this behavior.

Persistent Projections

Students using the website need to find courses to take. The fact graph is not optimized for search. It would be much better to project the facts into an infrastructure component designed for that purpose.

It is now time for the system operator to bring in domain knowledge. The application developers will provide components but not constrain how they are to be deployed. That decision was delayed until now. Let's look at those components.

The application developers provide both a specification and an index update function. The specification is written in Factual or a syntax like LINQ that compiles to Factual. It describes the projection of course data that needs to be indexed. The update function, for its part, sends those projections to the search engine.

The system operator decides how best to deploy these components. With the help of the development team, they encapsulate the specification and index update function into a lambda. The system operator needs to decide how best to integrate this indexer function.

One option is to connect the indexer function directly to the course catalog replicator as shown in Figure 6-6. This replicator already has all of the information that the indexer would need. This option is simple and easy to explain.

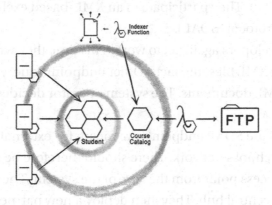

Figure 6-6. *The indexer function connects directly to the course catalog replicator*

Another option is to deploy an additional replicator downstream of the course catalog replicator. The subscription built into the indexing function will pull the necessary information down into that replicator. This option, shown in Figure 6-7, would isolate the course catalog replicator from the load of the indexer lambda.

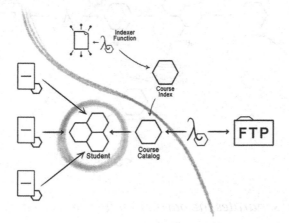

Figure 6-7. *The indexer function pulls facts through an intermediate replicator*

The system operator chooses the option shown in Figure 6-7. The replicator responds automatically to the specification described in the indexer. It pulls only the information from the course catalog that is to be indexed.

Data Firewalls

The school running this system collaborates with other nearby schools to transfer credits and allow student mobility. They participate in an XML-based exchange built on the Simple Object Access Protocol (SOAP).

The application developers again get to work. This time they write SOAP endpoints that translate incoming XML files into facts. Other endpoints query facts and project the results into outgoing XML documents. The system operator decides how to deploy this integration.

They recognize that the SOAP endpoints are meant for external consumers. They live on the edge of the school's network. There should therefore be an extra layer of security isolating this access point from the core of the system. The operator repurposes the student cluster as a central hub. They then deploy a new partner replicator, shown in Figure 6-8, so that they can isolate it using strict security rules.

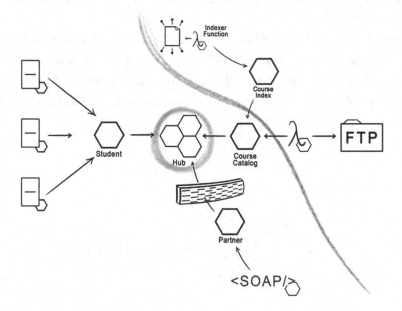

Figure 6-8. *A firewall separates the partner replicator from a clustered central hub*

Consider how the system operator decides where to deploy replicators. They make those decisions based on integration requirements and load. Compare this to a microservice-oriented architecture. When an application developer codes a new microservice, they impose constraints on the system architecture. But when an application developer codes a client to a replicator, they leave the infrastructure decision for later.

The deployment of replicators is orthogonal to the design of the historical model. Either can change without affecting the other. This is only possible because a replicator will adjust its behavior based on the model and the security rules that are deployed to it.

Specifications

The key to adjusting behavior on the fly is that applications describe expected behavior using specifications. A specification is not an implementation detail. It is a description of desired behavior. An immutable runtime generates behavior from specifications to project results, update user interfaces, refresh caches, exchange data, and enforce security rules.

Replicators receive all queries using a formal specification language such as Factual. The immutable runtime upon which an application is built translates the programmer's intent into Factual specifications. That runtime offers the application developer an internal domain-specific language (DSL) for representing specifications. For example, a .NET client library would use Language Integrated Query (LINQ) for specifications. The runtime converts specifications into Factual for processing.

At first glance, a Factual specification looks like a SQL query. Both are executed to produce results. However, specifications can also be transformed into other specifications. In one transformation, a specification is inverted to tell us when results change. In another, it is divided into feeds that control how facts flow from one replicator to another. And in a third, specifications are compared to determine who is allowed to read and write data. Let's see examples of each of these transformations.

Execution

Replicators encapsulate storage. That storage mechanism may, in fact, be a relational database. The schema for that database includes tables for facts and edges, not for domain entities. The replicator translates a specification into a SQL query in order to project results.

201

Suppose the education application we described earlier needs to run the following Factual query:

```
registrationsForOffering = (offering: Offering) {
  registration: Registration [
    registration→offering = offering
    ∄ {
      deleted: Registration.Deleted [
        deleted→registration = registration
      ]
    }
  ]
} ⇒ registration
```

The replicator will turn this specification into a query that it can execute locally. My reference replicator implementation, for example, is based on PostgreSQL. It has generic tables named fact and edge designed to store any directed graph. It converts the specification to a SQL query such as the following:

```
SELECT f2.hash as hash2
FROM fact f1
JOIN edge e1 ON e1.predecessor_fact_id = f1.fact_id AND e1.role_id = $3
JOIN fact f2 ON f2.fact_id = e1.successor_fact_id
WHERE f1.fact_type_id = $1 AND f1.hash = $2
AND NOT EXISTS (
  SELECT 1
  FROM edge e2
  JOIN fact f3 ON f3.fact_id = e2.successor_fact_id
  WHERE e2.predecessor_fact_id = f2.fact_id AND e2.role_id = $4
)
```

Notice that all domain words like offering, registration, and deleted have been removed from the query. These have become parameters. The query operates on generalized tables such as fact and edge. This allows replicators to be deployed independently of applications. There is no need to evolve the schema as the application model changes.

Inversion

Executing a specification only solves part of the problem. Another part is knowing when the results have changed. The results of a specification will either appear in a view that the user is interacting with or in a cache that provides rapid access to projected data. An inverse tells the immutable runtime when the view or cache needs to be updated and exactly how to update it.

Consider an application that displays the list of registrations we've just produced. If a new student registers for the offering, that application should add them to the list. And if they drop the course, they should be removed.

Part of the job of application development is predicting what actions will invalidate a view and then building in a mechanism to notify the view of the change. A lot of effort goes into getting this right. Some mechanisms commonly employed are reducers in the Flux pattern, the INotifyPropertyChanged interface in MVVM, observable collections in reactive frameworks, or any other form of the Observer pattern.[2]

An immutable runtime, however, can invert a specification to determine when results will change. It does so by pulling each of the labeled facts up into the parameter. When the runtime learns about that fact, the inverse tells it exactly which results to change and exactly how to change them.

Take the specification of registrations for an offering given previously. It contains two labels: registration and deleted. If we pull the registration label up to the parameter, we obtain an inverse that tells us which offerings have been affected and what to add to the list:

```
(registration: Registration) {
  offering: Offering [
    offering = registration→offering
  ]
} ⇒ registration
```

Look carefully at what this simple specification is saying. When we learn about a new registration, we look at its prerequisite offering. If the user is actively looking at a view of that offering, then we know that the view must be updated. In particular, we need to add a registration to the view. The registration we need to add is the result of this specification.

---

[2] Gamma, E.; Helm, R.; Johnson R.; Vlissides, J. M. (1994). Design Patterns: Elements of Reusable Object-Oriented Software. Addison-Wesley Professional. ISBN: 0201633612.

Next let's pull the deleted label up as a parameter. Now the inverse tells us what to remove and from which list:

```
(deleted: Registration.Deleted) {
  registration: Registration [
    registration = deleted→registration
  ]
  offering: Offering [
    offering = registration→offering
  ]
} ⇒ registration
```

When the runtime learns about a new registration deleted, it runs this specification. The specification looks up the registration and then the offering. If the user is looking at a view of that offering, then the view is out of date. But just as before, we don't need to re-run the whole query to get the updated results. The specification also tells us specifically which registration to remove from the view. It is the result of this specification: the registration that is the predecessor of the deletion.

When an immutable runtime learns about a new fact, it runs all matching inverses. It then notifies the application to update the associated view or cache. Computing the inverse is mechanical. The proof of correctness appears in Chapter 13.

Executing and invalidating queries is completely automated. The runtime can accomplish this with no domain knowledge. There is no opportunity for a human developer to make a mistake in the process.

Communication

As discussed previously, an immutable runtime performs all of its operations locally. It does not call out to a replicator to query or update remote data. Instead it operates on its own local replica. The specifications that it runs against that local replica tell the runtime what facts the application is interested in. The runtime transforms those specifications into feeds, similar to the topics found in message brokers such as Kafka or Apache Pulsar. But whereas developers design topics when using those components directly, the runtime performs this calculation automatically.

The runtime will convert a specification into a collection of feeds. Taken together, the feeds provide just enough information for the local replica to return a consistent result for that specification. You might expect that each feed contains a stream of facts, but that

is not the case. Instead, each feed contains a stream of tuples. The members of the tuples
are the facts identified by the labels within the specification. A single tuple contains a
group of labeled facts that together satisfy all of the conditions of the specification.

Let's expand upon the prior example to show this in action. Instead of returning
the list of registrations for an offering, we want to display a student roster: a list of all of
the registered students' names. We'll represent this with a projection that computes the
names of each registered student. The modified specification follows:

```
studentRoster = (offering: Offering) {
  registration: Registration [
    registration→offering = offering
    ∄ {
      deleted: Registration.Deleted [
        deleted→registration = registration
      ]
    }
  ]
} ⇒ {
  names: {
    name: Student.Name [
      name→student = registration→student
      ∄ {
        next: Student.Name [
          next→prior = name
        ]
      }
    ]
  } ⇒ name.value
}
```

This specification begins like the one before. It asks for registrations for the given
offering, and then the not exists clause filters out all of the registrations that have
been deleted. But now the projection is doing additional work. For each remaining
registration, the projection asks for the possible names of the student. It finds all of that
student's historical names and then filters out the ones that have been superseded.

You can envision a specification as a tree. It starts with the given fact at the root. Then each label defines another node in the tree. The tree branches when we enter an existential condition or a projection (i.e., when we encounter an open brace {). A path terminates when we reach the end of an existential condition or a set (i.e., when we encounter a close brace }). The tree for the student roster specification appears in Figure 6-9.

Figure 6-9. *The student roster specification describes a tree of labels*

The immutable runtime uses this tree structure to find paths through a specification. It traces each path from the root to a terminator. This particular specification, for example, produces four different feeds, one for each of four paths. The four paths are as follows:

- (offering, registration)

- (offering, registration, deleted)

- (offering, registration, name)

- (offering, registration, name, next)

Intuitively, you can imagine each of the feeds as handling a specific scenario. The first feed handles registrations from students who have not entered their name. The second communicates information about registration deletion. The third gives us the historical names of registered students. And the fourth tells us when a student has changed their name. When a developer designs a message structure, they might very easily overlook one of these scenarios.

The runtime receives tuples of facts from each of these feeds. Performing a transitive closure on each tuple produces a subgraph. The runtime then constructs the results of the roster specification after merging the subgraphs into its own replica.

Immutable runtimes reduce developer error. By automating the creation of feeds based on specifications, immutable runtimes provide a provably correct mechanism for exchanging facts asynchronously. The proof of correctness can be found in Chapter 12.

Security

Security is an essential function of any distributed system. All too often it is left until later in the process, where it is relegated to the edges of the network. Role-based rules are checked and then terminated. Interior components trust these edge components and one another. If an attacker can infiltrate the inner network or inject code that bypasses edge protections, then they will find a soft vulnerable interior.

An immutable runtime integrates security into the model. Replicators enforce security rules at every interface, not just at the edges. Application developers define rules describing which users should be trusted to author facts and which users need to learn about those facts. They do so by expressing rules in terms of specifications.

Authorization Rules

Authorization rules define which users are authorized to assert which facts. Given a fact, a rule lists the users that the replica should trust. It is expressed as a Factual specification returning user facts.

Let's continue with the education example. Suppose that an instructor is authorized to enter grades for their class offering. An authorization rule expressing that authority would look like the following:

```
authorizedInstructors = (grade: Grade) {
  assignment: Assignment {
    assignment→offering = grade→registration→offering
  }
  user: User {
    user = assignment→instructor→user
  }
} ⇒ user
```

Each replicator runs this rule upon receipt of a grade. It looks within its own data store for assignments of instructors to the course offering for which the grade is recorded. If the user who sent the grade is not one of those instructors, then the grade fact is rejected. It will remain in the queue until it can be accepted, for example, when the assignment reaches the replicator. Figure 6-10 illustrates the path the rule takes through the model.

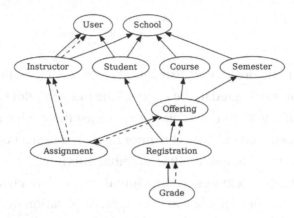

Figure 6-10. *An authorization rule traverses a model to determine which users are authorized to enter grades*

Not all instructors are authorized to enter grades for a given offering. Only those instructors assigned to teach this specific offering may do so. The assignment of an instructor to a course offering is itself a fact. A different authorization rule (not shown here) defines the set of users authorized to assert the assignment fact.

Each replicator enforces authorization rules on every fact that it receives. This prevents unauthorized facts from entering its data store.

Distribution Rules

Whereas authorization rules control writing, distribution rules control reading. A distribution rule describes the users who are allowed to query a given specification. It asserts that we may share a given specification with certain users. For example, a distribution rule might say that we can share a student's grades with that student.

```
share gradesForStudent = (student: Student) {
  grade: Grade [
    grade→registration→student = student
  ]
```

```
} ⇒ grade
with (student: Student) {
  user: User [
    user = student→user
  ]
} ⇒ user
```

The rule has two parts. The first describes the specification that the runtime might expect. The second describes another specification returning the users who can make that request. The two specifications start from the same given facts. Figure 6-11 shows the paths of those two specifications through the model, both starting at the student.

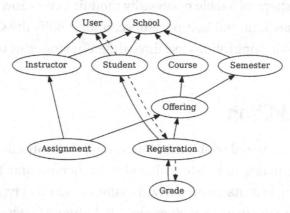

Figure 6-11. *A distribution rule traverses a model to determine which users are allowed to run a specification*

A replicator enforces distribution rules at the feed boundary. It first breaks the distribution rule into a set of feeds. Then it compares feed requests from peers against the feeds resulting from distribution rules. If the requesting user is among the users allowed to receive that feed, then the information is permitted to flow. This prevents the distribution of information to users who are not permitted to see it.

There is one important exception to this. All facts are sent upstream regardless of distribution restrictions. Upstream replicators act as central repositories of information. They receive facts without expressing any particular interest on behalf of a user. An immutable runtime employs additional controls to ensure the privacy of information flowing through untrusted centralized replicators. This mechanism is described in Chapter 9.

Application developers write security rules using specifications. System operators deploy those rules to replicators to control the flow of information. Replicators automate the process of enforcing security rules to reduce human error and improve safety.

Versioning

Over time, the application model will change. As it does, the replicator and runtime will need to absorb those changes while holding existing facts immutable.

Evolving a schema in a relational database often requires changing the shape of a table. When this happens, all rows in the table must also change to conform to the new schema. Evolving the shape of a table necessarily modifies every row.

But because facts are immutable, replicators cannot modify the shape of existing facts. Instead, immutable applications use three different strategies to respond to model changes.

Incremental Addition

The first strategy is incremental addition. The new model simply adds new fact types.

Most application changes to a historical model are incremental. For example, when an application adds a new mutable property, it defines a new fact type. Or when an application adds a new step to a business process, it defines a fact type to represent that decision. Since facts are immutable, they tend to be small. And as a result, most changes add new fact types to the code, rather than changing the shape of existing fact types. Replicators absorb these changes transparently.

When an incremental change occurs, some clients will be updated to take advantage of new features while others will not. Clients that don't know about the new fact types will not generate specifications referencing those types. They will therefore continue to function and collaborate exactly as they had before. Upgraded clients will interoperate with older clients while taking advantage of new features.

Structural Versioning

The second strategy is structural versioning. The structure of the fields and predecessors determines the version of the fact. Application developers will employ this strategy when they discover that they need to add a field or predecessor to an existing fact type. This changes the shape of facts within the programming language.

210

To absorb this sort of change, immutable runtimes treat the fact's structure as its version. Versions of facts are represented not as incrementing numbers, but by the set of fields and predecessor names and types. If an application developer changes the fields or predecessors in their programming language, the runtime would recognize that as a different version.

Depending upon the change, it might be impossible for the runtime to load old facts into the new shape. It may therefore offer a mechanism for application developers to provide multiple declarations in code for a given fact type. The runtime will then deserialize a fact into the matching structure.

Another issue related to changing the shape of a fact in code has to do with identity. The identity of the fact is determined by its type, its fields, and its predecessors. The immutable runtime computes a hash from the fields and predecessors. The type and hash together identify the fact. Therefore, if an old fact is loaded into a new structure, it would inevitably produce a different hash than it originally had.

To account for this, the runtime retains the hash of the original fact rather than recomputing it from serialized fields and predecessors. As a result, an old fact loaded from a replicator keeps its identity even as the structure of the application model changes. The application can evolve without requiring replicators be updated in lockstep.

One-Way Transformation

In extreme circumstances, a developer may determine that the shape of the graph needs to change. Information that used to be captured in one fact might need to be split across two. Or perhaps the predecessor-successor relationship between two fact types needs to be inverted. In these extreme cases, a developer can employ a one-way transformation.

The developer will write a function that maps a graph of facts from one structure onto another. Ideally, this function would be deterministic; any client running the function would produce the same output. If that is the case, then the function can be deployed at the edges and run on the client to migrate the model.

But sometimes the transformation cannot be deterministic. For example, it might need to generate a new unique identifier using a GUID or timestamp. In these cases, the function must be deployed in a central location. Application developers must ensure that the transformation runs only once for each subset of the graph. To do so, they will need to use a static journaling table. This table maps from old identities to new ones and keeps track of the work that has been completed. To transform a fact, the function first generates the new identity and stores it in the journal. Then, it produces the new fact using that identity. If the process is interrupted, the function can resume without risk of duplicating work.

Archiving

Replicators are append-only storage components. During its lifetime, a replicator's footprint will continually increase. This presents a challenge for system operators.

Fortunately, replication offers a solution. Operators can find opportunities to bring new replicators online and archive old ones. One-way transformations offer one such opportunity, although those are rare. An operator may choose to put the transform function between two replicators, thus isolating portions of the network using the new version from those using the old. Components are not upgraded in place but instead are deployed to the new network as they are upgraded. Once all components are upgraded, the replicators on the old network can be taken out of service and archived.

Operators don't need to wait for these extreme situations to archive replicators. They could instead rely upon the natural period of the application. Developers may employ the Period Pattern (described in Chapter 8) to subdivide the model by time. An application tends to create new facts only within the current period. It also tends to retrieve facts only within a small number of past periods. A system operator may choose to rotate replicators into service at a cadence roughly equivalent to the application period.

To perform a rotation, the system operator introduces a new network of replicators in the same configuration as the existing set. They configure these new replicators to connect as peers to the ones they replace. The resulting topology is shown in Figure 6-12.

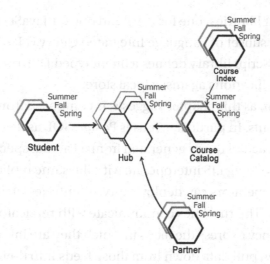

Figure 6-12. *A school network of replicators is cycled and archived at semester boundaries*

In this configuration, every specification pulls information through a new replicator, thus populating it with facts from old ones. Facts that do not appear in a specification are not replicated. Neither do the old replicators pull facts from the new ones. Eventually, the new replicator contains all of the information it needs to satisfy day-to-day specifications and no more. This doesn't typically take very long, just until the complete set of specifications has been executed. Operators can observe the flow of facts to verify that traffic has quiesced. Then on the next rotation, the oldest replicators are removed from service and archived. This periodic rotation can be automated to improve reliability and decrease cost.

Jinaga

As you may already suspect, the description of immutable runtimes and replicators described in this chapter is not purely academic. One such runtime already exists. Jinaga is an open source reference implementation of the ideas presented here. You may use it to experiment, to build immutable applications, or to inspire your own immutable runtimes.

Jinaga has two client libraries: one for .NET and one for JavaScript. The .NET client library converts a subset of Language Integrated Query (LINQ) into Factual specifications. The JavaScript library defines a fluent typed DSL using TypeScript. They each execute those specifications against a local store.

The Jinaga replicator, as this chapter suggests, is composed from existing infrastructure components. In particular, it uses PostgreSQL as its storage engine. The SQL shown earlier is an actual query generated from a Factual specification.

Both Jinaga.NET and Jinaga.JS interoperate with the same replicator. Application developers and system operators can deploy a mix of runtimes to the same heterogeneous network. The runtimes communicate with replicators using feeds, as described previously. They express the feeds in which they are interested using Factual specifications. They then pull data down from those feeds into their own in-memory replica and serve application queries from there. They can even be configured to use a durable store like SQLite or IndexedDB to support offline mobile applications and progressive web apps (PWAs).

I have learned quite a lot from constructing this runtime. I can now say with confidence that the goal of reducing human error is achievable. I have seen the runtime produce behavior from specifications alone that would take an entire team months to design and develop. And it does so flawlessly.

The code for the client runtimes and replicator can all be found at `https://github.com/jinaga`. The clients are in the jinaga.js and jinaga.net repositories. The replicator is in jinaga-server and jinaga-replicator. A fully deployable education example as explored in this chapter can also be found at that location. I hope that you will give Jinaga a try. But even more, I hope that you will consider immutable runtimes in whatever form they ultimately take. We have a lot of software to write, and the only way we are going to do it quickly and well is if we change the equation.

CHAPTER 7

Patterns

You now have a set of tools with which you can build systems that are naturally resilient and reliable. You might even have a good idea how to apply these tools to solve the business problems that your customers face. But there might be some gaps.

In this chapter, we will take a systematic look at how to apply the rules of historical modeling to solving real-world problems. Starting from common issues, we will derive historical solutions. Then using the analytical tools we've developed in the previous chapters, we will examine the consequences of those decisions. The result will be a catalog of patterns that we can reference as we construct new models. This catalog will not be comprehensive, but it will provide a good foundation for exploring new solutions to problems you will face in the future.

Structural Patterns

A large portion of the software that we write for business customers falls under the category of *forms over data*, sometimes known as *CRUD*. This is the kind of software that presents the user with the ability to create, read, update, and delete entities. It is not glamorous work, but it needs to get done.

Relational models and hypermedia models seem to be conceived with CRUD applications in mind. Databases map these four operations to the four primary commands: INSERT, SELECT, UPDATE, and DELETE. Hypermedia applications using POST, GET, PUT, and DELETE seem to reflect the basic operations of CRUD.

But the implementation of CRUD operations in a historical model is not so clear and direct. The most obvious point of dissonance is that a historical model does not allow for updates or deletes. The user wants to perform these operations, but the underlying model does not permit them. And so, we have to find a way to simulate these operations.

© Michael L. Perry 2024
M. L. Perry, *The Art of Immutable Architecture*, https://doi.org/10.1007/979-8-8688-0288-1_7

Where relational and hypermedia modeling provide direct analogs to CRUD operations, historical models require a bit more consideration. To reconcile the differences between the needs of CRUD and the capabilities of historical modeling, let's walk through the CRUD concepts one by one. We will construct patterns that allow us to simulate each of them within the strict rules of immutability.

Entity

Motivation	Represent the creation of an entity.

In a forms-over-data application, a user needs the capability of creating new things. Usually, they will click a button and be presented with a form. Once they fill it out and click another button, the system creates an entity and gives it identity.

The identity of a row in a relational database is sometimes generated by an auto-incrementing ID. This strategy is not appropriate for a historical model, as doing so would rely upon a location-dependent identifier. Different replicas might generate the same ID for different entities. A location-independent identifier is required.

Another point of difference is the initialization of a new entity. Relational databases have INSERT statements, which set all of the columns of a new row to their default or provided values. But in a historical model, it makes less sense for the construction of an entity to initialize its properties. Some future operation will want to modify those properties. The historical fact itself is immutable, so using it to store the initial version of a set of mutable properties is awkward. Doing so would make the initial version something different from the future updates. It would also make those initial values part of the identity of the entity, even after they have been subsequently changed.

The *Entity* pattern focuses on constructing a location-independent identity and avoids initializing mutable properties.

Structure

An entity is a historical fact that contains only identifying information. It contains a natural key, GUID, timestamp, or some combination of those and other location-independent identifiers.

```
fact Entity {
  identifier1: type
  identifier2: type
}
```

Issuing this kind of fact is equivalent to creating the entity. It represents both the identity and the creation of the entity itself.

Example

A product can be represented by a fact that simply captures the SKU (stock keeping unit):

```
fact Product {
  sku: string
}
```

The description, price, quantity on hand, back-order status, and other properties of the product are not stored within the fact. These properties are mutable. The fact is immutable. It represents the identity of the product and the fact that it was created.

Consequences

An entity must use location-independent identity. It cannot use auto-incremented IDs, URLs, or any other location-dependent identifier.

An entity does not contain mutable properties. Any mutable properties that should be associated with the entity are applied with a subsequent fact.

If two client machines create entities with the same identifiers, then they are the same entity. The clients may not be aware of each other at the time of creation, but any replicas who learn of the two entities will assume that they are the same.

If auditing information – such as the creator, location, or time of creation – is added to the entity, then that becomes part of its identity. Choosing to make that information part of the identity is one way of circumventing the previous consequence – that two entities with the same identifiers are the same entity. Do this only if it is important to the model. Otherwise, keep auditing information outside of the facts themselves.

Related Patterns

An entity that includes the identity of its parent follows the *Ownership* pattern.

While the entity's fact cannot be deleted, the *Delete* pattern simulates the removal of an entity.

Mutable properties are not included within the entity's fact. Instead, they are attached using the *Mutable Property* pattern.

Ownership

Motivation   Represent a strict hierarchy among entities.

It is not uncommon for a model to have a strict hierarchy. In Domain-Driven Design,[1] this structure is referred to as an *aggregate*. In a relational model, this is a special kind of *one-to-many* relationship where each child has only one parent, sometimes with a cascade delete constraint. This kind of strict ownership is often called a *parent-child* relationship.

Identifiers often reflect the strict ownership of an entity. In REST, resource identifiers have a path structure that reveals which ones are contained within others. In file systems, each folder exists strictly within one parent folder. The path to the folder includes the identity of the parent.

In a historical model, it is not strictly necessary to identify one predecessor as the owner of a successor. Yet this is often a relationship that occurs in the problem domain. We will therefore typically represent that special relationship via convention.

The *Ownership* pattern documents a strict parent-child relationship between a successor and one of its predecessors.

Structure

The parent of an entity is represented as a predecessor of its identifying fact, as in Figure 7-1.

---

[1] Eric Evans. Domain-Driven Design: Tackling Complexity in the Heart of Software. Addison-Wesley Longman Publishing Co., Inc. Boston, MA, USA ©2003. ISBN:0321125215.

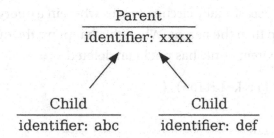

Figure 7-1. *Each child belongs to only one parent*

The parent predecessor is listed first within the child fact's fields. It precedes even the child entity's identifiers. While this convention does not make the parent behave differently than any other predecessor, it is a low-cost way of documenting the desired owner relationship.

```
fact Child {
  parent: Parent
  identifier: type
}
```

The child fact is sometimes given a name that includes the name of the parent fact. This is *not* a strict convention and may be violated when the relationship is obvious or names get too long.

```
fact Owner {
  identifier: type
}

fact OwnerItem {
  owner: Owner
  itemIdentifier: type
}
```

Queries for child entities often start from their parent. Given a parent, the query returns all children.

```
childrenOfParent = (p: Parent) {
  c: Child [
    c→parent = p
  ]
}
```

However, there are occasionally circumstances wherein a query references a child by some other relationship than the parent. When this happens, the query should include the condition that the parent entity has not been deleted.

```
childrenRelatedTo = (r: Relation) {
  c: Child [
    c = r→relatedChild
    ∄ {
      d: ParentDeleted [
        d→parent = c→parent
      ]
    }
  ]
}
```

Example

An order belongs strictly to the company to which it is placed. Each order also has a distinguishing attribute – a GUID – to separate it from other orders for the same company.

```
fact Order {
  company: Company
  orderGuid: guid
}
```

This fact does not use the conventional name CompanyOrder. The owner prefix in this case simply lengthens the name with no real value. It can be assumed that many of the entities in this system are owned by the company.

An order will contain line items. By convention, we give this child fact a composite name, which includes the name of the parent.

```
fact OrderLine {
  order: Order
  createdAt: timestamp
}
```

This fact *does* follow the naming convention, as otherwise it could not be assumed that a Line belongs to an Order. Perhaps the system also models Invoices with their associated InvoiceLines.

Both `Order` and `OrderLine` follow the convention of listing the owner first among the fields, even before identifiers of the child entities.

The `createdAt` time distinguishes among order lines within the same order. Timestamps are not sufficient identifiers on their own, but combined with other identifiers – such as the parent entity in this case – they can be effective. It is expected that order lines will be added by a single user from a single replica and that the number of order lines will be very small.

Also note that `createdAt` is a timestamp captured from the actual creation of the order line. It is the clock time of the workstation that the user was using. This is not the time at which a web server or some other downstream replica learned of the order line. It is the time that the user physically clicked the button in the browser or client app.

The resulting model appears in Figure 7-2.

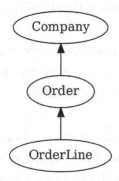

Figure 7-2. *An order line belongs to one order, which in turn belongs to one company*

Consequences

The identity of the parent is part of the identity of the child. Because predecessors are immutable, children cannot be moved to another parent. Ownership is nontransferable.

The parent must exist before the child can be created. Ownership does not apply to a collection of individual entities that are later grouped after they are constructed.

The *Ownership* pattern encourages multi-tenancy. The identity of a root owner tends to become part of the identities of most other entities. To do otherwise opens the possibility of contamination from neighboring replicas under the control of other organizations, especially if they tend to generate overlapping identifiers.

Related Patterns

If ownership needs to be transferred, consider the *Membership* pattern instead.

The *Ownership* pattern is a special case of the *Entity* pattern, where the entity's identifiers include the identity of an owner.

Delete

Motivation   Represent the deletion of an entity.

Historical facts are immutable; they can be neither modified nor destroyed. But deletion is a regular part of business applications. Deletion, therefore, is simulated by the addition of a new fact.

It is a common practice in a relational database to include a `deleted` column on a table. This is a Boolean flag that is set when the row is intended to be removed. All queries include a `WHERE` clause that excludes deleted rows. This is a pattern known as *soft deletion*.

The *Delete* pattern of historical facts, however, is a little different. Setting a flag is a modification. A historical model does not permit modification. Therefore, deletion cannot be simulated by setting a flag. It must be represented as the creation of a new fact. This fact is sometimes called a *tombstone*.

Structure

A deletion fact takes the entity that it deletes as a predecessor. By convention, the name of the deletion fact is `Deletion` appended to the name of the entity.

```
fact Entity {
  owner: Owner
  identifier: type
}

fact EntityDeletion {
  entity: Entity
}
```

Any query for that predecessor must include a not exists (∄) clause that excludes entities that have been deleted. For example, if the preceding entity had an owner, then the query for children would be expressed as follows:

```
entitiesInOwner = (o: Owner) {
  e: Entity [
    e→owner = o
    ∄ {
      ed: EntityDeletion [
        ed→entity = e
      ]
    }
  ]
}
```

Example

In a previous example, order lines were added to an order. If the application allowed a user to remove lines from an order, it would represent those as OrderLineDeletions, as in Figure 7-3.

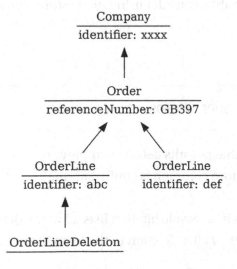

Figure 7-3. *An order line has been deleted from an order*

The query for lines in an order should exclude all deleted lines:

```
linesInOrder = (o: Order) {
  ol: OrderLine [
    ol→order = o
    ∄ {
      old: OrderLineDeletion [
        old→orderLine = ol
      ]
    }
  ]
}
```

Consequences

If the deletion fact has no identifiers to distinguish it from other deletions of the same entity, then the entity can only be deleted once. To allow future restoring of the entity, add a distinguishing identifier. A timestamp will be sufficient in most cases.

Related Patterns

If deletion should be reversible, consider using the *Restore* pattern.

Restore

Motivation   Reverse a prior deletion.

Almost every application that permits deletion employs one of two methods to mitigate accidental deletion. The more common is confirmation. But some will offer a way to restore a deleted entity.

Restoration may begin in a recycle bin that lists all of the deleted entities. Or it may only be available immediately after deletion in the form of an undo.

Structure

A restoration fact references a prior deletion. By convention, it appends the word `Restoration` to the name of the entity. The deletion has an extra identifier, usually a timestamp. The restoration has no extra identifiers.

```
fact Entity {
  identifier: type
}

fact EntityDeletion {
  entity: Entity
  deletedAt: timestamp
}

fact EntityRestoration {
  deletion: EntityDeletion
}
```

Any query for the entity includes a not exists (∄) clause on `Deletions`, which in turn has a not exists on `Restorations`. If the preceding `Entity` had an owner, the query for child entities would appear as follows:

```
entitiesInOwner = (o: Owner) {
  e: Entity [
    e→owner = o
    ∄ {
      ed: EntityDeletion [
        ed→entity = e
        ∄ {
          er: EntityRestore [
            er→deletion = ed
          ]
        }
      ]
    }
  ]
}
```

If the user is offered a recycle bin from which to restore entities, it displays the results of a query where a Deletion exists. Notice that this is exactly the same as the previous query except that the not exists (∄) has been changed to exists (∃) on EntityDeletion.

```
entitiesInRecycleBin = (o: Owner) {
  e: Entity [
    e→owner = o
    ∃ {
      ed: EntityDeletion [
        ed→entity = e
        ∄ {
          er: EntityRestore [
            er→deletion = ed
          ]
        }
      ]
    }
  ]
}
```

The symmetry of these queries makes the deletion and restoration activities atomic. Creating a Deletion both adds the entity to the recycle bin and removes it from the application. Later creating a Restoration both removes the entity from the recycle bin and reintegrates it into the application.

Example

In a previous example, we saw a model that supported deletion of lines from an order. To support restoration of deleted lines back to the order, we would add an OrderLineRestoration fact to the model, as in Figure 7-4.

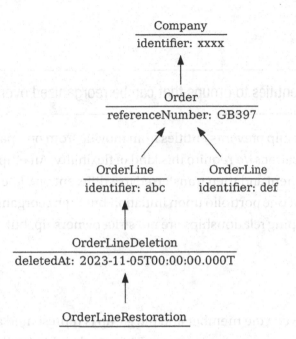

Figure 7-4. *An order line previously deleted from an order has been restored*

In the *Delete* example, the `OrderLineDeletion` did not require any additional identifier. However, to support *Restoration*, `OrderLineDeletion` now has a timestamp field.

Consequences

If the `Deletion` fact does not have an additional identifier – like a timestamp – then the entity can only be deleted and restored once. Thereafter, it would not be possible to delete the entity again. The second deletion would not be distinct from the first, which had been restored. This is almost certainly not the desired behavior. Therefore, the timestamp is effectively a requirement.

Related Patterns

Restore is an extension of the *Delete* pattern.

If the entity can be reconstructed under a new identity with no loss of fidelity, then consider using the simpler *Delete* pattern. This is often preferable when the entity has no mutable properties and does not participate in any sort of workflow. But if properties, workflow, or any other successors are possible, then the *Restore* pattern is more appropriate.

227

Membership

Motivation   Add entities to groups that can be reorganized over time.

Whereas strict ownership prevents entities from moving from one parent to another, some business applications *do* require this kind of flexibility. An employee can be added to one department and then transferred to a different one later in their career. A project may be part of one portfolio upon initiation but then reorganized into a different one later. These grouping relationships are not strict ownership, but a more flexible membership.

Structure

The relationship between the member and the group is represented as a fact having both the member and group as predecessors. The membership fact has an additional identifier – usually a timestamp – that allows a member to be removed and re-added to a group over time.

By convention, the member is listed first among the membership fields, before the group. Both appear before the differentiating identifier.

```
fact Group {
  identifier: type
}

fact Member {
  identifer: type
}

fact Membership {
  member: Member
  group: Group
  createdAt: timestamp
}
```

Whereas with *Ownership*, the parent is a predecessor of the child, in *Membership*, the group and member are not causally related. As Figure 7-5 illustrates, they have a common successor in the membership.

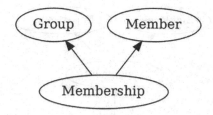

Figure 7-5. *Membership is a successor of both the group and the member*

To find all of the members of a group, query through the membership:

```
membersOfGroup = (g: Group) {
  ms: Membership [
    ms→group = g
    ∄ {
      msd: MembershipDeletion [
        msd→membership = ms
      ]
    }
  ]
  m: Member [
    m = ms→member
  ]
}
```

Example

Employees can be reassigned to different departments over time. Representing the assignment as a distinct fact – rather than a direct predecessor relationship between department and employee – allows the employee to be reassigned without changing their identity. Figure 7-6 depicts this relationship.

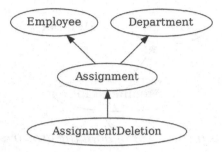

Figure 7-6. *An employee is assigned to a department and subsequently removed*

When querying for employees in a department, be sure to include only assignments that have not been deleted:

```
employeesOfDepartment = (d: Department) {
  a: Assignment [
    a→department = d
    ∄ {
      ad: AssignmentDeletion [
        ad→assignment = a
      ]
    }
  ]
  e: Employee [
    e = a→employee
  ]
}
```

Consequences

The model cannot enforce the business rule that an entity belong to only one group. There is no mechanism that prevents two membership facts from having the same entity predecessor.

Creation and addition to a group are not an atomic process. In the *Ownership* pattern, the parent is created before the entity. In *Membership*, however, membership is created *after* the entity. If the only queries that reach the entity are through membership, then this has little consequence. However, if there is another query that reaches the entity, it may be observable as an *orphan* for an indeterminate period of time. If the application developer wishes to hide orphans, they should add an exists (∃) clause to the query.

For example, if *Employee* defined previously included a *Company* owner predecessor, then the following query would include employees not assigned to a department:

```
allEmployeesOfCompany = (c: Company) {
  e: Employee [
    e→company = c
  ]
}
```

To exclude unassigned employees from the results, the developer adds an exists clause requiring that an Assignment has been made and not subsequently deleted:

```
allAssignedEmployeesOfCompany = (c: Company) {
  e: Employee [
    e→company = c
    ∃ {
      a: Assignment [
        a→employee = e
        ∄ {
          ad: AssignmentDeletion [
            ad→assignment = a
          ]
        }
      ]
    }
  ]
}
```

Related Patterns

If the model requires that the entity be a member of only one group, and that group cannot change, then consider using the *Ownership* pattern instead.

If the model requires that membership in one group be replaced with membership in another group, then consider applying the *Entity Reference* pattern. Represent membership in the group as a reference to the group fact, superseding prior references for the same entity. While this will not prevent concurrent changes, it will at least make removal from one group and addition to another an atomic operation.

Mutable Property

Motivation   Represent values that change.

Historical facts are immutable. They do not change. Yet users expect to be able to change properties. The *Mutable Property* pattern represents changes to properties over time using only immutable facts.

It is desirable in a distributed system for replicas to be able to act in isolation. A user should have the autonomy to change a property without requiring a connection to any other replica. The user might be on a mobile phone that is temporarily disconnected from the server. Or it might simply have a slow network connection, and the latency of performing a connected update would be undesirable.

With capability of autonomous change comes the possibility of conflicts. The disconnected user might change the same property as someone who is connected. Or two users on a slow connection might change the same property at more or less the same time. When each of their changes propagates to the other, the conflict will be detected. The system needs to include the capacity for resolving those conflicts.

Structure

A mutable property is represented as a fact having the entity as a predecessor and the value as a field. To keep track of changes over time, it records prior versions in a predecessor set.

By convention, the name of the fact appends the property name to the entity name. The set of prior versions is conventionally called `prior`. This set is empty for the initial value.

```
fact Entity {
  identifier: type
}

fact EntityProperty {
  entity: Entity
  value: type
  prior: EntityProperty*
}
```

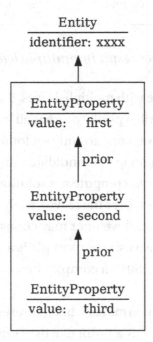

Figure 7-7. *In a chain of versions, each points back to its immediate predecessor*

As a user changes the property, the `prior` set captures only the most recent version. Under ordinary circumstances, this forms a linear chain of property facts, as Figure 7-7 demonstrates.

If two users (or one user on two devices) change a property concurrently, the graph will fork. The result will be a tree like the one in Figure 7-8 with more than one leaf.

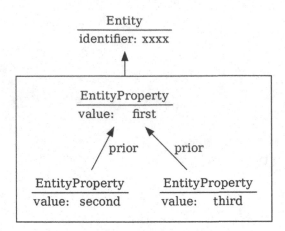

Figure 7-8. *Concurrent changes result in multiple leaves*

When a replica observes a tree with multiple leaves, it recognizes a concurrent change. In this situation, the application will typically present all leaves as candidate values. Each leaf represents a value that was concurrently set for the property and has not been superseded. The user can select among the candidate values and resolve the dispute.

Alternatively, an application can compute a resolution on its own. This is usually accomplished via a simple function over the leaves, such as a maximum. In rare situations, however, the application developer may choose to base the resolution on the nearest common ancestor of all leaves. One example is a source control system like Git that computes a three-way merge. Such a complex function is not appropriate for most applications.

In any case, the application determines what to present, but it *does not generate any new facts*. Facts are only generated as a result of a user's decision. When the user changes a property from a concurrent state, the system includes all of the leaves of the tree in the new fact's `prior` set. This results in a graph like Figure 7-9 that again has a single leaf.

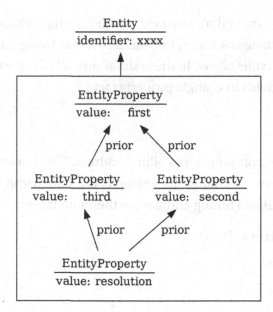

Figure 7-9. *A new fact references all prior concurrent changes and resolves the graph to a single leaf*

To compute the set of leaves, an application runs a query with a not exists (∄) clause looking for a next instance. A next version of the property would refer to the candidate version as prior. This clause excludes all versions for which a next version exists:

```
valuesOfProperty = (e: Entity) {
  p: EntityProperty [
    p→entity = e
    ∄ {
      next: EntityProperty [
        next→prior = p
      ]
    }
  ]
}
```

If the query returns one fact, then that fact represents the most recent version. If it returns many facts, then they represent the leaves and can be used as candidate values.

A property may have more than one field, not just a single `value`. It is not uncommon for multiple values to change as a unit. In Domain-Driven Design, this situation arises when a property uses a *value object*. In these situations, all of the components of the value object appear as fields in a single property fact.

Example

An order in our example company has a billing address. This is a set of fields that change as a unit. It makes no sense to change, for example, the state without also changing the city and street. The fields of a billing address are therefore treated as a single atomic fact.

```
fact OrderBillingAddress {
  order: Order
  street: string
  city: string
  state: string
  zipCode: string
  prior: OrderBillingAddress*
}
```

The current billing address of an order is given by the following query:

```
billingAddressOfOrder = (o: Order) {
  ba: OrderBillingAddress [
    ba→order = o
    ∄ {
      next: OrderBillingAddress [
        next→prior = ba
      ]
    }
  ]
}
```

If the query returns one fact, then that represents the most recent billing address. If, however, it returns multiple billing addresses, then concurrent changes have occurred and the facts represent the candidate billing addresses. The application presents all candidates to the user so that they can research and resolve the issue.

An order will also include a shipping address. This is represented as a separate fact from the billing address, even though it has mostly the same fields.

```
fact OrderShippingAddress {
  order: Order
  street: string
  city: string
  state: string
  zipCode: string
  prior: OrderShippingAddress*
}
```

A similar query gets the latest shipping address. While it is unusual to change only one part of an address at any given time, it is not uncommon to change only the shipping address or only the billing address. That is why the application developer chose to make them separate facts.

While concurrent changes to billing address will result in multiple leaves, concurrent changes between billing address on one side and shipping address on the other will not. The system will simply present the most recent billing address beside the most recent shipping address. This reflects the intent of the application developer, as expressed by the decision that shipping and billing address have no causal relationship between them.

Consequences

Applications observing the *Mutable Property* pattern can act autonomously. They can record a new value for a property without first connecting with any other replica to prevent concurrent changes.

Said another way, concurrent changes *cannot be prevented*. There is no mechanism within a historical model that would ensure that only one change can be made at any given time. Properties can neither be locked nor serialized.

Replicas will recognize that concurrent changes have occurred *post facto*. All replicas will eventually receive the same graph, compute the same leaves, and therefore come to the same conclusion. Concurrent changes do not result in conflict.

When a user attempts to modify a property, the application should first verify whether the value has actually been changed. The application might, for example, display a dialog box with "OK" and "Cancel" buttons. The user might click "OK" even if they made no change. If the application created a new fact without checking whether the value had changed, it would create an unnecessarily complicated history. Instead, it should perform a check like the following:

```
let leaves = query(valuesOfProperty, entity);

// Display the dialog box and get the user's input.

let value = input.text;
if (leaves.length != 1 || leaves[0].value != value) {
  createFact(new EntityProperty(entity, value, leaves));
}
```

The mutable property fact should not contain any auditing information. This allows two different users to change a property to the same value without introducing a concurrent update. If the fact contained, for example, the user or timestamp, then two concurrent changes in which the users each changed the property to the same value would appear as distinct facts. The result would be an unnecessary merge between similar changes.

The response to multiple leaves must be based only on the information in the facts themselves. It must not be based, for example, on the order in which the facts arrived at the replica. The result is a function that is commutative and deterministic; it computes the same result at every replica regardless of message order. That is why the results of queries are unordered *sets* and not ordered *lists*.

If an application computes a resolution to a concurrent change, it must do so only on read. It must not attempt to create a new fact to resolve the concurrent changes. To do so would be to introduce the possibility of a never-ending storm of concurrent resolutions. Consensus algorithms such as Paxos are carefully constructed to avoid these resolution storms, but without such careful consideration, storms can easily arise. At any rate, strong eventual consistency demands convergence without consensus. This is achievable if all replicas run the same deterministic function on read.

The *Mutable Property* pattern cannot guarantee that a property has a single value. The query will always result in a set. Applications must be written to expect that that set might have multiple values. While it is sometimes tempting to introduce a location-specific rule to prevent concurrent updates – only one user is allowed to change a property, or only one replica can be used to make that change – such rules are ultimately difficult to enforce and impose undesirable constraints on the system.

A query for the current value of a property could return an empty set. This represents the situation in which the property has not been initialized. On remote replicas, this could also indicate that the entity has been transmitted, but its initial properties have not yet arrived. Creation of an entity is not atomic with initialization of its properties. If an application developer intends to present only entities that have been initialized, they could add an exists clause based on the property fact.

Related Patterns

If the mutable property represents a relationship with another entity, the pattern becomes an *Entity Reference*.

Entity Reference

Motivation   Represent a mutable relationship between entities.

Where *Ownership* and *Membership* are strict grouping constructs, some relationships between entities are simple references. These references don't imply any kind of belonging or grouping, but rather just an association.

An entity reference is a property that points to another entity. In Domain-Driven Design, the referenced entity is typically an *aggregate root*, possibly in a different *bounded context*. In an object-oriented language, the entity reference is a pointer to another object. And in a relational database, it's a foreign key. The reference is typically mutable and often will be initialized to NULL.

A relational database will use foreign keys to represent *Ownership*, *Membership*, and *Entity Reference*. To distinguish among them, first, look to the cardinality. A many-to-many relationship typically denotes *Membership*. A one-to-many relationship that has a cascade delete constraint represents *Ownership*. A less constrained one-to-many relationship – especially one that allows NULL – is probably an *Entity Reference*.

Structure

The structure of an entity reference looks very similar to a *Mutable Property*. It is a fact having the primary entity and referenced entity as predecessors. The referenced entity is often nullable. Just as a mutable property does, the fact keeps the set of prior versions of the entity reference.

```
fact EntityReference {
  entity: Entity
  referencedEntity: ReferencedEntity?
  prior: EntityReference*
}
```

The distinction between the primary and referenced entity is an important one. The primary entity is the one with the reference property. Creating a new EntityReference fact changes the value of that property for the primary entity. The prior set will include other EntityReference facts that refer to the same primary entity.

Querying for the current value of an entity reference begins with the primary entity. Like a property query in the *Mutable Property* pattern, it matches references that have not been superseded. The query includes one additional clause that follows the entity reference.

```
referencedEntity = (e: Entity) {
  er: EntityReference {
    er→entity = e
    ∄ {
      next: EntityReference [
        next→prior = er
      ]
    }
  }
  re: ReferencedEntity [
    re = er→referencedEntity
  ]
}
```

Unlike *Mutable Properties*, entity references permit queries in the opposite direction. To query from a referenced entity back to all entities that reference it, include the not exists (∄) clause on next. This prevents the query from returning entities with references that have been superseded.

```
entitiesReferencing = (re: ReferencedEntity) {
  er: EntityReference [
    er→referencedEntity = re
    ∄ {
      next: EntityReference [
        next→prior = er
      ]
    }
  ]
  e: Entity [
    e = er→entity
  ]
}
```

Example

An order line references the product that was purchased. This relationship is optional: some order lines represent fees, discounts, or services not listed in the catalog. The OrderLine therefore has a reference to the Product entity.

```
fact OrderLineProduct {
  orderLine: OrderLine
  product: Product?
  prior: OrderLineProduct*
}
```

This creates the relationship demonstrated in Figure 7-10.

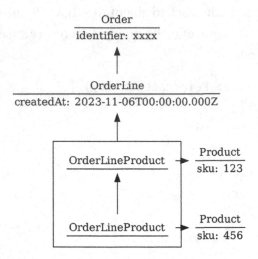

Figure 7-10. *Two versions of an order line, each referencing a different product*

A query for the product referenced by an order line begins like any other mutable property query. But then it contains an extra clause to get the referenced Product.

```
productForOrderLine = (ol: OrderLine) {
  olp: OrderLineProduct [
    olp→orderLine = ol
    ∄ {
      next: OrderLineProduct [
        next→prior = olp
      ]
    }
  ]
  p: Product [
    p = olp→product
  ]
}
```

Traversing the graph from the opposite direction, we can query for orders that purchase a given product. This query includes the same not exists clause.

```
ordersContainingProduct = (p: Product) {
  olp: OrderLineProduct [
    olp→product = p
    ∄ {
      next: OrderLineProduct [
        next→prior = olp
      ]
    }
  ]
  o: Order [
    o = olp→orderLine→order
  ]
}
```

This similarity between the two queries makes them behave atomically. When an order line is changed to reference a different product, both of the queries are affected. The first query will no longer return the previously referenced product, and the second query will no longer return the order.

Consequences

Just as with the *Mutable Property* pattern, an *Entity Reference* cannot guarantee that only one entity is referenced. The query for the current reference returns a set. An application must respond appropriately to a set larger than 1. This represents a concurrent update of entity references.

The results of the query could also be the empty set. This could occur – just as in *Mutable Property* – when the reference has not yet been initialized. But it could also occur when the reference has been set to NULL.

Related Patterns

This is a variant of the *Mutable Property* pattern in which the value of the property is a reference to another entity.

This is sometimes used as an alternative to the *Membership* pattern to indicate that an entity should be a member of only one group. While it cannot enforce that rule, it at least makes the transfer from one group to another an atomic operation.

Entity List

Motivation   Display a list of entities to the user.

In almost any application, the user will need to see a list of entities. The list will show a name, title, or other representative property of the entity. The user may select one of the entities to interact with it in some way.

Structure

This pattern combines the *Owner, Entity, Delete, Restore*, and *Mutable Property* patterns. Together, they allow users to add, remove, and modify elements of a collection.

To display the list, the application runs a query. The specification for that query includes a projection. One of the properties of that projection is a sub-specification that selects all current values of the mutable property:

```
entitiesInOwner = (o: Owner) {
  e: Entity [
    e→owner = o
    ∄ {
      ed: EntityDeletion [
        ed→entity = e
        ∄ {
          er: EntityRestore [
            er→deletion = ed
          ]
        }
      ]
    }
  }
```

```
    ]
} ⇒ {
  titles: {
    p: EntityProperty [
      p→entity = e
      ∄ {
        next: EntityProperty [
          next→prior = p
        ]
      }
    ]
  } ⇒ p.value
}
```

Example

A company's customer relationship manager system displays a list of customers. The list shows the customers' names. The data backing this list will include customers who have been deleted, restored, and will have undergone name changes. An example appears in Figure 7-11.

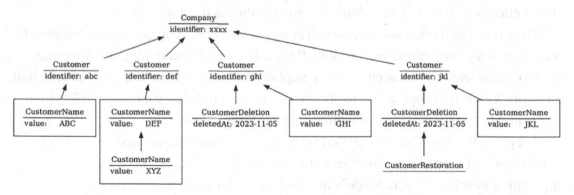

Figure 7-11. *Customers of a company in varying stages of change*

The application will run a query based on a specification that removes deleted customers. It ignores deletions that have subsequently been restored. It then projects the current name of each of those customers. As a result, the application displays a list that contains (in some order) the following:

- ABC

- XYZ

- JKL

Consequences

The results of any specification are an unordered set. For most patterns, this is usually not an issue, as the members of the set are not causally related to one another. However, when an application displays an entity list, the user expects some consistent order. They will get confused if the order changes while they are using the application, or while they move from one device to another.

An application should therefore sort the set before displaying a list to the user. If it sorts by a field of the entity fact, such as an identifier or creation date, then the order of the list will never change. If instead it sorts by a mutable property in the projection, then the order will adjust based on user interactions. It is often desirable, for example, to sort alphabetically by the same mutable property that the list displays.

The projected titles of each entity will also be sets. There is no guarantee that the title set will contain only one value per entity. If the title set contains more than one value, then a concurrent edit has occurred. The application must choose what to display in that scenario. A common approach is to choose one of the candidate values according to a deterministic function, such as the minimum value alphabetically.

A replica may learn about a new entity before it learns about the first version of its mutable property. In that circumstance, the projected set of titles will be empty. An application may either choose a default visualization for such untitled entities or might add an exists ($\exists$) clause to include only entities for which a title exists.

Related Patterns

An entity list is a combination of the *Owner, Entity, Delete, Restore,* and *Mutable Property* patterns.

Application Patterns

To put entities into context, we must consider the scope of the entire application. As shown in the previous section, many entities have owners. Those owners are themselves entities. That chain of ownership must stop at some point. The structure at the topmost layers of a model depends heavily upon the purpose of the application.

In traditional application design, it is permissible for an application to query across an entire database. A contact management system can execute a query with no WHERE clause to display all contact rows. In a historical model, however, this is not permitted. Every specification must have a starting point.

Application patterns help us determine how to structure the topmost layer of facts. They suggest ways to display the initial results for landing pages and home screens, where the user has yet to make their first selection, and thereby define a clear starting point. These patterns determine the starting points for the specifications of initial screens, based on how the application is designed to be used.

Personal Collection

Motivation   Each user manages their own collections of entities.

The simplest application pattern is a model in which each user has their own private set of information. They store their data on their own devices. These devices may be connected through replicators so that a user can move from one device to another. But their data remains private.

Structure

Each user has a fact that represents them within the model. This fact has a public key. The user maintains the private key outside of the model, typically in a keystore.

The user fact owns a set of entities, either directly or indirectly. Direct ownership is appropriate when the number of entities for a user is intended to be small. For example, the application might manage the books that the user has written. Unless the user is exceptionally prolific, the size of this set will remain manageable.

More often, however, entity ownership will be indirect to give the user more control over organization. The model includes an intermediate fact between the user and the entity. Let's generalize and call that fact a collection. The user fact owns a set of collections, and those collections own entities. Each collection is uniquely identified, either with a GUID or a timestamp. Users manage their set of collections, giving them names to differentiate them. Entities belong to collections.

```
fact User {
  publicKey: key
}

fact Collection {
  owner: User
  identifier: type
}

fact CollectionName {
  collection: Collection
  value: string
  prior: CollectionName*
}

fact Entity {
  collection: Collection
  identifier: type
}
```

Example

In a personal task manager, each user manages lists of tasks. A task list is a collection. Each task is an entity. The resulting model appears in Figure 7-12.

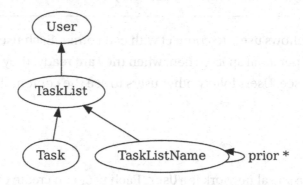

Figure 7-12. *A user has lists of tasks*

The first screen that a user sees in this application (after authenticating) is a list of their task lists. That list is generated with a specification that starts at the user fact. The act of authentication provides that initial fact.

Consequences

Collection names are not guaranteed to be unique. It is up to the user to name collections in a way that avoids confusion. A name collision is only a problem for the user. The application will still be able to distinguish the collections by their unique identifiers. The user will be able to change the name of one of the collections again to resolve the ambiguity.

A collection belongs to a single user. That user remains part of the identity of the collection. If the application developer wants to support collaboration, they can use the *Shared Project* pattern, described later in this chapter.

Related Patterns

The *Personal Collection* pattern is a specialization of the *Ownership* pattern. Collections are owned by users, and entities are owned by collections.

This pattern can be extended using the *Social Network* pattern. In such a model, users can publish their collections for other users to see.

Social Network

Motivation   Connect with content produced by other users.

A social application allows users to connect with each other. Each user can create content in their own personal space. Then, when they are ready, they can publish that content for others to see. Users follow other users to see the content that they have published.

Structure

The top-level fact of a social network is a User. Each user can create collections to organize their content. Each collection has a name and a set of content entities.

A user can then publish their content by creating a Publication fact. Other users can follow a user by creating a Follow fact. The relationships among these types of facts appear in Figure 7-13.

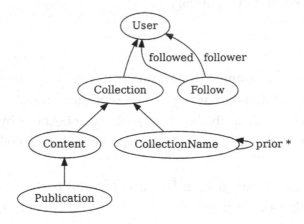

Figure 7-13.   *A user publishes content while other users follow them*

Based on the desired features, the application may choose to allow users to follow collections rather than other users. It may also permit further interaction with content, such as liking or commenting.

Example

A social network for sharing recipes allows users to follow each other. Users can create recipe books. They then publish recipes to make them available to others. The model appears in Figure 7-14.

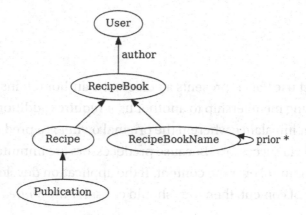

Figure 7-14. *A user manages recipe books and publishes recipes*

Other users can interact by uploading photos of their dishes. The original author can then approve those photos to be displayed alongside the recipe.

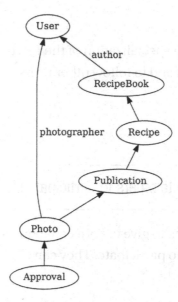

Figure 7-15. *A user uploads photos of their dishes, and the author approves them*

251

Security rules are used to control who can see what content. Create several distribution rules to define the layers of access. For example, one rule allows a user to see their own recipes. Another rule allows a user to see recipes that have been published by users that they follow. A third rule allows users to see photos that they themselves have uploaded. And a fourth rule allows users to see photos that have been uploaded to their own recipes.

Consequences

Because the topmost user fact represents a person, the author retains ownership of their content. Granting membership to another user requires additional successor facts. This would create an imbalance wherein the original owner is a predecessor, while new members are added via successors. Because predecessors are immutable, the original owner would retain control over the content. If the application developer wishes to support the transfer of content, then they should consider the *Shared Project* pattern instead.

The fact graph is not well suited to finding new content creators to follow. To make content searchable, the application should project published content into a search index.

Related Patterns

The *Social Network* pattern is a specialization of the *Personal Collection* pattern. It adds the abilities to publish content and to follow other users.

Shared Project

Motivation   A user can invite others to participate in their space.

Some applications are designed to give users a collaborative space. One user sets up the space and then invites others to participate. They can control the level of participation, including the ability to invite others.

Structure

As with the prior patterns, the top-level fact of a shared project is a `User`. But unlike the prior patterns, the user does not represent a person. Instead, it is a single-use principal created only for this project. This avoids the imbalance of having one user own the project while others are invited as members.

Membership is controlled by a `ProjectMembership` fact. This fact has a `User` and a `Project` predecessor. The relationship of project membership appears in Figure 7-16.

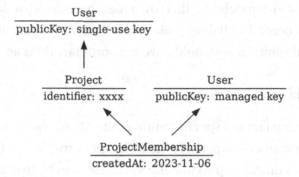

Figure 7-16. *A user creates a project and invites themselves as a member*

A new key pair is generated on the device. The public key is stored in this single-use user fact. The private key is used to create the project and the first invitation, wherein the user invites themselves. Then the private key is discarded.

The application defines different types of project membership facts to represent different levels of access. For example, an application might define `ProjectAdmin`, `ProjectContributor`, and `ProjectViewer` facts. These fact types appear in different authorization and distribution rules.

Consequences

If the application discards the private key after creating the project and the first membership, then the user enjoys no special privileges. They are a member of the project just like any other. That membership can be revoked.

Users of the application must trust that the application does not retain the private key. If the application does retain the private key, then more members can be added later. The model offers no guarantee that only one membership can be added with the single-use key.

If instead of a single-use key, the application evolves the shared project pattern to use a managed key, then the user retains ownership of the project. Their access cannot be revoked.

To prevent users from accidentally locking out all administrators, the application should prevent the user from deleting their own membership. This does not guarantee that a lockout cannot occur, but it does make it less likely. To delete all administrator memberships, two administrators would have to coordinate their actions.

Related Patterns

The project membership fact is a specialization of the *Membership* pattern.

To revoke project membership, apply the *Delete* pattern. Ensure that the project membership fact has a timestamp so that the same user can be invited again later.

Enterprise Domain

Motivation   Control access to all data in an enterprise.

Enterprise applications are typically custom built for a specific organization. When built using traditional tools like relational databases, it is not uncommon for an application to query across the entire database. Historical models, however, resist these kinds of queries. They require that every query has a starting point.

As a result, historical models encourage a multi-tenant approach to application design. An enterprise can take advantage of this approach by mapping tenants to environments.

Structure

The topmost fact in the enterprise domain model is a single-use user fact, similar to the *Shared Project* pattern. This single-use user is the owner for an environment. When setting up a new environment, an administrator creates this user. They then use it to create the environment and invite themselves as an administrator. The administrator then discards the private key for this user.

When deploying the application, the administrator configures the web app or mobile client with the public key for the single-use user. Then the client application can use this information to create the correct `Environment` fact.

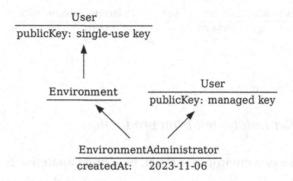

Figure 7-17. *An administrator creates a single-use user to set up a new environment*

Example

An online retailer creates an enterprise application to sell their products. An administrator creates a test environment to support the development of the application. They create a single-use user and use it to create the environment. They then invite themselves as an administrator.

During testing, the team creates catalogs and products. Once they are ready to deploy to production, the administrator creates a new environment. The production environment does not contain any of the test data. The environments are illustrated in Figure 7-18.

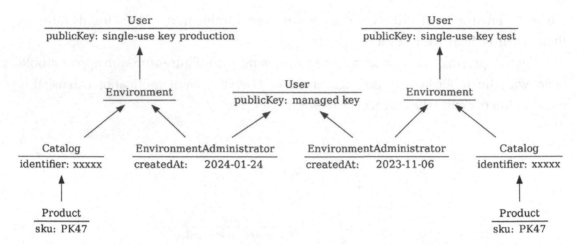

Figure 7-18. *A retailer isolates test from production*

It is likely that these two environments will be using isolated sets of replicators. Nevertheless, separating the environments helps to ensure that the test data does not leak into production.

Consequences

The environment is the penultimate owner in the enterprise domain model. All of the business entities roll up to the environment. By carefully crafting security rules, the enterprise can grant permission at the environment level.

Since the enterprise domain pattern sets up multi-tenancy within a single model, it is possible to host multiple tenants on the same infrastructure. This makes it possible to test applications on production hardware. A development team may choose to implement feature toggles at the environment level. After deploying new code, but before enabling the feature for the production tenant, they can test new features in situ.

Related Patterns

This pattern uses the same technique as the *Shared Project* pattern to create a single-use user. This technique allows administrators to be added and removed without permanently associating an environment with its creator.

Designing from Constraints

The patterns presented here are a starting point for building applications using only immutable historical facts. They emulate – as closely as they can – the behaviors that people have come to expect from business applications. And they do so using only the capabilities of immutable distributed data.

Where these patterns diverge from expected behavior, they reveal constraints about the medium in which they are rendered. A *Mutable Property* cannot have a single value. And we cannot enforce that an entity have *Membership* in only one group. Those truths reveal that the application is distributed across several replicas, each of which has autonomy to capture concurrent changes.

We cannot give the users of our applications exactly what they have come to expect from centralized systems. The rules of immutable architecture prohibit it. The reason is simple; those promises *cannot* be kept in a strong eventually consistent manner. Architectures that nonetheless provide these behaviors must compromise some aspect of their distributed nature in order to do so.

An application built according to these patterns acknowledges the constraints imposed by distributed replicas. It starts from those constraints and builds toward expected behavior, never promising more than what can be reasonably delivered.

These patterns are more than guidance on how to build a distributed application; they are a means of communication. They make it possible for application designers to talk to stakeholders about constraints without first teaching them about strong eventual consistency and the CAP Theorem. They permit us to speak in generalities without reasoning through specific scenarios in which distributed replicas might cause us problems. They frame a conversation about application design that helps all participants set expectations and keep them.

CHAPTER 8

State Transitions

Among the most powerful tools available to a software developer is the finite state machine. This mechanism – sometimes illustrated as a state transition diagram – describes a multistep process. The machine moves from one state to the next as it encounters input. Each unit of input determines which arc of the graph the state machine follows. That arc decides how the input is processed and what state the machine finds itself in to receive the next unit.

This tool is a natural choice for solving problems such as parsing computer languages and input files. The specification for the JSON data interchange format,[1] for example, is described in terms of state machines. The language is broken down into discrete structures, each defined by a state transition diagram. When the parser expects to see a particular structure, it enters into the states depicted in the graph. For example, the diagram for parsing an object can be drawn as Figure 8-1.

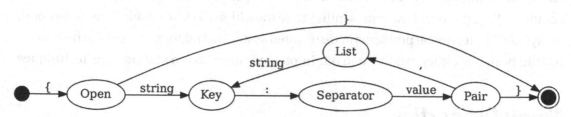

Figure 8-1. *State machine for parsing a JSON object, as described in ECMA-404*

The diagram as it appears in the specification is drawn a bit differently, but here we name each of the states and label the edges with the input that causes that transition. This is a common way of drawing state transition diagrams. A machine's state is mutable: it changes as the machine consumes input.

---

[1] The JSON Data Interchange Syntax. Standard ECMA-404. ECMA International. Second Edition, December 2017.

© Michael L. Perry 2024
M. L. Perry, *The Art of Immutable Architecture*, https://doi.org/10.1007/979-8-8688-0288-1_8

Given the expressive power of state machines, it is no surprise that many people have applied them to distributed systems. Chris Patterson, creator of the distributed systems framework MassTransit, recommends using state machines for managing sagas.[2] Jonathan Oliver, industry-recognized expert on distributed systems, observes that "Process is best implemented using a state machine."[3] These and other leaders in this space have demonstrated how to use state machines to manage business processes, break up long-running transactions, and protect against message duplication and ordering.

My experience, however, has shown that state machines are a poor choice for both understanding and implementing business processes in a distributed system. State machines are good for implementing parsers, but not distributed business processes. All of the input to a parser comes from a single source: a block of memory or a character stream. Input to a business process, on the other hand, arrives from many sources. It often represents business decisions made by different people with different views of the system. Parsing happens all in one place, so knowing the state of the parser is easy. But business processes happen in many locations simultaneously, making it difficult to know the single state of the system.

Let's explore some of the challenges that you can expect to face while applying state machines to distributed systems. We will first try to solve those problems using the tools readily at hand. But eventually we will find that the problem directs us toward a different solution. We'll discover how representing state transitions as immutable facts solves both analytical and technical problems in distributed systems. And then we will see how to rebuild both our understanding and our implementation on top of those new techniques.

Many Properties

When working on a supply chain management system, I ran into the first of the problems with state transition at scale. We were using an enterprise resource planning (ERP) solution to build the application. Like many ERP systems, the one we were using was extremely customizable. It allowed application developers to define their own entities, properties, and operations. It also allowed them to define a state machine.

---

[2] Chis Patterson, State Machine for Managing Sagas. Los Techies. 2009. https://lostechies.com/chrispatterson/2009/01/17/state-machine-for-managing-sagas/

[3] Sagas with Event Sourcing. https://blog.jonathanoliver.com/cqrs-sagas-with-event-sourcing-part-i-of-ii/

Within the ERP system, a developer would identify the states that an entity would transition through as it progressed along a business process. They would define which state transitions were permitted and which were forbidden. Each transition was an arrow between two states and represented a step in the process. Developers would attach actions to those steps in order to customize the process.

For simple state machines, this model was manageable. But as the system became more complex, we found ourselves multiplying new features by the number of existing states. It became apparent to us that the state of an entity represented more than one property. Sometimes those properties interacted, and other times they did not.

Shipping and Billing

To demonstrate the problem, let's examine a somewhat simpler example. Suppose we have built a system that accepts orders for products in a warehouse. Once the order is placed, the shipping department picks the product and ships it to the customer. Meanwhile, the billing department invoices the customer and receives payment. We want to allow these two operations to happen independently. Since we are using an ERP system that defines a state machine per entity, we design a graph of states that combines the two ideas, like the one in Figure 8-2.

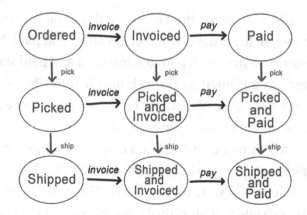

Figure 8-2. *States of an order: billing moves to the left, and shipping moves down*

This state machine allows shipping and billing to operate orthogonally. As the shipping department picks and ships orders, the state moves down the page. And as the billing department invoices and receives payment, the state moves across. Eventually, like a cab driver making their way through Manhattan, the state reaches the lower right.

Introducing Back-Orders

After the system has been in operation for a while, the company realizes that they are turning away business when they run out of stock. To remedy this situation, they expand their operations to include back-orders. When a product is out of stock, rather than picking it, the shipping department orders it from their supplier. They can either receive it themselves and then ship it to the customer or can ask the supplier to drop-ship it directly to its destination. The modified state transition diagram appears in Figure 8-3.

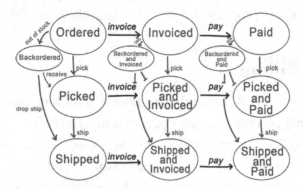

Figure 8-3. *Out-of-stock products are back-ordered. Back-ordering does not interact with billing*

Adding the back-order feature required us to add three states to the diagram. While the product is back-ordered, the order can still be invoiced and paid. We therefore need to combine the back-ordered state with both the invoiced and paid states. Because this new feature has no interaction with the existing billing feature, the new transitions have exactly the same actions associated with them. There is no difference between drop-shipping an order before or after it has been paid.

As we add features to this model, we will find that we multiply the number of new states by the number of existing states in independent features. There were three states in the billing process, so one new state became three. The more independent processes are at work within a single state machine, the larger this combinatorial explosion becomes.

Cancellations and Returns

After a bit more time, the company decides that it is not properly accounting for cancellations and returns. A cancellation occurs before the order is shipped and may involve a refund. A return, on the other hand, occurs after the order has shipped and requires restocking. The new state transition diagram is in Figure 8-4.

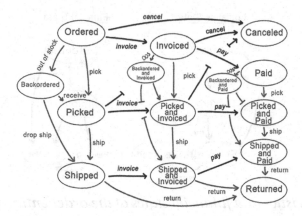

Figure 8-4. *Cancellations happen before shipping; returns happen afterward*

A cancellation is handled almost entirely by the billing department. Because the product has not yet been shipped, there is little work for the shipping department to do. They simply have to recognize that an order has transitioned and that the ship operation is no longer allowed. There is no arrow from the Canceled state labeled ship.

A return, on the other hand, is handled by the shipping department. The item has already been shipped, and so they need to restock it upon receipt. Only the transition from Shipped and Paid to Returned involves the billing department. In that situation, they must issue a refund.

When adding features that interact with existing states, we can often avoid a combinatorial explosion. However, we pay the price in terms of complexity. We must now examine every existing state to determine the correct course of action should that new operation occur at that time. Some of those transitions will require compensating actions, while others will not.

Parallel State Machines

An application developer faced with this issue might reach for the nearest solution at hand. This solution is not the best, but it is the most readily available. With a small refactoring, a single co-mingled state can be broken into two or more parallel states. In this particular example, the simple fix for the problem is shown in Figure 8-5.

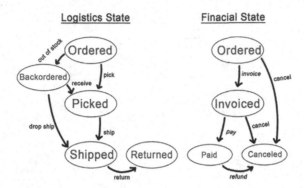

Figure 8-5. *The logistics and financial states of the order entity are separated*

Instead of a single state, the order entity has two. The logistics state keeps track of the process as seen by the shipping department. The financial state captures the process of the billing department. Insofar as those processes can progress independently, these two state machines run in parallel.

When those processes interact, however, an operation needs to be sensitive to both states at the same time. If an order is returned, we expect the logistics state to start from Shipped. The operation will transition it to Returned. However, it must also consider whether the financial state is Paid. If so, it must issue a refund. In any case, it must move the financial state to Canceled so that the customer is not charged.

Parallel state machines relieve the combinatorial explosion that occurs when one state models independent processes. They also make the complexity a little easier to express, because edge cases don't need to be considered for every distinct combination. They are near to hand for an application developer using mutation to build a system. But they are not the ideal solution; they still leave several problems unsolved. One of those problems has to do with aggregates – entities with many children.

Many Children

After solving the problem of an entity having many properties, we are still left with the problem of an entity having many children. On the one hand, each child might individually have its own state. But, on the other, the state of the parent might depend upon the state of the children. This leads to an interaction among state machines even as they are created and destroyed dynamically.

The parent state machine tracks an overall process. At a certain point, the process branches. Each child entity must individually progress through a child process in parallel. Only after all children have finished do we allow the parent to proceed. After the main process has advanced, adding a child might arrest progress and move the parent state backward. Deleting that child should again push the parent state forward.

Describing all of these interactions as state transitions becomes incrementally more tricky, as each new scenario spins a growing web of edge cases. Our first inclination is to create a mechanical solution: "When in this state and this happens, do that and move to that state." Such logic quickly becomes difficult to reason through. The web of edge cases becomes a hiding place for defects. We cut this Gordian Knot by representing state not as a mechanical set of transitions, but as a declarative function.

Software Issue Tracking

One of my clients uses a popular issue tracking solution for managing bug fixes, features, user stories, and other changes to their software. Like an ERP system, this program lets users customize their workflow by defining states and transitions. By default, a bug might start in Triage, transition through In Progress and In Test, and finally end up in Done. My client, however, has modified this workflow. They are required to ensure that all changes have been reviewed for regulatory compliance. They have therefore inserted Awaiting Review before the change is In Test. The modified state transition diagram of a defect appears in Figure 8-6.

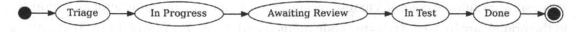

Figure 8-6. *The state transition diagram for a software defect, modified to ensure changes are reviewed*

Features go through a similar workflow. Every software change is motivated by a feature or a bug fix. Because of this, my client can be confident that every change that makes it to production has gone through the review step. This solves the problem that was originally before them: ensuring compliance. However, it creates others.

Every software change is a commit in the version control system. It may take several commits to fix a bug. It is common for developers to separate refactoring changes from fixing changes to make the intent more clear. And yet, the entire bug is reviewed as a single unit. Because this state transition diagram is implemented in a commercial issue tracking tool, my client is constrained in how they can break down the entities. The tool does not allow them to represent the state of a commit as it relates to an issue. And so, they capture the review at the Bug entity and not the Commit entity.

Child State

To solve this problem without modifying the issue tracking system, my client employs other third-party tools. One of them is a change review system that allows developers to comment on individual lines of each commit. Within this tool, developers and reviewers have a conversation over the code to discuss motivation, recommendations, and possible corrections. At the end of this process, the reviewer changes the state of the commit. The state transition diagram applied at the commit level appears in Figure 8-7.

Figure 8-7. *The state transition diagram of a commit, as implemented in a separate tool*

Combining these two tools requires discipline. A developer moves the issue tracking tool to Awaiting Review and then invites reviewers to join the conversation in the change review system. Reviewers move the commits through their individual workflows, requesting additional commits to resolve any issues that come up. Only after all commits in the branch are in Accepted is the code merged and the defect moved to In Test.

Composite State Transition Diagrams

Assuming that we could combine these two tools to suit our needs, a developer might choose to merge the two state transition diagrams. A bug would move through the parent state machine, and each commit would move through the child state machine. The composite state transition diagram appears in Figure 8-8.

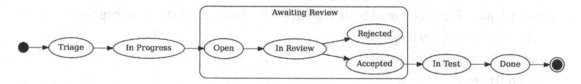

Figure 8-8. *A composite state transition diagram allows the parent to progress only after all children have reached a terminal state*

To implement this diagram mechanically, we need to consider how the state of the parent interacts with the state of the children. If the parent is `Awaiting Review` and a child becomes `Accepted`, check whether all other children are also `Accepted`; if so, transition the parent to `In Test`. If a `Rejected` child is removed from the branch, see if it was the last one; if all others are `Accepted`, move the parent forward. And if a parent is `In Test` or `Done` and a new child is added, move the parent back to `Awaiting Review`.

Does that mechanism account for all possible scenarios? It is difficult to tell. The burden of proof is on the developer implementing the solution. Verifying all of those edge cases is up to the tester. And as we add more states, the number of edge cases grows.

A Declarative Function of States

Rather than a mechanical solution, we can define a declarative one. Declarative solutions lend themselves to proof much more easily than mechanical solutions. It is easy to look at a declarative statement and see whether all possible conditions are listed. The function computes the overall workflow based on the states of the individual components.

We can describe the workflow of a bug as a function of the parent and child states. For this, we will invoke a *universal quantifier*. That's just a fancy phrase meaning "for all." The parent states `Triage` and `In Progress` map directly to the workflow. But the difference between `Awaiting Review` and `In Test` depends upon the child states. A bug is in test if, *for all commits in the branch*, the commit is in `Accepted`. Otherwise, it is awaiting review.

This logic can be written declaratively as in the following pseudo code:

```
workflow (bug) =
  if bug.state = Triage
    then Triage
  else if bug.state = InProgress
    then InProgress
  else if not for all commit in bug.branch, commit.state = Accepted
    then AwaitingReview
  else if bug.state = InTest
    then InTest
  else Done
```

The check for all commits being `Accepted` stops the workflow from progressing beyond `Awaiting Review`. It doesn't matter if the parent state has moved on; any child that is not completed will hold the workflow back. This declarative description means that we don't have to write a machine that handles every edge case. If a new commit is added while the bug is in test, the universal quantifier causes this Boolean expression to return to awaiting review. And if a commit is removed from the branch, the universal quantifier reevaluates and allows the workflow to progress. Without a declarative expression, a developer would have to code for those edge cases and prove that all possible scenarios have been explored.

The declarative function finds the edge cases caused by interactions between parent and child states. Writing the function in terms of states is a short step from managing state transitions through mutation. However, it still is not the ideal solution. Now that we have a couple of examples at our disposal and have explored a few candidate solutions, we can now dive into the more difficult issue of conditional validation. This will finally lead us to abandon solutions based on mutability.

Conditional Validation

As entities move through a process, they don't just change state. They also accumulate data. As we transition an entity from one state to the next, we will want to record that new data. We ideally perform both operations within a single transaction so that the presence of data is consistent with the current state.

Depending upon the state of the entity, data fields might be null, or they might require a value. The validation of the data fields is conditional upon the state of the entity. The type systems of our database and programming language tools typically do not capture such conditional validation. So we find ourselves weakening the declared types in order to compensate.

We've examined two examples: order fulfillment and software change tracking. In each of these examples, we found solutions to state transition issues as they arose. But we haven't analyzed the other fields of the entities. Let's take a look at those fields and see if we have any conditional validation.

Nullability Based on State

In the order fulfillment example, we want to record information about the order and each item that it contains. For the order, we record the customer, shipping address, and billing address. For each item, we capture the SKU, current price, and quantity. When we ship the item, we will also want to include the tracking number. Where does this belong?

At first, it might seem that the tracking number should be part of the order, as shown in Figure 8-9. When the order is placed, we don't yet have a tracking number, so we allow this field to be null. It is only filled in when the order is shipped. And so a shipped order will have a non-null tracking number. Setting the state to Shipped and filling in the tracking number would happen in a single transaction.

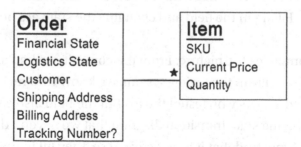

Figure 8-9. Tracking number is a nullable field in order, which also holds logistics state

But perhaps the logistics state should be part of the item, as in Figure 8-10. Each item can be back-ordered, picked, shipped, and returned individually. If so, it makes sense to put the tracking number on the item instead of the order. Again, when an item is added to an order, it doesn't have a tracking number. And so this field is null until the item is shipped.

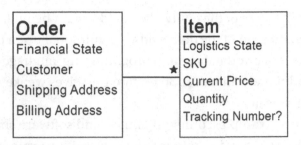

Figure 8-10. *Tracking number is a nullable field in item, where we have moved logistics state*

Whether we put the tracking number on the order or on the item, we face conditional validation. The tracking number must be null if the logistics state is Ordered, Backordered, or Picked. It must not be null if the logistics state is Shipped or Returned. Once we have passed a certain point in the workflow, the tracking number is expected to be present. Validation of this field is conditional upon the state of the entity.

Cycles in State Transition

Let's look at another customization that my client made to the software change tracking system. The system allows users to add custom fields to bugs and features. My customer added a field to keep track of the tester who verified the change. When the bug or feature is first created, this field is null. Once it has been tested, the tester fills in their own name and moves it to Done. Filling in the field and changing the state are both done in the same transaction.

This new field completes the picture. From the commit, we had a permanent record of who made the change. From the review system, we know who reviewed each commit. And now this new field tells us who tested the fix. But the field also creates a problem.

There's an arrow in the state transition diagram that we haven't drawn yet. A tester can evaluate a change and find that it is defective. If so, they fill in their name and move it back to Triage. This backward arrow creates a cycle, as shown in Figure 8-11.

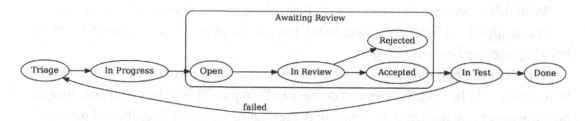

Figure 8-11. *Failing a test moves the bug back to the beginning of the workflow*

This cycle means that we cannot write the same kind of conditional validation that we saw earlier. We cannot say with certainty that if a bug is in Triage or In Progress, the Tester field is null. It will be null on the first time through, but not if the bug was previously failed. Worse yet, what happens if a different tester verifies the bug the second time? Which name ends up in the field?

Collect Data During Transitions

Conditional validation forced us to declare fields as nullable when they actually record required data. Once the state has progressed beyond a certain point, we want to ensure that that data is captured. We never want to allow tracking number to be null once an order has shipped, nor do we want to allow tester to be null once the bug has been tested. To change these fields so that they don't allow nulls, we need to remove them from their entities and place them in a new object. This object will be created only when the entity transitions to the target state.

For example, when an order is shipped, we can create a Shipment object, shown in Figure 8-12. The tracking number is not a field of the order, nor is it a field of the item. Instead, it is a field of the Shipment. This object records which items were shipped and collects other data generated at that time, such as the tracking number.

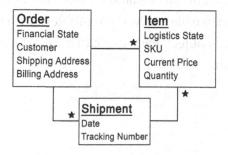

Figure 8-12. *An order has multiple shipments, each with a non-nullable tracking number*

With this model, we can enforce that the tracking number is not null. Before the order is shipped, no Shipment object exists. But afterward, the object is created, and the tracking number has to be filled in.

Consider the bug tracker example. What object we can move the Tester field into? When a tester fails a bug fix, they can create a Fail object. This object could capture not only the tester but also the description of the test failure, expected result, and perhaps screenshots, logs, and other supporting materials. Conversely, when a tester passes a bug fix, they can create a Pass object. This object captures the tester and any additional notes. These two objects are shown in Figure 8-13.

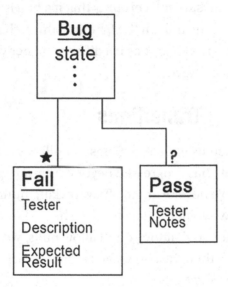

Figure 8-13. *A bug has many fail objects and zero or one pass object. These objects record the tester*

This model creates two new objects. Each object has a Tester field that cannot be null. We no longer have conditional validation; before the bug is tested, these objects don't even exist. In addition, we have solved the problem with state cycles. Each time a bug is tested, we create a new object. Each one can have a different Tester, and previous values are never overwritten.

Immutable State Transitions

By introducing new objects, we have solved the problem of conditional nullability. Before an entity moves beyond a certain state, the additional object does not exist. Afterward, the object contains non-nullable fields. We no longer need to store the field within the entity. This means that we don't need to compromise the field declaration to allow the weaker type.

We have also solved the problem of cycles. Each time an entity transitions through an iteration, it accumulates more data. Each pass is recorded in a separate object. Prior passes are not overwritten.

In either case, the new object is immutable. Each of these objects represents a historical fact. There is no reason to go back in time and change these facts. We've replaced mutation with object creation. Perhaps now we can use these immutable objects to eliminate even the mutable field recording the state itself.

The Question Behind State

The problems of many properties, many entities, and conditional validation have led us to a place where we record information about a state transition in an immutable object. Our models currently have one or more mutable state fields on each entity, in addition to the immutable historical records. The application both changes state and adds historical detail in a single transaction, ensuring that the two are consistent. This leads one to wonder: Is one of these redundant?

Translating a State Machine to a Historical Model

Let's go through each of the examples we've explored so far and construct a historical model of the state transitions. If we can compute the state of each entity from these historical facts, then we can be assured that the mutable state field is redundant. With that assurance, we can eliminate the redundant fields from data storage. To store something that could be computed from something else is to invite defects. When redundant fields exist, it is possible to store an inconsistent set of values. Eliminating the redundant field eliminates this class of defects.

Once we have a way of computing the current state, we can ask a larger question: What is the reason for determining the state of an entity in the first place? By examining what state is actually used for, we can map those questions down to the historical facts. This analysis will reveal that in many domains, we do not need to know the state of an entity at all. We can answer the questions behind state directly from the historical facts.

Order Fulfillment

In the order fulfillment system, we tracked the financial state of an order and the logistics state of an item through a pair of parallel state machines. Let's model each of these state machines as a history of facts, starting with the financial state. The documents that affect financial state appear in Figure 8-14. I've associated each document with its predecessors to represent causality.

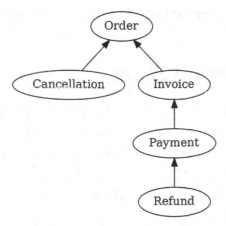

Figure 8-14. *Historical facts representing the documents that the billing department manages*

The financial state of an order can then be written as a function of these documents. We will use *existential quantifiers* or statements of the form "there exists." If there exists an invoice for the order, then the order has been invoiced. If there exists a payment for that invoice, then the order has been paid.

```
financial state (order) =
  if there exists Cancellation
    then Canceled
  else if there exists Invoice then
    if there exists Payment then
```

```
     if there exists Refund then
        Canceled
     else Paid
   else Invoiced
 else Ordered
```

Adding a new document to history affects the financial state of the order. We don't need any handlers to receive the documents and update the state. There is no machine for processing messages. The state is simply a declarative function on the existence of documents.

The logistics state is a little more complicated. We captured the tracking number in an immutable Shipment object to indicate that multiple items were shipped for a given order. The fact type diagram in Figure 8-15 retains that relationship between a shipment, its order, and the shipped items, while also accounting for other activities that affect logistics state.

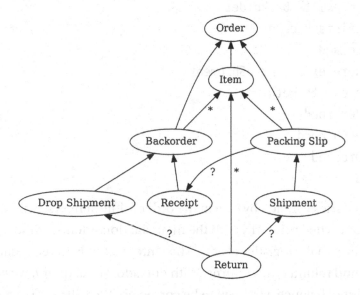

Figure 8-15. *Historical facts representing actions of the shipping department*

When the shipping department picks items from the warehouse, they produce a packing slip. The existence of a packing slip therefore indicates that those items have been picked. That package will later be shipped, at which time it receives a tracking number.

Meanwhile, out-of-stock items will be back-ordered. A set of back-ordered items can be drop-shipped or received. If received, the warehouse will create a new packing slip, resulting in a shipment.

Items can be returned from either a drop shipment or a warehouse shipment. The entire shipment need not be returned, so the return has to specify which items were included. The history of facts tells the story. The following function determines the current state of an item based on the existence of those facts:

```
logistics state (item) =
  if there exists PackingSlip
    if there exists Shipment
      if there exists Return
        then Returned
      else Shipped
    else Picked
  else if there exists Backorder
    if there exists Receipt
      then Received
    else if there exists DropShipment
      if there exists Return
        then Returned
      else DropShipped
    else BackOrdered
  else Ordered
```

These two histories live side by side in the order fulfillment system. The billing department is concerned primarily with the financial documents, while the shipping department deals with the logistics events. They intersect only in reconciling payments with shipments and refunds with returns. With one additional query, we can identify orders that are out of balance and need to be corrected. We will write that query a little later. Meanwhile, let's design a historical model for the software change tracking system.

Software Change Tracking

Taking another look at the software change tracking system, we can identify the state transitions that take place with respect to a bug or a commit. We've identified two such transitions already: Pass and Fail. The other transitions appear as arrows in the state transition diagram. In Figure 8-16, we label those arrows so that we can see the full set.

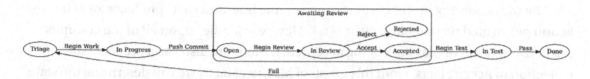

Figure 8-16. *Transitions in the software change tracking system are labeled with the actions that trigger them*

Pivoting from a state transition diagram into a fact type graph, each of these transitions becomes a fact. We associate the facts with the entities that they affect. We also associate each fact with the state transition that preceded it. This ensures that we cannot take a state transition too early. The resulting fact type graph appears in Figure 8-17.

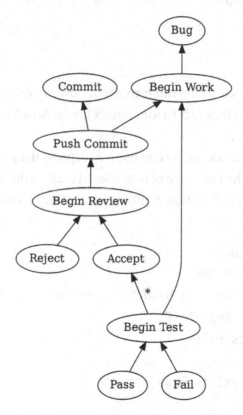

Figure 8-17. *A graph of facts representing the state transitions of a software change tracking system*

The transition `Begin Test` is performed on the bug, and so its predecessor is the last action performed on that bug: `Begin Work`. However, it relies upon all of the commits pushed as a result of that work being accepted. It therefore also has a predecessor collection of `Accept` facts. From this graph of historical facts, we can determine the state of an individual commit, or of the bug as a whole. Let's start with a function that gives the state of a commit. We express this function in terms of the `Push Commit` fact, as we don't need to consider commits that haven't been pushed.

```
state (pushCommit) =
  if exists BeginReview
    if exists Reject
      then Rejected
    else if exists Accept
      then Accepted
    else InReview
  else Open
```

This function expresses a subtle but important design decision: rejection vetoes acceptance. It tests for a `Reject` fact before it tests for an `Accept` fact. If somehow both exist, the commit is rejected.

Now that we have this function, we can use it to express the state of the bug. The bug's state is based not only on the existence of bug-related actions but also the state of all commits. For that reason, this function combines both existential and universal quantifiers.

```
state (bug) =
  if there exists BeginWork
    if there exists PushCommit
      if for all pushCommit in branch, state(pushCommit) = Accepted
      and there exists BeginTest
        if there exists Fail
          then Triage
        else if there exists Pass
          then Done
        else InTest
      else AwaitingReview
    else InProgress
  else Triage
```

Once again, failure vetoes passage. Furthermore, the bug requires both that all commits are accepted and that we explicitly begin testing. If either of these checks fails, it remains awaiting review. We don't have to code for the combination of these events to advance the state of the bug. The declarative nature of a state function takes care of that for us.

Reasons for Computing State

This exercise demonstrates that we can determine the state of an entity based on the existence of historical facts. Given this, we should drop the mutable state field from the entity records. Doing so eliminates the possibility that we fail to update it correctly while inserting a new historical fact.

Having dropped the mutable state field, we can now consider why we had it in the first place. Under what circumstances are we going to call these new declarative state functions? What is the question that we were using state to answer?

Handling the Next Action

State machine-based patterns show us one of the reasons that we want to know the state of an entity: to understand how to respond to the next action. A message handler usually follows a predictable series of steps:

- Look up the entity (by correlation ID or some other property of the message).

- Determine the state of the entity.

- Validate the message.

- Operate on the entity.

- Update the state.

The state determines how to perform the subsequent operations. We could run the declarative function to determine the current state and then from that state determine the strategy for handling a message. Or we could skip a step and simply determine the strategy directly from history. In many domains, deciding how to respond to an action is much simpler than determining state.

For example, in the order fulfillment system, the strategy for responding to a cancellation request depends upon the financial state of the order. If the order is `Paid`, then we issue a refund. If not, then we simply cancel the order. Determining the state of the order is somewhat complicated, as we saw earlier. And yet determining whether an order is paid is much simpler:

```
paid (order) =
  there exists Invoice
    such that there exists Payment
      such that there does not exist Refund
```

Furthermore, the work of determining whether an order is paid is exactly the work required to find the payments that need to be refunded. And so we can boil it down to a single Factual query:

```
nonRefundedPayments = (o: Order) {
  p: Payment [
    p→invoice→order = o
    ∄ {
      r: Refund [
        r→payment = p
      ]
    }
  ]
}
```

When we receive a request to cancel an order, we run this query. If it finds any payments that have not yet been refunded, we issue refunds for them. Doing so has the side effect of transitioning the order to the `Canceled` state if we were so inclined as to run it. But if we can determine how to handle the next action without running the state function, why run it?

Finding Work Items

In addition to determining how to handle the next action for an entity, states are often used to find all entities requiring a next action. Rather than looking up the state for a given entity, systems will query for all entities that are in a given state. One common reason for running such a query is to present the results to the user as a list of work items.

For example, a software change tracking system will commonly display issues in swimlanes. Each column represents a state. When a user is looking for work that needs to be done, they will scan the issues in a given state and select one to pull forward. A developer would look in the `Triage` swimlane for bugs that are ready to be worked on. Going through all of the bugs and running the state function would be a slow way to provide this user interface. Fortunately, a Factual query gives us those results directly from history.

```
bugsInTriage = (s: Sprint) {
  b: Bug [
    b→sprint = s
    ∄ [
      bw: BeginWork [
        bw→bug = b
      ]
    ]
  ]
}
```

For the sake of this query, we put all of the bugs in a sprint. This gives us a starting point for the query. We first look for all bugs in the sprint and then limit them to only those for which work has not yet begun. In other words, we only want the work items that will accept our next action. The developer can choose any one of them and create a new `Begin Work` fact, thus removing it from the swimlane.

That was a pretty simple example. What about something more complicated? A tester, for example, might be looking for all of the bugs that are `In Test` so that they can select one to verify. A bug is only in test if no commits have been reviewed and rejected.

```
bugsInTest = (s: Sprint) {
  bw: BeginWork [
    bw→bug→sprint = s
    ∄ {
      r: Reject [
        r→beginReview→pushCommit→beginWork = bw
      ]
    }
  ]
```

```
bt: BeginTest [
  bt→beginWork = bw
  ∄ {
    p: Pass [
      p→beginTest = bt
    ]
  }
  ∄ {
    f: Fail [
      f→beginTest = bt
    ]
  }
]
}
```

The last clause filters the list based on the next action. We are only concerned with bugs that have not passed or failed. Queries for work items always include a not exists (∄) clause based on the next action. Once we perform the next action, the query will no longer return the result. This updates the user interface and removes the work item from the user's list.

Executing Compensating Transactions

One final reason for knowing the state of an entity is to determine if there are any compensating transactions that need to be applied. This is one of the features for which the Saga Pattern[4] was originally invented. Most database management systems provide a mechanism for executing several operations in one atomic transaction. These transactions are intended to be short-lived. Holding a transaction open for an extended period of time can block other operations, seriously impacting the scalability of your solution. The Saga Pattern associates compensating transactions with intermediate steps so that they can be rolled back should a problem arise. Compensating transactions allow you to commit the intermediate database transactions and yet still handle long-running activities.

---

[4] Hector Garcia-Molina, Kenneth Salem. Sagas. Department of Computer Science, Princeton University. 1987.

Another way to think about compensating transactions is to consider whether a state is desirable or not. Ordinarily, database transactions would prevent a system from entering undesirable states, as the transaction can be rolled back. In a Saga, however, database transactions are committed more frequently to improve scalability. It is possible for a sequence of smaller database transactions to leave the system in an undesirable state. A compensating transaction is a corrective action that can be taken if the system is left in such a state.

One example from the order fulfillment system has to do with reconciling returns with refunds. It is undesirable for the financial state of an order to be Paid while the logistics state of its items is Returned. We can arrive at this state in a couple of ways: we can receive payment for items that have been returned, or we can receive a return for items that are already paid for. A state machine-based implementation of the Saga Pattern would look for each of these situations in a separate handler. The payment handler would look for items in the Returned state, and the returns handler would look for orders in the Paid state. But doing so duplicates logic that could simply be expressed in one place. The following Factual query identifies items that are both paid and returned:

```
itemsRequiringRefunds = (s: Seller) {
  i: Item [
    i→order→seller = s
    ∃ {
      p: Payment [
        p→invoice→order = i→order
        ∄ {
          rf: Refund [
            rf→payment = p
            rf→items = i
          ]
        }
      ]
    }
    ∃ {
```

```
    r: Return [
      r→item = i
    ]
  }
 ]
}
```

A service runs this query to determine which items need to be refunded. If it returns any items, then it processes those refunds. After doing so, adding a Refund fact removes the item from the preceding query. The service did not need to determine the state of items and their orders to find the entities that required compensating transactions. It ran that query directly against the history and then acted upon the results.

In most domains, I have found that querying history directly produced exactly the information I needed without determining state. To determine whether a button should be enabled, just query that its action does not yet exist. To distribute a queue to worker nodes, query for items not yet worked. Historical queries are more direct and less error prone than managing state machines. And it is not just for analytical reasons; they have a significant technical advantage as well.

Single Source of Truth

We've identified an alternative to state machine-based solutions for business problems. First, we modeled transitions not as changes to the mutable state of an entity, but instead as immutable records. And then, we wrote declarative functions that query the existence and absence of such records. These functions answer two questions: What is the next action for a given entity and what entities can accept a given action? Answering these questions directly from history turned out to be simpler than keeping track of states. As an additional benefit, we will find that it also solves some of technical problems that arise in distributed systems.

In order to process requests, a state machine needs to do two things. First, it needs to know with certainty the state of an entity. And second, it needs to determine whether the request is valid when the entity is in that state. As a consequence, clients have less autonomy. They must rely upon a privileged set of nodes to process requests on their behalf. Clients must consult the single source of truth to know what has happened as a result of their actions.

Orchestrators

Many state machine-based distributed systems employ message-driven architectures. In such a system, each step in the process is associated with a *command* message. A node called an *orchestrator* receives each message and executes the appropriate transaction. The orchestrator loads the current state from the entity identified by the *correlation ID* of the command. It determines which transaction to apply based on the state of the entity. The transaction modifies the entity, and the state machine determines the next state.

Consistent State

When we studied the CAP Theorem in Chapter 5, we defined consistency as the property that two nodes in a distributed system will report an entity as being in the same state. For an orchestrator to know the state of an entity, it must achieve consistency with other orchestrators in the system. This cannot be relaxed. Eventual consistency is not sufficient, because the state machine must process the command and provide a definitive result. To achieve consistency, orchestrators will often share a common database.

The orchestrator must be able to obtain a lock against an entity in order to determine how to process a command. For this reason, it is not uncommon to send all commands to a central set of orchestrators. This body of orchestrators and the database in which they maintain entity state becomes the single source of truth. It is the sole authority on the state of those entities.

Central Validation

A state machine determines which operations are valid based on the state of an entity. Payment can only be applied if the order is in the Invoiced state. A bug can only be failed if it is in the In Test state. In a distributed system, the users who initiate these operations are not co-located with the state machines. They are using clients.

A client issues commands for an orchestrator to process. Because the orchestrators must be consistent with one another, the CAP Theorem tells us that they must become unavailable in the face of a network partition. To overcome this, commands are often queued. An orchestrator will process the command at some later time, once the network partition has been healed.

Since the outcome of the command depends upon the state of the entity, the client cannot predict exactly what will happen. Clients lie outside of the single source of truth. They must wait for the command to reach the orchestrator and then for the result to make its way back to the client. And by the time the results make it back, the user has moved on.

By relying upon a consistent state to validate operations, the state machine-based solution has sacrificed autonomy. A client cannot predict the outcome of a request on its own. It cannot determine whether the request will succeed or fail, as other requests of which it is unaware may have moved the entity into a different state. Instead, clients must rely upon a single source of truth, push commands to a queue, and await the results.

Convergent Histories

Instead of relying upon a centralized static model as the single source of truth, we can allow each client to represent its own truth. The truth is whatever the user has done, it is not the responsibility of an orchestrator to validate the user's actions. It is the responsibility of the system to understand what has happened and to combine those histories into a cohesive story.

Define Immutable Records

To begin, we model each user action as an immutable record. This record captures the information that was produced at that time. Each record refers to previous actions as predecessors. These aren't simply a list of all events that occurred in the past; these previous actions are specifically the ones that lead to the new action. The predecessors represent the information that the user had while making this decision.

For example, a Shipment fact captures the tracking number. This information is produced when the user takes action. Furthermore, a Payment refers to a predecessor Invoice but is not related to any Shipments that might have already happened. The invoice is causally related to the payment, but the shipment is not.

Query for the Next Action

Once the immutable records are modeled, write a query for each kind of action. Query for all of the records that would be predecessors of that action. Add a clause including only those for which the action does not exist. This query tells you if this is the next action for an entity.

For example, for a `Commit`, query for `Begin Review` without a subsequent `Reject` or `Accept`. If that query returns one or more records, then the commit is still in review. Accept or reject is the next action. Furthermore, the records returned by the query are predecessors of the `Accept` or `Reject` records that will be created.

Write another query that begins higher up the chain. Instead of starting at a `Commit`, start with the `Sprint`. This query will list all entities for which a particular next action is required. This provides a set of work items to present to the user.

Capture Actions Locally

When the user takes an action, add the record to the local history immediately. Creating the record will influence the results of the queries. The user will immediately see the entity removed from one set of work items and added to the next. They will observe that the new next action of the entity has advanced. This gives them immediate feedback that their actions have been honored.

The user is making their decision based on the information that they have available. The system should not pause to check the current state, or take a remote lock to ensure that the user's action is consistent. It should not push the record to a queue and wait for an orchestrator to process it later. Commit the action to history at the client, and let parallel histories converge.

Define Compensating Actions

Finally, identify undesirable states that might arise due to convergent histories. Such states can arise because we've given clients the autonomy to act based on the information that they currently have available. Write a query to find entities in undesirable states and then design processes to perform compensating transactions.

It's possible that an order will have both a `Refund` and an unreturned `Shipment`. Create a query looking for orders in this state. Present the results to a representative, prompting them to call the customer asking them to either return the product or pay another invoice. It is up to the analyst to identify appropriate compensations for such situations and not the responsibility of a state machine to try to prevent them.

Users are the source of truth. They are distributed across the system. They do not participate in a consistent, orchestrated state machine. They do not care about the current state of an entity. They just need to know what has happened and how to interpret those parallel histories. They need the assurance that their actions will be honored and will become part of that convergent history.

Workflow Patterns

The preceding exploration of state transitions in distributed systems has revealed some valuable insights. We've codified those insights into some general advice.

We begin by capturing the work to be performed in an immutable fact. Its predecessors are the prior facts that the user consulted when making that decision. Then, we set up a query to identify which work items are ready for any given process. Finally, we capture the outcome of that process in an immutable way that atomically moves the work item along to the next step. Any unwanted concurrent decisions are discovered and resolved as late as possible, rather than prevented in real time.

Now let's document some patterns that help us to apply this advice. Rather than adding these patterns to the previous chapter, I decided to wait until I had given you that advice. Unlike the patterns in the previous chapter, which attempted to implement behaviors that users expect from stateful systems, these patterns take full advantage of the immutable nature of historical models. They give us atomicity in a distributed solution, task-focused interfaces for human processes, and a mechanism for aging out historical data on a human-centric cadence.

Transaction

Motivation   Capture a known state of an entity to perform an atomic unit of work.

The structural patterns that we explored in the last chapter allow an entity to change over time. The changes are captured as immutable facts, but the accrual of new facts as the user interacts with the system simulates changes to an entity. At some point, the user will decide to take some action. Any further changes to the entity after that point should not affect that action.

Users might be adding items to a shopping cart. They can remove items, replace them, and restore them back to the cart. They can change the quantity, product, shipping options, delivery address, and any other property. The structural patterns in the previous section allow those operations.

But then when the user submits the order, the items and all of their properties should be locked down. No additional items can be added, and no properties can be modified. Processing may begin at any time, and a change to an order in flight would be disruptive to business.

The *Transaction* pattern takes advantage of immutability for business processing. It records the information about a request for work in such a way that it cannot be modified after work begins.

Structure

A *Transaction* identifies as a predecessor an entity that it is acting upon. Whereas that entity was originally a starting point for children, mutable properties, and other successors, the transaction now seeks to lock it down. It does so by inverting the predecessor/successor relationship.

Where *Ownership* placed the parent as a predecessor of its children, *Transaction* makes children predecessors of parents. Successors can be added over time, but predecessors are immutable. Recording children as predecessors prevents further creation or deletion.

The transaction also identifies the specific versions of *Mutable Properties*. These become direct or indirect predecessors of the transaction. Again, the relationship is inverted so that any further modifications to those properties do not affect the transaction.

A TransactionItem as described as follows is a child of a Transaction. The Transaction has a set of TransactionItem predecessors. Furthermore, a TransactionItem captures one specific version of a mutable property.

```
fact TransactionItem {
  itemContext: ChildEntity
  property: ChildProperty
}

fact Transaction {
  transactionContext: ParentEntity
  items: TransactionItem*
}
```

The transaction and all of its items are captured at a single machine. This is typically the workstation that the decision maker is using. When a user decides to issue a transaction, the system captures the state of the objects as they are known to that user at that time. Creating a transaction does not require the machine to communicate with any other node, as all of the information required is local.

Example

When a customer submits an order, they lock down its current state. They cannot make further changes to the order. They can only request a subsequent return and new orders.

We start from the order structure that we built using the patterns *Entity*, *Delete*, *Mutable Property*, and *Entity Reference*. This structure is modifiable, as the customer can add or remove items and change products or quantities. Then we create a parallel model – demonstrated in Figure 8-18 – that inverts the predecessor/successor relationships. Items in the order become predecessors so that new items cannot be added.

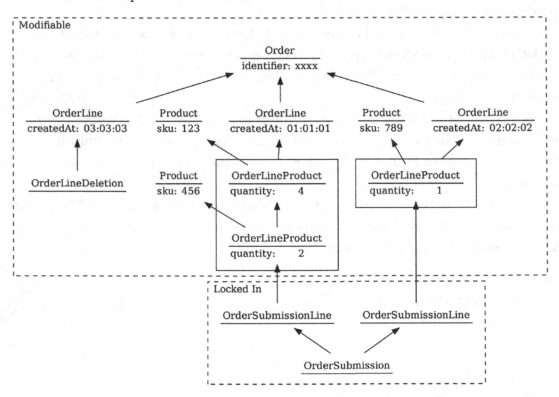

Figure 8-18. *An order submission inverts the model to lock in predecessors*

Any lines that have been deleted are not included in the OrderSubmission. Other lines might be subsequently deleted, or deleted lines later restored. Neither change will affect the OrderSubmissionLines that have been captured.

All of the arrows point out of the OrderSubmission. All of the information required to process the order can be found by traversing the graph in one direction. Given an OrderSubmission, any node will compute exactly the same order. This locks in the items, products, and quantities.

290

Consequences

Once a transaction is recorded, subsequent changes to the entities or properties will have no effect. All of the information in the transaction is recorded in predecessor relationships. Predecessors are immutable, so the transaction is locked down.

All nodes receiving the transaction see it in exactly the same state. The identity of a fact includes the identities of its predecessors. Any difference in predecessors such as transaction items or property versions would necessarily result in different facts.

A transaction is processed atomically. Items may arrive at a node ahead of their transaction. But processing begins with a query for a transaction, not an item. Items will remain dormant until the subsequent transaction arrives, at which time all items will take effect simultaneously.

All necessary information must be in the transitive closure of the transaction. Starting at the transaction fact, follow all predecessors. From those facts, recursively follow their predecessors. The transitive closure is the set of all facts thus visited.

Related Patterns

The *Transaction* pattern inverts the predecessor/successor relationship found in the *Ownership* and *Mutable Property* patterns.

A transaction is often placed in a *Queue* or an *Outbox* and is usually associated with a *Period*.

Queue

Motivation	Manage work to be processed manually.

Work that a person needs to handle is often presented in a list. The user interface shows the user a set of work items that require their attention. The user selects a work item and navigates to part of the application where they can handle it.

The user might get interrupted. So the work remains on the queue until they actually complete it. If another user observes the queue, they will be able to see the same work item.

The *Queue* pattern presents a set of work items that are ready for manual processing. It ensures that a work item is removed from the queue when it is completed. Note that this is not related to the first-in-first-out (FIFO) data structure of the same name. Order is not preserved.

Structure

A queue is nothing more than a query that returns projections representing work to be done. The query starts from some root-level entity – for example, an *Owner* – and matches children for which an action has not been performed.

```
workToDo = (o: Owner) {
  wi: WorkItem [
    wi→owner = o
    ∄ {
      a: Action [
        a→workItem = wi
      ]
    }
  ]
}
```

In the process of performing the requested work, the user will create an `Action` fact. The action records the outcome of the work.

Because the action appears in the not exists (∄) clause, the work item is removed from the query once the action has been performed. Recording the action and removing work from the queue occur in a single atomic operation.

Example

Once an order is submitted to our hypothetical company, the shipping department picks products to fulfill a submitted order and prints a packing slip. The logistics department, meanwhile, calls for a delivery truck. Each of these is a manual process. The relationship among order submissions, delivery, and packing slips is captured in the model depicted in Figure 8-19.

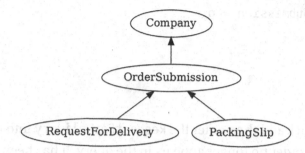

Figure 8-19. *An order submission triggers both the request for delivery and the packing slip*

The shipping manager knows what orders to pick based on a query. The query looks for order submissions that do not yet have a packing slip.

```
ordersToPick = (c: Company) {
  o: OrderSubmission [
    o→company = c
    ∄ {
      ps: PackingSlip [
        ps→orderSubmission = o
      ]
    }
  ]
}
```

Once the order is picked, the shipping manager prints a packing slip. The act of doing so removes the order from this queue.

Meanwhile, the logistics team runs another query to find orders that do not yet have a delivery request:

```
ordersToShip = (c: Company) {
  o: OrderSubmission [
    o→company = c
    ∄ {
      rd: RequestForDelivery [
```

```
        rd→orderSubmission = o
      ]
    }
  ]
}
```

They call for a truck and then enter the RequestForDelivery into the system. Once they do so, the order no longer appears in the query. It has been removed from the queue.

We have deliberately chosen not to have a predecessor/successor relationship between RequestForDelivery and PackingSlip. The delivery request can be made before the product is picked. Or, based on volume, the warehouse might find themselves backlogged and choose to delay the request for delivery.

When the shipping manager predicts that the warehouse is about to be backlogged, they notify logistics to switch to a different query. Now they wait for orders to have been picked before requesting delivery.

```
pickedOrdersToShip = (c: Company) {
  o: OrderSubmission [
    o→company = c
    ∃ {
      ps: PackingSlip [
        ps→orderSubmission = o
      ]
    }
    ∄ {
      rd: RequestForDelivery [
        rd→orderSubmission = o
      ]
    }
  ] .
}
```

The creation of a PackingSlip atomically moves the work from the shipping manager's queue into the logistics queue. The subsequent creation of the RequestForDelivery removes it from the logistics queue.

The packing slip is not a hard prerequisite. It is not a predecessor of the request for delivery. But by switching from one queue to another, the company can adjust its business process to better respond to circumstances.

Consequences

The action performed on a work item is used in the not exists ($\nexists$) clause of the queue. As a result, recording the action and removing the work item from the queue are a single atomic operation.

Unlike a FIFO (first-in-first-out) queue, the queue query does not impose an order on the work items. The results of a query are a *set*, not a *list*. If order is important, place a timestamp on the work item fact. Use that timestamp to order the set for presentation to the user.

Related Patterns

If work is to be performed automatically instead of manually, then the *Outbox* pattern is more appropriate.

Work items in a queue are often *Transactions*.

Work items are often grouped by unit of time. This recognizes a natural period that the business already recognizes. Application of the *Period* pattern has the extra benefit of preventing the queue query from slowing down as history accrues.

Period

Motivation	Bound the accrual of facts with discrete time slices.

The time required to query a historical model is governed by the number of successors that the starting point or intermediate fact has. If we start each query from the root of the graph, those queries would get slower over time. Starting further down the graph at a fact that has a bounded number of successors will keep performance constant as we accrue more facts.

Any feature of the system that limits the number of successors is a good candidate for subdividing the graph. The one that is most readily available is time. The *Period* pattern subdivides the historical graph by discrete units of time. While the total number of facts is expected to grow, the number *per unit period* will remain somewhat more bounded.

In addition to the performance benefits, associating facts with a period often captures an important business concept. Accountants tend to close their books on daily, monthly, and quarterly periods. They do this not just to limit the size of a ledger but also to give themselves reporting boundaries. The *Period* pattern seeks to do the same with application data.

Structure

A period is a fact that has one *Owner* predecessor to give it context and one discrete time value. The time is measured in coarse units; it is not a continuous timestamp.

```
fact Period {
  owner: Owner
  time: discreteTime
}
```

Typical choices for the discrete time unit are calendar or business day, month, quarter, or year. For high-throughput systems, units may go down to the hour, but rarely smaller.

Work items include a period as a predecessor. Queries for work start at the period.

```
workToDo = (p: Period) {
  wi: WorkItem [
    wi→period = p
    ∄ {
      a: Action [
        a→workItem = wi
      ]
    }
  ]
}
```

Results from two or more queries are unioned together to produce an overlapping query. The overlap is chosen to allow plenty of time for remote replicas to connect and share their work items and for those work items to be processed before the period rolls off.

The period has no additional fields, so that the owner and discrete unit of time produce a unique fact. All replicas creating work items produce the same fact. And each query for work items creates the starting point in the same way.

Periods are sometimes captured hierarchically. The largest period – say a year – falls directly under the owner. The next period down – for example, a quarter – has the larger period as a predecessor. Periods organized in this way must share a boundary; month and week cannot be organized in a hierarchy. This is usually done for reporting rather than performance reasons.

Example

In the previous example, we added order submissions directly to the company. As time passes, the system searches more orders within the company to find the ones that have not yet been picked or shipped. We can make things easier on the system and record an important dimension of the model at the same time.

The DateOfBusiness fact has one predecessor and one field:

```
fact DateOfBusiness {
  company: Company
  businessDate: date
}
```

We insert a DateOfBusiness between Company and OrderSubmission, as shown in Figure 8-20. This fact captures the date on which the order was submitted.

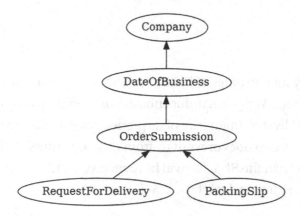

Figure 8-20. *An intermediate fact groups orders submitted to a company by date of business*

Date of business is not strictly determined by the computer clock. An order may be counted toward the next date of business if it is placed after hours, or if it occurs on a weekend or holiday. In fact, the company may even choose a policy wherein orders placed after 3:00 are associated with the next date of business. The period is an operational construct, not a physical one.

Not all replicas need to advance to the next period at exactly the same time. There is no need to rigorously synchronize the clocks across the workstations on which users are submitting orders. If one workstation starts submitting orders into the next date of business while another workstation remains on the current one, then those orders are simply counted in different periods. This will not cause any problems as long as there is no causal relationship between the order submissions. And the fact that the developer chose not to make one OrderSubmission the predecessor of the other indicates that there *should* be no causal relationship.

To determine the orders to pick for any given date of business, we find those that do not yet have a packing slip:

```
ordersToPick = (dob: DateOfBusiness) {
  o: OrderSubmission [
    o→dateOfBusiness = dob
    ∄ {
      ps: PackingSlip [
        ps→orderSubmission = o
      ]
    }
  ]
}
```

We run this query for two dates of business – the previous one and the current one – and union the sets. Any given order submission occurs in only one date of business, as indicated by the singularity of its predecessor, so this practice does not risk duplication. But the overlap *does* prevent us from missing orders. As long as the period is significantly longer than the SLA, we will have received and processed a day's orders before we roll the query forward too far.

Consequences

A work item should have only one associated period. If a unit of work is broken into smaller units, and those each have their own period, then it would be possible to split the work between two periods. Think of a train moving across a switch at the same time that the switch is thrown (ignoring the distance between the front and back sets of wheels). If the cars are not connected, then there is no problem. But if they are attached to one another, this could cause some unintended consequences.

Two or more periods should be queried for work items. The overlap provides a buffer of time for work items to arrive and be processed. If upstream replicas can be offline, the number and duration of overlapping periods must be chosen to allow them to reconnect. As long as the expected time to receive and process work items is significantly shorter than the duration of overlapping periods, then work will not typically be lost.

There is no mechanism in the model to guarantee, however, that work won't be delayed beyond the oldest period queried. The processing system should be flexible enough to be manually reset to pick up lagging work items. A query from the *Owner* one predecessor higher than the period can encompass all periods. While this query would be slower, it would look back in time for any missed work items. A business decision can then be made to determine the best corrective action.

Related Patterns

Periods are often used as the starting point for queries in the *Queue* or *Outbox* pattern. An unbounded queue gradually becomes a performance problem. But a queue bounded by the expected number of work items per period is much easier to manage.

The work items within a period are often *Transaction*s.

CHAPTER 9

Security

A common approach to application security is role-based access control (RBAC). Under this system, an administrator assigns individuals to roles and then authorizes those roles to perform certain actions within the system. As we adopt immutable architectures, RBAC becomes more challenging. Requiring an administrator to assign roles and permissions reduces the autonomy of individual users. Consulting a single source of truth for those roles and permissions reduces the autonomy of client nodes. The access control model begins to work against the advantages that we fought so hard to achieve.

RBAC is typically applied at the organization level. A team of administrators define the roles and operations within an organization. They manage a set of resources, upon which the operations are performed. That organization is the single beneficiary of the system. In a multi-tenant environment, however, the division of roles and responsibilities becomes much more complex. The myriad of tenants may not agree on a single body of administrators to manage access to their resources. Instead, they will seek to maintain autonomy over their own assets. This will lead them away from a centralized form of access control and toward more distributed trust models.

Our desire for autonomy drives us toward a decentralized model of access control. The expansion of distributed systems across multiple tenants removes the organizational structures that we might have otherwise depended upon. And so we look elsewhere for a solution. Instead of a role-based access model, we find inspiration in public key infrastructure (PKI) and delegation of authority. With these tools, we can build a system of security on top of a model of immutable facts.

Proof of Authorship

A historical record represents a decision that a person made within a distributed system. Before we can determine whether to trust that particular decision, we have to have some assurance of the identity of the person who made it. We seek proof of the authorship of

M. L. Perry, *The Art of Immutable Architecture*, https://doi.org/10.1007/979-8-8688-0288-1_9

a fact. Modern digital systems rely upon *public key infrastructure* (PKI) to provide that proof. PKI is based on the existence of a trapdoor function: a mathematical function that is easy to compute in one direction, but difficult to invert.

Key Pairs

Suppose that I have a pair of functions. Each function is the inverse of the other; if the outcome of one function is fed into the other, the original input will emerge. For example, the functions *x+3* and *x-3* are such a pair. Adding three and then subtracting three gives you back the original value. You could think of many more examples and probably come up with several different ways of generating new pairs.

If I gave you one of these functions – say *x+3* – you would probably be able to tell me what its inverse is. Computing the inverse of such a simple function is not difficult. But what if I gave you a function like $x^{37} \bmod 1829$? It might take you a bit to work out what the inverse is. A computer given the right algorithm could find it quickly enough: the inverse is $x^{823} \bmod 1829$, as demonstrated in Figure 9-1. But if I make these numbers significantly larger, then even the most powerful digital computer will have a hard time finding the inverse.

$$36 \rightarrow x^{37} \bmod 1829 \rightarrow 842 \rightarrow x^{823} \bmod 1829 \rightarrow 36$$

$$42 \rightarrow x^{823} \bmod 1829 \rightarrow 858 \rightarrow x^{37} \bmod 1829 \rightarrow 42$$

Figure 9-1. *Some functions that are inverses of one another can be used in asymmetric cryptography*

Functions of this form are examples of trapdoor functions. These were generated with a protocol known as RSA, named after its inventors Rivest, Shamir, and Adleman.[1] It is really easy for you to compute the modular exponent. It is really difficult for you to compute its inverse (known as the discrete logarithm). It's only because I generated this pair at the same time that I'm able to find the inverse myself.

If you look closely at these functions, you can see that they have an upper bound. The function $x^{37} \bmod 1829$ only has an inverse if *x < 1829*. This is a consequence of

---

[1] R.L. Rivest, A. Shamir, and L. Adleman. A Method for Obtaining Digital Signatures and Public-Key Cryptosystems. Communications of the ACM. February 1978.

the *pigeonhole principle.* The modulus 1829 limits the number of possible results the function can return; it determines how many pigeon holes you have. If you try to put more pigeons into the function, there will be at least two sharing the same pigeon hole. This function is deliberately constructed to ensure that every input has a distinct output, which is necessary to make sure it has an inverse within the same domain.

RSA gives us a protocol to generate a function and its inverse at the same time. If I give one of the functions to you, you will have a hard time finding the inverse; it's a trapdoor function. We'll call the one that I share the *public key.* The function that I keep is the *private key.* I can use this pair of inverse functions to prove authorship.

Digest

If you run a hash function over a stream of data, you'll produce a digest. The digest will have a fixed size, determined by the hash function you choose. It's important to choose a hash much smaller than the size of public/private key pair. Pad this digest with some random data and feed it into the private key function. The result is the signature.

If someone knew your public key, they could verify your signature. All they would need to do is run your signature through your public key function to get back your padded digest, as shown in Figure 9-2. They could then compute the digest of the message themselves and see if it matches with yours. If so, then they have confidence that the message came from you. This works because it would be very difficult to invert your public key to find your private key. Without your private key, they could not produce a signature that would contain the correct digest.

Digest

random + Digest → *private key* → signature → *public key* → random + Digest

Figure 9-2. *Running the digest of a document through the private key produces a digital signature*

If you wanted consumers of an immutable record to know that it came from you, you could produce a digest. The procedure must be repeatable to ensure that everyone produces the same digest. We must therefore choose a *canonical form* for immutable records. One procedure that I like to use is as follows:

- Serialize the record in JSON.

- Include the record's type as a field.

- Replace predecessors with objects having only a ref field, the value of which is the digest of the predecessor.

- Sort collections of predecessors by their digest and eliminate duplicates.

- Sort fields alphabetically.

- Remove extraneous whitespace.

- Encode the text using UTF-8.

- Compute the SHA-256 hash of the stream.

As an example, a forum post might be serialized as follows before whitespace is removed:

```
{
  "author": {
    "ref": "MSHFIBOX5JkupOYu7ZZuIKJHVtow3vtAK/7f4GYmKVqdcKMcVg9AURmg
U9RQAtJwQjaYguJSJZzlwFctOTqrCw=="
  },
  "forum": {
    "ref": "PQu2HVVqExAOr1kO9lK+rWHzui5Ysd07+g5VkgnNRsJqPnpsy5rzjSfIpnd79ae
a8jjoPe+YIiouOz3xcJvQUQ=="
  },
  "text": "Posted my first forum message.",
  "type": "ForumPost"
}
```

After removing whitespace, applying UTF-8 encoding, and taking SHA-256 hash, you can produce a signature using your private key. Any consumer of this record would compute the same digest. If they had your public key, they could verify your signature.

Insofar as only someone with your private key could produce a valid signature, they can be assured that the message was from you.

The immutable record itself does not contain a signature. It could not, because the signature is produced from the digest of the contents of the record. Instead, the signature is carried in an envelope. As one replica communicates a collection of immutable records to another, it provides with each a list of public keys and signatures.

Authorization

Having proved that you have authored a fact, you might next seek to establish that you are permitted to do so. How might you assert your claim of authorization in a distributed system? If we could appeal to some central authority, then perhaps it could validate your claim. But to retain autonomy, we would like to avoid such an authority. We must therefore establish a means of authorization that the recipient can verify on their own.

To begin, we will define a means of exchanging public keys. When a replicator interacts with an agent, it should be able to verify claims of authorship. Then, the recipient will consult a set of rules to determine which agents are authorized to produce which facts. These rules are based entirely upon related facts.

Principal Facts

The easiest way to exchange public keys is to make them part of the historical model itself. Every agent that is capable of producing facts is a *principal*. Users are principals; autonomous services are principals; authorized entities are principals. Every principal creates a historical fact that represents themselves.

The principal fact contains as a field the user's public key. It typically contains no additional fields. Because the identity of the immutable record is derived from its contents, the identity of the principal *is* its public key. For example, a user of forum software would be represented by the fact in Figure 9-3.

User
publicKey: MIIEogIBAAKCAQEAzPhOXAP...

Figure 9-3. A principal fact has a public key

A principal fact needs no signature. A signature would not prove anything useful. The principal fact contains no additional claims, so the signer would only be reasserting that this is their public key.

Authorization Rules

An important aspect of the model is who is authorized to perform which actions. Since a fact maps to a decision that a person has made, facts are the perfect proxy for the actions that a user can perform. We therefore model authorization rules as queries starting from the authorized fact.

Suppose, for example, that a user created a cart. We could capture the user's identity as a prerequisite.

```
fact Cart {
  createdBy: User
  createdAt: timestamp
}
```

Adding an order line to a cart can then be expressed as an authorization rule. Only the creator of the cart is allowed to add the order line. This is expressed using the authorize keyword.

```
authorize (ol: OrderLine) {
  u: User [
    u = ol→cart→createdBy
  ]
} ⇒ u
```

The body of the authorization rule is exactly like the body of a specification that returns a collection of users. If the user who initiated the action is in the specification results, then that user is authorized to perform the action.

Authorization Query

When a replicator receives a fact, the new fact is considered *contested*. The permission of the author to create that fact remains in doubt. The replicator must verify that the author has authority to create the contested fact. To do so, it will run an authorization query.

This query determines which principal facts are authorized to create the contested fact. If the envelope of that fact contains a signature from an authorized principal, then the fact is *permitted*. Only permitted facts are stored, used in subsequent queries, and forwarded to other replicas.

For example, the forum post that we recently observed is an example of the following kind of fact:

```
fact ForumPost {
  forum: Forum
  author: User
  text: string
}
```

To verify that the post is signed by the author, each recipient will run the following authorization rule:

```
authorize (p: ForumPost) {
  u: User [
    u = p→author
  ]
} ⇒ u
```

Overlaid on top of the fact graph, the authorization query appears in Figure 9-4.

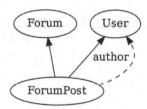

Figure 9-4. *A forum post with the authorization query that determines which user can create it*

This rule instructs the recipient to find the principal fact that is the `author` of the post. It uses the `publicKey` from that principal fact. If the envelope contains a valid signature from that public key, then the post is authorized. If not, then the recipient immediately rejects the fact.

When used as described previously, authorization rules can prevent others from forging messages. If your public key becomes well-known, then a would-be forger might attempt to create a new forum post with your principal as the author predecessor. However, without being in possession of your private key, they would be unable to create a matching signature. The forger would have to settle for generating a new public/private key pair. Such messages would be authorized, but their author would be a different principal. No recipient would be fooled into believing that the forum post was from you.

Initial Authorization

While the preceding authorization rule prevents forgery, it still permits any principal to post to the forum. In other domains, it is desirable to constrain behaviors to a restricted set of principals. Without relying upon a centralized authority to administer these restrictions, we will turn to the model itself to seed the initial authorization.

Suppose that instead of an open forum, we want to model a personal blog. Only the creator of the blog is permitted to post. The blog can be described with the following fact:

```
fact Blog {
  creator: User
  identifier: guid
}
```

An authorization rule verifies that the blog is indeed authored by its creator:

```
authorize (b: Blog) {
  u: User [
    u = b→creator
  ]
} ⇒ u
```

Now we can define a blog post with the following fact:

```
fact BlogPost {
  blog: Blog
  author: User
  postedAt: datetime
}
```

For this domain, we are leaving mutable properties such as the title, text, and tags as separate facts. Only the date and time distinguish one blog post from others by the same author in the same blog.

But the most important thing is that now we can write an authorization rule that allows only the creator of the blog to post to it.

```
authorize (p: BlogPost) {
  u: User [
    u = p→author
    u = p→blog→creator
  ]
} ⇒ u
```

The authorization rule for a blog post traverses the fact graph as shown in Figure 9-5.

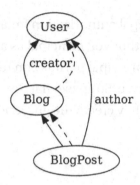

Figure 9-5. *A blog post can be authored only by the blog's creator*

This query will only return the author principal if they are also the blog's creator. If someone tries to create a fact claiming to be from an author other than the creator of the blog, then this query will return no results. Seeing no principals authorized to sign the fact, the recipient will reject it outright. Creating a blog provides the initial authorization list, without the need for any party to consult with a centralized administrator.

Grant of Authority

The authorization queries that we've written thus far return only the creators of the root entity. This is an ideal starting point for a decentralized system; if you made it, you alone control it. It cleanly dispenses with the need for a body of administrators to define roles and permissions, or to grant access to certain resources.

But this is only a starting point. For most domains, authorization cannot remain solely with the creator of an entity. The creator must be able to transfer authority to another party. Such transfers can either be limited or indefinite. If a transfer is limited, it is constrained in scope to one single occurrence. But if it is indefinite, then authorization persists.

Limited Authority

A creator can grant another principal authorization for a single instance of an entity. To do so, the creator identifies the authorized principal as a predecessor to the new entity. An authorization rule grants this principal permission to create successors.

This is best seen with an example. Suppose that the creator of a blog would like to invite a guest to post on the site. They create the guest post for the selected user.

```
fact GuestPost {
  blog: Blog
  guest: User
  createdAt: datetime
}
```

Only the blog creator can add a guest post. Clients use the following authorization rule to enforce this constraint:

```
authorize (gp: GuestPost) {
  u: User [
    u = gp→blog→creator
  ]
} ⇒ u
```

Guests are then authorized to set the title, write the text, and other subsequent operations. For example, to set the title, the guest issues the following kind of fact:

```
fact GuestPostTitle {
  post: GuestPost
  value: string
  prior: GuestPostTitle[]
}
```

The following rule authorizes the guest to issue these successors:

```
authorize (t: GuestPostTitle) {
  u: User [
    u = t→post→guest
  ]
} ⇒ u
```

The diagram of the authorization rule in this graph appears in Figure 9-6.

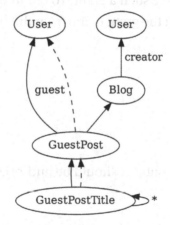

Figure 9-6. *Only the guest can set the title of the guest post*

The guest does not have authorization to create additional posts. Their permission is limited to the single child that has been created on their behalf.

Indefinite Authorization

When the creator of an entity wishes to share authority indefinitely with others, they can create a fact documenting that decision. The grant must be signed by the initial creator. It identifies the entity for which authorization is granted. And it names the principal with which authority will be shared. Then, recipients must be instructed to honor additional authorization rules.

Suppose, for example, that the creator of a blog wishes to invite others to post as well. They don't just want to give them a fixed number of guest posts. They want to share authorization indefinitely. To do so, the blog creator issues a grant.

```
fact BlogGrant {
  blog: Blog
  subject: User
  createdAt: datetime
}
```

Only the blog creator can issue such a grant. To enforce this, we write an authorization rule requiring that the grant come from the blog's creator:

```
authorize (bg: BlogGrant) {
  u: User [
    u = bg→blog→creator
  ]
} ⇒ u
```

Once the grant is issued, the subject should be authorized to post. We write a rule stating such.

```
authorize (p: BlogPost) {
  bg: BlogGrant [
    bg→blog = p→blog
  ]
  u: User [
    u = p→author
    u = bg→subject
  ]
} ⇒ u
```

This authorization rule zigzags through the fact graph as shown in Figure 9-7.

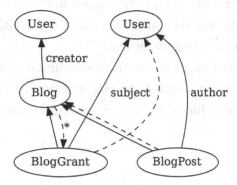

Figure 9-7. *Every subject of a grant is authorized to create a new blog post*

It's important to recognize that this authorization rule is *in addition to* the previous authorization rule for `BlogPost`. A client honoring both of these rules will allow the creator to post and allow all subjects granted authority to post. A client does not have just one authorization rule per type. Instead, the set union of all authorization rules defines the set of principals that will be validated. If the envelope contains a signature from any member of that set, then the fact is authorized.

Transitive Authorization

The authorization rule mentioned earlier permits the subject of a `BlogGrant` to post on another's blog. It does not, however, put them on equal footing with the blog's creator. It does not permit them to then extend that authorization to others by issuing further grants. If doing so would be a desirable feature of the domain, then clients will need to be given one more rule.

```
authorize (next: BlogGrant) {
  bg: BlogGrant [
    bg→blog = next→blog
  ]
  u: User [
    u = bg→subject
  ]
} ⇒ u
```

Even though the parameter next is a contested fact, the unknown bg must be satisfied by a permitted fact. This fact was once contested itself. It was permitted because of a prior authorization rule. The recursive nature of this definition implies that grants can be extended to any number of generations.

Just as with all authorization rules, this one is combined with others for the same contested fact. A different rule authorizes the blog's creator to issue grants. This one adds to it – via set union – authority for subjects to extend those grants to others.

Revocation

All of the approvals and grants documented earlier include a creation date. This is not mere audit detail. This is a design decision that allows for revocation. A one-time approval or an indefinite grant can be revoked by a subsequent fact. Authorization rules simply need to include a not exists clause to make it so.

If a blog creator wishes to revoke a prior grant, then they can issue a fact of the following form:

```
fact BlogGrantRevoke {
  grant: BlogGrant
}
```

The creator is authorized to issue revocations for their own blog. The authorization rule enforcing that is as follows:

```
authorize (r: BlogGrantRevoke) {
  u: User [
    u = r→grant→blog→creator
  ]
} ⇒ u
```

If other grantees are similarly empowered, then the following rule is added:

```
authorize (r: BlogGrantRevoke) {
  bg: BlogGrant [
    bg→blog = r→grant→blog
  ]
```

```
u: User [
  u = bg→subject
]
} ⇒ u
```

We can now add a not exists (∄) clause to the rule so that this fact revokes a previous authorization.

```
authorize (p: BlogPost) {
  bg: BlogGrant [
    bg→blog = p→blog
    ∄ {
      r: BlogGrantRevoke [
        r→grant = bg
      ]
    }
  ]
  u: User [
    u = p→author
    u = bg→subject
  ]
} ⇒ u
```

Adding the not exists clause to the authorization rule results in the diagram shown in Figure 9-8.

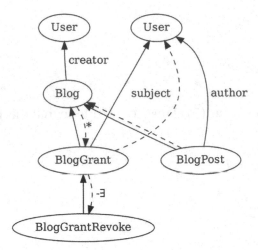

Figure 9-8. *The authorization rule checks for the existence of a blog grant revoke*

And this is where it becomes important to add a distinguishing field such as createdAt to the grant. Without it, authorization could only be granted to a subject once. Once revoked, there would be no way to create a new grant. It would be indistinguishable from the revoked grant.

Authorization Upon Receipt

Authorization rules are evaluated immediately upon receipt of a fact. They are not tested later to determine retroactively whether a fact should have been authorized. There are two important reasons for this: preservation and performance.

If authorization rules were evaluated retroactively, then revoking access would invalidate all prior actions that the party had performed. In most domains, this is not the desired outcome. An employee who is terminated should have their access revoked. Yet all of the work that they did for the company up to that point should be preserved. If the authorization rules were run for those work items after their termination, then those facts would be invalid.

The other consideration is performance. Retroactive evaluation is a recursive, time-consuming operation. If we wanted to use the authorization rules to validate facts every time they are used, we would have to apply them to all facts touched in a query. But to validate a fact, we must run its authorization rules. Those rules are themselves queries. Tracing these queries back to the facts that they touch, their authorization rules, and the queries for those rules leads to an explosion of validation up the historical graph. This process is not guaranteed to terminate, and even when it does, it is incredibly time consuming.

While evaluation upon receipt addresses these two important issues, it also causes a problem with respect to eventual consistency. One replicator may determine that a fact is valid, while another decides that it is invalid. This happens when one has received a revocation fact and the other has not. There is no causal relationship between the revocation and the contested fact. Neither is the predecessor of the other, so either one may occur first. Once this happens, no further messaging will bring these two replicators back into agreement.

Given the danger of inconsistency, revocation should be used with extreme caution. Provide the capability in the models that you design, but caution users to exercise that capability only sparingly. Build in some other mechanism to revoke privileges across the system. For example, control access to the private key for employees. When they are terminated, simply destroy the private key, rather than revoking grants of authorization. Or build a clock into the model. Periodically renew grants during the next period. If a principal leaves the group, simply neglect to renew their grant, rather than revoking past grants.

Confidentiality

The security considerations we've talked about so far have dealt with the ability to write data into the system. We now turn our attention to the ability to read data from the system. As with writes, we want to control reads without yielding to a centralized group of administrators. We will be conducting business over an evolving network topology that may include partner replicas outside of our direct control. And so we once again turn to PKI for inspiration on implementing trust without a central trusted authority.

The desire for autonomy is not one-sided. On the one hand, we want personal control for ourselves and our devices. We want to be assured that we can act without the need to connect to a central system of record. When working with partners in a distributed system, we should expect that they will want the same autonomy for themselves. We allowed them that autonomy by applying a *trust but verify* policy: we validated records for ourselves against an agreed-upon set of authorization rules. But granting them autonomy also gives them some degree of access to our sensitive information. We must now consider how to keep messages private in such an environment.

Untrusted Replicators

Confidentiality, as I'm using it here, means having reasonable assurance that the information that you wish to convey to a specific party will not be intercepted by others. The challenge in a distributed system is that the intended recipient might not be in direct communication. Messages might need to be stored on a third-party replicator that has greater uptime and accessibility than either of the parties' devices. Mail is stored on mail servers, not transmitted directly from sender to recipient. Direct messages are posted to shared channels. Records intended for one party can be found on untrusted intermediaries.

If we assume that we can trust our third-party providers implicitly, then we might be satisfied with simply encrypting data in transit. We might use a secure protocol like TLS to upload a private message to a social media provider, knowing full well that it will be decrypted on the server. It might even be stored in plaintext, to be reencrypted when the recipient initiates their own TLS connection to the same server. But if we do *not* want to assume that we can trust our intermediaries implicitly, then transport-layer encryption alone is not sufficient.

Asymmetric Encryption

As we saw in the "Proof of Authorship" section, public and private keys are nothing more than inverse functions. Put a number into one, and it produces an answer; put that answer into the other, and you get back the original number. We proved authorship by applying the private key first. We can send private messages by inverting the process.

If we wanted to send a number to a recipient, we can run it through their public key. The result can be stored on an untrusted replicator with little fear. Any party not in possession of the private key will have a very hard time inverting the function to find the original value. This is the basis for achieving confidentiality in a distributed system with third-party replicators. But before we can apply this protocol, we have to contend with the size limit.

Asymmetric Size Limit

If you recall, the functions that we produced using the RSA protocol only had inverses within a certain range. The function $x^{37} \bmod 1829$ – which we used as our public key – can only produce outputs in the domain *0-1828*. The pigeonhole principle prevented us from accepting any inputs that would cause us to double up on an output. And so this public key can only be used with 1829 distinct inputs; it only supports 10-bit messages. Real RSA key pairs are much larger: 2048 or 4096 bits in common usage. Nevertheless, there is a size limit. This was why we signed the *hash* and not the original message. And for the same reason, we cannot encrypt the original message using the recipient's public key.

Instead we will apply a *symmetric cypher* to the message. Symmetric keys don't have the same size limitation as asymmetric key pairs. They can be used to encrypt a message of arbitrary length. However, the same key is used both to encrypt and to decrypt the message. We must therefore keep the symmetric key private. That is what we pass through the recipient's public key.

Encrypt the Symmetric Key

And so the strategy that we use to ensure confidentiality in a distributed system is to encrypt the contents of immutable records before transmission. The sender first generates a random number to be used as the symmetric key. Effective symmetric keys can be significantly smaller than the size limit of a similarly effective public key. We can therefore pad and encrypt this symmetric key using the recipient's public key and store the result in the beginning of the immutable record. We can then encrypt the contents of the message using the symmetric key and store that encrypted blob at the tail of the record. The recipient can reverse the process, using their private key to reveal the symmetric key and extract it from the random padding. It can then decrypt the tail of the record to uncover the body of the message, as shown in Figure 9-9.

Figure 9-9. *The sender encrypts the symmetric key using the recipient's public key*

Third parties in the middle of this exchange will not be able to easily decrypt the record without the recipient's private key. We've succeeded in ensuring confidentiality when untrusted replicas lie between the participants. More than encrypting during transport – which exposes message contents to intermediaries – we've encrypted *prior to* transport. Even if the third-party replicator takes no additional precautions, we have protected the message at rest.

Encrypting Historical Facts

The protocol described previously is a popular mechanism for exchanging private messages over untrusted media. It is the core procedure in the OpenPGP protocol[2] used for private email exchange. It is commonly applied to messages stored on distributed file systems like IPFS, the InterPlanetary File System. In those and other scenarios, the protocol has a limit: it protects only the contents of the message, not the metadata surrounding the message. While an interceptor won't be able to read the contents of an OpenPGP email, they would be able to identify both the sender and the recipient. This is simply the consequence of the third party needing to know how to route messages. When this protocol is used within a historical model, the same limitation applies.

In a historical model, only the body of a confidential fact is encrypted. The type and – more importantly – the predecessors of that fact are not. The reason is that third-party replicas must be able to execute queries and return private facts. If the predecessors were encrypted, then the third-party replicator would not be able to determine which facts were the successors sought in the query.

For a similar reason, the identity of a confidential fact is based on the hash of its encrypted representation, not the original body. If other facts are subsequently recorded using the private fact as a predecessor, the intermediate parties need to understand that relationship. They need to be able to produce the hash of the record without decrypting it.

---

[2] Callas et al. IETF Network Working Group Request for Comments 4880. November 2007.

Limit the Distribution of Confidential Facts

Because the types and predecessor relationships are freely visible to intermediate parties, we still have to be careful with whom we share encrypted confidential messages. We can avoid shared distributed ledgers like blockchains that rely upon public scrutiny of metadata in order to function. We can limit the peers with which we directly share encrypted facts to only those that we can trust just enough not to infer meaning from the predecessor/successor relationships. We can even spread our trust among several intermediates so that no one of them has a complete picture of our interactions with other parties.

To prevent confidential facts from spreading further than they need to, these intermediaries must be given a set of rules by which they are permitted to release this information. Unlike the authorization rules previously discussed, we cannot execute these rules ourselves. We have to trust that the intermediaries that we choose to work with are enforcing them with each request. The rules tell them who is permitted to receive certain facts.

Distribution Rules

Whereas an authorization rule told us who was permitted to issue a fact, a distribution rule tells who is permitted to execute a query. We begin by defining the queries permitted. These can be expressed using specifications in the Factual query language, as we've already shown throughout the book. Give every replicator a list of allowed Factual specifications. Any client issuing a query not on this list is immediately rejected.

The next step is to identify the users who may receive the results of those queries. We do so with a second specification. The second specification begins at the same starting point as the first. It gives the list of users with whom we may share the results of the first specification.

Suppose that we have written the following specification for private messages sent to an individual:

```
privateMessagesToRecipient = (r: User) {
  m: PrivateMessage [
    m→recipient = r
  ]
}
```

A sufficiently restrictive replicator will not accept any queries until they have been provisioned to do so. It will not accept any query for `PrivateMessage` facts until it is given the preceding specification and the following distribution rule:

```
share privateMessagesToRecipient with (r: User) {
  u: User [
    u = r
  ]
} ⇒ u
```

This distribution rule is as simple as possible, but it demonstrates the important points. It identifies a specification, in this case the one defined just earlier. Then it adds a second specification identifying the users who are permitted to execute the query. This particular distribution rule allows only the recipient themselves to query for private messages.

Replicators turn specifications into feeds. Feeds provide all of the history required to execute a query from a particular starting point. This is the mechanism by which replicators communicate with one another, as detailed in Chapter 12. Distribution rules, therefore, are enforced at the feed boundary.

The controlled specification in each distribution rule is converted into a set of feeds. When a client or peer attempts to read from a feed, the replicator looks up all associated distribution rules. This results in a set of specifications listing the permitted users. If the client cannot prove that they are acting on behalf of at least one of those users, then the replicator will reject the feed request.

Evidence

Proving that a client is acting on behalf of a principal is not a trivial matter. How it is accomplished depends upon whether the query is coming from a client or another replicator. If the user is logged into the client, they will have an authorization token to share with the replicator. The token must have been issued by a *security token service* (STS) that both the client and the replicator trust. The client provided their credentials to the STS, and the STS signed the token. In this scenario, the replicator that the client is using directly will often be acting as a keystore as well. It will store the user's private key so that the user can log in from any device. This replicator must be completely under the user's control.

While client-server communication can be authorized by a token, server-to-server communication cannot. A replicator initiates a connection to another replicator without user intervention. There is no user to supply credentials to an STS and generate a token. Furthermore, the two replicators may not have an STS in common that they both trust. A security token would not provide satisfactory evidence that the query is on behalf of a given user.

To provide satisfactory evidence, the querying replicator must use the private key of the principal initiating the query. Given that this replicator is also likely to be the keystore, this process can be done without user intervention. The protocol begins with the querying replicator invoking a query from a certain starting point and identifying the principal's public key. If the target replicator determines that the identified principal is permitted to execute the query, it responds with a randomly generated challenge. The querying replicator answers the challenge in a way that proves that it is in possession of the private key. The trick is that it must not simply execute the private key and give back the answer. To do so would be to allow the replicator to use a message digest as a challenge, and thus generate a valid signature, or to execute a man-in-the-middle attack and produce a valid challenge response. Instead, a *zero-knowledge proof* protocol must be employed. Such a protocol proves that the querying replicator has the private key but does not allow the target replicator to gain any knowledge about it. David Chaum and his colleagues[3] give several protocols for proving that the querying replicator knows the discrete logarithm (inverse of an RSA key) of a given value without revealing that value.

Attacks and Countermeasures

None of these precautions, however, protect us from third parties that maliciously, negligently, or through legal compulsion share our information with others. For that, we may need to take additional precautions, based on the sensitivity of the metadata. Additional measures include the following:

- Periodically change key pairs to mask a party's identity.

- Mix one-time tokens with random users in key exchanges.

---

[3] Chaum, David; Evertse, Jan-Hendrik; van de Graaf, Jeroen (1987). An Improved Protocol for Demonstrating Possession of Discrete Logarithms and Some Generalizations. Advances in Cryptology – EuroCrypt '87: Proceedings. Lecture Notes in Computer Science.

- Generate a new key pair – and thus a new principal fact – for each interaction.

- Store identity mapping tables offline, or on a privately managed replicator.

- Generate a hum of meaningless facts between unrelated predecessors to hide the signal in the noise.

Such countermeasures are not necessary for every domain. But when the relationships among facts are valuable, and intermediate parties cannot be fully trusted, then additional care is warranted.

One more attack vector must be considered when storing encrypted facts on untrusted intermediate replicas. Data at rest is susceptible to offline attacks. Online services will throttle or block failed attempts to access data to prevent brute-force attacks. But when the attacker has the encrypted data in their possession, they can run as many attempts as their computing power will allow. Such an attack against modern cryptography algorithms will be expensive. But a determined attacker with a valuable enough payload might be willing and – eventually – able to discover the symmetric key.

There are several things that we could do to make their job easier. For example, the more that a symmetric key is reused, the more samples an attacker has to work with. And the longer the encrypted message, the more likely they are to discover an exploitable pattern. And so, to protect information from offline attacks, do exactly the opposite:

- Use a strong random number generator to produce symmetric keys.

- Use each symmetric key only once.

- Keep messages as short as possible.

- Pad messages with a large amount of random data.

- Generate additional meaningless facts to hide the valuable ones.

Even with all of these precautions in place, you must assume that the crypto systems that we use today will eventually become obsolete. This has been found true of the algorithms of the past, and we have no reason to believe that the future won't reveal weaknesses in today's technology. In fact, it's reasonable to believe that quantum computing will someday render all of today's asymmetric algorithms ineffective. Perhaps all that a determined attacker needs to do is wait.

My only advice to mitigate this problem is to ensure that the value of your information degrades over time. If you are exchanging payment information, make sure that those instruments expire before the encryption is broken. If you are collaborating on a secret plan, make sure that you execute before it's too late. If you have something that you want to keep secret forever, don't give it to a third party even if it is encrypted.

Secrecy

Employing PKI, distribution rules, and countermeasures, we have gained a level of confidentiality. We can now send a message to a specific recipient through untrusted replicas and have some assurance that the contents will remain private for some time. This form of confidentiality works well when communicating with one person. Many of our collaborations, however, involve groups. We will now generalize these techniques so that the group can communicate secretly.

We'll begin by defining a shared *workspace* in which the collaborators interact. This might take the form of a project containing work items, plans, and resources. Or it might be a department such as accounting, where payroll, accounts payable, and assets are all stored. Our goal is to control access within this workspace. We've already demonstrated the use of authorization rules to grant authority to create new facts in a workspace. Now we extend our strategy of confidentiality to keep those facts secret, visible only to those invited to the workspace.

Shared Symmetric Key

To keep the data within the workspace secret, we will create a shared symmetric key. Anyone in possession of this key will be able to decrypt the contents of the facts within the workspace. We must therefore have a protocol for exchanging that symmetric key with other members of the workspace within the historical model. We must do this without revealing it to untrusted third parties that store and forward the facts.

A workspace in a historical model takes the form of a fact. It has only one predecessor, the creator, and only one field, its identity. When a user initially creates the workspace, they generate a random symmetric key. This symmetric key is not stored in the workspace fact. Instead, it is shared with each participant individually.

To share the symmetric key with other participants, the creator sends invitations. An invitation is a successor to the workspace fact naming the recipient as a predecessor. Its only field is the shared symmetric key. The workspace creator sends the first invitation to themselves. The symmetric key is packed in random padding and encrypted using their own public key. Now the shared key is stored in the model in such a way that only the creator can decrypt it. The creator can send invitations to other collaborators immediately, or as they join the team.

A Secret Discussion Channel

To demonstrate this protocol, let's consider a secret channel to which collaborators can post messages. The channel itself is nothing more than a fact having an identifier. Invitations are successor facts sent to collaborators. The model appears in Figure 9-10.

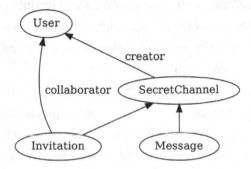

Figure 9-10. *A secret channel to which collaborators are invited*

The model is expressed in Factual as follows:

```
fact User {
  publicKey: string
}

fact SecretChannel {
  creator: User
  identifier: guid
}

fact Invitation {
  secretChannel: SecretChannel
  collaborator: User
  sharedKey: string
}
```

```
fact Message {
  secretChannel: SecretChannel
  sender: User
  body: string
}
```

Creating a Secret Channel

Alice wants to set up a secret channel so that she can talk with Bob and Charlie. She begins by following the Shared Project pattern described in Chapter 7. She generates a temporary key pair representing the creator of the channel. Then she creates a globally unique identifier and a random symmetric key. With these, she creates the SecretChannel fact and three Invitation facts. One of the invitations is to herself. The resulting facts are illustrated in Figure 9-11.

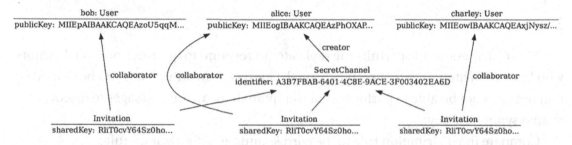

Figure 9-11. *Alice has created a private channel and invited both Bob and Charlie*

Even though the preceding diagram shows the plaintext contents of the Invitation facts, each one is encrypted using the public key of the associated collaborator. Each collaborator can individually decrypt their own invitation. Doing so reveals a shared symmetric key.

Team Distribution Rules

Even though the contents of the messages are encrypted using the shared symmetric key, it is still wise to limit the distribution of those facts. Assuming that the intermediate third-party replicas that we choose to use are well behaved, they will follow the rules that we define for distribution. Here is the query for secret messages and the corresponding distribution rule:

```
share messagesInSecretChannel = (sc: SecretChannel) {
  m: Message [
    m→secretChannel = sc
  ]
}
with (sc: SecretChannel) {
  i: Invitation [
    i→secretChannel = sc
  ]
  u: User [
    u = i→collaborator
  ]
} ⇒ u
```

This distribution rule permits the replicator to respond to queries from collaborators who have an invitation to that secret channel. Queries from other users will be denied so that they will not be able to perform offline cryptanalysis on the messages to discover the shared symmetric key.

Compare the distribution rule to the corresponding authorization rule:

```
authorize (m: Message) {
  i: Invitation [
    i→secretChannel = m→secretChannel
  ]
  u: User [
    u = i→collaborator
  ]
} ⇒ u
```

This rule authorizes every collaborator to post messages within the secret channel. It uses the same Invitation as the distribution rule. However, this need not be the case. We could define a different type of invitation called a ReadOnlyInvitation. By defining a distribution rule based on these types of invitations – but not defining a similar authorization rule – we can give some users read-only access to the messages.

Limit the Scope of a Shared Key

Just as we want to limit the distribution of encrypted facts, we want to limit the number of facts that are encrypted using the same symmetric key. Reusing a symmetric key provides a would-be attacker with more examples of ciphertext to analyze. When sending a fact to a single recipient, we were able to generate a distinct symmetric key for each message (commonly called a *session key*). Unfortunately, that same mechanism will not work for workspaces with large numbers of collaborators. The session key would need to be encrypted with the public keys of each collaborator in turn. Some of those collaborators may not have even joined the team at the time that the encrypted fact was created.

And so we must resort to reusing the shared symmetric key for all secret facts within the workspace. And in so doing, we run up against the problem of revocation once again. We want to be sure that we protect the ongoing work of the remaining collaborators after a former collaborator leaves the team. We can easily enough define an `InvitationRevoke` fact as a successor to an `Invitation`. With a not exists clause in the distribution rule, intermediate replicas will no longer distribute protected facts to the former collaborator. But that individual still has access to the shared symmetric key. If they were able to coerce the intermediate replicator to give up its cache of encrypted facts, they would have the tools to decrypt them.

Cohorts

One way to resolve the revocation problem is to move all of the remaining collaborators to a new shared key and issue them new invitations. The former collaborator would not have access to this new key. So while they could continue to decrypt the information they saw while a member of the project, they would not have access to any new information.

Moving collaborators to a new shared key is an inconvenience, but one that can be managed. All of the facts that they created before the move would be encrypted with the old shared key. The collaborators will want to create new facts using the new key but still have the ability to reference old facts as predecessors. Work must continue uninterrupted.

To model this solution, we insert a level of indirection. Between the workspace and the subsequent work, we inject a *cohort*. This fact represents the group of collaborators that all shared a symmetric key at the same time. All subsequent facts in the workspace are associated with a cohort, which tells us which symmetric key it was encrypted with. Modifying the secret channel model in Figure 9-10, the cohort fits in as illustrated in Figure 9-12.

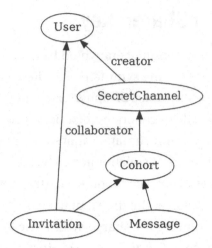

Figure 9-12. *Collaborators are invited to join a cohort*

Periods

Another solution to the revocation problem is to identify a clock within the domain. Use the clock as a cohort, as demonstrated previously. Each period of time gets its own shared symmetric key. All remaining collaborators receive new invitations at the beginning of each new period. Former collaborators fall away. While this leaves the window of attack open until the beginning of the next period, it has the advantage of being closely tied to the domain. A restaurant might define a period to be a single date of business. A school might define it to be a single semester. And such domains often align the boundaries of cohort membership with the clock. The *Period* pattern is covered in more detail in Chapter 8.

We've assembled a suite of tools that can help us control access to a historical model without relying upon an administrative body. Starting with the foundation of PKI, we've used public/private key pairs to identify principals, such as users or autonomous systems. Using the private key to sign a digest, we can prove authorship of each fact. Each replicator can then run authorization rules for itself to determine whether it believes that the author was authorized to perform the requisite action. And using the public key to encrypt a symmetric key, we can keep facts confidential whether intended for one individual or for a team. All of the information needed to enforce these rules lives within the model itself. This gives each replica autonomy to operate securely in a collaborative environment, without needing to rely upon the availability of a trusted third party.

PART III

Implementation

CHAPTER 10

SQL Databases

Immutable models are all about constraints. An application must not modify data. It is disallowed from deleting or overwriting information. These constraints are the axioms upon which the mathematical structure of immutable architecture is built. Ensuring that these constraints are met is the responsibility of every layer of the application stack, right down to the data storage system.

A sure-fire way to enforce immutability constraints is to use an immutable runtime. If you choose to do so, your work is done! But this option is not always available. You might, for example, need to gradually adopt immutability in a large stateful application. If so, this chapter will be your guide.

An immutable model can be backed by any kind of data store. One of the most powerful, flexible, and popular forms of storage engine is the relational database. Translating the constraints of the immutable model into a relational database takes discipline. We must avoid some of the capabilities that relational databases permit. To begin with, we must prohibit the use of UPDATE and DELETE. These two operations are part of the *Data Manipulation Language* (DML). Only the nondestructive DML command – INSERT – may be used in an immutable data store.

Limiting DML is a good start, but there is more we must do to store an immutable model in a relational database. We've defined queries against an immutable model using the Factual modeling language. As we discussed in Chapter 6, Factual specifications support not only execution but also inversion and decomposition into feeds. The specification language can only accomplish these things because of constraints that we don't ordinarily place on query languages like SQL.

A Factual specification must start at a set of known facts. It can only traverse the graph along predecessor/successor relationships. And it allows only existential conditions; data cannot be filtered by value. These constraints restrict our use of *Data Query Language* (DQL). DQL includes the ever powerful and composable SELECT, WHERE, and JOIN keywords. When storing an immutable model in a relational database, however, we must restrict ourselves to a subset of patterns.

333

M. L. Perry, *The Art of Immutable Architecture*, https://doi.org/10.1007/979-8-8688-0288-1_10

To work best with this subset of DQL, we will also constrain our use of the *Data Definition Language* (DDL). DDL statements use the CREATE keyword to define tables, indexes, and other objects. We will discover the subset of DDL that works best to define a schema for immutable records.

With all of these constraints, it would seem that we are losing the power and flexibility of relational databases. But in truth, we are gaining much more in exchange. The subset to which we limit ourselves will produce an extremely efficient data access layer. And where efficiency can be improved, we will find repeatable patterns of optimization. The steps we follow to produce DDL, DML, and DQL will be extremely mechanical. It will be so predictable that we will even be able to automate some or all of our SQL code generation.

To begin, we will learn how to write DDL to define a relational schema that stores an immutable model. The subset that we will use is carefully chosen to meet the constraints of immutable architecture. Designing to those constraints may at first appear to take capabilities away. But as we will see, it truly gives us capabilities that we could never have had before.

Identity

When we first introduced historical records as application data, we learned that a record is uniquely identified by the values of its fields and the identity of its predecessors. While this is a useful definition of identity for proving theorems about idempotence and convergence of histories, it is not very useful for database design. If every row were identified by the sum of its columns, then a foreign key would be a full copy of the parent table. This would not be at all practical.

A relational database requires that we identify historical records using some form of surrogate key. The most natural choice for most relational database systems is an auto-incremented ID. They provide the most optimal storage efficiency and query performance. They do, however, have the disadvantage of being location specific, as discussed at length in Chapter 5. We will therefore outline a mechanism for using auto-incremented IDs for their internal advantages but map them to content-based IDs to overcome the disadvantages.

Content-Addressed Storage

Conceptually, the content of a historical record *is* its identity. Practically, however, we need a stand-in for the content. The solution is to derive an identifier from the content using a hash function. This practice is known as *content-addressed storage*. This approach only works for content that does not change. And so it is an appropriate mechanism for identifying immutable records.

At first glance, this seems like an oxymoron. To load a record, you must know its address. Yet to find its address, you must first know its contents. It seems like you could never get started. In practice, however, it is not difficult at all to find a starting point. If someone is writing a record, then they know its contents. But if someone is reading a record, then they are given its hash. The starting point simply changes based on whether you are reading or writing.

Consider a blockchain on which a transaction needs to refer to a digital document. Space on the blockchain itself is far too expensive, which prohibits us from storing the document within the transaction. Instead, we store the hash. The actual document will be stored in a much less expensive distributed database, such as the InterPlanetary File System (IPFS).[1]

The author of the document has the original contents and can therefore compute the hash. Since the document is immutable, this hash will never change and can therefore be a reasonable surrogate for the document's identity. A reader of the transaction, on the other hand, does not have the original document. They cannot compute the hash to determine the identity. That's OK, however, because they can read the identity from the transaction.

Looking up a document in the distributed file system is a matter of fetching an object by its hash. Once retrieved, the reader can verify the identity of the document by computing its hash. Insofar as they can trust that it would be difficult to construct a fraudulent document with the same hash, they can trust that this immutable document has not been tampered with.

---

[1] https://ipfs.io

Advantages

In addition to the tamper-resistant nature of using a document's hash as its identity, we have several other benefits. Some of these were already covered in Chapter 5. Others will be new. Let's take some time, now that we have an understanding of how to model a system using immutable records, to evaluate these advantages.

As noted with the example of a document in a distributed file system, the writer computes the hash prior to storing the record. This implies that even before communicating with the server, the author of the record knows its identity. There is no need for the client to communicate with some external service before learning the identity. This gives it the autonomy to continue working, even creating other related records and referring to that identity, before it needs to connect to a peer.

There is also the advantage that every machine will compute the same identity for the same record. This provides a natural de-duplication benefit. Imagine if your photos were identified by the hash of their contents, rather than the folder that they occupy and the file name that the camera gave them. If that were the case, then you could never accidentally create duplicate photos by re-importing from digital media or sharing back and forth with friends. The same advantage exists in business applications. Preventing duplicates provides idempotence and avoids doubling the effect of a transaction.

Finally, consider the problem of merging data from disparate databases. If the identifier of those records was based on anything other than their contents, then two things could go wrong. First, it would be possible for two records with the same contents to have different identifiers, each allocated by a different database. And second, two distinct records could coincidentally share a common identifier. Both of these problems make it difficult to determine where the data structures intersect and where they diverge.

When using content-addressed storage, every machine computes identity in exactly the same way. If two records share an ID, they are the same record. And if they are the same record, they have the same ID. When any other mechanism is used, then IDs have to be re-mapped as data moves from one identifier space to another.

Avoid Hashes As Primary Keys

Hashes are fantastic identifiers. However, they are poor primary keys. The most obvious reason is size. Most modern computer systems have a natural word size of 64 bits. Relational database management systems take advantage of that word size for their native types and data structures. Hashes, on the other hand, are typically 160, 256, or 512 bits, depending upon the algorithm chosen. Larger identifiers can be noticeably slower and more cumbersome to manage.

Large primary keys can lead to bloated logs, as log entries must use the entire key to refer to rows. This impacts not only storage but also performance. Committing a transaction involves writing the log stream. Replication requires shipping it to other machines. Both of these operations take time.

Large identifiers will also bloat indexes. Scanning an index with larger identifiers means loading more pages to find the data that you want. Rebuilding indexes takes longer. And query operations cannot take place at the machine's native word boundary. The result is slower overall query performance.

Finally, most relational database systems will use the primary key as a clustered index. This means that the physical storage of the records will be sequenced according to this key. The most optimal way to allocate space for the next record is to append it to the block. The least optimal way is to insert it randomly somewhere in the middle. Hashes appear random. Using a hash as a clustered index will cause fragmentation and frequent page splitting.

Table Structure

We can apply this knowledge to constrain the Data Definition Language to produce well-behaved immutable models. To get the advantages of content-addressed storage while retaining the efficiency of auto-incremented IDs, we will store both. The auto-incremented ID will be the primary key of the table. Its value, however, will never leave the database. To the outside world, it will appear as if each record is identified only by its hash. We will impose a uniqueness constraint on the hash so that we have the necessary duplication protection.

Since a hash is larger than the word size of the computer, most database engines do not map them to native data types. Instead, they are typically stored in binary or text columns. If stored as text, they are base-64 encoded. This makes them easier to view as a human operator but increases the storage requirements by one-third. In the following examples, we will use the text option, as that is more portable. But please consider whether binary would be better for your application.

Let's recall one of the very first historical facts that we documented. This was a
`Catalog` fact having nothing other than a natural key to distinguish it from other catalogs.
We will convert this into a SQL table.

```
fact Catalog {
  referenceNumber: string
}
```

The table for a fact will contain the primary key, the hash, and a column for each
immutable field. This example has only one field, so the resulting table has just three
columns. This is how the table would be defined in PostgreSQL.

```
CREATE TABLE catalog (
  catalog_id SERIAL PRIMARY KEY,
  catalog_hash VARCHAR(88) NOT NULL UNIQUE,
  reference_number VARCHAR(50) NOT NULL
);
```

The reason for choosing 88 characters is that this application uses a 512-bit SHA-2
hash. When encoded in base-64, a 512-bit number takes 88 ASCII characters. To
find this value for any hash size, divide the number of bits by 24, round up, and then
multiply by 4.

It is tempting to define a uniqueness constraint covering the fields of the table.
We know that the values of those fields identify the fact, and so no other fact can have
those distinct values. In the preceding example, we might want to define a uniqueness
constraint on the reference number. While this would work for this specific example,
it breaks down in practice. We will see this more clearly when examining predecessors
with cardinality *many*. In all cases, the uniqueness constraint on the hash is serving the
same purpose. We will therefore rely upon that constraint alone.

To compute the hash of a record, find a canonical form. I prefer to use JSON with the
fields sorted alphabetically and all whitespace removed. Compute the hash of the UTF-8
encoded string representation.

```
$ echo -n '{"reference_number":"AX247"}' | \
> openssl dgst -sha512 -binary | \
> base64
8rCOhVD...ifdw==
```

This table structure permits insertion without the need to wait for the primary key to be generated. The caller already knows the hash of the record, and that is all that is required to uniquely identify the row. When the `catalog_id` is needed later, it can be retrieved by `catalog_hash`.

If the application attempts to insert a duplicate record, the uniqueness constraint will prevent it. There is no reason to treat this as an error. The application has simply confirmed that the record had been stored. Most relational database engines will allow you to ignore a uniqueness constraint violation. In PostgreSQL, for example, use the clause `ON CONFLICT DO NOTHING`.

```
INSERT INTO catalog
  (catalog_hash, reference_number)
  VALUES ('8rCOhVD...ifdw==', 'AX247')
  ON CONFLICT DO NOTHING;
```

Relationships

When we translate predecessor relationships into relational tables, they become foreign keys. To gain the space and performance advantages of integers, the foreign key will reference the auto-incremented ID of the predecessor, not the hash. This keeps our indexes small and fast. But these foreign keys do not leave the database.

Predecessor relationships come in three cardinalities: *one*, *optional* (0 or 1), and *many* (0 or more). If the relationship allows exactly one predecessor, then we represent it directly as a foreign key in the fact table. For example, we can translate a product residing in a catalog into a table. The Factual definition of the product is as follows:

```
fact Product {
  catalog: Catalog
  sku: string
}
```

The resulting table has an auto-incremented ID, a hash, the fields, and foreign keys for predecessors. The hash will be based only on the fields and the hashes of predecessors, not their database-generated IDs. Be sure to create an index on the foreign key, as most relational database systems will not do this automatically.

```
CREATE TABLE product (
  product_id SERIAL PRIMARY KEY,
  product_hash VARCHAR(88) NOT NULL UNIQUE,
  catalog_id INT NOT NULL REFERENCES catalog,
  sku VARCHAR(50) NOT NULL
);

CREATE INDEX product_catalog
  ON product (catalog_id);
```

Inserting Successors

Now with the schema defined, we can determine how to best structure our Data Modification Language. When inserting successor rows, the caller does not know the ID of the predecessor. That's because the ID never left the database. This was an important design decision to protect location independence. As a consequence, we need the database to look up the predecessor ID whenever it performs an insert.

We will look up the ID of the predecessor using the hash of the predecessor. Performing a lookup within an INSERT statement requires the INSERT ... SELECT syntax. The calling application computes the hashes of the predecessor and successor fact. The query looks up the predecessor ID by hash and inserts the successor hash directly.

```
INSERT INTO product
  (product_hash, catalog_id, sku)
  SELECT 'fKo2Oge...5GFw==', catalog_id, 'PK47'
    FROM catalog
    WHERE catalog_hash = '8rCOhVD...ifdw=='
  ON CONFLICT DO NOTHING;
```

To compute the hash of a successor from a canonical form, the hash of the predecessor must be used. In the canonical JSON that I prefer, the predecessor is represented by an object having a ref field. The value of that field is the hash of the predecessor. Predecessors are sorted alphabetically among the rest of the fields.

```
$ echo -n '{"catalog":{"ref":"8rCOhVD...ifdw=="},"sku":"PK47"}' | \
> openssl dgst -sha512 -binary | \
> base64
fKo2Oge...5GFw==
```

Optional Predecessors

An optional relationship allows zero or one predecessor. In the canonical JSON form, the *zero* case is represented by a `null` value for the predecessor field. And in a relational table, the foreign key column allows NULLs. Foreign keys that can be null are cause for concern in relational database design. The sorts of queries that we will perform, however, tend to avoid these concerns.

In some relational database systems, an index on a nullable column will skip rows in which the column is null. As a result, queries for NULL values will perform a full table scan. Fortunately, the forms of queries that we will build will join on non-null values. The indexes on predecessor foreign keys – even the nullable ones – will always be used in these kinds of queries.

Many Predecessors

Storing the foreign key directly in the fact table is appropriate for cardinalities *one* or *optional*. It does not work for cardinality *many*. Relationships with many predecessors require an associative table. By convention, I call these associative tables *predecessor tables*. The reason is that they conceptually hold the predecessor references of a given fact. They borrow their name from the fact that declares them.

To see an example, let's look at the price of a product. This property could change over time. Each individual price change is recorded as a `Price` fact. Following the *Mutable Property* pattern, this fact has many `prior` predecessors.

```
fact Price {
  product: Product
  value: decimal
  prior: Price*
}
```

The `price` table is constructed from this fact using the patterns already discussed. The table has an ID and a hash. It also has a column for each of the fields and *one* or *optional* predecessors. It does not, however, have any columns for *many* predecessors.

```
CREATE TABLE price (
  price_id SERIAL PRIMARY KEY,
  price_hash VARCHAR(88) NOT NULL UNIQUE,
```

```
  product_id INT NOT NULL REFERENCES product,
  value DECIMAL(10, 2) NOT NULL
);
```

```
CREATE INDEX price_product
  ON price (product_id);
```

The *many* relationship is represented with an associative table. The name of the table is derived from the successor – the fact that defines the relationship. The table contains only the foreign keys of the predecessor and successor rows, neither of which can be null. The pair of foreign keys is unique, encoding the truism that predecessor collections are *sets*, not *lists*; they cannot contain the same predecessor for any given successor. Both of the foreign keys are independently indexed.

```
CREATE TABLE price_predecessor (
  price_id INT NOT NULL REFERENCES price,
  prior_price_id INT NOT NULL REFERENCES price,
  UNIQUE (price_id, prior_price_id)
);
```

```
CREATE INDEX price_predecessor_price
  ON price_predecessor (price_id);
```

```
CREATE INDEX price_predecessor_prior_price
  ON price_predecessor (prior_price_id);
```

And now it should be a bit more clear why we do not add uniqueness constraints on the fields of a fact. If we defined such constraints on a table that had an associated *predecessor table*, then the predecessors would not be included in the unique index. In this case, had we defined a uniqueness constraint on the fields, it would be impossible to insert two `prices` with the same product ID and value, even if they had different `prior` sets. This is precisely what happens when a price returns to its former value.

The predecessors of a fact are part of its identity. But the predecessor references are stored in a different table. Uniqueness constraints cannot cross table boundaries. Therefore, we leave off uniqueness of the fields altogether. The uniqueness constraint on the hash solves the problem perfectly well.

Canonical Hash of a Set

The hash of a fact having many predecessors is based on all of the hashes of those predecessors. The canonical form that I recommend represents many predecessors as a JSON array. If there are no predecessors, the array is empty rather than `null`. If there happens to be one predecessor, the array contains one reference object. Reference objects are sorted alphanumerically by base-64 encoded hash so that there is only one canonical representation of the set. For example, the first price of a product would be identified by the hash of the following JSON document with whitespace removed:

```
{
  "prior": [],
  "product": {
    "ref": "fKO2Oge...5GFw=="
  },
  "value": 256.98
}
```

The subsequent price would get the hash of the JSON document with one prior reference:

```
{
  "prior": [
    {
      "ref": "ZlUYAZV...ZQZA=="
    }
  ],
  "product": {
    "ref": "fKO2Oge...5GFw=="
  },
  "value": 220.98
}
```

Inserting Many Predecessors

A fact with an empty predecessor set can be inserted exactly as we've done before. This row represents a complete fact with no related rows in the predecessor table.

```
INSERT INTO price
  (price_hash, product_id, value)
  SELECT 'ZlUYAZV...ZQZA==', product_id, 256.98
    FROM product
    WHERE product_hash='fKO2Oge...5GFw=='
  ON CONFLICT DO NOTHING;
```

When inserting a fact with one or more predecessors in the set, however, the DML needs to be extended. Rows are inserted into predecessor tables at the same time as the successor. Inserts are performed within a database transaction to avoid the possibility of using a partially written fact in a query.

```
BEGIN TRANSACTION;

INSERT INTO price
  (price_hash, product_id, value)
  SELECT 'DRFoFgF...BNpw==', product_id, 220.98
    FROM product
    WHERE product_hash='fKO2Oge...5GFw=='
  ON CONFLICT DO NOTHING;

INSERT INTO price_predecessor
  (price_id, prior_price_id)
  SELECT successor.price_id, predecessor.price_id
    FROM price as successor, price as predecessor
    WHERE successor.price_hash = 'DRFoFgF...BNpw=='
      AND predecessor.price_hash IN ('ZlUYAZV...ZQZA==')
  ON CONFLICT DO NOTHING;

COMMIT TRANSACTION;
```

By using the IN clause in the predecessor insert statement, we can list the hashes of all predecessors that we want to insert. The database will produce all of the primary keys in a single statement.

In this particular example, the predecessor and successor tables are the same type. For that reason, the insert statement needed to create aliases to disambiguate the predecessor and successor rows. This will not always be necessary, but you may wish to always use these aliases for the sake of consistency.

Queries

We've converted fact specifications into constrained statements in the Data Definition Language and Data Manipulation Language. We will now convert specifications into Data Query Language. This is a two-stage process.

The first stage is to turn the specification into a pipeline. A pipeline transforms one set of facts into another through a series of steps and filters. The second stage is to convert the pipeline into SQL. In this stage, we turn each step of the pipeline into a join and each filter into a subquery. With practice, you'll be able to write a SQL query from a specification directly. But seeing these two stages independently will make the process more approachable.

From Specification to Pipeline

A specification written in the Factual Modeling Language describes the types and relationships among facts. It gives the conditions under which certain facts should be included. A Factual specification is a declarative statement of the results that we seek. This description needs to be translated into something actionable.

A specification that we studied in Chapter 5 identified the lines in a cart, excluding those that had been ordered.

```
linesRemainingInCart = (c: Cart) {
  ol: OrderLine [
    ol→cart = c
    ∄ {
      o: Order [
        o→orderLines = ol
      ]
    }
  ]
}
```

We overlaid that specification on the fact type graph as shown in Figure 10-1.

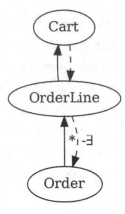

Figure 10-1. *The specification visualized as a path over the fact graph*

The dotted arrows indicate the path along which the instance graph will be traversed. It describes how we will execute the specification. We can formalize that process as a pipeline.

A Set of Unknowns

A specification is a set of *unknowns*. Each unknown gives a name to a set of facts. The only unknown in our example specification is `ol: OrderLine`. This unknown can take on the identity of any order line that matches a set of conditions.

There are two kinds of *conditions* associated with an unknown: path conditions and existential conditions. This simple specification has one of each. The path condition `ol->cart = c` traces a path back to the given cart. The existential condition states that there does not exist ($\nexists$) a related order line. We'll deconstruct the existential condition later. First, let's focus on the path condition.

A Sequence of Steps

Paths are written as an equation. The left side of the equation starts with the unknown. The right side starts with another labeled fact. It might be a given, or it might be a previously defined unknown. In this case, the right side starts with the given cart `c`.

Both sides follow predecessor *roles* up from their starting point. They meet at a common ancestor. We can convert a path into a sequence of *steps* by walking first the right side and then the left side of the equation.

Each role on the right side becomes a predecessor step. A predecessor step takes us from a set of facts to a set of predecessors along a role. In the example specification, the path `ol->cart = c` has no arrows on the right side. It therefore has no predecessor steps.

Then each role on the left side becomes a successor step. A successor step takes us from a set of facts to a set of successors along a role. In the example, `ol->cart = c` has one arrow on the left. It therefore has one successor step. If the path has more than one role on the left, those roles must be reversed to produce the correct sequence of steps.

Following these rules, we convert a path into a sequence of steps. Each step moves from one fact type to another along an edge. The edge is the predecessor/successor relationship between the two facts. Each edge has a role: the name given to the predecessor within the successor's type definition. So we can define a step between facts of types A and B as going up to the predecessor or down to the successor along an edge with a given role.

Our example produced a single successor step. Given a cart, this step finds all successor order lines in the role "cart." We can draw this step as shown in Figure 10-2.

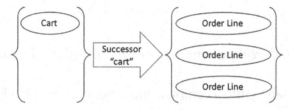

Figure 10-2. *The first step in the pipeline takes a set of carts to a set of order lines*

Each node in this pipeline is a set of facts. The first set contains only the single given cart. The second contains all matching order lines. Following the rules described here, we can convert a specification of unknowns and path conditions into a sequence of steps taking us from the given to the results. Now let's add existential conditions.

Filter by Existential Condition

Some components within the pipeline will not be steps at all. They will not move up to a predecessor or down to a successor along an edge. Instead, they will filter the incoming set based on an existential condition. Each condition's quantifier is either exists ($\exists$) or not exists ($\nexists$). The body of the condition is another specification, which starts at the fact type where the filter is applied.

In the example specification, we filter out all order lines that are not a part of an order. We accomplish this with an existential condition based on the unknown `o: order` with the path `o->orderLines = ol`. Following the rules described previously, we convert this subspecification into a successor step. It finds all orders that are successors of the order lines `ol`.

The existential condition filters the order lines based on the results of this successor step. It keeps only those order lines where no results exist. And so we add a filter component that feeds each fact into a subordinate pipeline. This component is shown in Figure 10-3.

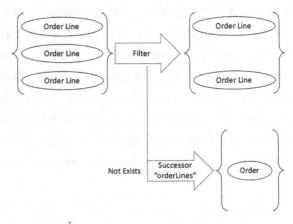

Figure 10-3. *A pipeline component filters order lines based on a subspecification*

Joining these two halves into a complete pipeline, as shown in Figure 10-4, gives us a mechanism for executing the specification.

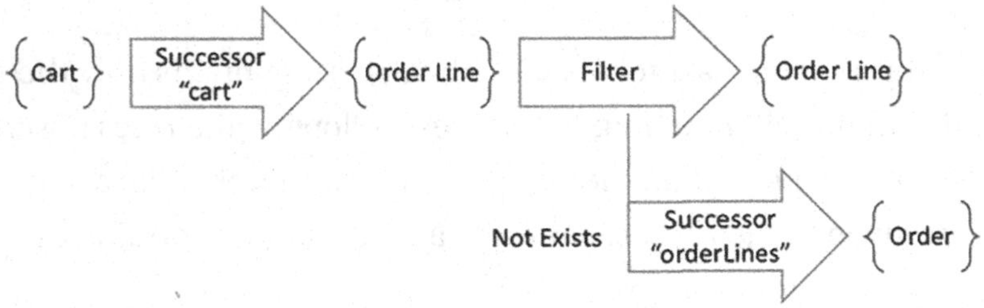

Figure 10-4. *A pipeline composed of three operations*

These rules give us a mechanism for converting a simple specification into a pipeline. Through a series of components, the pipeline takes a given to a set of resulting facts. Along the way, we pass through labeled sets defined by unknowns. We can compute projections from these labeled sets. But sometimes, those projections are themselves specifications.

Child Specifications

Let's examine another specification from earlier in the book. Chapter 7 gave an example of the Entity List pattern. This complex specification combines ownership, deletion, restoration, and a mutable property.

```
entitiesInOwner = (o: Owner) {
  e: Entity [
    e→owner = o
    ∄ {
      ed: EntityDeletion [
        ed→entity = e
        ∄ {
          er: EntityRestore [
            er→deletion = ed
          ]
        }
      ]
    }
  ]
} ⇒ {
  identifier: e.identifier
  titles: {
    p: EntityProperty [
      p→entity = e
      ∄ {
        next: EntityProperty [
          next→prior = p
        ]
      }
    ]
  } ⇒ p.value
}
```

This specification has a projection, which selects the identifier and titles of each entity. The identifier comes directly from the entity. But the titles require a subspecification.

The specification for entities and the specification for titles comprise two halves of the whole. We can create a pipeline for each of these specifications. The first specification selects the entities:

```
entitiesInOwner = (o: Owner) {
  e: Entity [
    e→owner = o
    ∄ {
      ed: EntityDeletion [
        ed→entity = e
        ∄ {
          er: EntityRestore [
            er→deletion = ed
          ]
        }
      ]
    }
  ]
}
```

It produces the pipeline in Figure 10-5.

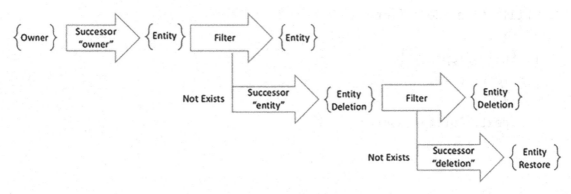

Figure 10-5. *A pipeline returning all entities that have not been deleted*

Given a single owner, this pipeline finds successor entities and then filters out those with deletions for which there is no restore. The result is a set of entities.

The second half is the specification that produces the titles of an entity.

```
titlesOfEntity = (e: Entity) {
  p: EntityProperty [
    p→entity = e
    ∄ {
      next: EntityProperty [
        next→prior = p
      ]
    }
  ]
}
```

By the rules defined earlier, this specification produces the pipeline in Figure 10-6.

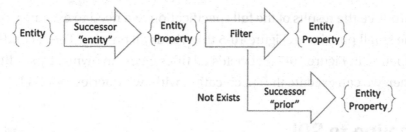

Figure 10-6. *A pipeline returning all properties of an entity that have not been superseded*

Given an entity, find all of the entity properties and filter out the ones for which a next version exists.

We don't execute the second pipeline directly. After all, we are given an owner, not an entity. If we executed the second pipeline directly for each entity, we would end up with what is called an "N+1 Query" problem. The number of queries we execute would be based on the number of entities in the dataset. Instead, we concatenate the two pipelines. This produces the combined pipeline in Figure 10-7.

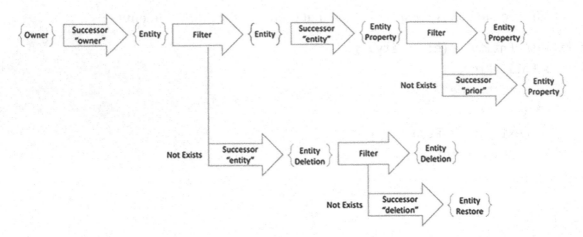

Figure 10-7. *Concatenating two pipelines produces one that finds all properties of all entities*

Now to produce the results of the full specification, we need to execute two pieces. The first is the small pipeline in Figure 10-5 that yields all entities. The second is the combined pipeline in Figure 10-7 that yields all titles given an owner. By shuffling the results together, we can execute the specification with two queries, not N+1.

From Pipeline to SQL

We have a mechanism for converting a specification into a set of pipelines. All pipelines start from the same given facts. Now we need to convert those pipelines into SQL queries so that we can execute them. We'll start where the pipelines do, at the givens.

Given Facts

Every pipeline has a starting point. We express the starting point by its hash. The ID never left the database, so we cannot start a query from an ID. The initial shape of the query selects FROM the starting type and lists the hash in the WHERE clause.

```
SELECT reference_number
FROM catalog
WHERE catalog_hash='8rCOhVD...ifdw==';
```

The initial query is almost never used in its basic form. Any application that can provide the hash probably already has the fields. Instead, we start from that initial query and add steps from the pipeline. Each step becomes a SQL join.

Joins

Every step in a pipeline follows a role up to a predecessor or down to a successor. The role has cardinality *one*, *optional*, or *many*. A step following a role with *one* or *optional* cardinality becomes a simple foreign key join. If it is a step up to the predecessor, then the foreign key is in the current table. If it is down to the successor – as in the following query – then the foreign key is in the remote table:

```
SELECT product_hash, sku
FROM catalog
JOIN product ON catalog.catalog_id = product.catalog_id
WHERE catalog_hash='8rCOhVD...ifdw==';
```

Steps always produce inner joins. There is no need to define left, right, or full outer joins. Ordinarily a left join would help an application find results for which there are no children. In Factual, however, children would be expressed as a projection with a subspecification. The developer would convert that specification into two pipelines. The first would produce results whether or not the second produced children.

For steps following a *many* predecessor role, we need to join through the *predecessor table*. We will see an example of that when we dive down to the subquery.

Correlated Subqueries

When we process a filter in the pipeline, we translate that into a subquery. In particular, it becomes a *correlated subquery*, as it depends upon the values of the current row. A filter will either use the quantifier exists ($\exists$) or not exists ($\nexists$). These translate directly into SQL EXISTS and NOT EXISTS clauses.

Suppose we want to select the current price for a product. The pipeline for this query appears in Figure 10-8.

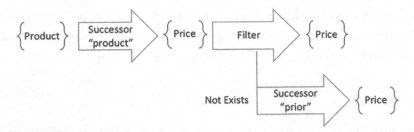

Figure 10-8. *The pipeline for the current price of a product filters prices based on a subquery*

We start with the product. Define a WHERE clause based on its hash. We will then walk down to the successor prices for that product.

```
SELECT price_hash, value
FROM product
JOIN price ON price.product_id = product.product_id
WHERE product_hash = 'fKO2Oge...5GFw==';
```

At this point, the pipeline sends us into a filter. The subquery starts at a price. It steps to a successor price using the prior role. This becomes a join using the price_ predecessor table.

```
SELECT price_hash, value
FROM product
JOIN price ON price.product_id = product.product_id
WHERE product_hash = 'fKO2Oge...5GFw=='
  AND NOT EXISTS (
    SELECT 1
    FROM price_predecessor
    WHERE price_predecessor.prior_price_id = price.price_id
  );
```

This query will skip the prices that have been replaced. It will only return the current prices. The filter in the pipeline becomes a correlated subquery containing all of the steps of the subordinate pipeline.

Optimization

From the examples earlier, you should have an appreciation for the richness and complexity of DQL that a pipeline could produce. But you might have some concerns with the less-than-ideal constructs that they sometimes generate. In the previous examples, we translated directly from pipelines to SQL. Now we will optimize that SQL to implement the same pipeline, but in a more efficient way.

Spurious Joins

One problem is that a direct mechanical translation sometimes produces a join that is not needed. These spurious joins will often arise when the pipeline steps to a predecessor and then immediately down to a different successor. For example, to find the name of a student enrolled in a class, we might use the pipeline shown in Figure 10-9.

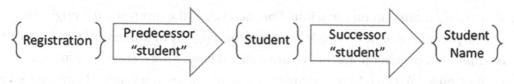

Figure 10-9. *Finding the name of a registered student involves stepping up to the student and then down to the name*

A direct translation of this pipeline to SQL would produce a query with two joins:

```
SELECT name
FROM registration
JOIN student
  ON registration.student_id = student.student_id
JOIN student_name
  ON student.student_id = student_name.student_id
WHERE registration_hash = 'xxxxx...yyyy=='
```

Careful inspection, however, reveals that the join to the student table yields no additional information. The student ID is already known. We can therefore optimize away the intermediate join.

```
SELECT name
FROM registration
JOIN student_name
  ON registration.student_id = student_name.student_id
WHERE registration_hash = 'xxxxx...yyyy=='
```

Joining directly from one sibling to the next without going through the parent is possible because we don't need any additional information. If some field of the parent *is* required, however, then this optimization is not available to us. A SQL generator could look for this pattern and produce the optimized query. Such an optimization would produce a more efficient query plan.

Covering Indexes

As you analyze the query plans produced by these kinds of queries, they will be dominated by *index seeks* and *index scans*. An index seek is the most efficient way that a database engine can implement a join. For each key in the input set, the engine seeks to a specific place in an index to find the corresponding key in the output set. An index scan is similar but used for joins that return many related rows – successor joins or *many* predecessor joins. We can take advantage of these fast query operations because we have created indexes for all foreign keys.

At the end of the query plan, however, you will usually find a *clustered index lookup*. The query has produced a set of primary keys through the various index seek and index scan operations. It is now using those primary keys to look up rows in the table to extract the values in the SELECT clause. This last operation might take a significant portion of the query time.

To speed up queries that select additional columns, it is sometimes wise to include those selected columns in a *covering index*. When creating an index based on a foreign key, you can include data columns. The values in those columns will be copied into the index so that they are readily available.

```
CREATE INDEX price_product
  ON price (product_id)
  INCLUDE (value);
```

While this could improve the performance of heavily used queries, covering indexes incur a cost. Since the index includes additional data, it will consume more space. Inserts will take slightly longer, and index operation will take a little extra time. It will be less time than the index seek followed by the clustered index lookup, but the difference in performance should not be ignored. Covering indexes should be used sparingly and only after profiling your queries.

WHERE NOT EXISTS

The most significant performance concern arises from existential conditions. Many of the queries that we produce in real-world applications will include a WHERE NOT EXISTS clause. The clause arises most often from the Delete, Mutable Property, and Queue patterns. It results in an *anti join*. This is an index scan that only returns input rows for which *no* output row is produced. In and of itself, this is not a slow operation, especially because it can use a foreign key index. The issue arises when it is performed over a large input set, even when it produces a small output set.

The index scan will be performed for every input row. Performance is not related to the number of output rows. This means that performance problems can hide in queries that seem small. Based on the way the pattern is used, we can estimate how many keys will be scanned vs. how many results will be produced. You could define the percentage of *waste* to be ratio of excluded inputs to the total number of inputs. For performance to be roughly correlated with value, we would like waste to be bounded and reasonably low.

Mutable Properties

If the WHERE NOT EXISTS clause occurs in a query for the current value of a mutable property, then the input set will include all historical values. The output set will contain only those versions that have not been superseded. The waste, therefore, would be the ratio of superseded versions to total versions. For a mutable property that changes frequently, waste would be high. But if the property changes relatively infrequently, waste is low.

For this reason, the Mutable Property pattern should only be applied to slowly changing properties. Things that change often over the lifetime of an entity produce significant waste. Slowly changing properties are things like a person's name or a company's address. Frequently changing properties are things like status or progress. Workflow patterns are often better alternatives for frequently changing properties.

Deletion

Another place in which `WHERE NOT EXISTS` often appears is a query that excludes deleted entities. The input set will include all entities that have ever existed. The output set will contain only those that still exist. The waste is the ratio of deleted entities over all entities. When most entities are deleted, waste is high.

Think back to the last CRUD application that you built. There was probably one large table that included the primary entity that the app worked with. Perhaps it was a customer table, which you queried frequently to produce a large list of current customers. Since customers come and go, more and more customers were deleted over time, compared to a relatively stable number of current customers.

If you used an actual `DELETE` statement, then you kept waste bounded. But if you used a soft delete, then waste grew over time. With a soft delete, you set a field to simulate a deletion and then selected only those rows where the flag is not set. The soft delete preserved data, but it came with a performance cost.

A deletion in a historical model is similar to a soft delete in a CRUD model. It preserves data but incurs the same performance costs. Fortunately, we have a couple of options for regaining that performance.

The first option to consider is to add a clock to the model. Please see the Period pattern in Chapter 8. A clock is a starting point for a query that slowly advances over time. Some models have natural periods, like dates of business in a retail system or semesters in an academic domain. In others, the clock is a bit more artificial. In either case, a query based on a small number of periods limits the amount of waste due to deletions. Only survivors move from one period to the next.

If no reasonable clock can be found, then a more drastic solution might be called for. Measure your performance and calculate the actual percentage of waste. If you find that most entities are deleted, and that that is affecting query performance over time, then consider a managed index. This solution is most applicable to queues, so we will examine it from that context.

Queues

The Queue pattern, as documented in Chapter 8, includes a successor fact that records the outcome of taking action upon a work item. The queue is fed by a query that selects work items for which no outcome exists. These translate into pipeline filters, which eventually become WHERE NOT EXISTS clauses in SQL. The input set to the anti join is the set of all work items. The output set contains only the work items not yet processed. Since every work item will eventually be processed, this query approaches 100% waste.

When relying upon an anti join, we are taking away the SQL engine's most valuable tool: direct addressability. The items in the queue are not directly addressable. Instead, the index stores specifically those items that are *not* in the queue. The engine has to scan that index for every work item to see which ones are not excluded. It would be much faster if we could convince the SQL engine to directly index those that were included.

To so convince the engine, we need to provide it something that it can directly index and address. Something that represents the *absence* of a successor. One option is to re-examine the soft delete flag.

A soft delete as implemented in a CRUD system is an UPDATE that takes the place of a DELETE. Instead of completely destroying the record, the application updates it to set a flag. Such a flag can be indexed to provide direct access to those records that have not been marked deleted. When relatively few of the rows are marked, the index is not selective. Most query engines will avoid a nonselective index because a table scan would turn out to be faster. But if most of the rows are marked – as in work items processed from a queue – then the index becomes quite selective. The query engine can use the index to directly address the relatively small number of unprocessed work items.

Even when it is selective, an index on a flag has a space disadvantage. All rows are indexed, even the ones for which the flag is set. The index will never be used to find the flagged work items, because the query specifically looks for the non-flagged ones. We could save some space if we excluded completed work items from the index altogether.

Some database management systems include a *partial index* feature. If this feature is available, you can create an index that has a condition. Specify that condition to include only unprocessed work items in the index, and that index will be used to directly address those items.

```
CREATE INDEX work_item_unprocessed
  ON work_item (queue_id)
  WHERE processed = FALSE;
```

But even if your database management system does not support this feature, you can simulate it. Create a table that you will use as an index yourself. Insert rows into this table to indicate that the flag is *not* set, and delete them to indicate that it *is* set.

```
CREATE TABLE work_item_unprocessed (
  queue_id INT NOT NULL,
  work_item_id INT NOT NULL UNIQUE
)

CREATE INDEX work_item_unprocessed_queue
  ON work_item_processed (queue_id);
```

Whether you add a mutable flag and define a partial index or you add a table to store unprocessed work items, you will have to manage the index yourself. For this reason, I call this technique a *managed index*. I recommend using triggers for index management. While the index could be managed by the application, it exists to address a database performance concern. The solution should therefore be entirely specified within the database.

To use the index table approach, create two triggers. The first inserts into the index table when a new work item is created. The second deletes from the index table when the outcome is created. For example, the following pair of triggers manages an index table for a queue:

```
CREATE FUNCTION insert_work_item_unprocessed() RETURNS TRIGGER AS $$
  BEGIN
    INSERT INTO work_item_unprocessed
      (queue_id, work_item_id)
      VALUES (NEW.queue_id, NEW.work_item_id);
    RETURN NULL;
  END;
$$ LANGUAGE plpgsql;

CREATE TRIGGER work_item_created AFTER INSERT ON work_item
  FOR EACH ROW
  EXECUTE FUNCTION insert_work_item_unprocessed();

INSERT INTO work_item
  (queue_id, description)
  VALUES (47, 'Do some work');
```

```
CREATE FUNCTION delete_work_item_unprocessed() RETURNS TRIGGER AS $$
  BEGIN
    DELETE FROM work_item_unprocessed
      WHERE work_item_id = NEW.work_item_id;
    RETURN NULL;
  END;
$$ LANGUAGE plpgsql;

CREATE TRIGGER work_item_outcome_created AFTER INSERT ON work_item_outcome
  FOR EACH ROW
  EXECUTE FUNCTION delete_work_item_unprocessed();
```

Join through the index table instead of using the WHERE NOT EXISTS clause. The query optimizer will use the table to directly address items remaining in the queue. It will not need to perform a scan over all historical work items in order to perform an anti join. The results will be much faster, especially for work items where 100% of them are eventually excluded from the query.

Integration

Not all of an application's features will be served out of an immutable database. Some queries do not lend themselves to traversing predecessor and successor relationships from a single starting point. Some table structures are better denormalized. When a mutable, state-based structure is more appropriate, use that structure. Integrate between the immutable database and the mutable one.

In separating mutable from immutable data, be sure to keep the data structures isolated from one another. Do not mix the two table structures. Do not include foreign keys from one model within the other. And avoid any form of cross-joining between the two models. Even though it may make sense to use the same relational database engine for the two models, do not combine them into the same database. They have distinct purposes and patterns of use.

Legacy Application Integration

When introducing immutable architecture to an organization, you will not have an opportunity to rewrite all of your systems in this style, nor should you seek such an opportunity. It would introduce a great deal of risk with rewards that would be realized far too late. Instead, let legacy applications continue to exist having stateful, mutable data models. Find the best integration points to work with those legacy applications with minimal risk and rework.

Some legacy applications might have been written with event-driven architectures in mind. If so, leverage those integration points as places where historical facts are produced and advertised. More likely, however, a legacy application will simply be a collection of stateless behaviors on top of a mutable data model. It will not throw off events that could be turned into facts. There will not be an easy way to modify the application source code to create those integration points.

In these cases, I suggest using the database as a point of integration. This is not to say that two applications should share a common database: that practice leads to tight coupling and rapid stagnation. Instead, use the tools inherent in the database to extract facts from state changes. These tools include scanners, triggers, and change data capture.

Scanners

The most direct way to extract facts from data is to scan for them. A scanner is a handwritten query that projects the current state of an application into the set of facts that gave rise to that state.

To design a useful scanner, you must understand which parts of the model might change and which parts are immutable. Relational database engines don't have many tools to enforce or document immutability, but they have a few. One such tool is the uniqueness constraint.

When a table is given a uniqueness constraint, the designer is documenting the fact that the included columns form a natural key for the row. Those columns represent an identity independent of the auto-incremented surrogate key. Even though the database engine does not strictly prohibit an application from changing these columns, doing so would change the identity of the entity. If a database designer has gone through the trouble of declaring a uniqueness constraint, you can be fairly confident that the columns are immutable.

Begin by producing a series of queries that select out the immutable data from the source system. You should be able to project these results directly into facts. If those facts already exist in the target immutable model, then no harm done; they will not be duplicated. Just project these results and insert the corresponding facts.

Next, you will be left with the mutable data. Projecting these will require a bit of history. To help keep track of its work, the scanner should keep a scratch pad of the mutable values that it last saw per entity. When it finds different values, it can use this scratch pad to find the prior versions and make those facts predecessors of the new facts. The specific details of the scratch pad depend heavily upon your application and chosen technology stack. Suffice to say that it should contain enough information to fully reconstruct the historical tree of prior versions.

It is common practice for a stateful database to be designed with auditing columns. These record the date on which the row was inserted and the date of the most recent update. A scanner can take advantage of these auditing columns to restrict the amount of work that it must do. Keep a bookmark in the scanner's scratch pad, separate from either the source database or the target immutable model. Include a WHERE clause that limits the scanner to rows that have been inserted or updated after the bookmark. Update this bookmark only after you are confident that the new facts have been persisted.

When migrating from any legacy database into an immutable data store, the scanner is always the first tool to build. You can construct the scanner layer by layer, first scanning for high-level facts having no predecessors and then building scanners for successors lower down in the graph. As you build the successive layers, continuously deploy the scanner to production. Scanning is not done just once. It will be done many times over the life of the project. Do not make the mistake of treating this like a one-and-done data migration. Invest the time in making the process repeatable.

Triggers

Triggers are perhaps the most contentious tool in the data modeler's toolkit. Perhaps they were overused in the past, leading several application developers to shy away from them and even warn others away. But for extracting information from a database, database tools are the most appropriate, especially if our aim is to minimize changes to legacy code.

We already used triggers to optimize queries for work items that had not yet been processed. We can also use them to infer facts from data modification operations. The original intent may be locked away in application code that we dare not modify, but the effect of that intent can be readily observed. Some well-crafted triggers can translate an INSERT into a new entity, an UPDATE into a mutable property, and a DELETE into a tombstone. They can insert these new facts into a set of staging tables to be processed through the same channels as user actions.

Triggers of this kind cannot take the place of scanners. They will have been put into place after the stateful data model has been in operation for some time. A trigger cannot go back in time and fire on all of the inserts, updates, and deletes of the past. A scanner is still required to bring in all of the legacy data.

Triggers, if implemented, will need to work in conjunction with scanners. At some point, you may choose to turn off the scanner while simultaneously enabling the triggers. Do this only if you have sufficient confidence that the triggers will catch all possible changes. If you use bulk inserts, for example, triggers may not fire. Alternatively, you may choose to implement triggers *using* the scanner. Write the scanner as a series of stored procedures. Then the trigger simply fires the scanner whenever it detects information being modified. This gives us the best of both worlds: a scanner running on a timer to collect bulk data changes and triggers running in real time to provide lower latency.

Change Data Capture

The patterns described previously can be implemented in any database management system. Some systems, however, provide more support. Microsoft SQL Server, for example, provides specific features that can be leveraged to extract changes from a database. The most powerful of these is change data capture.

When configuring change data capture, an administrator defines source tables. When DML operations against any of these source tables enter the transaction log, the capture process is notified asynchronously. The process inserts a record of each change into a corresponding change table. An application process can periodically pull records from the change tables and convert them into historical facts.

Change data capture has the advantage of using the transaction log to asynchronously identify changes. Triggers, on the other hand, fire synchronously with the DML command. This means that they have the potential to block or even break the legacy application. Change data capture is built into the database management system, whereas triggers need to be coded by hand. On the other hand, triggers could be customized to handle more complex scenarios. The choice between the two is by no means clear.

We have explored several alternatives for extracting facts from a stateful database. Legacy application integration must of course work in both directions. For getting information *into* a legacy application, please see the Outbox pattern in Chapter 11 or use the techniques described for reporting databases in the following section.

Reporting Databases

Executing reports directly from an immutable database can be challenging. The queries that compute the current state of an entity tend to work well for singular starting points. They are not well suited to aggregation, as is often required in reports. They are also not well equipped to group by mutable properties, as is common in reporting scenarios. For effective reporting, an immutable data model should be projected into a denormalized reporting model.

To build an effective reporting database from an immutable model, decide which facts will be reflected in the stateful database. Not all immutable records need to be reported against. Perhaps you can even subdivide the reports into categories and produce separate projections of the data for each. Top-level predecessors are fed into all of the reporting projections, but successors might only influence a few.

Once identified, write a job that will call a procedure for each fact in a historical table. This might be a scheduled database job, an application cron job, or even driven by a trigger. The choice depends upon your tolerance for latency and the degree to which you feel the application should be involved. This job runs completely within the scope of the immutable data store. The procedures that it calls, however, run within the reporting database.

Those procedures should in fact be stored procedures. They take as parameters all of the fields of the fact that they are processing. The procedure transforms an entity fact into an INSERT statement, a tombstone fact into a DELETE, and any mutable property or workflow fact into an UPDATE. The stored procedure then returns the ID of the row that it just affected. This helps the job to keep track of predecessors.

As the job calls procedures to handle facts, it keeps a map. It maps the hash of each fact to the ID that the handling procedure returned. Then, when it calls a procedure for a successor fact, it passes the mapped ID in place of the predecessor. This gives the stored procedure all of the information it needs to set up foreign keys.

The work of transforming facts into database changes is done completely within stored procedures. This keeps the information about the reporting database schema localized to the database. The individuals in charge of producing and optimizing reports will find this choice of tool to be near at hand. This solution provides the proximity, convenience, and autonomy required to produce the best reporting solution.

Integrating an insert-only historical database with a denormalized stateful reporting database gives you to the tools to solve issues on both the read and write sides. Design tables historically to faithfully record the user's intent while providing the best transaction processing behavior. Then use all of the mechanisms at your disposal to transform that history into its stateful analog. The constraints of immutable data structures give you confidence in the correctness of the transformation and provide opportunities to optimize.

CHAPTER 11

Communication

Many of the architectural choices that we make constrain the way in which messages are delivered and the way in which they are processed. Two common categories of message delivery are synchronous APIs and asynchronous queues or topics. Synchronous APIs include REST, GraphQL, and gRPC, while asynchronous queues or topics include Kafka, RabbitMQ, and SQS. Which one you choose often dictates how requests are processed. With a synchronous API, the server processes the request and sends back the response on the same channel. With an asynchronous queue, the server processes messages as it pulls them from the queue. It publishes the results, if any, to a different queue for downstream consumption. Patterns for communication and processing are tightly bound.

Immutable architectures give us a way to separate those two concepts. We can make choices about communication based on how close the sender is to the recipient, whether they are controlled by the same organization or whether they are more or less permanently connected. On the other hand, we can make choices about processing based on how a conversation is intended to progress and whether the initiator expects a response. We can choose how to exchange facts between services irrespective of our choice of how those services process the messages.

The models that we have analyzed and constructed define *what* the services are talking about. They do not define *how* those services will talk. To maximize autonomy, each service will have just the subset of the model that it requires to serve its users and make its decisions. They all participate in an information exchange to share subsets with one another. To make the most appropriate communication choices, we need to understand those subsets, the needs of each service, and the constraints of different communication protocols.

© Michael L. Perry 2024
M. L. Perry, *The Art of Immutable Architecture*, https://doi.org/10.1007/979-8-8688-0288-1_11

Delivery Guarantees

As the parable of the Two Generals taught us, a machine cannot know whether the message it just sent will be received. It has no guarantee based solely on the sending of the message. Instead, it only learns about successful delivery when it receives a subsequent message from the remote machine. Knowledge is delayed. Guarantees can only be fulfilled by retrying until that knowledge arrives.

Fortunately, we can build more reliable delivery guarantees on top of less reliable protocols. This is evident in the OSI model of networking, shown in Figure 11-1, which subdivides the stack into seven layers. The model describes many quality-of-service factors, not just delivery. To focus just on delivery guarantees, we only need to examine three layers: network, transport, and application.

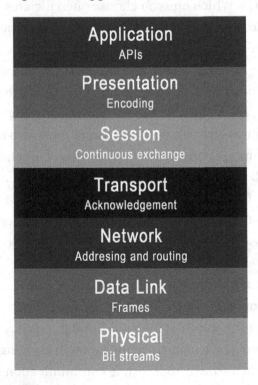

Figure 11-1. *The OSI model of network communication divides protocols into seven layers of abstraction*

At the network layer, no communication protocol offers a delivery guarantee. The network is concerned with addressing, routing, and error correction, but not with delivery. It is not responsible for establishing long-lived connections between machines, retrying failed packets, or even reporting on success or failure.

At the next level up, the transport layer takes on the responsibility of reporting successful delivery back to the sender. It provides confirmation, but not necessarily disconfirmation. It is often not possible to prove that a message was *not* received. But ultimately, the transport layer must give up at some point. It cannot make a guarantee before sending a message that it will keep trying until the message is received.

It is only at the application layer that protocols begin to offer such guarantees. If a message is given to a durable protocol, then it will do everything that it can to ensure that the message makes it to the intended recipient. It will keep trying to send the message until it knows that it was received. It will resume after a power failure. Some protocols even make additional promises about the order, uniqueness, and latency of delivery. The more a durable protocol promises, the more expensive it will be. We will therefore accept the weakest promise that we can tolerate.

Best Effort

The term "best effort" is an unfortunate moniker. While it would seem to imply that there is no greater effort that could be applied to solving the problem of delivery, it in fact means the opposite. A best-effort service will not try to resend a message upon failure. In fact, it will not even report on the success or failure of delivery. It is the quality-of-service (QOS) equivalent of a shrug.

All protocols at some point are built on best-effort layers. In most modern applications, this usually means the Internet Protocol (IP). Some protocols extend that limited quality of service up to the application layer. These include User Datagram Protocol (UDP) and IP multicast. When latency is more important than delivery, these are appropriate choices. They can be used alongside more durable protocols to provide services such as presence, streaming, and health monitoring.

To build on top of a best-effort protocol, the recipient must provide feedback upon receipt. This gives the sender confirmation that the message has been delivered.

Confirmation

At the transport layer of the OSI model, some protocols rely upon confirmation that a packet has been received. This is often done to throttle communications, holding some packets back until earlier packets have been confirmed. But in many cases, this is also used to establish a duplex connection between the two machines. The most prominent example is the Transmission Control Protocol (TCP), which is built on top of IP.

When a duplex – or two-way – connection has been established, each machine knows that it can successfully route packets to the other. That connection offers a tunnel through which messages can be sent and received. Peers can rely upon the fact that if bytes are received, they arrive in order and with a very low probability of error. As long as the connection remains open and has not timed out, the TCP protocol will retry packets until they have been confirmed. No application intervention is required.

Many application protocols rely upon duplex connections to provide delivery confirmation to their consumers. The examples are too numerous to examine, but certainly the best known and most widely used is the Hypertext Transfer Protocol (HTTP). Despite "hypertext" in the name, this protocol has become the de facto standard of all sorts of information exchange on the Web, not only HTML but also SOAP, JSON, and gRPC. HTTP upholds delivery guarantees by constraining how machines may change state upon receipt of various messages.

Safe Methods

The HTTP specification speaks of two properties of methods: safety and idempotence. The first category of methods that we will examine is those that have the property of safety. A *safe method* should not change the state of the server upon receipt. Verbs like GET and OPTIONS are safe.

Upon receiving a safe request, a server may retrieve information, but it may not *alter* its state in any observable way. Caching a response, while technically a state change, is not directly observable to a client. Caches are therefore allowed for servers processing safe methods.

As a client, you can feel confident in sending a safe request that you will not trigger any unwanted state changes. You can retry a GET on a different connection if you did not receive a response. The server should theoretically respond in the same way, assuming that no state changes occurred in the interim. Of course, there is no way for the client or the protocol to *enforce* this convention. It is entirely up to the server to refrain from changing state in response to a safe method.

Idempotent Methods

The second property of methods that HTTP defines is idempotence. This promises that the state of the server will change only upon the first receipt of a distinct message, not a subsequent receipt. All safe methods are by default idempotent; the server will not change state on even the first receipt, let alone the second one. And so the second category that we examine is idempotent, but not safe.

As we've learned in Chapter 5, idempotence is an important property of a message handler. It allows peers to retry messages without fear of changing state. If the first message was indeed received, then the second receipt will not change state further. In HTTP, PUT and DELETE are examples of idempotent verbs.

While idempotence is required for reliable message delivery, the reason for these verbs being labeled idempotent is *not* to permit retries and recover from duplication. It is simply based on the semantics of updating or deleting a resource. An update sets the state of a resource to a known quantity. Logically, one would anticipate that upon duplication, the resource is already in the desired state. Updating the resource again would have no effect. A similar argument applies for deleting an already-deleted resource.

Unfortunately, this line of reasoning only considers duplicates without intervening changes. If the resource changes between the original update and the duplicate, then the duplicate will reset the state of the resource *back* to a previous state. An eventually consistent handling of the message would ignore the duplicate, rather than applying it.

Consider the example in Figure 11-2. The first client issues a PUT request to update the value of a resource to "Bob." That command takes effect, but the connection is interrupted before the response gets back. Meanwhile, a second client issues a PUT request to update the value of the same resource to "Robert." That client sees their response. The first client makes a new connection and retries the message. If the server changes the value back to "Bob," as the HTTP protocol would suggest, then it is not ignoring the duplicate message.

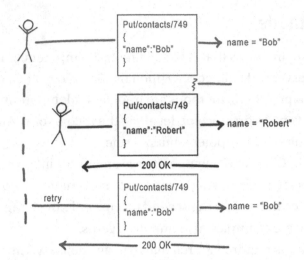

Figure 11-2. *A server responding to a duplicate request after a different request has intervened*

The HTTP server is behaving in an idempotent manner. And yet, the system is not eventually consistent. The problem is that idempotence is not sufficient. As we showed in Chapter 5, a protocol must also be commutative to ensure eventual consistency. If the server in Figure 11-2 had responded in the same way regardless of message order, then the outcome would have been better. Suppose that it treated "Bob" followed by "Robert" the same way as "Robert" followed by "Bob," for example, by allowing the resource to be in a superposition of the two candidate values. Then, the subsequent receipt of the duplicate message would simply be ignored. Recall the diagram from Chapter 5, repeated in Figure 11-3, illustrating this solution.

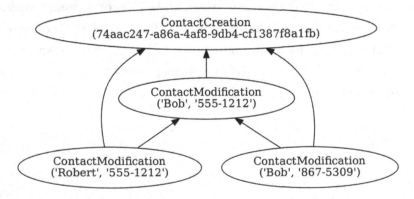

Figure 11-3. *A data structure that allows a resource to have multiple simultaneous versions is both idempotent and commutative*

The HTTP guarantee of idempotence is only semantic. The kinds of actions that idempotent verbs represent tend to bring a resource to a known state, even after the second application. But they offer no protection against message duplication. HTTP offers no guarantees of commutativity.

Non-idempotent Methods

The third category to consider is the methods that are neither safe nor idempotent. These methods offer no guarantees. They may change state upon every receipt. The POST verb is an example of this kind.

The semantics of POST make it likely that a change will in fact occur. In response to this request, a server creates a new resource and returns its identity in a 201 Created response. Presumably, the identity of the resource was not already known to the client before the request. If it was, the response would not need to include the URL. We can reasonably assume that in most implementations of POST, the identity was generated on the server.

When the identity is generated on the server, then there is little a client can do to prevent duplication. If the connection is lost before it receives the 201 Created response, the client has no recourse but to try again or report the error to the user (who is likely to try again). A second try will likely result in the creation of a second resource. HTTP makes no guarantee that the server will do any different.

Retry Within a Connection

Whatever the state-change guarantee of the HTTP method, the transport layer can only provide confirmation within the scope of a connection. Connections are relatively short-lived and reside entirely in memory. They represent a single-threaded communication channel between two peers.

Applications built on connection-oriented protocols need not retry messages on the same connection. TCP guarantees byte order, which implies that the retry would not be received until after the original message. But if the connection fails, then all bets are off. The sender has no knowledge of whether unconfirmed messages were received or not.

A connection can use delivery confirmation to guarantee that a message *has been* received. It cannot guarantee that a message *will be* received at some point in the future. Confirmation is a necessary but not sufficient condition for durability. While HTTP only forwards the connection semantics from the transport layer, other application-layer protocols add durability.

Durable Protocols

When the user of an application initiates a command, they would like to have some confidence that the effect of their command will last. The protocols described in the previous section will simply force them to wait until a remote peer confirms receipt of their message. But doing so robs the user of some autonomy. They can no longer make a decision and issue a command without involving the remote peer. To have the greatest autonomy, they should be able to work in isolation. And so they demand more from their protocol.

A *durable* protocol is one that guarantees that a message will eventually be delivered. Delivery confirmation is necessary, but not sufficient. Durable protocols need to continue to retry until such confirmation is received, even over long periods of time or power outages. Durable protocols therefore require durable storage at the sending side, which can only be provided at the application layer of the OSI model. Two of the most common forms of durable message storage are queues and topics. Popular examples of these forms are Advanced Message Queuing Protocol (AMQP) and Apache Kafka.

Queues

AMQP is a standard application-layer protocol for exchanging messages in queues. It is implemented by such queuing systems as RabbitMQ, Apache ActiveMQ, and Azure Service Bus. AMQP is a configurable protocol, offering several levels of service. Some of those service levels provide *at least once delivery* or the guarantee that the sender will keep trying until a message is received. This promise survives beyond a single connection or session. It even survives power outages.

This promise begins when the message reaches the broker. Before that, the client has no guarantee that the message will be delivered. The now-deprecated Microsoft Message Queue (MSMQ) provided client-side storage to narrow this window. AMQP-based brokers, however, do not generally provide this feature. Instead, they operate under the assumption that the connection between the client and the broker is fairly reliable. Clients must await confirmation before they can be assured that their message will be delivered.

A broker cannot guarantee that a message will be delivered only once. When a service retrieves a message from a queue, the broker holds it in reserve. Other service instances pulling from the same queue will not see that message. The service, for its part, must inform the broker when it has successfully processed the message. Only then will the message be removed from the queue. If that signal is interrupted, whether because the service failed or because the network was partitioned, then the message will be unlocked. It will then be available for another service instance to process it a second time.

Topics

Where AMQP defines queues, Kafka defines topics. A topic is a persistent stream of records. Unlike a queue, records in a topic are not removed when they are consumed. This allows a Kafka topic to support multiple subscribers, each of which receives all messages.

In addition to multiple subscribers, message retention allows topics to provide a stronger delivery guarantee. Since all past messages are still in storage, a topic can determine whether a message is a duplicate. It can ignore the duplicate, preventing it from being sent to the subscribers. This level of guarantee is referred to as *exactly once delivery*.

Duplicate detection only lasts as long as the messages are persisted. Not all topic implementations store messages indefinitely. Kafka topics, for example, have a configurable retention period that defaults to seven days. If a duplicate message arrives after the retention period expires, then it will be sent to subscribers.

For immutable architectures, at least once delivery is sufficient. Such applications are based on data structures that persist historical facts indefinitely. If a duplicate is received, it will be detected, as the fact is already in storage. And since records are identified by their content-based address, collisions are prevented at the storage level. Even though a durable protocol might offer exactly once delivery guarantees, enabling that configuration might prove to be as expensive as it is unnecessary.

Message Processing

In addition to delivery guarantees, we must also consider the timing of message processing when evaluating communication protocols. *Synchronous* protocols require that the message be processed immediately upon receipt, as the peer is actively waiting on the result. *Asynchronous* protocols allow the recipient to process the message later. These protocols tend to offer greater autonomy, as remote services are not waiting on one another.

An application based on immutable architecture tends to value autonomy over most other factors. Each service has precisely the subset of information that it needs to support the decisions that it and its users will need to make. Therefore, asynchronous protocols tend to be preferred.

Most Protocols Are Asynchronous

This choice between synchronous and asynchronous message processing is not completely isolated from the choice of delivery guarantee. A protocol offering only best-effort delivery is not going to inform the client about the success or failure of the message. It is certainly not going to wait for the server to process the request. These protocols therefore only support asynchronous message processing.

On the other extreme, protocols that offer durability guarantees will make that promise immediately upon storing the message in the broker. The actual communication with the server might take place shortly thereafter or might be deferred for a long period of time. The protocol has no way of signaling back to the client application that the message has been delivered. Such protocols therefore typically do not require that the remote peer process the request immediately and tend to be asynchronous in nature. Immutable architectures favor these kinds of protocols.

Only in the middle, where the client application receives a delivery confirmation, does it make sense to require synchronous message processing. The client application is actively waiting on a response. That response could well include the results of processing the message.

HTTP Is Usually Synchronous

HTTP by default is a synchronous protocol. When a client sends a request, it waits for the server to make a response. That response is both a delivery confirmation and the results of the message processing. HTTP response codes include such information as whether a resource was created (201 Created), whether the client was authorized to access that resource (403 Forbidden), or whether the processing resulted in a conflict (409 Conflict). These responses imply at least some degree of synchronous processing.

HTTP does not, however, require that the server process the response immediately. Some HTTP response codes (most notably 202 Accepted) are intended to reflect that the processing will happen asynchronously. In this case, information about the outcome of the process is not included within the response. It only serves as delivery confirmation.

In the current application landscape, most traffic over the public Internet is based on HTTP. Asynchronous protocols are not quite as popular outside of the firewall. AMQP can be tunneled over TLS and is sometimes exposed on the Internet. But more frequently, it is kept secured within an organizations datacenter, or exposed on the boundary between organizations. Mobile applications favor HTTP over other protocols, and browser-based clients use HTTP almost exclusively. Perhaps in the future, using asynchronous protocols on the Internet will become more commonplace. But for now, attaching a public client to a server usually involves HTTP. But this does not mean that we have to use it synchronously. Even request/response protocols can be used asynchronously.

Data Synchronization

The word "synchronization" is another unfortunate term when applied to data. Synchronization literally means to make two systems progress at the same time, or at least the same rate. Two people can synchronize their watches so that they both read the same time. But synchronizing data is specifically *not* about time. The goal is autonomy, not synchrony. What we seek when we synchronize data is *consistency*. If you ask two nodes the same question, they will give the same answer. They can do this because they have the same information, not because they are operating at the same time.

Machines in an immutable architecture have a subset of data at their disposal. This allows the users and processes on that machine to make decisions without consulting other machines. The procedure that we refer to as *data synchronization* is just the process of exchanging immutable facts with peers so that their data structures converge. Each machine will have only the subset that it requires, but where those subsets overlap, the rules of conflict-free replicated data types (CRDTs) guarantee that consistency has been reached when the procedure is complete.

Building on top of immutable data structures, we can now decide independently which protocols to use in this procedure. What kind of delivery guarantees do we require? Should messages be processed synchronously or asynchronously? Are we restricted to common open protocols, or can we choose bespoke options with more desirable characteristics? Will peers be addressable, or will we have to wait for them to call us? Will machines be permanently connected, or will they connect only occasionally?

To answer these questions, we will examine three main use cases. Each of these represents a different communication structure that is commonly found in immutable architectures. Each one requires a slightly different set of protocol choices.

For communication between servers within an organization, we will favor less ubiquitous but more asynchronous protocols such as AMQP and Kafka. This will help us to build an immutable microservices architecture. For communications between organizations, we will instead favor the more common REST APIs and webhooks, leading to lower infrastructure coupling. And for occasionally connected clients like mobile apps and progressive web apps (PWAs), we will use HTTP as an asynchronous protocol.

Within an Organization

Data synchronization within an organization is a bit of a luxury. One group controls all of the servers, all of the data stores, and the entire network. We have the luxury of selecting our preferred tools, meaning that we can use AMQP or Kafka if we choose. We also have the luxury of a fast, always-available connection between microservices. We will not abuse this luxury by calling from one to the other on every request, but we can keep their data stores synchronized.

With this kind of luxury, it is easy to get complacent. Intraorganizational architectures will sometimes share databases between services. They will often relax security controls within the firewall. And they will ignore versioning concerns, since they could deploy both sides of a connection at the same time. Each of these compromises to architectural integrity comes at a cost to future flexibility. They increase the coupling between services for the sake of convenience. When deploying microservices within a single organization, you can take advantage of the luxuries that you have while still avoiding unnecessary coupling.

To understand exactly *how* we are going to synchronize data between microservices, we must first determine *what* they are. Then we can analyze the boundaries between them to decide the best means of integration. The outcome of the analysis from Chapter 4 is your guide to where the boundaries should be drawn.

Pivots

When producing a historical model, we identified regions. These were areas of the model in which all of the facts originated from a particular kind of actor. When a predecessor/successor relationship crosses a boundary between two regions, two actors are collaborating with one another. I call such a predecessor/successor relationship a *pivot*.

The diagram that we used to introduce regions is reproduced in Figure 11-4. I have highlighted the pivots.

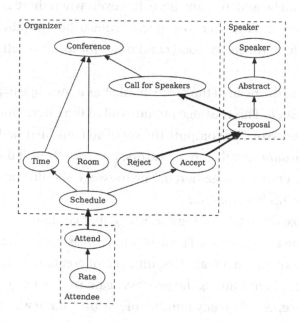

Figure 11-4. *A model highlighting the pivots, where arrows cross region boundaries*

During the analysis phase, a region represented the responsibilities of a single actor or set of actors. As we transition into implementation, we will construct a microservice for each audience. And so each region now represents a microservice. In this example, conference organizers have a microservice for collecting proposals and defining schedules. Speakers have a microservice for viewing calls, submitting proposals, and learning about acceptance. Finally, attendees have a microservice for viewing a conference schedule, selecting sessions to attend, and submitting ratings. The pivots are points of integration among these microservices.

The microservice at the head of a pivot needs to publish the predecessor fact so that the microservice at the tail can subscribe to it. Let's begin with the topmost predecessor in the causal chain, the call for speakers. This fact is in the organizer microservice.

Multiple Subscribers

Pivots at the top of the causal chain tend to be places where facts are published for multiple subscribers. The publisher might not have one specific use case in mind, and future subscribers could be added at any time. But even when there is a known use case, as in this example, sending a message to a specific subscriber introduces unnecessary coupling. And so top-level pivots are good candidates for topics, such as those provided by Kafka.

The microservice at the head of the arrow publishes a message to a topic when the predecessor fact is created. This message includes all of the information contained in the fact and all of *its* predecessors. To compute the set of all facts included in the message, perform a *transitive closure* over the predecessors. Recursively visit the predecessor relationships until the entire set is gathered. The message should contain all of this information, and *only* this information.

Two problems arise when publishing a message that contains more than the transitive closure of the predecessors. The first is that message is not deterministic. If the message contains internal database IDs, the time of creation, or any other detail not already part of the facts, then running the process again produces a different message. The process could be repeated for any number of reasons: there was an infrastructure glitch, the fact was produced by two redundant instances, the user clicked the submit button twice, and so on. If any of these situations arise, we want the process of generating a message from a fact to be deterministic so that the downstream consumer can practice idempotence and ignore the duplicate.

The second problem is that the message might contain information in successor facts. Successors can be created either before or after the message is published. If the message contains successor information, then subscribers will not learn of new successors created after the fact. In the example in Figure 11-4, the transitive closure of the call for speakers fact includes the conference. It does not include times or rooms. If speakers needed to know (for some reason) the number of rooms at the conference, this information might or might not be available at the time of publication. If a room is added later, they will not learn about it.

There are some successors that you will *want* subscribers to learn about. For example, the conference date (not shown in Figure 11-4) will be an important part of knowing whether to submit a proposal. Given that that is likely to be a mutable property of a conference, it will be modeled as a successor. Analysts have two options for resolving this problem: they can turn the successor into a *predecessor* of the published fact, or they can publish the successor.

To turn the successor into a predecessor, apply the Transaction pattern described in Chapter 8. An example is shown in Figure 11-5. The published fact is a transaction that brings together all of the successors that are current at the time of publication. This brings those successors into the transitive closure. An organizer can change the date or location of the conference after publishing a call for speakers, but they now have a clear indication of the information that a speaker had when they proposed their sessions. They can use this information to publish a new call for speakers and contact the speakers who replied to the earlier one.

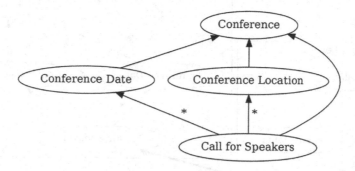

Figure 11-5. *A call for speakers is a transaction that captures the current date and location*

To publish the successor, produce an additional topic. Subscribers to the pivot can also subscribe to this topic. They will correlate the messages between the two topics using their common predecessor, in this case the conference. If the conference date is changed after the call for speakers has been published, then the subscriber will see that change and update their data store.

Responses

Facts on the tail of a pivot represent responses to messages. Responses are directed back toward earlier microservices. It therefore makes sense to use queues instead of topics for these kinds of messages. The producer of the original message includes the name of a response queue. Subscribers post response messages to the given queue. This manages coupling between publisher and subscriber, because the queue name is provided dynamically. In Figure 11-4, the proposal fact is a response to the call for speakers. It is directed toward the organizer microservice. That microservice will therefore create and manage a queue specifically for accepting proposals.

The response message, like the original message, is composed from the transitive closure of the fact. In this case, that means that the proposal contains information about the abstract and the speaker. If successors are required (such as speaker name), then the response should follow the Transaction pattern, as shown in Figure 11-6. Notice also that the message contains the call for speakers. The original message is a predecessor and will therefore be part of the transitive closure. This gives the original microservice sufficient information to correlate the responses.

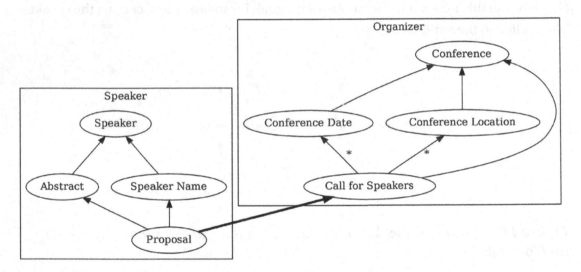

Figure 11-6. *A proposal gathers together all of the facts that will be necessary for the organizer to make a decision*

Since the speaker microservice knows about the call for speakers topic, it is tempting to also have it know about the proposal queue. Doing so would seem not to increase coupling between the two services. But that would be a mistake. Only the organizer microservice knows *how* it will respond to proposals. It might change the topology in a future release. It alone should be responsible for deciding where the response queue is located.

Pivots further down in the causal chain also represent responses. In Figure 11-4, the reject and accept facts are responses to the proposal. These kinds of responses should follow the same pattern. When the speaker microservice generates the proposal message, it includes the name of *its own* response queue.

Notifications

Not all responses are direct successors of pivots. And not all two-way conversations between microservices appear as arrows crossing region boundaries in both directions. Sometimes the relationships are hidden a little deeper in the model.

Every conversation between microservices ends with a message that has no response. This message serves only as a *notification*. It informs the recipient of the outcome of a process. These appear as leaves in the model below pivots. The rate fact is an example in Figure 11-4.

When a conference attendee rates a session that they have attended, they are simply giving feedback to the organizer. They do not expect any response to that rating. There is therefore no further pivot below the rate fact indicating that the conversation continues. The rating is pushed to a queue that the organizer provides, just as any other response. The name of that queue will be included in the schedule message, as that is the predecessor of the nearest pivot.

Between Organizations

When servers are not under our direct control, we lose a bit of the luxury that we might have had within a single organization. We can no longer choose from all available protocols to select the best possible fit. And we don't have any governance over the way in which peer systems will be modeled. Partners might not even be using immutable architecture. We adapt by implementing additional constraints and transforming our services to be more familiar.

One of the constraints of crossing organization boundaries is that the communication protocols need to be supported by both sides. This usually means that asynchronous protocols like AMQP are replaced by synchronous protocols like HTTP. The timing of message processing is not the issue; it is simply adoption. The more widely adopted protocols today tend to be those that support synchronous processing by default. A compromise can often be reached by using HTTP in an asynchronous manner.

Async over HTTP

External organizations will often need to publish messages to your services. Semantically, these are *commands*, instructing your service to perform some kind of business function. In a historical model, these are simply predecessors of a pivot, created in a remote region of the model. If we were working entirely within the scope of a single organization, we might choose a topic or queue to publish these messages. But since we are providing an endpoint for a partner, we will instead use HTTP. We can design the endpoint with additional constraints, not part of the HTTP specification, to make it work well with immutable architectures.

According to the HTTP specification, POST is neither required to be safe nor idempotent. However, an endpoint provided to partner organizations will clearly benefit from idempotence. This does not rule out HTTP POST. It only means that we implement the server to uphold stronger guarantees than the specification requires.

First, we ensure that the body of the message contains enough information to generate a unique identity. When we receive this request, we will generate a fact. The contents of this new fact need to be completely determined by the contents of the message. We will not use the time of receipt, a server-generated ID, or any other nondeterministic data to produce this fact. This guarantees that if the partner repeats this request, they will generate the same fact. That is the first step to making POST idempotent.

Second, we generate the URL of the resource using only information from the new fact and computing the transitive closure of the new fact to find the graph of all predecessors. Pull fields from these predecessors, and assemble them into a path. Append that path to the host name of the exposed endpoint to compose the URL. Assuming that we have used all of the fields, this generates a one-to-one mapping between facts and URLs. When the partner makes a subsequent call to the endpoint, we will be able to pull the components out of the path and reconstruct the fact.

And third, respond to the POST immediately after the new fact is stored. Do not wait until the request is processed. Before storing the fact, you will have the opportunity to run the authorization rules to make sure the partner is authorized to make this request. But there is no need to wait until the request is processed. You can complete processing asynchronously.

An endpoint implemented according to these constraints will be idempotent. Any subsequent POST of the same request will yield the existing fact. Because the service is using content-addressed storage, it will recognize that the fact already exists. It simply responds with the same URL as it had originally produced.

Such an endpoint is also durable. It does not respond until the fact is stored. A side effect of storing the fact might also be adding it to a topic or queue for further processing. The delivery confirmation of 201 Created indicates that this storage has occurred and has been committed. The sender may stop sending at that point; the message has been saved.

Finally, this endpoint is location independent. The URL does not contain any server-generated IDs. The URL path is based only upon the transitive closure of the fact. We are free to reorganize our infrastructure, fail over to a backup datacenter, or mirror requests to different geographical regions. None of these implementation details will be visible to our partners.

Webhooks

If our infrastructure were completely within our control, we could just post responses to a queue. When working with partners, though, we sometimes don't have the luxury of using queuing protocols. Yet we still want to pass the names of queues across organizational boundaries to reduce coupling between peer services.

The equivalent of a response queue in HTTP is a webhook. A webhook is an HTTP endpoint intended for use as a callback, a place to which to send responses. One service registers a webhook with another by providing an endpoint URL. The other service POSTs to this endpoint whenever there is new information to report about the topic.

A response in a historical model appears as the immediate or eventual successor of a pivot. We should generate webhooks based on the pivot's predecessor. As described previously, compute the transitive closure of the predecessor and extract all fields of those facts. For example, the speaker microservice might generate a webhook to receive a response from a conference organizer related to a proposal. The transitive closure of the proposal includes the conference, the call for speakers, the speaker, and the abstract. The path might therefore look something like this: /kcdc/2024/michael-perry/historical-modeling/. Construct a path and append it to a host name. That URL can now be used as a webhook. The service listening at that host can reconstruct the predecessor from the path.

Since the path contains all of the information necessary to reconstruct the predecessor, the body of the message does not need to include it. The body is all of the information necessary to create the successor fact *except* for the predecessor identified in the path. The service handling the webhook will follow all of the constraints of the command endpoint described earlier to ensure that responses are idempotent, durable, and location independent.

Emulating REST

In many integrations, an organization that has adopted immutable architecture will be integrating with one that has not. We might not have the luxury of defining the API so that it works well with immutability. We might have to adhere to an API that the partner has defined or provide one that is more familiar to them. In those situations, we can both consume and implement REST APIs from immutable services.

To consume a REST API from an immutable model, apply the Outbox pattern as described at the end of this chapter. The Outbox pattern creates a bridge between a historical model and a third-party API. The caller maps facts that the partner needs to know about into API calls. They record a journal of the responses from those API calls indexed by the hash of the facts. While this pattern cannot turn a REST API into an idempotent, durable data exchange, it provides at least a little protection against infrastructure failures. The rest is up to the partner.

To produce a REST API with an immutable model, we apply the Structural patterns in Chapter 7 to map all of the incoming requests into semantically equivalent facts. A POST maps to an Entity fact and likely one or more Mutable Property facts. A PUT or PATCH maps to one or more Mutable Properties. A DELETE generates a Delete fact. Based on the semantics of the domain, other patterns could be brought into play.

Where possible, generate URLs as described previously using only information found in the transitive closure. Ideally, all of the information needed to generate the fact will be present in the request. That would produce a truly idempotent API. However, this will not always be possible. In particular, Mutable Property facts cannot be generated based only on the desired value of those properties. They need to know their predecessors, which is not something traditionally given in a REST API.

To find the predecessors of a Mutable Property, the service will need to run a query. Find all facts that have not been superseded.

```
valuesOfProperty = (e: Entity) {
  p: EntityProperty [
    p→entity = e
    ∄ {
      next: EntityProperty [
        next→prior = p
      ]
```

```
    }
  ]
}
```

If the query results in one fact, and the value of that fact matches the desired value in the PUT or PATCH, then ignore the request. The property already unambiguously has the desired value. But if the number of results is *not* 1, or the current value is different, then create a new property fact having these results as predecessors. This algorithm allows the client to resolve conflicts by putting the desired value. Unfortunately, it does not capture what the client *actually believed* the original value to be and therefore record the real causal graph. Only a client participating in the immutable model and using an appropriately designed API could do that.

To GET a resource from a historical model, you will need to run several property queries. Generate the starting entity fact from the URL as described previously. Then run queries for all properties that you intend to return. If any of those queries returns more than one result, apply a conflict resolution function to determine the desired result. REST consumers are not used to properties having more than one value. Do *not* save the results of your conflict resolution. GETs are supposed to be safe.

A REST API produced from a historical model will compromise some of the benefits of immutability. It will only be as idempotent as a traditional REST implementation. It will not have the commutativity guarantees of an end-to-end immutable architecture. But it will be more familiar to partners who have not yet adopted these strategies.

Occasionally Connected Clients

The third common scenario for integrating with an immutable architecture is to support offline mobile or web clients. Whereas most mobile apps and websites in use today must have a reliable connection to a back-end API, an offline client can interact with the user even when that connection is interrupted. They have their own storage, their own outbound message queue, and can participate in conflict detection and resolution. Native mobile applications have storage capabilities from the operating system; web clients can use advanced browser features, operating as progressive web apps (PWAs).

Mobile and web applications designed to be used in this way are typically *offline first*. All of the data presented to the user is loaded from local storage, not an API call. Every user action is stored locally and pushed to a queue, not sent to the server. Synchronizing local storage with server history takes place in the background. The user can see the progress of that activity, but they are not blocked by it.

Occasionally connected clients will greatly outnumber servers. They will come online with nothing more than a download or a bookmark from the user. They might be used for a long period of time, or they might be visited once and quickly abandoned. When a client leaves the ecosystem, the server will not receive any notification. It would therefore be wasteful for servers to keep track of meta-information on behalf of the clients. The protocol for synchronizing an occasionally connected client puts the storage burden entirely on the client.

Client-Side Queue

As the user interacts with the client application, it will generate facts. These facts will be stored in its local subset of the historical graph. They will also be added to an outgoing queue. The user is permitted to continue interacting with the application as soon as the fact is stored and the message is queued. They do not have to wait for it to be sent to the server.

Mobile applications can use a local SQLite, Core Data, or one of many other databases for both fact and queue storage. To design the fact storage, see all of the advice given in Chapter 10. The outgoing queue is simply a record of which facts have not yet been sent to the server. It could be as simple as a table of foreign keys into the fact storage.

Progressive web applications can use IndexedDB to store facts and queues. This browser feature is not as rich as a SQL database. Instead, it is simply a set of name/value pair collections. Consider using one collection per type of fact. The keys of these collections are the hashes of the facts. In addition, the PWA has a collection for the outbound queue, indexed using a monotonically increasing key.

To send the outgoing messages to the server, the mobile application or PWA calls an HTTP endpoint. This is *not* a RESTful endpoint providing the usual semantics of POST, PUT, PATCH, and DELETE. That kind of endpoint compromises the value of an immutable architecture and is intended for use by clients that do not participate in the historical model. Instead, this is a more constrained endpoint to which messages can be POSTed in an idempotent and commutative way, as described for intraorganizational command transfer.

To reduce latency and make the most efficient use of the network, clients will batch several outbound facts into a single request. The contents of a POST will be a collection of facts of various types. My favorite way to encode a batch is as a JSON object in which the keys are base-64 encoded hashes. This makes it easy for the server to find incoming facts by their hash and helps to ensure that a fact is not unnecessarily duplicated within the same batch. The body of each fact contains the type, the fields, and the hashes of its predecessors.

Assuming that the predecessors were already known to the server before the upload began, it would have no trouble finding them by their hash and establishing the link in its own database. However, this assumption cannot be guaranteed in practice. A client might not be talking to the same server from one session to the next. Servers may be spread across different datacenters to gain redundancy or geographic proximity. It is therefore wise to include the transitive closure over the predecessors of all outgoing facts. This is why it is important to eliminate unnecessary duplication within the batch.

When the server receives the batch, it must store each of the facts in turn. Storing a fact requires executing authorization queries and setting up foreign keys. For those reasons, the server must have already stored the predecessors. It therefore processes the incoming batch in *topological order*. It recursively visits all predecessors before handling each message. When it visits a fact, it first looks in a temporary data structure to see if it has already visited that fact. If not, it verifies the hash and then looks in its own database for that record. If it is present, it moves on. If not, it runs the authorization rules and saves the new fact.

When it is done, the server responds with a 200 OK message. After that, the client can delete all facts sent in the batch from its outbound queue. The client continues until the queue is empty.

Client-Side Bookmark

Because clients outnumber servers, all of the meta-information is kept on the client. This includes the outbound queue that we just discussed. And it also includes information about *inbound* facts. Rather than keeping a per-client queue on the server, each client keeps its own *bookmark*.

A bookmark is a placeholder within a sequence of facts. It describes the position of the last fact that the client has received and stored. The client can ask for a batch of facts *greater than* a given bookmark, and the server will respond with both a collection of facts and a new bookmark. That new bookmark corresponds to the last fact in the batch.

Because we need to know which facts came after a given bookmark, these positions must be *totally ordered*. A total order is one that allows us to compare any two elements in the sequence. We can tell for sure whether one element is before or after another. In every other sense, however, facts are *partially ordered*. You know that a predecessor came before a predecessor, but you cannot compare two facts that are not causally related. Furthermore, facts are usually identified by their hash, which does not obey any kind of order. We therefore need a new method of describing the position of facts for use with a bookmark.

The position of a fact within a sequence must be monotonically increasing. Facts cannot be inserted into a sequence; they must be appended. If that were ever violated, then a client using a bookmark later in the sequence would miss inserted facts on subsequent requests. Timestamps alone are not sufficient for this purpose, as two facts could be stored at exactly the same time. An auto-incremented ID is the best choice. Even then, extra precautions must be taken to avoid reading a later ID before earlier IDs have been committed. One such precaution is to remove facts from the end of the batch until one is found that is old enough for concurrent writes to have settled. This implies that clients might not receive the absolute latest information until a subsequent read, but it mitigates against writes that happen out of order of ID allocation.

Imposing a total order on a partially ordered collection has a serious drawback. It means that bookmarks are location specific. If the mobile device or PWA were to connect to a different server on a subsequent fetch, the bookmark that it received from the last fetch would be meaningless. Different servers might have put the partially ordered facts into different total orders. For this reason, the client needs to keep a separate bookmark for each data store it contacts.

A datacenter having a load-balanced cluster of servers all sharing a common database is not a concern. No matter which server the client uses, the shared database generates the monotonically increasing IDs. The issue only arises when servers use different data stores. So bookmarks are really per database, not per server. Each database should generate its own unique identifier and use that to distinguish its bookmarks from those of other databases.

The client sends all of its bookmarks with the request. The server determines which bookmark is associated with the database it is using. If the client has no bookmark for that database, it starts at the beginning. The server then responds with a batch of facts, the database ID, and the new bookmark. The client stores all of those facts and updates its bookmark for that specific database. It repeats until the request yields no new facts.

In most network topologies, including a database ID is an overabundance of caution. The entire population of mobile clients can be served from a single database. As long as that remains true, then the clients will each have one bookmark that marches steadily forward. However, if the day ever comes that the database needs to fail over to a standby, then there is no guarantee that the order of insertions will be consistent between the two. Clients will find themselves redownloading the data set, but they will be able to detect and ignore duplicates. They will also be guaranteed not to miss any information as a result of data stored in different orders across different databases.

Choosing a Subset

A mobile or PWA client rarely needs to fetch the entire contents of the data model. These clients will have a single user, and that user will have access to only a subset of the data. Occasionally connected clients should fetch only the facts that their user needs. Based on an understanding of the model and how it will be used, we can divide facts into subsets. A particular user will have access to a small number of these subsets. The client will therefore need to keep track of separate bookmarks. It has one bookmark per database per subset.

A subset of a model can be defined by a single root fact. The subset includes all of the direct and indirect successors of that root. Imagine a cone extending down from the root and gathering together everything it touches, as illustrated in Figure 11-7. That is the subset of the model that the user needs to interact with that root.

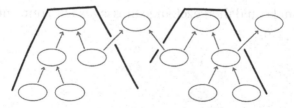

Figure 11-7. *A subset of a model is the cone of direct and indirect successors of a given root*

There are two kinds of facts that make for good subset roots: groups and periods. A group is a top-level fact participating in the Membership pattern defined in Chapter 7. A membership fact has two predecessors: a group and a user. It grants the user membership into the group and therefore access to its resources. Membership facts often determine authorization and distribution rules. A user need not see facts outside of the groups of which they are a member.

A period is a near top-level fact participating in the Period pattern from Chapter 8. This fact breaks successors down across time. A natural clock within the problem domain moves forward and points to the current period. This might be a date of business at a restaurant or a semester at a school. New facts are added to the current period. So client apps can focus only on recent periods and ignore older ones.

When a user interacts with an occasionally connected client, they only need the successors of the groups to which they belong and the most recent periods. But to understand a successor, they also need the transitive closure of its predecessors. For this reason, the subset that is actually downloaded to the device includes predecessors of those successors. The cone bounces back up the graph, forming a lattice structure as illustrated in Figure 11-8.

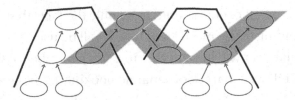

Figure 11-8. *The facts downloaded to a device include the cone of successors of a root and all of their predecessors*

Recall the example of the secret channel that we studied in Chapter 9. In this example, the creator of a secret channel sent an invitation to their collaborators. Members of the channel could then exchange messages with one another. The diagram is recreated in Figure 11-9.

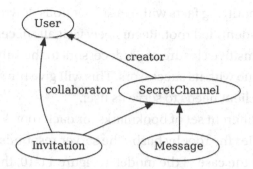

Figure 11-9. *A secret channel is a group to which collaborators are invited*

If we were to construct an occasionally connected mobile app or PWA for this model, SecretChannel would be an excellent choice of a fact that identifies a subset. If the user of the app is the creator or a collaborator in the channel, then they would expect all of the messages to be downloaded to their device. The group defines a subset of the graph containing the transitive closure of its successors.

This example illustrates one more root fact and one more rule of subsets. The user themselves should be the first root. This gives them a subset of all of the groups that they have created or been invited to join. That subset, however, should stop at the roots of other subsets. In Figure 11-10, for example, Alice both created a channel and was invited to Bob's channel. The subset with Alice as the root includes her channel and the invitation but does not include the messages in her channel. She specifically needs to pull those messages from that subset.

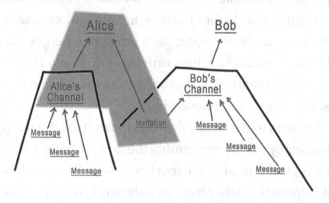

Figure 11-10. *The subset of facts under Alice includes her channel, but not the messages in her channel*

The algorithm for identifying facts within a subset boils down to a recursive traversal of the graph. Start at the identified root. Recursively visit all successors of that fact. Add that successor and its transitive closure of predecessors to the subset. If the visited fact is not itself a root, continue with its successors. This will give the set of facts that an occasionally connected client needs to serve its user.

Each client keeps a different set of bookmarks for each root. When it fetches facts from the server, it identifies the root by hash. The server responds with a batch of facts that are in that subset. In the case of the model in Figure 11-10, the first root is the logged-in user. That fetches the channels that they have created and the invitations that have been sent to them. With that information, the client makes additional requests for each of those channels. This fetches the subset of messages that the user can see. And each channel has its own bookmark.

The algorithm described here is simple enough for an application developer to apply on their own data model. It is usually sufficient for carving out subsets of the historical graph that a client would be interested in. However, this is not a rigorous proof, and a developer might make a mistake while applying it. Chapter 12 describes an algorithm that computes subsets that provably achieve consistency within the scope of interest. That algorithm is designed for immutable runtimes. It is not something that an app developer would typically apply when coding APIs by hand.

Avoiding Redundant Downloads

With queues for uploading facts and bookmarks for downloading them, we are starting to construct an algorithm for background data synchronization in an occasionally connected app. But as we put the two together, a problem emerges. All of the facts that a client uploads will be appended to the total order on the server. They will be greater than the client's bookmark. That means that they will be downloaded again to the client the next time it fetches. This is a waste of bandwidth.

We would like the client to fetch only the facts that it itself did not upload. We can get close to this behavior by simply performing the download first, then the upload. The client downloads facts greater than its current bookmark. It stops when the fetch returns no new facts. Then it uploads batches from its outgoing queue. It stops when the queue is empty.

At that point – ideally – the only facts greater than its bookmark would be the ones it just uploaded. So if we could update the bookmark without redownloading those facts, we would avoid the redundancy. The problem is that other facts may have been added in the meantime. Other clients might have uploaded their facts, or other processes might have created information that should be sent to the client. And so we cannot assume that we can update the bookmark without missing something that happened concurrently.

A good optimization is to send with the fetch request a list of hashes. These are the facts that the client just finished uploading. The server will filter out these facts from the response. In the ideal scenario, no new facts have been added, and so the entire download batch is filtered. In this case, the server returns an empty collection and a new bookmark. The client updates their bookmark, and we have avoided redundant downloads.

If, on the other hand, new facts were added concurrently, then the server would return only those new facts. It would also return the latest bookmark, including the new and the filtered facts. Upon seeing that response, the client would store the concurrent facts and update its bookmark. We achieve the correct behavior and avoid the redundant downloads.

This solution keeps all of the meta-information on the client. The client keeps track of the uploaded fact hashes in memory during the background sync operation. The server receives this information in the request and only uses it to filter that response. It does not store any per-client information in order to optimize network usage. And if something fails on the client, then it simply falls back to the correct, if suboptimal, redownloading of facts.

Outbox

Motivation   Send work to an external system that does not follow immutable architecture principles.

Distributed systems are heterogeneous. Components designed with differing architectural constraints will need to interact with one another. We will find ourselves sending requests from an immutable system into a location-dependent system.

At the boundary between immutable and location dependent, we have an API, whether RESTful or otherwise. The immutable system runs a service that calls the API whenever a fact appears in a *Queue*. It then records the results of that API call in a new fact that removes the work from the queue.

A single instance of a service would be easy to implement, but it would ensure neither high availability nor high throughput. For those properties, we need redundancy. And that's where implementing a service gets difficult.

When sending work to a location-dependent API, it is often beneficial to limit the number of duplicate requests. If the system is not idempotent, it might incorrectly duplicate the work. If so, we would like to ensure – as nearly as we can – that requests are sent exactly once. But even if the downstream system *is* idempotent, multiplying every request by the number of parallel services is unnecessarily wasteful.

The *Outbox* pattern provides a mechanism by which parallel services avoid sending duplicate work requests to third-party systems. It cannot prevent duplication altogether, but it can take steps to reduce it.

Note that there is no corresponding *Inbox* pattern. When information is received from an external system, it is simply turned into a fact. No special conversion pattern is necessary in this direction.

Structure

The *Outbox* pattern integrates with location-dependent services by becoming location-dependent itself. Unlike the other patterns presented in this book, the Outbox pattern is not implemented entirely within the rules of immutable architecture. Instead, it uses a stateful journal to keep track of successful API calls.

Journaling

The journal records the result of API requests made to the remote system. The index into the journal is the hash of the work item fact that triggered the API call. The journal contains all pertinent data received from the API. It only records successful API calls.

When everything works correctly, the service performs the following actions in order:

1. Receive a work item fact from a queue query.

2. Call the API.

3. Store the results of the API call in the journal.

4. Create a fact with the results of the API call.

The fact created in step 4 also has the effect of removing the work item from the queue. The next time the service runs the query, the work item fact will not be present. This is the "happy path."

When things don't work correctly, the service may fail partway and find itself repeating these steps. The journal is intended to reduce the probability that the API will be called more than once. It does so by providing a way to skip the API call in step 2 in some failure scenarios.

After a service receives a fact (step 1), it checks the journal for a matching row. The journal is indexed by the hash of the work item fact. If a matching fact is found, then a previous or parallel invocation of the service had completed step 3. The service reads all of the information about the result of the API call and proceeds to step 4 to create the fact.

After the service makes the API call and receives a successful result, it attempts to insert that information into the journal. The journal, however, has a uniqueness constraint on the work item fact hash. The insert will therefore fail if a parallel service inserted its results first. When this happens, the service has just detected a duplicate call to the API. It aborts and lets the parallel invocation finish the job. The full flow of the journaling algorithm appears in Figure 11-11.

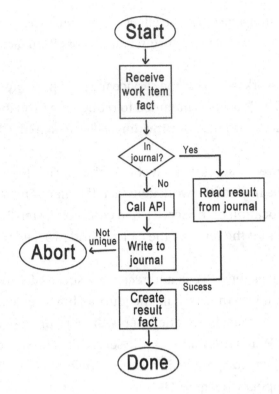

Figure 11-11. *Journaling reduces the likelihood of duplicate API calls*

Random Processing Delays

Journaling reduces the chances of duplicate successful API calls, but it does not prevent them. One of the ways in which duplication can still occur is for two services to process the same work item in parallel. We can take additional steps to make parallel execution less likely.

The simplest way to reduce the likelihood of parallel execution is to introduce a random processing delay. Consider a service that uses polling to query the queue for work items. It wakes up at regular intervals and runs its query. If it finds some work items, it processes *one of them* and runs the query again. It does not process all of them, because doing so adds time during which a different service could wake up and run the same query. It simply selects one work item at random and leaves the rest in the queue.

We can configure all of the nodes to wake up the service on the same schedule. Perhaps we simply create a cron job that runs once a minute. But to reduce the likelihood of parallel execution, we wait a random number of seconds before running the query.

This is a very simple technique. Combined with the journal and a relatively fast downstream API, it can be quite effective. But it is only appropriate for low-throughput interfaces. It introduces unnecessary latency and limits the frequency with which work items can be processed.

Rendezvous Hashing

When low latency and high throughput are required, a more sophisticated mechanism can be employed. Rendezvous Hashing[1] is a technique for uniquely allocating objects to services. It is often used in distributed caches. We will adapt it to instead allocate work item facts to services. A similar algorithm – Consistent Hashing[2] – can be adapted just as well.

To begin with, each service instance generates a random number when it starts up. It registers its number with the other services. The service registry could be implemented with a gossip protocol, a distributed hash, or even the same database that is used to keep the journal. The only requirement is that the other services become aware of this new member shortly after the service comes online.

Once it has registered, a service subscribes to new work items entering the queue. Unlike the random processing delay solution, services do not poll. They are notified via webhooks, broadcast, or a publish-subscribe message queue as soon as work is available. Which mechanism they use depends upon your chosen communication infrastructure.

When a service receives a work item, it computes the hash. But before it checks the journal, it pairs the fact hash with each of the random numbers of all of the registered services, including itself. It computes the hash of each pair, producing a *weight*. The service with the highest weight is the one that should process the work item. If that winner is the service itself, then the service checks the journal and processes the work item. The algorithm is depicted in Figure 11-12.

[1] Thaler, David; Ravishankar, Chinya. "A Name-Based Mapping Scheme for Rendezvous." University of Michigan Technical Report CSE-TR-316-96.

[2] Karger, D.; Lehman, E.; Leighton, T.; Panigrahy, R.; Levine, M.; Lewin, D. (1997). Consistent Hashing and Random Trees: Distributed Caching Protocols for Relieving Hot Spots on the World Wide Web. Proceedings of the Twenty-ninth Annual ACM Symposium on Theory of Computing. ACM Press New York, NY, USA. pp. 654–663.

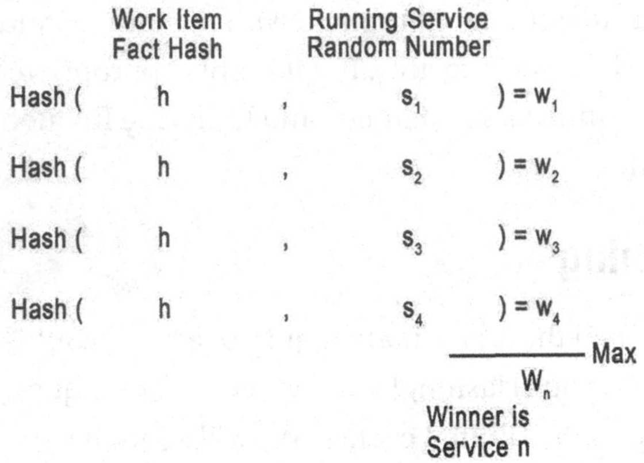

Work Item Fact Hash		Running Service Random Number		
Hash (	h	,	s_1	) = w_1
Hash (	h	,	s_2	) = w_2
Hash (	h	,	s_3	) = w_3
Hash (	h	,	s_4	) = w_4

$$\frac{}{W_n} \text{ Max}$$

Winner is
Service n

Figure 11-12. *A service computes weights for one work item to determine the winning service*

All services will compute the same weights for a work item. They will therefore all select the same winner. Only that winner will process the work item, resulting in less chance of parallel execution.

Service Failure

Unfortunately, services fail. When a service stops responding, its work items will remain in the queue longer than expected. Fortunately, the other services can detect this.

Since all services compute the weights for all work items, each service can see where it falls in the rank. If a service determines that it is the second-place winner, then it keeps track of the work item. If it sees it again after a timeout, then it assumes that the first-place winner has failed. It processes the work item and removes the failed service from the registry.

If a service that has *not* failed finds itself removed from the registry, it just creates a new random number and comes back in. The timeout should be high enough to make this scenario unlikely, but low enough that failures don't go undetected for too long.

Failure detection can be generalized beyond the second-place winner. Third-, fourth-, and higher-place winners can set longer timeouts on the work items. This will mitigate against a simultaneous failure of multiple services, as such would be caused by an infrastructure or network outage.

Example

We are integrating our example company with a third-party accounts receivable system. When an order is submitted, we send it off to be invoiced. Our first step is to define a queue of orders to invoice.

```
ordersToInvoice = (dob: DateOfBusiness) {
  o: OrderSubmission [
    o→dateOfBusiness = dob
    ∄ {
      i: Invoice [
        i→orderSubmission = o
      ]
    }
  ]
}
```

With that in place, we create a service that subscribes to this queue. As a service starts up, it generates a random number and inserts a record into a shared Redis cache. When a new OrderSubmission is created, the client that created it broadcasts a notification. The service subscribes to that notification to learn about new work items.

Upon notification, the service runs the query to find work items. It pairs the hash of each work item with the random number of each service in the Redis cache. It hashes this pair to compute the weight of that work item for that service. All of the work items for which the service itself has the highest weight continue to the next step.

The service checks a shared SQL database for a journal entry by that work item's hash. Finding none, it makes the API call and inserts the resulting invoice number into the journal. After that insert succeeds, it creates an Invoice record containing the returned invoice number.

If the service had found an existing journal entry, it would have instead loaded the invoice number and created the Invoice fact without calling the API. And if the insertion failed because of a uniqueness constraint violation, it would abort the processing of that work item after alerting the operations team of a likely duplication. Figure 11-13 shows the pair of artifacts that make up the outbox.

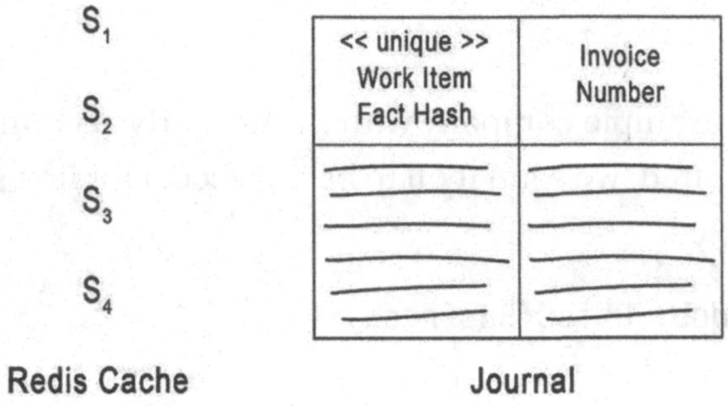

S_1

S_2

S_3

S_4

<< unique >> Work Item Fact Hash	Invoice Number

Redis Cache   Journal

Figure 11-13. *Services share a distributed cache and persistent table to support the Outbox pattern*

Consequences

There is no guaranteed mechanism to prevent duplicate calls to a third-party API. Even with this pattern in place, duplication will occasionally happen. Downstream services should be coded to be idempotent.

Upon service startup, a delay in notifying other services leaves open a window in which both could believe themselves to be the first-place winner. To mitigate against parallel processing in this scenario, delay processing by the new service until enough time has passed for all other services to finish processing any work items in flight.

The fact generated from the results of the API call must not contain any information not captured in the journal. If it contains, for example, auditing information such as the timestamp or IP address when and where it was recorded, then the fact would be different from other facts representing the same API call. The model would contain duplicate data even when the journal prevented duplicate API calls.

Related Patterns

For manual processes, present a *Queue* to the user using a simple query.

The work items in the outbox are typically *Transaction*s.

The query for the outbox usually begins at a *Period*. Overlap periods by significantly greater than the downstream SLA to prevent loss of work items.

CHAPTER 12

Feeds

The mathematics of conflict-free replicated data types (CRDTs) guarantee that two replicas will achieve consistency after they have received all updates. If you ask two replicas the same question, they will give you the same answer. There's a trick to how CRDTs accomplish this: they guarantee that the replicas reach the same internal state. That implies that *any* question – so long as it is deterministic and based only on the internal state – will yield consistent answers.

But there's an issue with this way of solving the problem. What if your replica is the size of an entire enterprise database? Are we expected to replicate the whole of its internal state to every client device and microservice? That would be highly impractical and destroy any benefit we hoped to gain by using immutable records.

Instead, we seek a weaker guarantee. Given a *specific set* of questions, show that two replicas will produce the same responses after they have both received a *subset* of all updates. Moreover, we will determine that subset based on the set of questions. That is what we will accomplish in this chapter.

The algorithm that we will derive is essential to the correct implementation of an immutable runtime. Without it, the runtime might share too many facts with its peers, thereby wasting bandwidth and storage. Or it might share too few and cause replicas to behave inconsistently. This algorithm finds the Goldilocks zone in which each replica has just the right facts to serve its needs.

Interest

In Chapter 11, we manually decided how to share facts with peers. We found pivots within the model – predecessor/successor relationships that crossed regions. These became points of collaboration not only between users but also between replicas. Then we decided how to express that collaboration: queues, topics, REST APIs, webhooks, and others. Now we will examine a way to automate that decision and take it out of the hands

© Michael L. Perry 2024
M. L. Perry, *The Art of Immutable Architecture*, https://doi.org/10.1007/979-8-8688-0288-1_12

of the human software developer. We replace it with an algorithm for automatically determining what facts a replica needs to know about. Immutable runtimes will exchange information among peers to express *interest* in the facts that they want.

A replica is interested in a fact if and only if the existence of that fact changes the behavior of the replica. The behavior of a replica depends upon the specifications and projections that it will execute and starting points of those queries. If a fact influences the results of a projection from an expected starting point, then the replica is interested in that fact.

To understand a fact, a replica must also know about all of its predecessors. When a replica expresses interest in a fact, it implicitly expresses interest in those predecessors. Those facts, of course, have predecessors of their own. The runtime computes the transitive closure of the interest set to find all of the required facts.

Tuples

When two replicators talk to one another, they exchange specifications. But unlike a GraphQL, OData, or SQL conversation, the requester is not asking for the results of the specification; they are asking for evidence. They want to know what facts are necessary for them to produce the results themselves.

To produce this evidence, the responder breaks the specification into feeds. They then produce a stream of tuples for each feed. The streams obey rules that guarantee that the requester will receive all the evidence they need. Let's begin by understanding how those tuples arise.

Labels

A specification defines a set of labels. These are named facts of known types. Let's take another look at a model we studied in Chapter 4. In a restaurant system, we want to know the parties seated at tables to which a server is assigned. We can write that specification as follows:

```
partiesForServer = (s: Server) {
  a: Assignment [
    a→server = s
  ]
```

```
sp: SeatParty [
    sp→table = a→table
]
}
```

In this specification, we have labeled three facts: the server, assignment, and seat party. One of those labels is a given. The other two appear within the body of the specification.

Each label picks out one fact in the model. Labels that appear as givens must match the starting point of the query. But labels that appear in the body can match any fact in the model, provided that all of the attached conditions are satisfied.

Let's look at an example set of facts. Suppose that the server Kaela asks for the seated parties. The labels in the specification then take on the identities of the server, their assignments, and the seated parties. I have indicated these labeled facts with boxes in Figure 12-1.

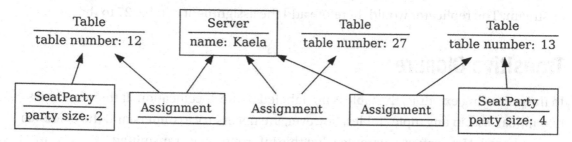

Figure 12-1. *A server sees all of the seated parties at their assigned tables*

Notice that the tables are not labeled in this particular specification. They are implied as common ancestors to labeled facts but not given names themselves. Also notice that the assignment to table 27 is not highlighted. Because there is no seated party, no tuple including table 27 satisfies all conditions. The feed produced by this specification therefore produces only two tuples:

- (Server Kaela, Assignment to table 12, SeatParty size 2)

- (Server Kaela, Assignment to table 13, SeatParty size 4)

The responding replicator provides a feed containing these tuples. It does not simply provide the results, the seated parties. That allows the requesting replicator to integrate these facts into its own knowledge and produce the results.

Will this be enough evidence to produce results consistent with another peer? Already in this example, we see the delicate balance between correctness and efficiency. According to the responder's knowledge, the requester does not need to know about the assignment to table 27. It will not affect their behavior. However, the requester might know about a party seated at table 27. With this knowledge, the assignment absolutely would change its behavior. If the responding replicator knew about that seated party, it would share the table assignment.

Our goal is to share only the facts necessary to produce consistent results. To prove that this algorithm accomplishes that, we must take into account the relationships among replicators. As discussed in Chapter 6, we deploy replicators in a hierarchy, where downstream replicators share all of their facts with their upstream peers. This ensures that upstream replicators have a superset of the information that their downstream replicators contain. This in turn guarantees that the upstream replicator has the evidence to correctly determine whether a downstream replicator needs to know about each fact. In this example, if a party was seated at table 27, the client would share this fact upstream. The replicator would therefore add the assignment of table 27 to the feed.

Transitive Closure

In the preceding example, the table is not labeled in the specification. It therefore does not appear within any tuple. Tables, however, are necessary to understand the evidence that is shared. How can we guarantee that this information is transmitted?

Upon receipt of a tuple, the requesting replicator checks its internal database. If it already knows about the facts in the tuple, then its job is done. But if it doesn't, then it asks the upstream replicator to provide those details. The upstream replicator then performs a transitive closure on the unknown facts and responds with a complete graph.

The transitive closure includes all predecessors. It also recursively includes the predecessors of those predecessors. All ancestors of the unknown labeled facts are shared through this process.

A path within a specification can only follow predecessors of labeled facts. There is no syntax for indicating successors. We can therefore assert that all facts along the path are either labeled or ancestors of labeled facts. The transitive closure must contain all relevant information.

By the way, some implementations of replicators may choose to include the transitive closure within the feed rather than waiting for a second request. While this reduces the number of round trips, it increases the likelihood of sharing facts that the requester already knows about. To mitigate this, implementations may choose to have the client provide the identities of known facts so that they can be filtered out of the response. These choices make different trade-offs between bandwidth and latency but do not affect the correctness of the algorithm.

Generating Feeds

A replicator given a specification will produce a number of feeds. The specification we just analyzed produced only one feed. That was sufficient to return all of the tuples necessary – with the help of transitive closure – to provide complete evidence.

That one feed was sufficient because the specification contained only path conditions. A path condition traverses the graph from labeled facts upward to common ancestors of other labeled facts. If a fact would influence the behavior of a replicator, then it will be included within the transitive closure of those tuples.

Sometimes, however, a specification requires more than one feed to generate the required evidence. This happens when the specification includes existential conditions or projections. Let's see how to turn those constructs into feeds.

Positive Existential Conditions

Specifications may contain conditions that test for the existence of related facts. These appear as exists (∃) or not exists (∄) clauses. Positive and negative existential conditions are treated very differently, so we will examine each in turn.

A positive existential condition constrains the tuples to only those for which additional labeled facts exist and satisfy their own conditions. The requester needs to know about these additional facts in order to compute consistent results. Without them, they would exclude results that should otherwise be included. We therefore treat positive existential conditions as extensions to the feeds that they constrain.

Let's modify our example specification to see this in action. Suppose that a manager needed to approve every table assignment. The server would therefore be interested only in the approved assignments.

```
partiesForServer = (s: Server) {
  a: Assignment [
    a→server = s
    ∃ {
      ap: Approval [
        ap→assignment = a
      ]
    }
  ]
  sp: SeatParty [
    sp→table = a→table
  ]
}
```

The requester is only interested in the assignments for which an approval exists. Furthermore, they need to know about that approval. We therefore flatten the specification so that the approval becomes a member of the tuple. The resulting feed is defined by the following specification:

```
(s: Server) {
  a: Assignment [
    a→server = s
  ]
  ap: Approval [
    ap→assignment = a
  ]
  sp: SeatParty [
    sp→table = a→table
  ]
}
```

This feed produces tuples with four members: server, assignment, approval, and seat party. These four members represent the Cartesian product of facts that simultaneously satisfy all path conditions. These are the facts necessary for the requester to produce consistent results. This is the only feed produced from this specification.

Being a Cartesian product, this feed would multiply the number of approvals by the number of seated parties. While this satisfies the correctness proof of the algorithm, the performance implications should not be taken lightly. If a replicator blindly returned all tuples in this product, then it would needlessly waste bandwidth. An intelligent replicator implementation would optimize its response. The requester is only interested in the distinct facts contained within those tuples. In practice, the replicator removes duplicates before responding. For simplicity, however, we will continue to talk as if it returned the complete stream of tuples.

Negative Existential Conditions

Whereas positive existential conditions are flattened into their supporting feed, negative existential conditions necessarily split the specification into two feeds. The requester is interested in the facts that match the specification. Moreover, they are also interested in the facts that exclude results from the specification. These two sets of facts cannot appear in the same tuple and must therefore be returned in different feeds.

Let's give these two feeds names to make it easier to talk about them. The first we will call the *ordinary* feed. This returns the tuples that would produce results from the specification. These are the tuples for which the negative existential condition is satisfied.

The second feed we will call the *excluding* feed. It produces evidence that certain results should be excluded. The tuples that it returns are those that demonstrate that the negative existential condition is false.

That's a double negative. We need a concrete example to clarify things. Let's again modify the restaurant specification, but this time to require that an assignment is not deleted.

```
partiesForServer = (s: Server) {
  a: Assignment [
    a→server = s
    ∄ {
      ad: AssignmentDeleted [
        ad→assignment = a
      ]
    }
  ]
```

```
sp: SeatParty [
  sp→table = a→table
]
}
```

The requester is interested in all of the tuples for which this negative existential condition is satisfied. These tuples will contain only the three facts labeled at the top level of the specification: server, assignment, and seat party. These tuples cannot contain assignment deleted; if such a fact existed, then it would exclude the tuple. The ordinary feed is therefore defined by the complete specification, including the negative existential condition. For brevity, we won't repeat it here.

The requester is also interested in all of the deleted assignments. These provide evidence that associated results should be excluded. Because assignment deleted cannot be returned in the ordinary feed, it must be returned in the excluding feed. The excluding feed would be defined with the following specification:

```
(s: Server) {
  a: Assignment [
    a→server = s
  ]
  ad: AssignmentDeleted [
    ad→assignment = a
  ]
}
```

This feed contains tuples of three facts: server, assignment, and assignment deleted. It provides the requester enough evidence to remove results that it would otherwise compute.

Unlike the positive existential condition feed shown earlier, the excluding feed does not continue on to match the seated parties. This is a choice made for optimization rather than for correctness. It would be just as correct to include seated parties in the feed, thereby limiting the deletions to those that would truly make a difference. This, however, would increase the number of distinct facts in the tuples of the feed. The trade-off made here risks sending unnecessary deletions in order to not also send the seated parties. The assumption behind this optimization is that exclusions tend to require fewer facts than the results that they are intended to exclude. Either choice would produce the desired consistency.

Nested Negative Existential Conditions

A negative existential condition might itself contain negative existential conditions. When this happens, we include only one level of existential condition in the ordinary feed. That prevents tuples from reappearing in the middle of a feed that a peer might already be consuming. We will return to this idea in more detail in the upcoming section on bookmarks.

Instead, the evidence for a nested negative existential condition appears as the excluding feed of an excluding feed. We will call this the *restoring* feed. Again, an example is necessary to demonstrate this idea.

Nested negative existential conditions arise in several scenarios, most notably in the Restore pattern described in Chapter 7. And so, let's apply the restore pattern to our example specification. Not only can an assignment be deleted, but it can also be restored.

```
partiesForServer = (s: Server) {
  a: Assignment [
    a→server = s
    ∄ {
      ad: AssignmentDeleted [
        ad→assignment = a
        ∄ {
          ar: AssignmentRestored [
            ar→deleted = ad
          ]
        }
      ]
    }
  ]
  sp: SeatParty [
    sp→table = a→table
  ]
}
```

The ordinary feed contains only one level of negative existential condition. It returns the tuples containing server, assignment, and seat party for which the assignment has not been deleted.

411

```
(s: Server) {
  a: Assignment [
    a→server = s
    ∄ {
      ad: AssignmentDeleted [
        ad→assignment = a
      ]
    }
  ]
  sp: SeatParty [
    sp→table = a→table
  ]
}
```

The excluding feed then picks up the deletions. This time, however, it includes a negative existential condition to remove tuples for which the assignment has been restored.

```
(s: Server) {
  a: Assignment [
    a→server = s
  ]
  ad: AssignmentDeleted [
    ad→assignment = a
    ∄ {
      ar: AssignmentRestored [
        ar→deleted = ad
      ]
    }
  ]
}
```

The excluding feed, having a negative existential condition, requires an excluding feed of its own. This third feed – the restoring feed – provides evidence that an assignment has been restored. That evidence does not appear in either of the other two feeds.

```
(s: Server) {
  a: Assignment [
    a→server = s
  ]
  ad: AssignmentDeleted [
    ad→assignment = a
  ]
  ar: AssignmentRestored [
    ar→deleted = ad
  ]
  sp: SeatParty [
    sp→table = a→table
  ]
}
```

The restoring feed *does* in fact continue with the specification. It includes the seat party label. That is because a second-level negative existential condition is positive in nature. It indicates tuples that will contribute to the results.

In this example, one specification produces three feeds. The ordinary feed tells the requester about parties seated at assigned tables. Tuples are removed from this feed when the assignment is deleted. Those deletions appear in the excluding feed. When an assignment is restored, however, we don't reinsert it into the ordinary feed. A peer replicator that has read past that point would miss the reinsertion. Instead, the restore appears in the restoring feed. Taken together, these three feeds provide sufficient evidence to produce consistent results.

We've named these feeds ordinary, excluding, and restoring just to keep things clear. The algorithm, however, has no such distinction; it works to any depth. It simply applies the rule of negative existential conditions recursively. But it does need to keep track of whether it has applied this rule an even or odd number of times. Each even-numbered level of negative existential condition produces a positive feed. Positive feeds include additional evidence required for the results. In our nomenclature, ordinary and restoring feeds are positive.

Projections

The last piece of syntax that a specification could contain is also the one that gives it the greatest richness. Many of the specifications we use in real applications will include projections. And quite often, those projections contain child specifications.

Producing feeds from a projection is a recursive process. First, produce the feeds from the unprojected specification. About half of these will be positive in nature; they represent tuples for which results are expected to exist. The ordinary feed and restoring feed are both positive. Then, append the feeds produced from the child specifications appearing in the projection. Recursively produce feeds from the projections of those child specifications.

There's a lot happening in that one description. Let's unpack it using another example. This time we will use the Entity List pattern described in Chapter 7 as that produces the most intricate projections.

Suppose that we want to show the list of servers at a restaurant. For each server, we want to display their name and their hourly pay rate. Both of these properties are mutable. In addition, employees can be terminated and rehired. This produces the following rather involved specification:

```
listOfServers = (r: Restaurant) {
  s: Server [
    s→restaurant = r
    ∄ {
      st: ServerTerminated [
        st→server = s
        ∄ {
          sr: ServerRehired [
            sr→terminated = st
          ]
        }
      ]
    }
  ]
} ⇒ {
```

```
names: {
  sn: ServerName [
    sn→server = s
    ∄ {
      next: ServerName [
        next→prior = sn
      ]
    }
  ]
} ⇒ sn.value
rates: {
  sr: ServerRate [
    sr→server = s
    ∄ {
      next: ServerRate [
        next→prior = sr
      ]
    }
  ]
} ⇒ sr.value
}
```

The unprojected server specification produces three feeds. The ordinary feed returns tuples containing the restaurant and server. The excluding feed returns restaurant, server, and server terminated. And the restoring feed returns restaurant, server, server terminated, and server rehired.

One of those feeds represents results that should be excluded. We do not want to extend that feed with name or rate, as the requester won't need that information. However, the other two feeds – the ordinary and restoring feeds – do need to be extended. They both represent positive results of the specification.

The specification for server names produces two additional feeds. The first is the ordinary feed yielding the server name. The second is the excluding feed yielding both server name and next. Appending them to the ordinary feed of the server produces these two feeds:

```
(r: Restaurant) {
  s: Server [
    s→restaurant = r
    ∄ {
      st: ServerTerminated [
        st→server = s
      ]
    }
  ]
  sn: ServerName [
    sn→server = s
    ∄ {
      next: ServerName [
        next→prior = sn
      ]
    }
  ]
}
(r: Restaurant) {
  s: Server [
    s→restaurant = r
    ∄ {
      st: ServerTerminated [
        st→server = s
      ]
    }
  ]
  sn: ServerName [
    sn→server = s
  ]
  next: ServerName [
    next→prior = sn
  ]
}
```

Appending those feeds to the server's restoring feed produces two more. And then, applying the same logic to rates produces another four feeds. In total, this one specification gives us eleven feeds: three for servers, four for names, and four for rates.

Given our knowledge of the domain and the Mutable Property pattern, we could get that number down to seven. We know that the next name fact and the next rate fact are successors of the server in their own right. By eliminating the negative existential condition, we know that we could reduce the number of feeds necessary for the client to have all the evidence that they need. Unfortunately, there is not enough information in the specification for the replicator to make this optimization automatically. That would be a good improvement for future research.

A developer solving this problem manually would almost certainly not arrive at eleven or even seven feeds. They would probably come up with no more than three. When developers do all of the work of reasoning through the solution, manually implementing it, and testing it, they are not only putting in more effort. They are also running the risk of forgetting scenarios.

This algorithm produces all of the feeds necessary to communicate the subset of facts required to guarantee consistent results. The upstream replicator has more information than its clients, meaning that it can produce just the right evidence. The transitive closure over the tuples includes all facts visited in every path condition. Positive existential conditions are included in those tuples. Negative existential conditions produce additional feeds to explain why tuples are excluded. The order of tuples in each feed is preserved; tuples may be removed, but they can never be reinserted before the end. Instead, they reappear in other restoring feeds. And finally, projections produce still more feeds all starting from the same point so that complete information is returned to the requester.

Unused Givens

There is one more syntactic construct in a specification that needs to be considered. A specification may start from more than one given. We haven't shown any examples in this book, but they do appear occasionally in practice. For example, a user might be interested in all posts for a blog, but only the comments that they themselves authored. Here's a minimal version of that specification:

```
commentsForUser = (b: Blog, u: User) {
  p: Post [
    p→blog = b
  ]
} ⇒ {
  url: p.url
  myComments: {
    c: Comment [
      c→post = p
      c→author = u
    ]
  }
}
```

Whenever a specification has more than one given, it will necessarily include an unknown with more than one path condition. In this example, the comment has one path condition relating it to the post and another relating it to the author. This is the pigeonhole principle at work again. Every label introduces an unknown, adding one disjoint graph. Every path condition at best joins two graphs, reducing that number by one. The specification must describe a connected graph; the desired number of disjoint graphs is one. Therefore, for N labels, we need at least N-1 path conditions. If one label is a given, then N-1 labels are in the body. But if more than one is a given, then fewer than N-1 are in the body. Those labels must support the necessary N-1 path conditions. Therefore, at least one label in the body has at least two path conditions.

When you turn the specification into feeds, you will subdivide the path conditions. Not all feeds will reference all labels. In this example, the posts are related only to the blog. The post feed should therefore reference only the given blog:

```
(b: Blog) {
  p: Post [
    p→blog = b
  ]
}
```

The comment feed, however, relates to both the blog and the user. It should therefore include both givens:

```
(b: Blog, u: User) {
  p: Post [
    p→blog = b
  ]
  c: Comment [
    c→post = p
    c→author = u
  ]
}
```

Following this algorithm gives us a set of feeds all starting from the same givens or a subset thereof. Each feed is represented by a flattened specification containing no positive existential conditions, no projections, and at most one level of negative existential conditions. The starting point and the feed specification give us a stream of tuples that a peer can consume. Each peer will keep track of their position within that stream using a bookmark.

Bookmarks

A client or downstream replicator will connect upstream to fetch data from feeds. Each time it does so, it will resume reading the feed from the place that it left off. It keeps track of this position within the stream using a bookmark. A client or peer keeps a bookmark for each upstream replicator that it connects to.

To prove that a client will not miss any important information, we will demonstrate that the bookmark is monotonically increasing. Furthermore, if any tuple appears before the bookmark, then the client has already received that tuple. We will do this by ensuring that the stream is sequential and append-only.

All throughout this book, we have extolled the power of partial order. Chapter 5 demonstrated exactly how partial order allows groups of replicas to achieve consistency. Why then are we now imposing a total order on a feed?

The partial order that we've been so fond of is still carrying the bulk of the load. It governs the order among facts. It permits any number of replicas to reach consistency with one another. The total order we impose here is among tuples. It exists only within a single replicator and controls how its peers consume its feeds.

Location-Specific Fact ID

To achieve a monotonically increasing append-only feed, we can start where Chapter 5 warned us not to go: the auto-incrementing ID. This has two of the benefits that we are looking for: it increases every time we insert a fact and facts only appear at the end of the sequence.

But why did Chapter 5 warn us not to use auto-incrementing IDs? It was because they are location specific. The number that we assign to a fact will only be meaningful at that location. The same fact in another location would get a different number.

In this scenario, that is perfectly fine. We only need a way to monotonically order a feed at a specific location. Clients connecting to an upstream replicator will keep a bookmark specifically for that replicator. When they connect to another one, they will keep a different bookmark. There is no assumption that bookmarks or fact IDs will be consistent from one replicator to another.

Furthermore, bookmarks will be opaque. From the outside, they will lose their connection to the facts contained within the tuple. They will only be used to determine how much of the feed the client has already read. If a tuple appears earlier in the feed than the bookmark, then the client has already received it. That's what we will prove here.

Adding Tuples to a Feed

Consider again why feeds contain tuples. The tuple represents a set of labeled facts that taken together satisfy all conditions of a specification. We've now seen how to construct a feed. We know that the specification that describes a feed includes only path conditions and one level of negative existential conditions. How then does adding a new fact affect the tuples in a feed?

A new fact may become a labeled member of a new tuple. If it satisfies the path conditions of a feed with a group of existing facts, then a new tuple forms from that group. Indeed, one new fact could form several new tuples simultaneously. All of the other facts in that tuple were already in place but simply lacked this new fact to complete a chain of path conditions.

A new fact cannot cause a new tuple to appear without itself being a member. Recall that the labeled facts in a specification can only join to their predecessors. A predecessor cannot appear where its successor is already known. Predecessors must come before. We therefore cannot complete a chain of path conditions except by adding a labeled fact.

And finally, we don't need to worry about negative existential conditions causing a new tuple to appear. Such a condition is true as long as no matching fact exists. Once it appears, that condition becomes false. We permit only one level of negative existential condition. Therefore, no fact can cause it to become true again.

Consider again the simple feed we started with, which determined which parties were seated at an assigned table.

```
(s: Server) {
  a: Assignment [
    a→server = s
  ]
  sp: SeatParty [
    sp→table = a→table
  ]
}
```

Only two kinds of facts could cause new tuples to appear in this feed. First, the replicator could learn of a new assignment. In that case, the tuples related to the parties seated at that table would all simultaneously appear. Second, the replicator could learn of a new seated party. In that case, the tuples related to existing assignments would all appear. No other fact could form a tuple. If the replicator learned about a new table, for example, that table would have neither assignments nor seated parties. Those are both successors and would come later.

Vectors

With that understanding, let's return to the problem of denoting positions within a feed. A feed contains tuples, not individual facts. Positions within a feed cannot, therefore, be represented by fact IDs alone. They must somehow encode the IDs of all facts contained within the tuple. And they must do it in a way that is monotonically increasing and append-only.

We know that a tuple forms around a new fact and that that fact is always a labeled member of the tuple. We will therefore use that new fact's ID as the most significant component of the tuple's position. Any tuples prior to that fact are necessarily at a lower position. We also know that one new fact could add multiple tuples to a feed simultaneously. A single fact ID is therefore not sufficient to differentiate the positions of these new tuples.

Instead we will define the position of a tuple as a vector. Include the ID of every labeled fact within that vector. Sort the components in descending order. Compare vectors component by component. If the first component of vector a is less than the first component of vector b, then a is less than b. If they are equal, move to the second component.

Let's see how this works in practice. Suppose that the server Kaela is fact ID 1. Table 12 is fact ID 2. Then Kaela is assigned to table 12 (fact 4) and a party is seated (fact 6). The resulting tuple of server, assignment, and seated party is facts 1, 4, and 6, respectively. The vector of this tuple is that set of IDs sorted in descending order: [6, 4, 1]. The table fact (2) is not a member of the tuple and therefore not included in the vector. The diagram in Figure 12-2 highlights the facts that are in the tuple.

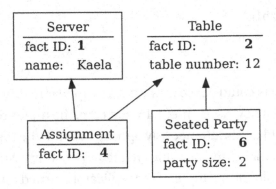

Figure 12-2. *A seated party completes a tuple*

I deliberately skipped some facts. Table 13 was fact number 3. A party was seated at that table in fact number 5. When Kaela is assigned to table 13 in fact number 7, that forms a new tuple. The vector of the new tuple is [7, 5, 1] as illustrated in Figure 12-3.

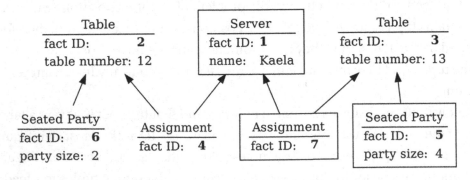

Figure 12-3. *A table assignment completes a tuple*

The first tuple in the feed formed around the seated party. The second tuple formed around the table assignment. Even though the party was already seated before the first tuple formed, it gets sorted to a later position in the feed. The vector ensures that tuples are appended to feeds, regardless of which fact causes them to form.

A client pulling from a feed will receive a set of distinct facts listed in its tuples. It will also receive the position of the last tuple that it read. The client will merge the new facts into its own replica and store the position as a bookmark. The next time it talks to that upstream replicator, it will use that bookmark. The replicator will only return tuples at positions later than that bookmark. Because those positions are vectors of fact IDs, they are monotonically increasing. The client will not miss any tuples because none will be inserted before its bookmark.

Security

If feeds are the means of distribution in an immutable architecture, then they must be secured. Recall distribution rules, which we introduced in Chapter 6. They describe who is permitted to ask what questions. They gate the distribution of facts. Feeds are where we apply distribution rules.

A distribution rule is expressed in the form `share <specification>` with `<specification>`. Both specifications start from the same givens. The specification following `share` is the one that users are permitted to query. The specification following `with` lists the users permitted to make that query.

To apply a distribution rule, a replicator breaks the first specification into feeds following the algorithm described previously. When a client or peer makes a request of a feed, the replicator looks up the applicable distribution rules based on that feed specification. It then executes the user specification from the same starting point to determine which users are permitted to read from that feed. If the requester can prove that they are acting on behalf of one of those users, then the replicator permits access.

The proof of identity varies based on network topology and deployment. Replicators deployed as backends for frontends (BFFs) will be configured to honor bearer tokens. Those deployed at integration points between organizations might instead use client certificates or API keys. And replicators belonging to the same organization might use service principals. The operator configures the appropriate mapping from credential to in-model identity.

Operators may also decide which distribution rules to apply. Replicators at the edge will have the most restrictive of distribution rules. They will limit the information that they share to just what the client or partner system needs to know. Centralized replicators will have more permissive distribution rules. Operators choose distribution rules in order to control the flow of information through the network.

As described so far, distribution rules determine which *users* can execute which specifications. But now that we can see how distribution rules are applied, I must confess that that is not entirely accurate. An identity might not refer to a single user, but instead to a group, a department, or even an organization. As operators deploy more permissive distribution rules to centralized replicators, they wouldn't express those rules at the user-by-user level of granularity. Peer replicators would be overwhelmed trying to prove that they are acting on behalf of a large group of users. Instead, they prove that they are acting on behalf of all users in that group. The rule is expressed using the Membership pattern described in Chapter 7.

While distribution rules are an essential tool in securing immutable architectures, they are not the only tool. Recall from Chapter 9 that we can also deploy encryption and public key infrastructure (PKI) within the model. This allows us to protect secrecy even as facts flow through untrusted replicators. While we trust the operators of our own organization's infrastructure, we know that at some point some information must flow beyond our borders. Distribution rules protect the feeds. Encryption protects the facts.

Losing Interest

A feed specification, as constructed using the algorithm described earlier, can contain negative existential conditions only at the first level. Any positive existential conditions will have been flattened into the feed. And any nested existential conditions will be moved into additional feeds.

A negative existential condition has an interesting effect on the stream of tuples that the feed produces. While new tuples appear at the end of the stream, the condition removes tuples from somewhere in the middle. Clients who have already read past the point of removal will already know about the tuple. But clients who have not yet read to that point will never learn of them. We must demonstrate that those two clients will nevertheless produce the same results from the specification. We will do so by examining two patterns in which this situation most often arises: Delete and Period. The Delete pattern is presented in Chapter 7, and the Period pattern is presented in Chapter 8.

Interest in Deleted Entities

The Delete pattern uses a fact to indicate that an entity has been deleted. When a replica learns about that fact, it loses interest in all information about the entity – all information, that is, except for the knowledge that the entity has been deleted. That has to be preserved.

Consider the feed for items in a menu, including their names. The negative existential condition in the feed excludes deleted menu items. When a menu item is deleted, the replica loses interest in the name of the menu item.

```
(m: Menu) {
  mi: MenuItem [
    mi→menu = m
    ∄ {
      d: MenuItemDeletion [
        d→menuItem = mi
      ]
    }
  ]
  n: MenuItemName [
    n→menuItem = mi
  ]
}
```

New clients reading from this feed will never learn of the menu items or their names. This avoids the problem with the transaction pipeline described in Chapter 5. A device introduced into a running system will not download the entire history just to be told to ignore half of it. However, the client *does* need to learn about the deletions. It does so with an additional feed:

```
(m: Menu) {
  mi: MenuItem [
    mi→menu = m
  ]
  d: MenuItemDeletion [
    d→menuItem = mi
  ]
}
```

This feed informs clients, both old and new, that they are not interested in the menu item. It does so in a way that does not share the properties of the menu item, such as the name. And so, even though a replica is interested in the entity and its deletion, it is not interested in the properties of deleted entities.

This is a subtle and important optimization of the interest set. You might think that a replica will not be interested in the deleted entities at all. Once an entity is excluded by the deletion filter, then it no longer appears on the user interface. If it does not appear, then why would a replica be interested in it?

The reason for the continued interest becomes clearer as you consider how interest propagates through a network of replicas. Suppose a new replica comes online and does *not* learn about deleted menu items. Then suppose that it communicates with a peer that has not yet learned that a particular menu item has been deleted. The peer will helpfully tell the new replica about the menu item, its names, its prices, and its other properties. The new replica will believe that this menu item exists and display it to its user. And so a replica that does not retain interest in deletion facts will incorrectly display deleted entities.

You may have observed this behavior in some popular synchronization engines. For example, if you use Microsoft Active Directory, it is possible to observe lingering objects if a domain controller is disconnected beyond the tombstone lifetime.[1] A *tombstone* in Active Directory is a record of an entity's deletion. It is analogous to a `Deletion` fact. Active Directory does not preserve tombstones indefinitely. Instead, it defines a lifetime of between 60 and 180 days, depending upon the operating system. If a replica is disconnected for longer than that lifetime, or if the clocks have drifted significantly, then its peers may discard the tombstone. That causes the deleted entity to magically reappear.

The only truly fool-proof way of defending a replica against deleted entities is for it to continue to be interested in the entity facts and their deletion facts. A replica needs to learn about the tombstones no matter how old they are. This seems like a large set of data to retain, but in fact it prevents an even larger set of data from lingering. Sharing this complete list of tombstones prevents a replica from becoming interested in all of the property changes and other actions associated with these entities.

---

[1] Information about Lingering Objects in a Windows Server Active Directory Forest. Microsoft Knowledge Base 910205.

Retaining interest in deleted entities has traditionally been one of the more controversial results of immutable architectures. I have had countless conversations with peers who attempt to solve the problem with rules about when a system can forget about entities. The results are always similar to the lingering-object issue that Active Directory faces. If you remain unconvinced, then perhaps the interaction between interest and the Period pattern will provide a more palatable solution. Periods are a way of imposing lifetimes on interest without falling into lingering-object defects.

Interest in Past Periods

The Period pattern describes regularly occurring spans of time during which activities take place. The duration of a period is a time frame that makes sense for the application: a date of business, a calendar month, an academic semester, or a fiscal year. When an activity occurs at a particular replica, that replica believes the system to be in one single period. It records the activity as a successor of the period fact.

Each replica determines its own interest set. Different replicas will express interest in different periods. Replicas closer to the edge of the network tend to operate only within recent periods. A point-of-sale terminal might only display data within the current date of business. It serves the needs of its users in the short term and leaves long-term history to reporting servers living closer to the center of the network.

To respect the bandwidth and storage limitations of smaller edge devices, we wish to limit their interest set to only the more recent periods. Replicas get to choose the starting points of their queries. If those queries start with the current period, then the replica is no longer interested in the past.

The period clock advances for each individual edge replica. Close to a time boundary, different replicas might believe the system to be in different periods. But this will not cause any problems sharing facts with more central replicas. Edge replica clocks don't need to agree so long as central replicas accept facts outside of what they believe to be the current period.

To apply this solution, a replica starts its queries not from a top-level owner, but from a period defined *within* that owner. For example, the front-of-house terminal within a restaurant that the host uses would begin not from the `Restaurant` fact, but from a successor `RestaurantDateOfBusiness`. As its clock progresses, the front-of-house terminal loses interest in the previous date of business for the restaurant. Instead, it starts its queries from the new date of business. It rotates its internal database so that prior periods are discarded.

This strategy allows edge replicas to limit their storage requirements, while central replicas take on the storage burden. Different replicas get to decide their own interest set. Edge replicas express interest in recent periods by providing a query that starts with a period. Central replicas express interest in deep history by starting from the periods' predecessor.

Purging Facts

As time passes, replicas will lose interest in facts. When an entity is deleted, replicas will no longer be interested in their properties and relationships with other entities. As the clock advances, replicas lose interest in the day-to-day decisions that occurred within a period. Even though facts are immutable and cannot *conceptually* be deleted, it sometimes makes sense for a replica to actually delete data.

Replicas at the edge of a network tend to be personal devices. These are relatively small machines with limited storage, bandwidth, and connections. To respect their limits, it is practical to avoid storing and transmitting facts that they have lost interest in.

A sufficiently sophisticated immutable runtime can recognize when a new fact has removed other facts from its interest set. It can tell, for example, that a `Deletion` fact has caused an existential condition to become false. It would lose interest in all of the properties of the associated entity. The runtime could then remove such facts from storage. Before this strategy is applied, however, a couple of caveats must be observed.

First, before the facts are removed, the edge replica must have shared those facts with more permanent peers. If the user of a personal device has modified the property of an entity just as another user has deleted it, then the device might learn about the deletion before it has a chance to upload the property change. If the property change – which the device is no longer interested in – is deleted from storage, then no other replica will ever learn of it. When the deleted entity is restored, or a historical report is run, the user's decision will be lost.

The second caveat is that no other replica can depend upon this device as a source of facts. Edge devices tend to connect upstream to more central devices to receive new facts. The only facts that they upload are the ones that the user of the device created themselves. But if the personal device is itself upstream of an even more remote edge device, say a smartwatch, then its data store cannot be purged. A smartphone to which such a companion device is attached must retain the history of facts that its satellite might need, even if it itself has lost interest in them.

If this sophistication proves to be too complex or cumbersome for an immutable runtime, a simpler strategy exists. The runtime could periodically swap one data store into the background and start filling up a new store. Projections are served out of both data stores, the background one providing stability of past data and the foreground one contributing freshness of new events. Over time, all of the facts that the replica is interested in are copied to the foreground store, and all of the outgoing facts are drained from the background queue. At that point of quiescence, the background store can be purged with no loss of information or change of behavior.

Whatever the strategy, it is important to recognize the difference between the practicality of purging facts and the inductive rigor of retaining interest. A replica must retain interest in deleted entities and their tombstones in order to correctly defend against lingering objects. As long as a replica is interested in a fact, that fact cannot be purged. Only under the strictest of conditions can facts be removed from storage. This can only happen on edge replicas, only after durably sharing that fact with a more central replica, and only when interest is truly lost.

Implementations

The feed mechanism as described here depends upon auto-incrementing fact IDs to generate bookmarks. It uses specifications that can easily be converted into SQL statements with WHERE NOT EXISTS clauses. A relational database provides the most direct implementation.

However, we could do better. Relational databases are not intended to be used in this way. Streaming databases are a more natural fit. Many examples exist, including Kafka, Redis, Event Store, and Apache Storm.

An immutable runtime does not replace these infrastructure components; it automates them. Instead of a relational database, it can choose one of these options for storage and communication. A runtime designed to use purpose-built infrastructure components would inherit all of their reliability and performance characteristics. At the same time, it would protect developers and operators from the complexities of configuration and deployment.

When application developers manually configure a streaming database, they make important decisions based on domain knowledge and intuition. For example, they decide what kinds of events to put in different kinds of topics. Should a topic be homogeneous, or should it contain events of many types? If a consumer is interested in some events but not others, at what point should we separate them? And how do we tolerate the lack of order guarantee between topics when we do so?

As described in Chapter 11, a historical model provides some guidance on topic design. That chapter describes pivots, which inform the boundaries for both topics and queues. Pivots, however, are not mathematically rigorous. To guarantee consistency among consumers, we need to apply an algorithm for which we can write a proof. Feeds provide that guarantee while automating topic configuration. They keep performance high while eliminating entire classes of defects.

To use a streaming database as a storage and communication mechanism, the immutable runtime creates a topic for each feed. Rather than generating its own bookmarks for consumers of those streams, it relies upon the infrastructure component to do what it does best. When a replicator learns about a new fact, the runtime adds new tuples to the appropriate topics. It also uses the database's compaction feature to remove tuples for which negative existential conditions are no longer satisfied.

How then does the immutable runtime determine which feeds are affected by a new fact? That mechanism – inversion – is the topic of the next chapter.

CHAPTER 13

Inversion

Mathias Verraes' joke about two hard problems in distributed systems is based on a saying by Phil Karlton formerly of Netscape. He quipped, "There are only two hard things in Computer Science: cache invalidation and naming things."

I am notoriously bad at naming things (as you have no doubt discovered in earlier chapters). However, I have a rock solid solution to cache invalidation. *Inversion* determines not only which caches should be invalidated but also precisely how they should be updated.

When we think of caching, we often think of improving performance or scalability. But there are other caches in a system. The streams of tuples that we produced with the previous chapter's feeds are one example. The user interface is another. User interfaces are caches of projected results stored temporarily in view models and browser DOMs. When that cache is invalidated, the user expects their view to automatically update. Failure to update the UI leads to a frustrating user experience.

On the face of it, you would expect caching of immutable data to be easy. If data doesn't change, the cache is always up to date. The point of the cache, however, is not to store a copy of the immutable facts. It's to store a copy of projected results. It is projected results – not raw facts – that appear on a user interface. And so we must find a strategy for determining when a projection's results have been affected.

The results of a query change as new facts are introduced. For each new fact, we must answer two questions:

1. Which caches, feeds, or UI components are invalidated?

2. What results should be added to, removed from, or modified in those caches?

Inversion answers both of those questions. The caches that are affected can always be found by traversing the query from the introduced fact back to the givens. The results to add or remove can be found by examining the other labeled facts. After that, we can adjust the cache, distribute to the feed, or update the UI without rerunning the original query.

© Michael L. Perry 2024
M. L. Perry, *The Art of Immutable Architecture*, https://doi.org/10.1007/979-8-8688-0288-1_13

Mechanizing the Problem

Determining what to update when certain events take place is the bread and butter of application development. We do it intuitively all the time. Whether responding to user-input events, API commands, or messages in a queue, a developer decides what state is out of date and how to update it. It might be a view model that needs to raise property changed events or an array of results that needs to be flushed and reconstructed. Developers make those decisions intuitively.

Intuition, however, fails in two important ways. First, it is easy to miss dependent state that needs to be updated. And second, update logic needs to be revisited as requirements are added. For the first problem, we simply test until we think we've found all of the reasons for a view to change. And for the second problem, we analyze each new feature for how they interact with existing behaviors. We add these as acceptance criteria, modify all affected areas of code, and test for regressions. Because of this, new changes take longer to make and have a greater chance of introducing bugs.

A better solution is to remove cache invalidation and UI update decisions from developer's hands. If the runtime could decide which caches to rebuild and which user interface components to update all on its own, then that logic would not clutter the code. The decisions can be made mechanically without the risk of human error. And they can be updated automatically as the application grows, keeping each new feature as quick and safe to add as the first one.

The good news is that the runtime already has enough information to make cache invalidation decisions. Every cache, feed, and user interface component is initially populated with a specification. That specification describes a path through the system's data that yield the results to store, distribute, or render. By processing the specification when it is first executed, the runtime can determine what new facts will affect the results in the future. All we need to do is invert the specification and begin watching for those new facts.

The Affected Set

The first question that an inverse answers is which caches, feeds, and views are affected by a new fact. It identifies those components by the starting point from which the specification was first executed: the givens.

Every specification has a set of givens. Any particular cache, feed, or user interface component holds the results of a specification for a specific set of given facts. Let's focus on UI components for now. Different users will be running the same specifications, but each will start at a different fact. Hence, their views will be different. As they navigate through the user interface, they will render components by running specifications. While many of these components will run the same specification, each one will start from a different fact. The starting point of a specification determines which user interface component to update. The same logic also applies to caches and feeds.

In Chapter 4, we showed an example of a view displaying the table assignments for a server at a restaurant. The wireframe appears again for reference in Figure 13-1. Each server will log into the system and bring up the same page. They will see different results because, even though the user interface component always uses the same specification, each user will start from a different fact. When a new Assignment fact is introduced, the system computes the affected Server to determine which view to update.

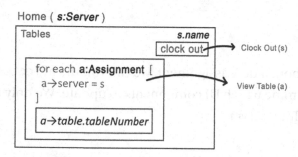

Figure 13-1. *The user interface component showing assigned tables starts at the server fact*

Computing the Affected Set

When the table list view first loads, it runs the specification shown in the wireframe. That specification determines which tables to show in the list. But that specification also provides all of the information needed to compute the affected set of any subsequent Assignment. That is the role of the inverse.

The affected set is the set of givens that a new fact will affect. For example, when a new Assignment fact is recorded, we can determine which server is affected. They are the predecessor of that assignment. We can express that as a specification.

First, let's write out the specification in the wireframe:

```
tablesForServer = (s: Server) {
  a: Assignment [
    a→server = s
  ]
  t: Table [
    t = a→table
  ]
} ⇒ t.tableNumber
```

Then we can write the specification for the affected set:

```
affectedServer = (a: Assignment) {
  s: Server [
    s = a→server
  ]
} ⇒ s
```

When we learn about a new assignment, we can run the `affectedServer` specification to determine which UI components to update. We only update those that started from the resulting server.

Increasing the Complexity

The preceding example is simple. If a human developer was working on the problem, they wouldn't think twice about determining whether a new assignment affects a particular server's view. It would be obvious.

But if we increase the complexity, we'll start to uncover scenarios that a developer would have to think about. These scenarios often appear in user stories and are the subject of both automated and manual tests. Let's look at an example.

Suppose that we want to show the server a list of parties seated at tables to which they are assigned. Let's remind ourselves of the model. First, a party requests a table. Then the host seats the party at a table. That table is assigned to a server. The model appears in Figure 13-2.

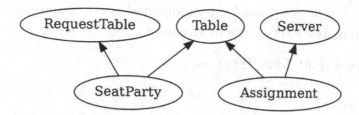

Figure 13-2. *A model describing the process of seating a party at a restaurant*

Now we can write a specification based on that model. We will find the seated parties by server as follows:

```
seatedParties = (s: Server) ⇒ {
  a: Assignment [
    a→server = s
  ]
  t: Table [
    t = a→table
  ]
  sp: SeatParty [
    sp→table = t
  ]
  rt: RequestTable [
    rt = sp→requestTable
  ]
} ⇒ {
  name: rt→name,
  partySize: rt→partySize,
  tableNumber: t→tableNumber
}
```

Let's see what can affect this specification. The user interface will need to be updated whenever a new table assignment is made. The affected set of a new `Assignment` fact is the same as it was previously. It is simply the server to which the assignment is made: the predecessor of the assignment.

Also, the user interface will need to be updated whenever a new party is seated. The affected set of a new SeatParty fact is more complex.

```
affectedServers = (sp: SeatParty) ⇒ {
  t: Table [
    t = sp→table
  ]
  a: Assignment [
    a→table = t
  ]
  s: Server [
    s = a→server
  ]
} ⇒ s
```

Starting from the SeatParty fact, we zigzag through the model to find the affected servers. Computing the affected set is not difficult, but neither is it obvious. We need to run the specification backward from seat party to server rather than the other way around. This intuition will help us to generalize this process so that it can be fully automated.

Are there any other facts that could affect this specification? What does your intuition tell you? Think through whether there are any scenarios that we missed. Are there any cases that the analyst failed to specify, that the developer failed to code, or that the tester failed to validate? We will return to the question of completeness when we make inversion rigorous. But first, we need to understand how to apply updates.

Targeted Updates

Once we have determined the affected set, we need to update the cache. What that actually means depends upon the type of cache. It might mean storing an object in memory, creating a view model to bind to a UI component, or appending a tuple to a feed. Whatever form the cache takes, its elements are projected results.

We always have the option to invalidate the cache and re-run the projection. This is the default option in many scenarios using traditional runtimes, such as in-memory caches of database query results. It's simple to understand and guaranteed to produce correct results. However, it may not yield the best performance. We would likely get a faster system by targeting the update to specific results. It's best to know precisely which results to insert, remove, or modify. We can accomplish this with inverses.

When the cache takes the form of a set of view models bound to a view, targeted updates become even more important. Re-running the query not only takes time, causing lag in the UI, but it also runs the risk of taking the user out of context. They might be in the middle of editing data on the UI. Or perhaps they have selected some items in a list. Maybe they have scrolled partway down the list. If the UI is completely refreshed, the user might lose their edits, selections, or scroll position. It's better to target only those results that have actually changed.

New Results

Sometimes a new fact will cause one or more new results to appear in a projection. When that happens, we can insert those new results directly from the inverse. No additional queries are required.

Let's look again at the specification to list seated parties by server.

```
seatedParties = (s: Server) ⇒ {
  a: Assignment [
    a→server = s
  ]
  t: Table [
    t = a→table
  ]
  sp: SeatParty [
    sp→table = t
  ]
  rt: RequestTable [
    rt = sp→requestTable
  ]
} ⇒ {
  name: rt.name,
  partySize: rt.partySize,
  tableNumber: t.tableNumber
}
```

Previously we computed the affected sets for a new Assignment or SeatParty fact. Now let's see what new results those two inverses would yield. The complete inverse determines both the affected set and the new results simultaneously. It includes the

437

projection of the original query, since that already describes the shape of a result. The inverse of the preceding specification for a new assignment would be as follows:

```
(a: Assignment) ⇒ {
  s: Server [
    s = a→server
  ]
  t: Table [
    t = a→table
  ]
  sp: SeatParty [
    sp→table = t
  ]
  rt: RequestTable [
    rt = sp→requestTable
  ]
} ⇒ {
  name: rt.name,
  partySize: rt.partySize,
  tableNumber: t.tableNumber
}
```

Notice that the server and assignment have swapped places. Originally, the server was a given. Now, the assignment is the given. The server has moved into the body of the specification to become an unknown.

After that, the specification continues just as it does in the original. We find the table associated with the assignment and then find all parties seated at that table. Finally, with all of that information, we can compute the projection. It is the same projection as the original specification.

This specification provides two outcomes from a new assignment. First, it gives us the affected set: the server identified by the first unknown. Second, it gives us the new results. We find the caches that started from the server and add these results to it. A similar operation gives us new results when a party is seated.

Removed Results

A new fact does not always lead to a new result. Sometimes it tells us that we need to remove a result. This happens when the original specification contains a negative existential condition.

Let's update our example to add such a condition. The server wants to see all parties currently seated at their tables. We want to exclude those for which the table has been bussed. As a reminder, bus table was introduced into the model as a successor to seat party, as shown in Figure 13-3.

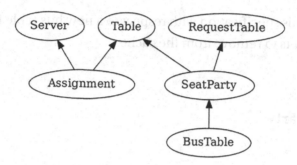

Figure 13-3. *When a table is bussed, it indicates that the party previously seated has left*

The revised specification now includes a negative existential condition. It returns only the seated parties for which a bus table fact does not exist.

```
seatedParties = (s: Server) ⇒ {
  a: Assignment [
    a→server = s
  ]
  t: Table [
    t = a→table
  ]
  sp: SeatParty [
    sp→table = t
    ∄ {
      bt: BusTable [
        bt→seatParty = sp
      ]
    }
```

```
  ]
  rt: RequestTable [
    rt = sp→requestTable
  ]
} ⇒ {
  name: rt.name,
  partySize: rt.partySize,
  tableNumber: t.tableNumber
}
```

Now let's invert this specification with respect to a new bus table fact. The inverse will tell us which results to remove from the cache.

```
(bt: BusTable) ⇒ {
  sp: SeatParty [
    sp = bt→seatParty
  ]
  t: Table [
    t = sp→table
  ]
  a: Assignment [
    a→table = t
  ]
  s: Server [
    s = a→server
  ]
  rt: RequestTable [
    rt = sp→requestTable
  ]
} ⇒ {
  name: rt.name,
  partySize: rt.partySize,
  tableNumber: t.tableNumber
}
```

From the new BusTable fact, we identify the seated party and the table. Then we find all assignments to that table in order to identify the server. That is our affected set. From here, we let the specification continue as it did before, bringing in the request table fact and projecting the results. These are precisely the results that we want to remove from the cache. In this application, we find the associated view model and remove it from the bound collection, hence updating the view.

Modified Results

Finally, a fact might neither add nor remove a result. It might just modify an existing one. This happens when the projection of the original specification contains a child specification.

Take a closer look at the specification that we've been studying. Its projection picks fields from labeled facts. What can you say about those fields? Can they change?

Facts, as we are well aware by now, are immutable. Therefore, a projection that picks fields from facts will also be immutable. The results of those projections cannot be modified.

Let's take another specification from Chapter 4 to explore results that can be modified. Here is a specification that lists the names of all of the items on a menu:

```
menuItems = (m: Menu) ⇒ {
  i: MenuItem [
    i→menu = m
  ]
} ⇒ {
  names: {
    n: MenuItemName [
      n→menuItem = i
      ∄ {
        next: MenuItemName [
          next→prior = n
        ]
      }
    ]
  } ⇒ n.value
}
```

This specification begins by finding all menu items associated with the given menu. Then, for each menu item, it finds all names that the menu item has had. It returns only those that have not been superseded by a next name. The names property of the projection is the set of the resulting values.

When the application learns of a new menu item name, it needs to modify an existing result already appearing on the screen. First, it must determine the affected set. Which menu was affected by this change? The one to which the menu item belongs.

Second, it must determine the result within that cache (in this case, which view model) to modify. For the menu view, we find the view model associated with the predecessor menu item of the fact.

And third, it must determine how to change the result. Results of child projections are sets, not single values. The application needs to remove the prior menu item name from the set and add the new one. The inverse describing the value to remove is as follows:

```
(next: MenuItemName) ⇒ {
  n: MenuItemName [
    n = next→prior
  ]
  i: MenuItem [
    i = n→menuItem
  ]
  m: Menu [
    m = i→menu
  ]
} ⇒ n.value
```

This inverse computes the affected set: the menu unknown m. It also computes the affected result: the menu item unknown i. Finally, it projects the value to remove from the names collection of that affected result. We look for the affected view starting at the menu, find the affected menu item, and then remove the name.

The original specification has a second inverse. The inverse describing the value to insert is as follows:

```
(n: MenuItemName) ⇒ {
  i: MenuItem [
    i = n→menuItem
  ]
  m: Menu [
    m = i→menu
  ]
} ⇒ n.value
```

Just like the first, the second inverse computes the affected set and the affected result. But this one projects a value that should be *inserted* into the names set. The application finds that view model and updates the set.

When we studied the Mutable Property pattern in Chapter 7, we showed that this pattern has the advantage of representing concurrent changes. The set of names is the candidate values of the mutable property. When the set contains more than one name, then a concurrent change has been detected. There is no fair and consistent definition that tells us which concurrent change is correct. That is simply a consequence of the distributed nature of this restaurant system.

The important idea as it relates to inversion is that modifiable results contain sets. Modifying a result is therefore achieved by adding or removing a projection in those sets. Modification is exactly the same as addition or removal, just one level deeper in recursion.

Computing Inverses

To demonstrate how to use inverses, we examined a couple of examples. Those examples gave us an intuition about how inverses are computed. But intuition is not proof. How do we know that an inverse always exists? How do we prove that it always works? And how can we program inversion into an immutable runtime? Let's derive an algorithm while generating the proof.

The claim that we would like to prove is that an inverse finds all updates to a cache. Updates include additions and removals of results. As noted previously, modifications are simply additions or removals at some depth of recursion. An inverse finds all updates if, after the introduction of a new fact, it updates every cache of the specification that would contain different results because of that new fact. It correctly updates the cache if it modifies the results in such a way as to be indistinguishable from running the specification again. Given a specification, I claim to have an algorithm that will compute all such inverses. The inverses will find all caches that need to be updated. And they will apply the updates correctly.

This is a tall order, so let's begin.

Tuples

We first studied tuples in Chapter 12 with respect to feeds. There, we discovered that feeds don't contain individual facts; they contain tuples of facts. The elements of the tuple are the labeled facts within the specification. An instance of a tuple represents a particular set of facts that simultaneously satisfy all conditions of the specification. We can use tuples again to prove our claims about inversion.

Consider a specification with an immutable projection – that is a projection containing no child specifications. The specification has a set of unknowns and the conditions applied to them. Those conditions may include existential conditions, which have their own unknowns and conditions recursively. To begin, consider only the top-level unknowns.

```
(a: A) {
  b: B [
    ...
  ]
  c: C [
    ...
  ]
} ⇒ {
  ...
}
```

The top-level unknowns, combined with the givens, make up a set of labels. These are the labels that appear within the tuples in the products of the specification. Specifically, we produce the Cartesian products of labeled facts that simultaneously satisfy the conditions of the specification and match the givens. For example, for the label a in the specification shown previously, if the fact a0 is a given fact, then the following set describes the matching products:

$$\{ (a, b, c) \in (A, B, C) \mid \textit{specification conditions hold} \land a = a_0 \}$$

The cache produced from the specification evaluated at the givens contains one result for each product. The result is simply the outcome of applying the projection to the product. Since the projection is immutable, this is a deterministic operation.

Now, remove the constraint that the givens match provided facts. Once you do, the set of results is the union of every cache that could be generated from that specification. Supplying given facts simply selects a subset.

$$\{ (a, b, c) \in (A, B, C) \mid \textit{specification conditions hold} \}$$

We want to prove that an inverse finds all updates, where an update is an addition or a removal. Let's first consider only additions. We'll evaluate removals later. Adding a result means adding a projection of a product. If introducing a new top-level fact c_n causes the addition of a result into a cache, then that product is a tuple containing c_n. Note this is only true for top-level unknowns. We will evaluate lower-level unknowns later. Furthermore, if the cache was produced from the given a_0, then that product also contains a_0. There must therefore be a tuple containing both a_0 and c_n that satisfy the specification conditions.

$$(a_0, b, c_n) \in \{ (a, b, c) \in (A, B, C) \mid \textit{specification conditions hold} \}$$

If we rewrite the specification as if c was the given, then we will find a_0. The inverse will find all affected sets.

$$(a_0, b, c_n) \in \{ (a, b, c) \in (A, B, C) \mid \textit{specification conditions hold} \land c = c_n \}$$

Furthermore, the inverse finds all products that yield results that must be added to the cache generated by the affected set. The inverse will find all additions.

This argument generalizes for any number of givens in the original specification. The inverse will always contain only one given, and it will not be among the original set of givens.

Rewriting Specifications

We'll start building the algorithm by rewriting the input specification to make each of the top-level unknowns in turn the only given. That will produce a collection of inverse specifications that each causes an addition to a cache upon the introduction of a new fact. We'll use these specifications as follows.

Pass the new fact in as the given into all inverses that match its type. Run each inverse specification to compute the products. Pick out the members of the products corresponding to the original givens. Those are the affected set. Use them to identify caches produced from those givens. Finally, insert the projections of those products into those caches.

We have a procedure for executing a specification. Now we need a procedure for rewriting specifications into inverses. Each inverse moves one of the unknowns into the given position and the givens into unknowns. While it does, it preserves all of the conditions so that the inverse computes exactly the same products as the original specification. We are still only considering the top-level unknowns.

Look again at those top-level unknowns. They will each have a set of conditions. Let's start by looking at only the path conditions. Each unknown will have at least one path condition. Every path condition starts from the associated unknown and relates to a prior label.

```
(a: A) {
  b: B [
    b→... = a→...
    ...
  ]
  c: C [
    c→... = b→...
  ]
}
```

These constraints guarantee that the specification represents a connected graph. By convention, the unknown appears on the left-hand side of the equation; the prior label appears on the right.

First, demote all givens to unknowns having no conditions. This is no longer a valid specification, but it is a helpful interim step.

```
() {
  a: A [
  ]
  b: B [
    b→... = a→...

    ...
  ]
  c: C [
    c→... = b→...
  ]
}
```

Next, move one given to the head of the list. As you do so, move all of its path conditions into the unknowns that they reference on their right-hand side. Swap the left and right sides of the equation in the process.

```
() {
  b: B [
    ...
  ]
  a: A [
    a→... = b→...
  ]
  c: C [
    c→... = b→...
  ]
}
```

The unknown that you are moving might contain existential conditions that reference other unknowns that it passed. If so, move the existential condition into the lowest referenced unknown. This ensures that each existential condition only references the current and previously defined unknowns.

447

After this process, the unknown that has shifted might still contain existential conditions. If so, those conditions depend only upon the unknown. Promote this unknown, including its conditions, to the given.

```
(b: B [
  ...
]) {
  a: A [
    a→... = b→...
  ]
  c: C [
    c→... = b→...
  ]
}
```

This specification is once again valid. Nowhere else in this book have we seen a specification with an existential condition on a given. It does not arise except in inverses. The interpretation is that when the existential condition is not satisfied for the given, the specification produces no results.

Reorder the Graph

During the algorithm described previously, it is possible to find more than one unknown with no path conditions. Only the unknown that will eventually be promoted to a given should be devoid of path conditions. This keeps each unknown connected to the labels that came before it, making execution much easier. We can reorder the graph during these intermediate steps to ensure that inverses are well behaved.

Suppose that we are moving an unknown that is further down in the list. As it rises above other unknowns, it deposits each path condition into the other unknown that the path references.

```
() {
  c: C [
  ]
  a: A [
  ]
  b: B [
```

```
      b→... = a→...
      b→... = c→...
   ]
}
```

That target unknown might end up with more than one path condition, while the previous given will still have none. Let's define a reordering sub-algorithm to resolve this situation.

Consider the specification as having two parts. The head of the specification contains the new given (c in the preceding example). The tail of the specification contains all other unknowns. The head has no path conditions that join it to the tail, since it appears first in the specification. Remember, all paths join an unknown to a previous label.

Scan the tail for the first unknown that contains a path condition joining it to any label in the head. You are guaranteed to find one, since the graph is connected. That was proven based on the structure of the original specification. If that unknown is not already at the top of the tail, move it up into that position, depositing its path and existential conditions into other unknowns as it rises.

At this point, the unknown that just moved still has at least one path condition. We selected it because it had a path condition joining it to a label in the head. It still has at least that one, since it didn't rise above any head labels. Now you can expand the head to include that unknown. The tail is now one label smaller. Repeat until the tail is empty.

```
() {
  c: C [
  ]
  b: B [
     b→... = c→...
  ]
  a: A [
     a→... = b→...
  ]
}
```

When this reordering is finished, the only unknown with no path conditions will be the first one. All others will be listed in an order that connects them to prior labels.

This process usually has the effect of reversing the list of unknowns. That is why you will often observe the resulting products of inverses listed in reverse order.

Positive Existential Conditions

We now have an algorithm for computing inverses from top-level unknowns. These inverses cause additions to caches in the affected set. But we don't yet have a complete list of inverses. We must evaluate the effect of adding a fact that matches a lower-level unknown. Let's first look at unknowns that appear within positive existential conditions.

Consider a specification that contains a positive existential condition on a top-level unknown.

```
(a: A) {
  b: B [
    b→... = a→...
    ∃ {
      d: D [
        d→... = b→...
      ]
      ...
    }
  ]
  c: C [
    c→... = b→...
  ]
}
```

That existential condition itself contains second-level unknowns. If a new fact is introduced that matches a second-level unknown, it might cause the addition of a product. I say "might" because that product might already be in the set.

To compute the inverse based on this second-level unknown, promote the unknown to the top level. Move the existential condition, minus the unknown itself, into this new position. If this is the only unknown in the existential condition, then drop the condition altogether.

```
(a: A) {
  b: B [
    b→... = a→...
  ]
  d: D [
```

```
      d→... = b→...
      ∃ {
        ...
      }
    ]
    c: C [
      c→... = b→...
    ]
}
```

Moving the remainder of the positive existential condition into the unknown keeps the constraints satisfied. Every existential condition references only the unknown in which it appears and prior labels. Since the existential condition contained a complete graph, we know that the remainder references the unknown.

Now promote the unknown to a given as before.

```
(d: D [
    ∃ {
      ...
    }
]) {
  b: B [
    b→... = d→...
  ]
  a: A [
    a→... = b→...
  ]
  c: C [
    c→... = b→...
  ]
}
```

This new specification will produce at least one tuple for each product of the original specification. The difference is that the new products will contain an additional fact.

(d, b, a, c)

Find the subset of each product corresponding to the top-level facts of the original specification.

(b, a, c)

Each product of the inverse is evidence that the subset satisfies the original specification.

(d, b, a, c) ⇒ *(b, a, c)*

We can now add the projected results to the affected cache if the product is not already present. Every cache needs to record not just the results of the specification that generated it, but also the products that projected to those results. When deciding whether to add to the cache, determine whether the product already exists. If it does not, add it and the corresponding result. This resolves the uncertainty about whether the new fact "might" introduce a new result.

Negative Existential Conditions

So far we have only considered additions of new results. Now it is time to find removals. A new fact causes the removal of a result when it matches an unknown in the body of a negative existential condition.

Consider a specification with a negative existential condition in a top-level unknown.

```
(a: A) {
  b: B [
    b→... = a→...
    ∄ {
      c: C [
        c→... = b→...
      ]
```

```
    ...
  }
 ]
}
```

The specification produces products with labels matching its top-level unknowns.

(a, b)

Compute an inverse by pulling a second-level unknown from the negative existential condition.

```
(c: C [
  ∄ {
    ...
  }
]) {
  b: B [
    c→... = b→...
  ]
  a: A [
    b→... = a→...
  ]
}
```

This inverse produces products with additional labels, just as with positive existential conditions. But now, these products are evidence that their subsets no longer satisfy the specification.

(c, b, a) ⇒ not (a, b)

The cache keeps track of the product that generated each of the results that it contains. We search the cache for the subset. If it is present, we remove the product and its associated result. If it is not, then the product was already removed and this new evidence has no effect.

Nested Existential Conditions

Now that we have a strategy for handing positive and negative existential conditions of unknowns at the top level, we can consider existential conditions nested deeper in the specification. Fortunately, we've already performed an operation that reduces the problem.

While processing existential conditions of top-level unknowns, we promoted each of its unknowns to the top level itself. Each time we did, we brought with it all of *its* existential conditions. All of those nested existential conditions were now one level higher. We can apply the same algorithm recursively from this point to bring those now-second-level unknowns up to the top. We continue the recursion until every nested unknown has been promoted to a given.

Every time we promote a negative existential condition, we flip the sign. We either transition from an inverse that adds to one that removes or transition from one that removes to one that adds. But here we have to be careful. When transitioning from removal back to addition, we need to perform an extra check.

This situation arises when we apply the Restore pattern. Let's look at a concrete example to better understand the issue. A menu item can be deleted from a menu and subsequently restored.

```
itemsInMenu = (m: Menu) ⇒ {
  i: MenuItem [
    i→menu = m
    ∄ {
      d: MenuItemDeleted [
        d→menuItem = i
        ∄ {
          r: MenuItemRestored [
            r→deleted = d
          ]
        }
      ]
    }
  ]
} ⇒ i
```

This specification produces products (m, i) that initialize a cache. As the system learns about new facts, it uses inverses to update that cache. Let's take a look at those inverses one at a time.

The first inverse adds results as new menu items are added. Notice how the existential condition stays with the given menu item, since it doesn't depend upon any other unknown.

```
(i: MenuItem [
  ∄ {
   d: MenuItemDeleted [
      d→menuItem = i
      ∄ {
        r: MenuItemRestored [
          r→deleted = d
        ]
      }
    ]
  }
]) ⇒ {
  m: Menu [
    m = i→menu
  ]
} ⇒ i
```

The first inverse produces products (i, m) that satisfy the specification. It only produces results when the menu item was not subsequently deleted. All of these results can be added to the cache. So far there's no problem.

The second inverse arises from the negative existential condition. Since it is the first negation, an odd number, it removes results from the cache. In this scenario, it removes results as menu items are deleted.

```
(d: MenuItemDeleted [
  ∄ {
   r: MenuItemRestored [
     r→deleted = d
   ]
  }
```

```
]) ⇒ {
  i: MenuItem [
    i = d→menuItem
  ]
  m: Menu [
    m = i→menu
  ]
} ⇒ i
```

The second inverse produces products (d, i, m). Each product is evidence that the subset (i, m) no longer satisfies the specification.

(d, i, m) ⇒ not (i, m)

Those results are removed from the cache. Again, no problem.

The problem occurs when we reach the third inverse. This one arises from the second nested negative existential condition. As a negative of a negative, it flips the sign back to positive. It re-adds results as menu items are restored.

```
(r: MenuItemRestored) ⇒ {
  d: MenuItemDeleted [
    d = r→deleted
  ]
  i: MenuItem [
    i = d→menuItem
  ]
  m: Menu [
    m = i→menu
  ]
} ⇒ i
```

This specification produces products (r, d, i, m). Each product is evidence that the subset (d, i, m) no longer satisfies the specification.

(r, d, i, m) ⇒ not (d, i, m)

However, this cannot be taken as irrefutable evidence that the subset (i, m) *does* satisfy the specification. The inverse cannot be taken as true.

---

not (d, i, m) ⇏ (i, m)

The issue is that the menu item might have a second deletion. Only one of those deletions has been restored. The second one should prevent the item from being re-added to the cache.

To check for this condition, we need to reapply the negative existential conditions on the menu item. The correct inverse is as follows:

```
(r: MenuItemRestored) ⇒ {
  d: MenuItemDeleted [
    d = r→deleted
  ]
  i: MenuItem [
    i = d→menuItem
    ∄ {
      d2: MenuItemDeleted [
        d2→menuItem = i
        ∄ {
          r2: MenuItemRestored [
            r2→deleted = d
          ]
        }
      ]
    }
  ]
  m: Menu [
    m = i→menu
  ]
} ⇒ i
```

The new `MenuItemRestored` fact acts not only as the given r but can also serve as the unknown r2. Its presence prevents its predecessor deletion from excluding the item. But it does not prevent *other* deletions from doing so. With this modification, the inverse checks that no other deletion exists, thus proving that the menu item can indeed be re-added.

To generalize, whenever a negative existential condition transitions the inverse from adding to removing, we must remove the existential condition from its unknown. But when transitioning from removing to adding, we must add it back again. This guarantees that we will not re-add a product that has another reason for having been removed.

Be careful when recursively applying this procedure. Do not add the negative existential condition back into the specification before the recursion. Doing so may cause it to be processed again, leading to infinite recursion.

Child Specifications

Up till this point we have considered only specifications that have immutable projections. Those projections depend only upon the labeled immutable facts in the product. It requires just a few more steps to extend this proof to projections with child specifications.

Consider a specification with a projection that contains a single child specification.

```
(a: A) {
  b: B [
    b→... = a→...
  ]
  c: C [
    c→... = b→...
  ]
} => {
  children: {
    d: D [
      d→... = c→...
    ]
```

```
e: E [
    e→... = d→...
]
    }
}
```

The body of the specification produces Cartesian products, tuples of labeled facts that simultaneously satisfy a set of conditions.

(a) ⇒ (a, b, c)

The child specification produces products with additional labels.

(a) ⇒ (a, b, c, d, e)

We can add those child products to the parent projections. Find the parent whose product is a subset of the child product.

Projection of (a, b, c) contains (a, b, c, d, e)

In this chapter, we've constructed an algorithm that transforms the parent specification into a set of inverses, some of which cause additions to the cache. These we will call the positive inverses. If the set of all positive inverses is complete, then they describe all conditions under which a product should be included in the cache. To populate their projections, we add the child products.

Let's append the child specification to all positive inverses of the parent specification. This gives us the products that we need to add to the parent projection once it is in the cache.

(b) ⇒ (b, c, a, d, e)

(c) ⇒ (c, b, a, d, e)

In addition, we must take all of the inverses of the child specification. These will tell us how to modify the results already in the cache.

We saw a similar result in Chapter 12 related to feeds. Just as before, the Entity List pattern provides the best example. Suppose we were to complete the menu item specification to include the mutable property of menu item name. For brevity, we won't write the complete specification here. That specification would produce products containing menu and menu item.

(m) $\Rightarrow$ *(m, i)*

The projection of those products would be results containing menu, menu item, and menu item name.

Projection of (m, i) contains (m, i, n)

Now consider the positive inverses of the parent specification. There are two. One is the top-level inverse giving the menu item and the menu. The other is the second negation giving the restore, delete, menu item, and menu.

(i) $\Rightarrow$ *(i, m)*

(r) $\Rightarrow$ *(r, d, i, m)*

Now consider the inverses of the menu item name property. There are two of these as well. The top-level inverse gives the name and the parent subset. And the first negation gives the next, name, and parent subset.

(n) $\Rightarrow$ *(n, i, m)*

(next) $\Rightarrow$ *(next, n, i, m)*

These inverses tell us how to update the name of a menu item that is already in the cache. Subsets of these products lead us to the result that we must modify. The subset (m) gives us the affected set. And the subset (i, m) gives us the item projection result in that set. The remainder of the product tells us what to update about that result: either add or remove a candidate name. If the parent and child inverses are complete, then this set of modifications is also complete.

It is important that the runtime executes the parent inverses before the child inverses. Consider the case of re-adding a previously deleted menu item. The parent inverse will add the menu item back into the cache. The child inverses will repopulate the properties of that projected result. If executed in the wrong order, the child inverses will not find the result that they should modify.

This argument generalizes to projections with more than one child specification. Just process each child independently. And then to generalize to child specifications with projections that have their own child specifications, apply the argument recursively.

Proof of Completeness

We have finally assembled all of the pieces to construct an algorithm and prove that it is complete. The algorithm takes a specification and returns a set of inverse specifications. That set is complete in two ways: it includes all inverses, and those inverses find all updates. Let's summarize how it accomplishes this.

For a new fact to cause an addition, removal, or modification of a result, that new fact must match one of the unknowns somewhere in the specification or its projection. Facts that match top-level unknowns cause direct additions. Facts that match second-level unknowns cause indirect additions when appearing in positive existential conditions, or indirect removals when appearing in negative existential conditions. And facts that match deeper unknowns within existential conditions have recursively more indirect effects. That inference path switches sign as it passes negative conditions, and rechecks conditions every time it switches to a positive.

Facts that match unknowns within a projection cause modifications to results. Those modifications are either additions or removals in sets within those results. The inverses account for every scenario that could cause the addition of the result that they modify.

The algorithm visits each unknown in the specification. It visits top-level unknowns directly. Then it visits unknowns in existential conditions by raising them to the top level. Furthermore, it visits unknowns in deeper existential conditions by raising their parent up one level and acting recursively. Finally, the algorithm visits each unknown in a projection by acting recursively on every child specification. That recursion always produces new inverses because it uses the positive inverses of the parent, and every specification has at least one positive inverse (i.e., the direct top-level inverse).

This algorithm produces a lot of inverses. It's eye opening how many scenarios it must account for in order to cover every possible update. To me, this only strengthens the case for immutable runtimes. A human developer is likely to miss some of these scenarios. Fortunately, the number of inverses is bounded. It is based only upon the complexity of the specification, not the size of the data set. A well-optimized immutable runtime can calculate inverses once and then execute them quickly as it learns about new facts.

You can find a reference implementation of the algorithm described here in the open source project Jinaga.JS. Source code is available on GitHub in the Jinaga organization. Please see the book's website on Apress or at `http://immutablearchitecture.com` for more details.

Consequences of Inversion

Specification inversion is the most complex result of my research into immutable architecture. At the same time, it is also the most fruitful. It completes the promise that I made at the beginning of this book. And it enables the behaviors that we seek from immutable runtimes.

The promise that I opened with was to define a new process by which to build distributed systems. This new process relies upon a rigorous system of specification, a mathematical proof of correctness, and a mechanical translation into machine behavior. Factual specifications are that rigorous description of intent. And inverses are the mathematically proven translation into machine behavior.

The motivation for this system was to improve the reliability, predictability, and security of distributed software. Specifications and inversion achieve those goals. They rigorously define intent in a way that allows for analysis and prediction of results. Security rules are expressed in the same specification language. And the implementation of behaviors described by specifications is generated mechanically through inversion.

When humans are responsible for designing the ins and outs of software systems, they will inevitably make mistakes. These mistakes lead to defective behavior. We call them "bugs" and pretend that they are inevitable. But as we've seen several times throughout this book, it is possible to prove theorems about the behavior of software. If humans write the data access layer, business logic services, and view models for the user interface, then it is possible for them to introduce bugs. But if an immutable runtime is computing inverses according to mathematically proven rules, then we can have confidence that the system will behave correctly.

Let's look at just a few examples of desirable behaviors that inversion unlocks.

Real-Time Notification

The most exciting consequence of inversion emerges when it is applied to feeds. Recall that a feed is a stream of tuples that match a particular specification. The inverses of that specification capture all of the scenarios in which a tuple is added to or removed from a feed. The result is real-time notification of peer replicas.

Imagine a network of replicators similar to the one we constructed in Chapter 6. The clients at the edge are built on immutable runtimes that contain their own replicas. They request information from the replicators in the network by sharing specifications. Those replicators forward those specifications to one another, thus constructing a chain of feeds leading back to the client. Along the way, they compute the inverses of those feed specifications.

When new information arrives at a replicator in the form of a small graph of facts, the replicator executes those inverses. The results tell it precisely which feeds are affected and what tuples to add to those feeds. At this point, the replicator doesn't need to wait for its peer to check the feed. It can notify its peers in real time. They will in turn notify their peers until the cascade of pushes finds its way back to the client.

Compare this with the real-time notification mechanisms that we currently use. SignalR, for example, requires that developers explicitly describe the users and groups that should be notified of each message. Message-oriented middleware (MOM) frameworks require developers to implement handlers and decide for themselves how state should evolve. Kafka requires the explicit design of topics to match the use cases and achieve consistency. These mechanisms are coarse-grained and manually configured. Developers encode business logic into the communication patterns of these infrastructure components, making that logic difficult to change later.

API Isolation

Another place where inversion provides an improvement over existing behaviors is the point of integration with an API. Let's think about our network of replicators again. If we need this network to access a third-party API, we would deploy a service to an edge node or a serverless function. This service would use the Queue pattern from Chapter 8 to subscribe to a specification. The inverse of that queue specification is what triggers the API call.

You may have recently used an application that makes third-party API calls synchronously. Many mobile applications like podcast players and social network aggregators check RSS feeds and call APIs directly from the device. This results in a poor user experience, as the end user is often left waiting for the request to succeed. And when the third-party API call *is* made from the back end, it is often performed synchronously. It takes extra developer effort to isolate the app from external systems with a set of message queues. The Queue pattern and inversion make this a more natural and reliable interaction.

As they grow in popularity, immutable applications will run side by side with stateful applications. API integration points will be common. Using the Queue pattern, the Outbox pattern, webhooks, and emulated mutability, developers of immutable applications will find ways to bridge those gaps. Over time, they will publish those integrations as reusable components for other immutable application developers. The integration points will become small immutable applications living on their own within the architecture, proxies for external services.

Low-Latency Projections

There are many use cases for which a historical model is a poor fit. Business intelligence systems often need to aggregate over the current state of large numbers of entities. Search engines need to find information by the values of properties, not just by predecessor/successor relationships. There are data structures better suited to these needs than a fact graph.

If you've built enterprise systems, I'm sure you have worked on reporting. It's ubiquitous. A best practice in reporting is to separate the data warehouse from the transactional database. Quite often that takes the form of a batch-oriented extract, transform, and load (ETL). We extract data from the transactional system, transform it into a reportable schema, and then load it into the data warehouse.

Batch processes are a great way to maximize bandwidth. Entire data sets can be processed in seconds. However, that comes with a trade-off: increased latency. Results are often delayed by some duration governed by the schedule of the batch job.

Specifications provide a single way to express the desired transformation (what we've been calling the projection). They can be executed to produce results and quickly seed a database. Then, they can be inverted to identify precisely when that database needs to be updated. By switching between the two, we can achieve the right trade-off between latency and bandwidth.

A component that stores the results of a specification in a data warehouse or search index will be a common part of any immutable deployment. The inverses of that specification will perform the update as soon as new facts become available.

Collaboration

The previous examples of the benefits of inversion all describe machine-to-machine collaboration. But ultimately, the real benefit is to the collaboration among people. People using the distributed systems constructed with historical models will collaborate with one another through the creation of facts. It may be developers writing Factual specifications, but those specifications are actually an expression of the *user's* interest and intent. Inverses empower users by directing their facts toward their collaborators.

And it's not just the collaboration among users that is improved. It is also the collaboration among the people who build the software. Through a historical modeling workshop, stakeholders can express their intent and share common workflow scenarios. Analysts capture that intent with historical models, specifications, and annotated wireframes. Developers encode that intent directly into immutable runtimes, allowing the system to infer the desired behavior.

This process is iterative. A team begins with a simple model, describing the most basic interactions and the most common scenarios. As they and their stakeholders test and use the system, they will discover gaps and opportunities. That will lead to refinement of the model, the specifications, and the projections. The team builds up a working application over several iterations.

The immutable runtime maintains consistency throughout that evolution. At no point can developers express one intent to the data access layer and a different intent to the networking subsystem. They cannot introduce bugs based on disagreement between infrastructure components. All behavior is generated from the expression of intent. This gives the team the confidence to explore new business solutions and the autonomy to try new ideas.

I believe that immutable architecture will give you that confidence and autonomy as well. Continue your journey at `https://immutablearchitecture.com` with example models and reference implementations. Go build something awesome.

Index

A

Acyclic graphs, 52, 53, 189
Advanced Message Queuing Protocol
(AMQP), 165, 374, 375, 377,
378, 383
Aggregate root, 38, 39, 239
Aggregates, 38, 58, 118, 135, 136, 264
Alistair Cockburn, 195
Application-defined invariants, 156
Application patterns, 247
Architecture
API, 192
domain model, 192
infrastructure, 192
Asynchronous Model View Update,
29, 44, 45
Asynchronous queues/topics, 367
Auditing information,
217, 238, 402
Authority
authorization
indefinite, 312, 313
receipt, 316, 317
transitive, 313, 314
limitation, 310, 311
revocation, 314–316
transfers, 310
Authorization, 305
initial authorization, 308, 309
principal facts, 305
query, 306–308, 310
rules, 207, 208, 306, 316

Auto-incremented IDs, 8, 9
database management systems, 141
environment dependence, 142, 143
foreign keys, 141
issue, 142
object identifier, 142
parent-child insertion, 143, 144
remote creation, 144
unique primary keys production, 141
Autonomy, 22, 24, 28, 29, 55, 159, 189, 232,
257, 284, 286, 287, 301, 317, 367,
374, 375
Availability, 156–158, 160, 163, 330, 396

B

Backends for frontends (BFFs), 423
Bidirectional data flow, 43
Blockchains, 23, 25, 26, 58, 149, 150
Bookmarks, 390, 391, 419
adding tuples, 420, 421
fact IDs, 420
partial order, 419
vectors, 421–423
Business intelligence systems, 464

C

C#, 93
Caching, 196, 370, 399, 431
CAP Theorem, 257
ACID properties, 156
algorithm testing, 159–161

M. L. Perry, *The Art of Immutable Architecture*, https://doi.org/10.1007/979-8-8688-0288-1

Printed in the United States
by Baker & Taylor Publisher Services